# transforming
## the COMPANY

'A thought-provoking and refreshingly broad look at achieving corporate change.'

**Personnel Today**

'This book is essential reading for all managing directors and management consultants.'

**Management Consultancy**

'A fantastic opportunity to continue to stay ahead for those who won't consider losing as an option. Colin offers practical advice for success in an intensely competitive business environment.'

**Hamid Aghassi, European Consulting Director, Logica plc**

'One of the most stimulating and refreshing books on corporate transformation available. Coulson-Thomas's approach is both pragmatic and inspirational.'

**Vern Zelmer, formerly Managing Director, Rank Xerox (UK) Ltd**

'An authoritative, convincing and realistic guide. Colin Coulson-Thomas's invaluable and encouraging book reveals that fundamental change can be achieved if a practical and holistic approach is adopted.'

**Martin Bartholomew, Managing Director, Nortel-Periphonics EMEA**

'Packed with crystal clear, step-by-step practical guidance on how to address the issues and create the strategy and implementation plan to achieve changes in the enterprise.'

**Harvey N Parr, formerly Managing Director, OSL Ltd**

# transforming the COMPANY

## Manage Change, Compete & Win

COLIN COULSON-THOMAS

RECOMMENDED BY
INSTITUTE OF DIRECTORS

KOGAN
PAGE

## Dedication

To Yvette, Vivien and Trystan Coulson-Thomas

This book has been endorsed by the Institute of Directors.

The endorsement is given to selected Kogan Page books which the IoD recognizes as being of specific interest to its members and providing them with up-to-date, informative and practical resources for creating business success. Kogan Page books endorsed by the IoD represent the most authoritative guidance available on a wide range of subjects including management, finance, marketing, training and HR.

The views expressed in this book are those of the author and are not necessarily the same as those of the Institute of Directors.

First published in 1992
Reprinted 1993
Second edition 2002

Kogan Page Limited
120 Pentonville Road
London N1 9JN
UK

Kogan Page US
22 Broad Street
Milford CT 06460
USA

**British Library Cataloguing in Publication Data**

A CIP record for this book is available from the British Library.

ISBN 0 7494 3651 4

Typeset by Saxon Graphics Ltd, Derby
Printed and bound in Great Britain by Biddles Ltd, Guildford and King's Lynn
*www.biddles.co.uk*

# Contents

failure to communicate and share 78; Corporate transformation or corporate butchery 79; Moving from machine to organism 80; Mechanical and intuitive approaches 80; Vision and the network organization 80; Turning vision into reality 81; Rooting the vision in reality 82; Focus and horizon 82; The international dimension 84; Visioning winners and losers 85; Beginning in the boardroom 87; Roles and responsibilities 88; Effective communication 89; The effective communicator 89; The potential for differentiation 90; Differentiating winners and losers 91; Breaking out 92; Danger areas 94; Vision and communication 94; Checklist 95; References 96

**5   Winning Business and Building Customer Relationships      97**
Corporate transformation and the customer 97; Staying close to the customer 98; The challenge of implementation 98; Something is wrong 99; Reactions to a changing business environment 100; Caring 100; The customer in rhetoric 101; The customer in reality 101; How losers treat their customers 102; The bureaucratic organization and the customer 103; Size and responsiveness 104; What winners do differently 104; People and the network organization 106; Values and the network organization 107; Creating new relationships 107; Learning from the customer 109; Building relationships with customers 110; Reconciling integration and focus 111; Thinking it through 112; Barrier analysis 112; Speed of response 113; Tackling sources of delay 114; Segmentation, prioritization and differentiation 115; Who is responsible for the customer? 116; Who speaks for the customer in the boardroom? 117; The fate of the functional director 117; Checklist 118; References 119; Further information 119

**6   Transformation Intentions and Business Development      121
Outcomes**
Aspiration 121; How much transformation? 121; Incremental or fundamental change 123; Transforming the leviathan 123; Rhetoric and aspirations 125; Senior management preoccupations 126; The implications of change 127; Moving from the particular to the general 128;

# Acknowledgements

I would like to thank my colleagues at Adaptation Ltd, ASK Europe plc, Cotoco Ltd, Policy Publications Ltd, The Networking Firm, the e-Business Innovations Awards and the National Centre for Competitiveness, and the team at Kogan Page for their encouragement and support. I owe a special debt of gratitude to Yvette, Vivien and Trystan Coulson-Thomas to whom this book is dedicated for their understanding and forbearance while I was on board 'Solar Eclipse' updating 'Transforming the Company'.

Since the first edition of this book I have either led or been the Process Vision Holder of a number of major change and business development programmes. This experience has convinced me that the core messages of 'Transforming the Company' are more relevant than ever. I would also like to thank those who are involved with these and other initiatives for being so willing to share what they have learnt with others.

I continue to be particularly grateful to former Xerox colleagues, and especially the team at Xerox PARC, for first alerting me to the extent of the latent talent and unrecognized potential that exists in both people and organizations. If only a little more of this were tapped, released and applied to creating new offerings and more effective ways of working and learning our lives would be immeasurably richer.

# About the Author

**Prof. Colin J Coulson-Thomas** helps boards and entrepreneurial teams to manage change, compete and win through successful transformation, rapid business development and the creation, management and exploitation of new offerings and relevant knowledge and understanding. He counsels individual directors and entrepreneurs and has advised over 60 boards on change management, differentiation and corporate venturing, transformation and learning. A regular speaker at corporate events and international conferences he has given some 300 presentations in over 20 countries.

An experienced businessman, Colin is currently Chairman of ASK Europe plc; Cotoco Ltd; Adaptation Ltd and Policy Publications Ltd; Chairman of the Judges for the e-Business Innovations Awards and Professor of Competitiveness at the Centre for Competitiveness at Luton University. He leads the winning business best practice research programme (see Appendix) and reviews processes and practices for winning competitive bids, building customer relationships and managing change and knowledge.

Colin is also a member of the Council of the Parliamentary Information Technology Committee; the European Commission's Team Europe; and the Institute of Director's Professional Standards Committee, Board of Examiners and Chartered Accreditation Board.

A Visiting Professor at the Management Development Institute, Delhi since 1997, he was Hooker Distinguished Visiting Professor at McMaster University, Canada in 1995; and Visiting Professor at East China University of Science and Technology, Shanghai in 1996. From 1994 to 1997 he was the Willmott Dixon Professor of Corporate Transformation, Dean of the Faculty of Management and Head of the Putteridge Bury campus at the University of Luton and a Senior Associate at the Judge Institute of Cambridge University.

Colin was a member of the Board of Moorfields Eye Hospital for ten years, and Deputy Chairman of the London Electricity Consultative Council for six years. He served two terms on the Council for Professions Supplementary to Medicine, nine years on the National Biological Standards Board, five years on the Council of the Foundation for Science and Technology and four years as Corporate Affairs Adviser to the British Institute of Management. He is a past Chairman of the Crossbencher Parliamentary Liaison Programme and a past Chairman and past President of the Focus Group.

Colin has served on the governing bodies of representative, professional, learned, and voluntary institutes, societies and associations, including as Chairman and President. He led the European Commission's COBRA initiative that examined business restructuring across Europe, and was the principal author and co-presenter of the 'employment and training' module of the CBI's European single market initiative.

Colin has led various change management, re-engineering and transformation projects and surveys of entrepreneurial and boardroom issues, attitudes and practice for the Institute of Directors, Institute of Management, Institute of Personnel Management, Government Departments and the NHS. Practical lessons derived from these surveys and his work with particular entrepreneurs and various boards are summarized in over 30 books and reports.

Colin was educated at the London School of Economics (Trevennon Exhibitioner), the London Business School, the EAESP – Fundacao Getulio Vargas (Brazilian Government Scholar), and the

Universities of Aston, Chicago (Deans List) and Southern California (Graduate School Distinction). He obtained first place prizes in the final examination of three professions. He can be contacted by telephone: +44 (0) 1733 361149; fax: +44 (0) 1733 361459; e-mail: adaptationltd@cs.com; Web site: www.ntwkfirm.com/colin coulson-thomas.

# RECENT BOOKS WRITTEN BY PROF. COLIN COULSON-THOMAS

*Creating the Global Company: successful internationalisation* (McGraw-Hill, 1992)

*Transforming the Company: Bridging the gap between management myth and corporate reality* (Kogan Page, 1992)

*Creating Excellence in the Boardroom: A guide to shaping directorial competence and board effectiveness* (McGraw-Hill, 1993)

*Developing Directors: Building an effective boardroom team* (McGraw-Hill, 1993)

*Business Process Re-engineering: Myth & reality* (Kogan Page, 1994 and 1996)

*The Responsive Organisation: Re-engineering new patterns of work* (Policy Publications, 1995)

*The Future of the Organisation: Achieving excellence through business transformation* (Kogan Page, 1997 and 1998)

*Developing a Corporate Learning Strategy: The key knowledge management challenge for the HR function* (Policy Publications, 1999)

*Individuals and Enterprise: Creating entrepreneurs for the new millennium through personal transformation* (Blackhall Publishing, 1999)

*The Information Entrepreneur Changing requirements for corporate and individual success* (3Com Active Business Unit, 2000)

*Shaping Things to Come: Strategies for creating alternative enterprises* (Blackhall Publishing, 2001)

All of these publications can be ordered from the bookshop of the networking firm Web site: www.ntwkfirm.com/bookshop.

# 1

# Management Theory and Corporate Reality

*'Flood plains flood'*

## THE OPPORTUNITY

For over a decade there has been an unprecedented and historic opportunity to transform the capacity of companies to serve customers. A revolution could occur in the working relationships between people, and the
extent to which their individual talents could be harnessed and their
personal requirements satisfied.

This is not wild speculation, but a tantalizing prospect. Many people, in
different roles in a variety of organizations, have glimpsed the potential to
break free of a range of traditional constraints. Most of those that remain
are self-imposed and susceptible to appropriate action.

All the individual elements, from attitudes to processes, that are
necessary to achieve the transition have been identified. These are already
in place in leading-edge companies. The secrets of the individual and
collective release of capacity, and the fulfilment of personal aspirations
and corporate ambitions, are no longer hidden. Their use has been demonstrated and documented, and their utility is clear.

It can be done. However, it is not clear that it will be done. For many
companies the failure to question, anticipate and 'think things through'
means that frustration has been snatched from the jaws of success. There is
disappointment where there should be elation.

# THE FRUSTRATION

If so much is known, why is the new Jerusalem not with us today? Why has so much aspiration, intention and vision had such apparently limited impact upon reality? Why has the talk and hype been accompanied by ineffective action? Why are we not 'getting it together'?

Senior managers in many companies are maintaining a stoic attachment to the public line that 'it will come out right'. However, in private many are experiencing a mixture of anguish and despair. Too many outcomes and events are different from expectations. It is not happening, and they believe something is missing.

Corporate management is not lacking in plans, programmes or initiatives. Major companies such as BP with its 'Project 1990', BT with its 'Operation Sovereign', and ICL and IBM, have attempted fundamental corporate transformation programmes.

The lives of many thousands of people have been significantly affected by these 'flagship' programmes. Their experiences are shared by those in a wide variety of smaller companies that have quietly, and sometimes painfully, sought to bring about change.

Directors and senior managers feel they know what they want. Their desires are being reflected in corporate activity. Organizations are actively seeking a transition to more flexible and responsive forms, based upon teamwork and trust. Networks are being established that embrace customers, suppliers and business partners.

In the case of some companies, the extent to which corporate survival depended upon successful transformation was both clear and quite explicit. However, the widespread desire for change is not always matched by an awareness of how to bring it about. The issue is not whether to change, but *how* to change.

Corporate transformation is taking much longer to achieve than was first thought. Momentum is being lost, and attitudes and behaviour are proving stubbornly resistant to change. In many organizations a wide gulf has emerged between expectation and achievement.

Those who copy the pioneers, and emulate their initiatives, tend to accumulate 'examples', prototypes, experiments, individual innovations, islands of potential, that do not 'come together' to have a significant impact upon the total corporation. They collect some 'lovely pieces', but not enough of them to play a new game successfully.

Many managers who have a genuine desire to achieve results, are disappointed. They are failing to spot interrelationships, make connections, think ahead, 'manage through' the obstacles and 'line up' all the elements needed to 'make it happen'.

## TEN YEARS ON

That was the opportunity and the frustration set out ten years ago in the first edition of my book *Transforming the Company*. Much has changed since its publication – enough to justify a rewrite rather than a reprint. However, there is still a large gap between management myth and corporate reality that needs to be bridged.

Human nature remains a constant and most managers still rely upon fads rather than original thought. Hence many sections of my initial text are unaltered, while most of the comments quoted then have a familiar ring about them and are still valid. Many could have been uttered yesterday. I hope their repetition may yet spur action.

E-commerce has become e-business, a generation after the invention of the Internet and its use by early pioneers. The laggards – the great bulk of managers – have caught up with the Internet. Some may wish they hadn't. Although discounted by hype and rhetoric, the fundamentals of business success remain unchanged. As investors in many 'new economy' ventures discovered when the 'dot.com' bubble burst we ignore them at our peril.

After a decade in which a succession of further management fashions have come and gone, layoffs, downsizing and drives to cut operating costs are still discussed in many boardrooms. W R Grace, a supplier of specialist chemicals, has created a new role of Chief Restructuring Officer to oversee a process that has become a recurring if not continuous feature of corporate life.

Despite high spending on associated consulting and new technologies many managers remain insecure. They still struggle to become and remain competitive. Even former superstars like the computer suppliers Dell and Compaq have not been immune from the need to make significant job cuts. In Compaq's case, the response included merger negotiations with Hewlett Packard.

In growing markets some survive in spite of themselves. However, every so often the threat of recession returns. It lurks in the shadows of our perceptions at some times and hovers menacingly over us at others. When like old age it catches up with us, the cracks appear. The business cycle may have lengthened but the risk of a slowdown or downturn is always present. Creating expensive overheads is like building houses on a flood plain. Sooner or later disaster will strike.

## THE ANGUISHED MANAGER

The extent of frustration felt by senior decision makers was evident in the comments of many of those interviewed in the course of the surveys upon which my original book was based. Consider the following selection:

*We say one thing and do another. People are not fools, they look for results. So far it's just words on paper. Nothing has happened out there.*

*Our actions undermine our words. Until top managers start acting as role models things won't begin to happen. People need to see that it is for real.*

*After a time you get totally immune to concepts, theories, and the blandishments of consultants and gurus. What is the point if you cannot put it into effect?*

*Too many visions remain as blue sky hidden by a layer of fog. Even if a few of them attract your attention, they do not reach your wallet because they have not been translated into products and services.*

*All over the world politicians say whatever is necessary to 'hang on in there'. Why should it be different for corporate politicians facing employees, shareholders and customers? You have to say things to hang on to these people.*

*Never before has so much commitment and effort resulted in such disappointing outcomes. Something must be missing, something obvious that we haven't seen.*

*Would you believe someone who turned up with half a roof and a few bricks to make a house? People know what it takes, and they know it is not going to happen.*

## DAWNING REALIZATIONS

As organizations flatten, and growth projections are revised downwards, more managers have to seek satisfaction in current roles rather than in future prospects. They can no longer move on before 'adverse consequences' or a lack of results 'catch them up'.

Management teams are having to live with the outcomes of their own decisions, initiatives and advocacy. Where it matters, many of them know they face a gap between aspiration and achievement. They are also conscious that they themselves are held responsible for bringing outcomes more in line with both desires and claims.

In some cases, there have been premature celebrations of success. The false dawn makes continuing darkness even more unbearable. The following comments illustrate the extent of the anguish:

*Our internal journals have made the most of isolated successes, but we don't know how to apply the lessons to the whole company.*

*Everyone knows about our one team that is doing great things with the latest of everything. They produce all sorts of amazing projections of what would happen if we all worked the same way. What they don't know is the cost and management time involved. To do the same everywhere would kill us.*

*Past initiatives have been like forest clearings. They're great, but when you move on the old habits and ways of doing things grow back again.*

*If you achieve a breakthrough, it's best to keep quiet about it. Tell the centre and they will want it everywhere. They are desperate for results, but you can't replicate what we've done that easily.*

## THE DANGERS IN AN AGE OF HYPE

Economic recession and slowdown has always had a sobering impact. As one chief executive officer (CEO) put it: 'We can't rely on economic growth to solve the problem. This one is not going to come right without us, or in spite of us.' Those who are in a pit are seeking a way out and adversity has made them more desperate for a 'handle' or a 'lifeline'.

The situation is ripe for exploitation by the plausible, and the assault of the packaged. Instant solutions and the quick fix abound. Never has there been such an age for hype. The limiting factor is cynicism, fed by a continuing stream of disillusionment with the results of past panaceas. The safeguard is, paradoxically, a failure to implement, which protects some of the naïve from their own gullibility.

It is an age of temptation. There are more people alive today than have died throughout all eternity. And, given some forethought, most of them can be reached in seconds by one means or another. The technology of communications allows the deepest recesses of the most remote regions to be reached by a variety of media.

Industry sectors have grown up that are hungry for new messages to spread. Creative talent can turn the banal into an 'appeal' or a 'proposition' that lures with its appearance of profundity and insight. The 'management audience' has been a lucrative target for many years.

Never before has it been so easy to spread the latest fad. Never before has the organized peddling of simplistic notions offered such returns. The palate for the new and the catchy seems never to jade. The time of self-deception, group-think and the contagion of myth has surely come.

## THE SEARCH FOR SOLUTIONS

If directors and managers are to turn their backs on hype, to whom should they look for the 'real solutions'? The answer is 'To themselves'.

Handing the problem to someone else, while continuing as before, does not work. Like people, organizations can die even when almost all their individual elements are in satisfactory, if not perfect, working order. No amount of external help of the highest quality that is devoted to honing parts of the body corporate to perfection can grant life if the will to go on is lacking, if a vital organ fails or if a crucial flow is blocked.

In most cases devoting more resources to the problem will not help. A superior technology of itself may not have a significant impact. People without direction, motivation and relevant skills may add more to costs than to output.

Well thought-out programmes, even a variety of distinct initiatives that in themselves are worthy, may not be enough. Their introduction, along with changes of structure, may fail to influence attitudes and behaviour. Their combination may not be sufficient to 'make it happen' in the unique context of a particular company.

A more holistic approach is required. One that involves:

- understanding the critical success factors for competitive success;
- an emphasis upon vision, goals, values and objectives;
- establishing and nurturing relationships;
- empowerment and motivation, and the harnessing of potential;
- tolerance and encouragement of diversity, and a culture of learning;
- the introduction of a range of new skills and approaches;
- the appropriate use of a comprehensive and complementary armoury of accessible tools, techniques and processes;
- a focus upon attitudes and behaviour, and obstacles and barriers; and
- the identification and delivery of key priorities.

If progress is to be made, all the element need to be in place. When they are, the results can be dramatic. Given a holistic approach to the achievement of corporate transformation, getting it right may turn out to be easier than doing it wrong.

# THE LATENT REVOLUTION

The extent of frustration and concern should be viewed as a source of hope. Change emerges slowly and reluctantly from the soil of complacency.

Thomas Kuhn, following a study of the history of scientific discovery, concluded that revolutions in thought or a 'paradigm shift' tend to occur when, increasingly, what has been regarded as 'normal science' no longer appears to 'fit' or explain a growing number of observed situations and circumstances (Kuhn, 1970). Prior to each watershed, individuals in different locations tend separately to challenge the *status quo*.

There is a parallel with the contemporary management world. Too many management theories appear no longer to match reality. In many cases, promising ideas have been crudely and unthinkingly applied. Our perceptions of them derive from their use and application in a world that is rapidly passing into folklore. A President of Philips, Jan Timmer, has recognized that in order to achieve corporate transformation a 'mental transformation' must first occur.

There has been a succession of challenges to management orthodoxy and behaviour over a period of years, but the revolution in thought has not yet occurred. Prophets exist with perception and insight, but their various ideas are not being brought together in the form of workable corporate change programmes based upon the factors that actually make a difference between winning and losing.

## CORPORATE ASPIRATION

The desire for change, and for particular changes, is genuine enough. Chief executives, directors and senior managers consistently rank general organizational capabilities such as adaptability, flexibility, responsiveness and the ability to learn above 'single issues' in terms of importance. As one CEO put it: 'Without these qualities in our organization, and in our people, how can we hope to achieve any of our other objectives and survive in a changing environment?'

Those interviewed for my original book did not rank very highly the prospect of corporate survival, unless their organizations could achieve a 'transition' or 'transformation'. Many of those from the largest companies considered these giants to be the most vulnerable. Sheer scale is perceived as a source of weakness when it is not accompanied by flexibility.

Why this strong and continuing desire for corporate transformation? Flexibility and responsiveness was not being sought for its own sake, but in order to cope with the realities of the business and market environment.

According to Sir John Harvey-Jones (1989):

Organizational flexibility is essential. Rates of change have speeded up. The hierarchical organization is slow to respond. Decisions taken at the centre are too far away from the coal face. While the centre seeks local and relevant understanding, delays in decision making result.

In today's turbulent business environment speed of decision making is critically important. Windows of opportunity quickly open and close. Adaptability and change must be continuous. The organization that learns to learn will survive. To do this its people must also learn to learn.

## CHALLENGES

In an ever-changing, at times bewildering and generally demanding business environment, companies face multiple challenges and opportunities. For example:

- international markets have become more open as deregulation and privatization have become global phenomena;
- more intense competition has strengthened the bargaining position of consumers *vis-à-vis* suppliers, and there is pressure upon prices and margins;
- demanding customers now expect quality and reliability. There is a need to find new sources of differentiation to avoid falling into the 'commodity products' trap.

These bracing and competitive market conditions give the advantage to companies that empower those who are closest to the customer; are alert, astute and act quickly; and operate with limited 'overheads'. Those whose thoughts, activities and various elements are co-ordinated and in harmony seize the opportunities.

The slow, cost-heavy bureaucracy is a threatened species. Size, reputation and track-records of past achievements are no guarantee of future success. Without the flexibility and responsiveness that comes from different values, attitudes, behaviour and processes, all may be lost. To freeze in the glare of the headlights of external challenge is to court the risk of calamity.

In response to both longer-term trends and short-term economic pressures, CEOs are seeking to create more flexible, responsive and adaptable organizations. As one chairman put it:

> I used to boast about our size, the number of people we employed, and how many buildings we had. I now see these as a source of weakness. We lumber forward under the burden of a capability we cannot use flexibly in order to quickly serve our customers. The central issue is the transformation of the company.

The scale of readjustment that may be needed to adapt to changed market realities can be dramatic. For example, Olivetti reduced its workforce by a quarter over a two-year period.

## CHANGE IMPERATIVES

Companies do not seek to turn the worlds of their people upside down without good reason. The imperatives of change vary from company to company. The following concerns led some companies to seek fundamental change:

> We were not moving quickly enough. Our competitors were beating us to the punch.

> Customers are wanting things tailored to their particular needs. We have to be able to treat them all as individuals.

*The underlying technology is entering a digital revolution. The impacts will be felt throughout the organization.*

*My people are imprisoned in self-contained functional boxes. I cannot get at them. We can't use them more widely.*

*It's not coming together. Different parts of the company seem to have their own agendas.*

*How do you best prepare for the unknown? We don't know that much about what may happen tomorrow.*

*Now that we are all multiskilled we know a little about lots of things but not much about anything in particular. We have wiped out all our specialist expertise and our key customers are looking elsewhere.*

Recognition of the stark nature of reality can stiffen the resolve. There is little point in attempting corporate transformation unless there is a strong change imperative.

Many organizations find it difficult to summon up the collective energy needed to succeed unless 'backs are to the wall'. In a world in which time can be spent listening to the rustle of the leaves in the trees, it does not make sense to cause disruption, anguish and frustration, or to nourish false hopes when there is not a realistic prospect of success.

## INCREMENTAL OR RADICAL CHANGE?

In the past many companies coped with changes in the business environment by responding and adjusting incrementally, as and when particular challenges arose. There are those who take the view of one interviewee: 'So what's new? We've always been faced with changes, from great crashes to world wars, and we are still here. History is full of social and economic revolutions. Every generation thinks it's facing unprecedented challenges.'

The bureaucratic organization adjusts to discrete changes by taking relatively small, self-contained and incremental steps (see Halperin, 1974). Over a period of time this can lead to a better accommodation with a slowly changing environment. As more portraits of past chairmen appear on the panelled walls of the boardroom, a warm glow of pride in a heritage of achievement can lead to complacency.

An incremental approach is unlikely to cope with a sudden rush of multiple challenges. Many of the pressures faced in the past were not 'life-threatening', and in the case of those that were, many people felt they had more time to make whatever adjustments were necessary. There was the security of 'protection against foreign suppliers', the cartel and the cabal.

With hindsight, competition appeared less intense. As one director put it: 'We did not have a pack of wolves snapping at our heels.'

Since the 1980s the perception has been different. Directors and senior managers are aware of a multiplicity of changes in the business environment that have had far-reaching consequences for their companies (Table 1.1). Many of the changes represent a discontinuity, a break from the past. Their number and nature has led the management teams of many companies to conclude that incremental adjustment to change is no longer enough. A 'first principles' transformation is required.

**Table 1.1** The changing business environment

| Old | New |
| --- | --- |
| Confidence and rigidity | Insecurity and openness |
| Permanence and certainty | Turbulence and uncertainty |
| Incremental change | Revolutionary change |
| Opinions and theories | Facts and values |
| Logic | Intuition |
| Boundaries and disciplines | Interests, issues and problems |
| Constraints | Priorities |
| Organization | Adaptation |
| Attitudes | Feelings |
| Personalities and vested interests | Principles and business philosophy |
| Quantity | Quality and post-quality |
| Getting ahead | Achieving balance and harmony |
| Drives | Needs |
| Producer centred | Customer centred |
| Focus on activity | Focus on output |
| Conflict and rivalry | Co-operation and consensus |
| Command and control | Two-way communication and sharing |
| Direction and management | Facilitation and support |
| Power | Empowerment |
| Resources | Enablers |
| Bureaucratic hierarchy | Horizontal relationships |
| Absolutes | Solutions relative to context |
| Simplicity | Diversity and relative complexity |
| One-dimension maximization | Multi-dimensional trade-offs |
| Answers | Questions |
| Solutions | Temporary accommodations |
| Authority | Consent |
| Sanctions | Encouragement |
| Departmentalism and procedures | Business processes |
| Sequential activities | Parallel activities |
| Discrete problems | Holistic issues |
| Uninformed customers | Demanding customers |
| Homogeneous customers | Diverse customers |
| Standard products and services | Tailored products and services |
| Local customers | International customers |
| Established relationships | Integration and fragmentation |

| | |
|---|---|
| Sales | Account management |
| Individuals | Teams |
| The self and the company | The group and the environment |
| The 'here and now' | The consequences and the future |
| Unsupported | Facilitating processes and technology |
| 'Hoarding' by the few | Empowerment of the many |
| Protected information | Ubiquitous information |
| Single discipline | Multi-disciplinary |
| Diversification | Focus |
| Generalization | Segmentation |
| Knowledge | Competence |
| Teaching | Learning |
| Specialist teaching institutions | Integration of learning and working |
| Initial qualification | Continual updating |
| Lifetime practice | Functional mobility |
| Job descriptions | Roles |
| Career ladders | Succession of projects |
| Standard employment | Various patterns of work |
| Commodity products | Search for differentiation |
| Limited competition and barriers to entry | Open competition and diversity of supply |
| Cartels and oligopolies | Competition and choice |
| Zero-sum relationships | Positive-sum collaboration |
| Independence and dependence | Interdependence and partnership |

# TRENDS

What avenues are being explored by those who are seeking to transform their organizations? The following trends were identified over a decade ago:

- Externally, priority is being given to building closer relationships with customers in order better to understand their requirements, while internally the focus is upon harnessing human talent in order to deliver greater customer and shareholder value.
- There is recognition of the need for both individuals and organizations to learn. In particular, there is a strong desire to integrate working and learning and to free both from dependence upon particular locations.
- Responsibility is being devolved to groups and teams with specific tasks. The focus is shifting from 'input' to 'output', and the organization is becoming a portfolio of projects.
- The membership of teams is being drawn from a wider spread of functions, locations, nationalities and organizations. Heterogeneous groups are generally more creative than those which are homogeneous.
- Awareness is growing of the importance of access to the approaches, skills, processes and supporting technology that can facilitate team working and shared learning.

- Companies are increasingly thought to be competing on the basis of their know-how, processes, attitudes and values rather than their products and services, or their technology, all of which can be copied. Money, information and other resources are 'there' in the environment, ready to be 'picked up' by the companies with the processes, attitudes and values to make the best use of them to generate value for individual customers.
- The management of corporate transformation is recognized as a strategic challenge in its own right, requiring a distinct perspective and a special kind of awareness.
- Successful transformation is increasingly seen as dependent upon securing changes of attitudes and behaviour, and the co-ordinated bringing together of those 'transformation elements' that are particularly relevant to the change needs and barriers of each organization.

Transformation cannot be achieved without fundamental change. Within organizations, interest in rules and procedures has waned and a desire for new processes for generating and delivering value for customers, and achieving adaptation and change, has grown. In particular, companies are becoming conscious of the need for continuing learning, adaptation and change.

## THE NETWORK ORGANIZATION

The shape of the 'emerging organization' that is desired, and to which managements aspire, is becoming clearer. Ten years ago CEOs were describing and defining their organizational goals in network terms (Coulson-Thomas, 1992). Their jottings and doodlings are summarized in Figure 1.1.

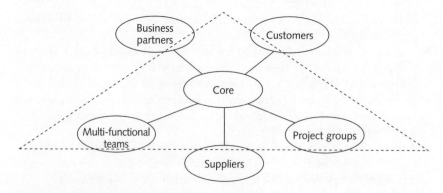

**Figure 1.1** The network organization

*Source: Coulson-Thomas and Brown (1990)*

There was a fair degree of consensus as regards the 'end point' of transition, or the nature of the transformed organization:

- A high priority was being given to creating network organizations that were increasingly independent of particular geographic locations and more adaptable and responsive to the changing needs of their customers and employees. Organizations are becoming more fluid, facilitating networks rather than bureaucracies (Figure 1.1).
- As fewer companies are able by themselves to deliver 'total value' to customers, increasingly they are creating networks of relationships, with electronic links forward into customers, backwards to suppliers and sideways to business partners.
- The boundary of the organization is becoming blurred. It is no longer a 'hard shell' surrounding all that which is owned or all those who are employed. Members of the network community are colleagues, peers, participants and partners, their membership being negotiated and a matter of choice.
- Networks and supply chains are becoming global, bringing together all those who share a common vision or a particular mission. The network community resembles a cooperative collective or confederation of entrepreneurial teams and of groups with a particular focus.
- As a consequence, the formulation and implementation of information technology (IT) and other strategies increasingly involves co-operation and collaboration across organizational and national boundaries. These links, common access to ubiquitous information, and shared vision and values, hold together a constellation of entities of diverse natures, nationalities, shapes and sizes.
- Departmental barriers fade as more work is done by groups, teams and project groups. The corporation is emerging as flatter, leaner and tighter. Processes are replacing procedures and, increasingly, organization is by key process rather than by function.
- Within the network an internal market operates, groups and teams buying and selling services to and from each other. Some members of the network might be both collaborators and competitors.
- There is delegation, devolution and decentralization, and greater accountability and responsibility. Reward is increasingly linked to outputs that result in value for customers or the achievement of business objectives.

These changes and developments are ongoing. While start-up companies may have the option of going straight to the network form of organization, most enterprises have a past. The organizational heritage from which escape is sought may be complex, and the bonds of corporate culture can be difficult to break. For example, the constraints of an entrenched matrix form of organization can confuse, bind and entrap like a spider's web.

Across companies in general, progress has been made in such diverse areas as defining competency requirements, identifying empowerment methodologies, introducing self-managed work groups and installing facilitating processes. However, the relative significance of these various change elements, and how they should be brought together within the framework of an overall change programme, is rarely understood.

In the main, the 'end point' has not been reached. After a further decade of trying hard, the network organization remains an aspiration.

## AREAS OF UNCERTAINTY

While there is some agreement as to the general shape of the organizational 'end point', there is little consensus as to how best to get there. The extent of the uncertainty is illustrated by the following selection of comments:

*Should we go straight to our end goal, or establish intermediate forms of organization? Will this help or confuse?*

*We drew the conventional pyramid, but couldn't agree what to do with it. Turning it upside down with the customer on top put us [the board] in our place in terms of helping others to serve the customer. But to show cross-functional processes we needed the customer over to one side. We ended up rotating the triangle, twisting it, looking at it this way, looking at it that way… it went on and on.*

*I worry about what new sets of problems are likely to emerge. None of us know anything about running the sort of organization we are trying so hard to create.*

*We have our innovations, but how do we spread them through the organization? What happens when we let go? Will revolution and chaos break out all over the place?*

*No one knows who the experts are. People make claims, but as these organizations we are all seeking don't yet exist, how do they know? Who knows what we might find?*

*I do try to benchmark, but it is difficult to judge who is ahead, or how much might be applicable to our situation. Will today's benchmark be tomorrow's disaster?*

It is beginning to dawn upon a number of advocates and agents of change that, for all the fanfares and bravado, many organizations set out on an uncertain journey with little in the way of experience, or the equivalent of a compass, to guide them. They did not know what the effect of a certain combination of change elements might be, and were not in a position to know until these had actually been brought together.

The degree of acceptability of the individual elements of a change programme in different national and cultural contexts is also not easy to determine. For example, an organization with aspirations to become an international network must recognize that while flexibility may be valued in some cultures, it is frowned upon in others. A willingness to change may be interpreted as a lack of consistency and 'backbone'. Reliability and predictability may be highly valued qualities. Those thought to move according to whatever way the wind blows are not respected.

Pursuing the analogy with a journey, people are aware that there are winds and currents, and that choppy patches and occasional storms may well be encountered. The hope is that a degree of organizational unity and common purpose will allow the storms to be ridden out. However, the various possible effects of different combinations of wind and current make the drift and destination problematic.

## ATTITUDES AND VALUES

More progress has been made in shaping the intended structure of the network organization than in building the attitudes and values, and in encouraging and rewarding the behaviour, that will allow its full potential to be achieved. Few organizations reward on the basis of contribution to customer value, let alone role model behaviour or commitment to learning.

Wherever there is uncertainty, a common vision and shared values can allow commitment and unity to be sustained for longer than might otherwise be the case. The vision or purpose of a network, and its values, are key sources of differentiation. Much effort needs to be put into articulating a distinct, shared and compelling vision that can hold a network together.

The bureaucracy was held together by a mixture of power, fear and guile, buttressed by the voluminous procedures manual. Gatekeepers hoarded information. There were those who played the power game like medieval bishops, willingly abetted by supine bootlickers and supplicating crawlers.

Given its potential for dispersing power and loosening many of the traditional forms of control, the evolving and moving network organization can fragment without the gravitational pull of a common vision and shared values. As one CEO put it: 'Unless we all have the same end point vision, I can see us rushing off in all directions. Unless managed in new ways, the network and all these teams are a recipe for disaster.'

Commercial success can generate considerable rewards for those whose noses are in the incentives and options trough. However, many people who seek to amass personal wealth have little idea of how to generate value for others. When greed is widespread, making money has come to be regarded as an objective in its own right rather than as a consequence of getting other things right. Credibility, the extent to which people will believe that an organization can deliver, is emerging as an important differentiator. In a commodity product marketplace, the opportunity will go to those who can 'make it happen'.

# A DECADE OF EXPERIENCE

Some companies assemble many of the building blocks needed for effective adaptation to changing circumstances. Even so, successful corporate transformation cannot be taken for granted. People can develop or acquire and bring together most of what is required to succeed and still screw up.

Xerox Corporation faced off a determined onslaught from formidable Japanese competitors and held a winning hand. Thanks to its Palo Alto Research Centre its technology led the world in several critical areas. The company won many awards for management best practice. It recruited energetic and talented people and was advised by the brightest and the best. Yet its golden heritage and outstanding prospects were squandered. A decade after its selection in the last edition of *Transforming the Company* as a model of best practice, the corporation teetered on the edge of insolvency.

Other transformations have been more successful. After the fall of the Berlin wall British Aerospace faced a grim future. In order to bank the 'peace dividend', governments across the free world had cut back defence procurement. However, the company discovered a new sense of purpose as BAe Systems, the world's largest supplier of defence electronics. Notwithstanding the difficulties, the chief executive Dick Evans managed to instil a collective belief that it could be done.

Like Xerox Corporation, the Swiss watch industry was challenged by new low-cost competitors. Swatch reinvented itself by making the wrist watch a fashion item. Mobile phones and a variety of other products have also since become wardrobe products. Individual items are selected from the collection according to the mood and occasion.

Other boards have also undertaken bold moves. Britannica.com took the plunge and made the entire contents of its encyclopaedia available on-line. However, daring needs to be matched with realism. The greater the steps the more important it is to ensure that consumers will keep up and not trip up. For many in Europe, genetically modified crops and foods have been a bridge too far.

# THE AIM AND FOCUS OF THE BOOK

So why have some companies failed to transform and reinvent themselves while others succeed? This book reviews a further decade of corporate experience. During this period the author became the first Professor of Corporate Transformation, led EU-supported pan-European re-engineering initiatives and assumed a process vision holder role within projects to revolutionize certain national and international markets.

Many of the research-based conclusions presented in the first edition of *Transforming the Company* remain valid and are restated in largely unchanged form. In place of the supporting survey findings, they are now complemented with the key factors that distinguish winners and losers in the struggle to become and remain competitive. These derive from more recent work undertaken by the Luton-based Centre for Competitiveness (see Appendix) and the author's experience of helping entrepreneurs to build their businesses and boards to achieve substantial improvements in corporate performance.

The purpose of this book is to explain why some boards and management teams end up as losers in the struggle to survive and grow while others who find themselves in similar situations, facing equal challenges and with comparable resources behind them, emerge as winners. It highlights the critical success factors that account for these very different outcomes. It aims to cut through the rhetoric of management speak and distinguish approaches that court financial disaster from those which achieve sustained business success.

Another aim of this book is to help facilitate the process of corporate transformation by sharing selected insights. The focus and subject matter of the book is not what should be in an ideal state, but what is, and what could be in the reality of the marketplace.

At various points in the course of the text there will be discussion and analysis of:

- what companies have set out to do, in terms of 'the words', myth or expectation;
- their experiences, ie typical problems and difficulties;
- what can be done to bridge the gap between vision and reality; and
- the key factors that distinguish winners from losers in the struggle to become and remain competitive.

When considering the many gaps between aspiration and perception, and corporate reality, value judgements should be avoided. Misperception and misunderstanding should not be regarded as an aberration. They should be assumed in complex and changing contexts, when there is uncertainty and there are other players in a competitive game.

# CRITICAL SUCCESS FACTORS

Understanding the circumstances and causes of business failure is an occupational priority of government inspectors and investigating accountants and lawyers. Thinking managers and directors are interested in the general lessons to be learnt from an analysis of root causes that might enable others to escape the same fate. Could other enterprises change how they operate to avoid the obstacles, pitfalls and traps into which the unwary and unprepared blunder? Are there steps which new ventures should take to increase their resilience and improve their prospects when the going gets tough?

This book addresses such questions. It examines gaps between intentions and outcomes. Liquidation may represent an extreme case but the failure to achieve targets or to successfully manage the transition from one state or situation to another is widespread.

We draw upon work undertaken by the author in recent years with both individual entrepreneurs and a wide diversity of corporate boards. The emphasis of this activity has been upon corporate transformation, business development, the creation and exploitation of knowledge and intellectual capital, differentiation and the creation of new income streams. The relatively long-term relationships involved enable the consequences of alternative approaches to be compared.

The losers are those who do not accomplish what they set out to achieve. The winners attain desired objectives, whether to bring about particular and significant changes or generally build a competitive business. Some people have been sorely tested. They faced severe challenges and came close to disaster. Yet they avoided nemesis and prospered.

We will learn from battle-hardened corporate warriors who have coped and emerged wiser and stronger from their experiences. When we review what they have been through, certain common factors stand out that increase the prospects of success. In many cases the firm foundations that enabled them to endure periods of difficulty and accomplish their aims needed to be in place ahead of both opportunities and challenges.

We will examine the key factors that distinguish winners from losers in the struggle to achieve sought after outcomes, seize opportunities, face up to threats and confront the challenges of transformation. In each case we will look first at the characteristics of 'losers', the boards and management teams of businesses that struggle to change and cope, before turning to the 'winners', those responsible for competitive enterprises that ride out storms, grow and develop.

## Losers

Losers:

- become lost in a world of trendy management concepts, fashionable fads and panaceas;
- seek single solutions to problems;
- are lured by, and become preoccupied with, ideas that are interesting for their own sake;
- are attracted by those who appear positive and claim to have answers to questions that concern them;
- may need to be subjected to a degree of hype and a relatively high level of generalization before their attention is captured;
- recognize what they want and may have a genuine desire to change, but are uncertain as to how to bring it about;
- experience anguish and frustration when people and events do not turn out as they might have hoped;
- are preoccupied with their own aspirations and requirements and largely oblivious to what is going on around them;
- ignore the very different requirements for the successful management of the new forms of organization, different ways of working and more collaborative relationships that are emerging;
- ultimately fail to transform either themselves or their organizations.

## Winners

Winners:

- keep their feet on the ground and address the critical realities of the situation they are in;
- recognize that the solution of a problem may require a combination of elements;
- would not cross the street for an interesting idea that was not relevant or capable of implementation;
- are attracted by those who focus upon critical success factors and concentrate upon what is important;
- become engaged when they perceive the relevance of what is being suggested and the specifics of what needs to be done are addressed;
- consciously set out to make their aspirations a reality;
- expect reverses and disappointments and are not distracted or inhibited by them;
- track and understand what is happening in the business environment and think through the implications for themselves and their customers;
- are aware of the attitudes, qualities and approaches required to successfully manage alternative forms of organization, ways of working and types of relationship;
- accomplish sufficient personal and corporate transformation to remain relevant and vital.

# AN OVERVIEW PERSPECTIVE

Wherever possible, points will be made through actual quotes from a selection of the CEOs, directors and managers who were interviewed during the survey programme (Coulson-Thomas, 1992). These are not attributed, as openness and frankness was encouraged by a guarantee of confidentiality.

The perspective of this book is that of the organization as a whole. A considerable degree of self-discipline has been required to avoid going in great detail into particular aspects of corporate transformation in order to ensure the reader is presented with an 'overview' and a holistic approach.

No attempt has been made to sound catchy or to serve up a new set of buzz-words. There is little value in concepts that cannot be used. Ideas, however interesting, have been weeded out if they are not thought to be of practical value. In the main, the views expressed are those of real and 'hard-nosed' people who are running real companies.

# THE PURPOSE

Every company is unique. How the reader should apply the lessons of this book will depend upon the situation and circumstances of his or her own company. Key points are made, and questions are raised which could be posed in the context of a particular enterprise.

It is hoped that the reader will gain a more balanced perspective on what is involved in transforming a company, and some guidance on how to manage the transformation process. No attempt has been made to hide the areas that are proving difficult, or to 'play down' likely obstacles and barriers. These must be recognized, confronted and tackled if success is to be achieved. The author's concern is that single and simplistic solutions should not be sought to a challenge as fundamental as transforming a company.

Successful transformation depends critically upon the relevance of the selection, combination and application of change elements to the require-ments of the situation at each stage of the change process (Coulson-Thomas, 1992). Certain combinations and applications of change elements do work, and can 'bear fruit' when they are correctly applied.

In spite of the evidence that a carefully-selected set of complementary change elements is needed, many organizations adopt a simplistic approach to the achievement of change within organizations. Too often people continue to believe in the general applicability of standard solu-tions, even though warning signals have been issued.

# THE AUDIENCE

The point has already been made that this book is primarily based upon the experiences of those who occupy key roles in actual companies. Hence, its messages are rooted in reality. It should be of value and interest to all those practitioners, whether directors, managers or consultants, who are seriously trying to bring about change.

Because it is based upon practical experience and a comprehensive programme of questionnaire and interview surveys, the book should also be suitable for those undertaking executive and MBA programmes.

Organizational transformation is affecting the public sector as well as the private. In the UK, for example, there has been an extensive programme of 'privatization', 'contracting out' and the introduction of executive agencies and internal markets. These changes are now occurring in many countries around the world. Hence, the book should also be of benefit to those in the public sector. What can and should be promised to the citizen in terms of outcomes and expectations will depend critically upon what it is felt could, with reasonable certainty, be delivered.

## WINNING AND LOSING

Much management literature is glib and assumes success. Less is written about failed attempts to 'manage change' and the negative consequences of re-engineering and corporate restructuring. Yet the financial collapse of weaker competitors is an intrinsic element and inevitable consequence of a competitive economy.

If some are to win others must fail. We assume that a proportion of new initiatives, start-up ventures and product launches will fall by the wayside. If more than one proposal is submitted, bidders need to accept the prospect of losing.

Financial crises free up resources. They are the primary source of income for company doctors, receivers and liquidators. Handling them engages and generates significant fees for many other professionals. Animals rarely die alone. Stragglers and corpses provide rich pickings for predators.

Escape artists draw crowds. Military minds prize withdrawals from difficult situations. With managers the problem is often concealment and self-deception rather than failure per se. An issue has to be acknowledged before it can be addressed.

## CRISIS SITUATIONS

Root causes must be identified if the non-achievement of desired outcomes is to be remedied. Let's take one extreme of the performance spectrum. We think we know why businesses fail. Their consequences are widely reported. Quick assessments of their immediate causes are made and expressed in sound bites. The arrival of a receiver or liquidator is usually linked to one or more causes such as customers deserting or a pressing event such as a cash flow crisis.

Behind every business failure lurks a particular situation and an individual story. Each case is likely to be unique and traumatic for the people involved. Eventually the company's bankers may have become impatient with unrealistic forecasts. Maybe they felt unable to extend or increase an existing facility.

The triggers of financial disaster can be sudden and dramatic. The company may not be able to pay its bills or meet other financial commitments when they fall due. However, after reflection the circumstances of a collapse may be perceived differently. What was described at the time as the main catalyst of an eventual meltdown might well itself be the result of other causes. It could be a consequence of an earlier sequence of events or combination of factors, and a symptom of underlying problems. Losers remain unaware of them until after the event. Winners identify and tackle them before it is too late. They bounce back.

## WINNERS AND LOSERS

Losers are like walkers in a fog. They are unaware of what is to come. They do not foresee the consequences of their actions. Oblivious to danger and unaware of commercial realities, some jog rather than walk. Too rapid an expansion can lead to over-trading. Pressures sometimes quickly build. Excessive dependency upon a small number of customers makes a company vulnerable when major contracts are unexpectedly lost.

In the short term most overheads may be fixed. During an economic downturn when sales drop, a business may be unable to cover them. Losers create inflexible attitudes, structures, roles, processes and systems. They do not adapt quickly to changing situations and circumstances. When events go according to plan all may be well. When they don't the directors of such enterprises find themselves in deep trouble.

Some thrive when the heat is turned up. They come alive. Others cannot or do not rise to the challenge of coping with crisis situations. Instead they look after themselves. They may sense the game is up. Sometimes when they are most needed key players simply resign. They leave an organization without effective leadership and a diminished capability to respond.

In difficult conditions priority is often given to self-interest and the preservation of managerial reputations. The various parties involved may give differing accounts of events and their own roles in them. Some may endeavour to avoid blame and strive to put a gloss upon their own particular contributions. They rewrite history.

## A MESSAGE OF HOPE

Ultimately, this book should be a source of encouragement. Moving from concern to action is a question of taking the first steps. The areas that need attention have been identified, as have most of the change elements that are needed. In many companies the more complex and difficult individual change elements are already in place. When the missing and complementary elements are put into position 'things could start to happen'.

There is also a new determination in many companies to 'make it happen'. For too long a growing business may have concealed the lack of progress in certain areas. Illusions have now been stripped away by the realities of economic downturn.

Few companies sail effortlessly to world-class performance. Most of the organizations which do appear to be achieving changes of attitude and behaviour share the common experience of having travelled along a rocky path. Almost all have suffered a degree of insecurity and anguish along the way.

Among the many directors and managers who were interviewed are some with the quiet confidence of those who have 'peered into the pit' and 'avoided the abyss'. They are both thinkers and doers. They release the energies and talents of others as they fulfil themselves. These are the champions of corporate transformation.

## CHECKLIST

▶ Does your company have a compelling reason for existing?

▶ What would the world lose if it ceased to exist tomorrow?

▶ Does your company have clear and agreed vision, goals and values?

▶ Who within the company has thought through what the vision and these goals and values mean for its relationships with people, whether as customers, suppliers or business partners?

▶ Is there an overview of what the company is trying to achieve in terms of its various objectives?

▶ Are all the objectives expressed in terms of measurable outputs?

▶ To what extent are you and management colleagues frustrated with what has been achieved in the area of corporate transformation?

▶ What are the symptoms of non-achievement?

▶ Is there a process in place within your company to root out the underlying causes of gaps between aspiration and achievement?

▶ Is the complex nature, and full extent, of the corporate transformation challenge fully appreciated?

► Has thought been given to whether particular change elements are missing from the transformation jigsaw puzzle?

► How genuine is the desire to change in each functional component and business element of your organization?

► Is there an agreed vision of a more flexible and responsive 'end point' organization?

► To what extent have the changes which have been introduced into your company to date influenced attitudes, values and behaviour?

► Have the cross-functional and inter-organizational processes that are necessary to achieve desired outcomes been identified?

► Have relevant roles and responsibilities been allocated, and the required resources been lined up?

► Are people equipped, empowered and motivated to do what is expected of them?

# REFERENCES

Coulson-Thomas, C (1992) *Transforming the Company: Bridging the gap between management myth and corporate reality*, Kogan Page, London

Coulson-Thomas, C and Brown, R (1990) *Beyond Quality*, BIM, London

Halperin, M H (1974) *Bureaucratic Politics and Foreign Policy*, Brookings Institution, Washington, DC

Harvey-Jones, J (1989) A commentary, in *The Responsive Organisation, People Management: The challenge of the 1990s*, ed C Coulson-Thomas and R Brown, BIM, Corby

Kuhn, T S (1970) *The Structure of Scientific Revolutions*, 2nd edn, University of Chicago Press, Chicago

# 2

# Aspiration and Achievement

*'If the river meanders, the journey is longer'*

## CORPORATE ASPIRATION

A company is a community of people who have come together in order to increase their collective capability to turn aspiration into achievement. If the network organization is to hold together, its members must share a feeling that the prospects of 'making it happen' are enhanced when they work as a group rather than separately.

While a company transitions to a more responsive and flexible form, other activities will be ongoing. Corporate transformation may be but one of a number of strategic programmes that are under way. Each of these initiatives, and the teams behind them, will have aspirations. Corporate transformation needs to facilitate, enable and support these other developments.

Many companies have set ambitious objectives for their change programmes. Alcoa, a US corporation, has sought to invert the organizational pyramid in order to put the front-line business units that serve the customer 'on top'. Such a change, when followed through, can have a traumatic impact upon how many people view their contribution and worth.

The aspiration can be international. BP has encouraged networking across national borders in order that groups and teams can be brought together, independently of location, to tackle particular tasks.

The more profound the change, and the further its reach, the greater the number of barriers and obstacles that may be encountered. On the other hand, a certain level of scale, and perceived urgency and importance can increase the prospect that senior management attention will be secured and sufficient resources might be obtained to 'break through'.

# CORPORATE REALITY

In view of the uncertainties involved in transforming companies to more flexible forms, it is not surprising that achievement generally lags behind aspiration. The first edition of this book (Coulson-Thomas, 1992) revealed:

- A growing gap between management theory and corporate experience, between expectation and achievement, and between rhetoric and reality.
- As a result of the achievement or delivery gap a number of arenas of confrontation were emerging. Perspectives were in conflict. People could not agree the sources or root causes of problems being encountered, or the next steps to be taken.
- Patience and goodwill are not inexhaustible. In some companies there already appeared to be a search for scalps and scapegoats.
- Many well-intended actions of boards and management teams were having unforeseen and counter-productive consequences. These were a source of angst, recrimination and division.
- The phenomenon of the 'herd instinct' or 'groupthink' was widespread. Groups were 'going automatic'.
- While there remained a desire for corporate transformation, its achievement was generally taking longer than expected and was often fraught with difficulties.
- The single-minded pursuit of particular panaceas appeared to be driving some companies into the ground. A sense of balance was being lost, as a desire for outcomes resulted in management teams putting excessive, and sometimes blind, faith in 'solutions' such as 'quality' or 're-engineering'.
- As a result of unforeseen delays, some transformation programmes were being overtaken by events. The requirement was substantially changed before the outcomes or results that were initially agreed could be achieved.
- As a consequence of the above, there was widespread disillusion, cynicism and despair.
- People in many companies were beginning to lose faith in the 'vision', and were critical of the 'standard' solutions and simplistic generalizations of consultants, business schools and gurus.
- In general, many people within companies that were being subjected to fundamental change needed both reassurance and practical help.

In many companies considerable effort is still being devoted to initiatives that are doomed to failure. Reputations and much goodwill are being squandered upon approaches that are likely to lead to unintended consequences and disappointment.

One survey concluded that:

> *Many managers have 'had enough' of forever 'doing more with less', when the reality of the vision they are offered is corporate survival for another few months... The life of the manager has become a tough one... It was almost impossible to interview... without feeling both respect and sympathy for many hardworking and 'unsung heroes'. Realistic and dedicated, open and frank, they 'battle on' until they are 'dropped'.* (Coulson-Thomas and Coe, 1991)

These findings are consistent with other work which has suggested that activities such as delayering and downsizing are often undertaken with little thought as to the consequences or concern for how people should be equipped to operate in changed circumstances. Scase and Goffee suggest that many managers feel themselves caught in a treadmill from which they cannot escape (Scase and Goffee, 1989).

The problems that emerge are sometimes embarrassingly visible. Organizational change is increasing the awareness of failure. Such results call for a greater work-life balance:

- The bureaucratic organization protected some people from their own deficiencies. Departmental barriers and a penchant for secrecy prevented damage and knowledge of failure from spreading, inadequate implementation reduced the adverse consequences of bad decisions.
- In the more open corporation, the emphasis given to corporate communications ranging from videos to posters, and new-found enthusiasms for sharing visions, have seen to it that expectations have been raised and hopes are high. When gaps between words and deeds arise, more people know about it.

One chairman summed up a new challenge faced by many companies:

> *I rue the day we decided to invest so much in hype. We have so wound them up that many of those in the field are rushing about mouthing slogans and thinking we're on the way to great things. How do we get them to understand that it's just not working without totally disillusioning them? Imagine the reactions, for us and them.*

## ACKNOWLEDGING THE EXISTENCE OF GAPS

If aspiration is to be translated into the reality of achievement, companies need to become and remain competitive. This requires continuing vigilance across a range of critical success factors in key areas such as winning business and building customer relationships.

Palm, a supplier of handheld computers, was one of the first to appoint a Chief Competitive Officer. However, many leading companies do not have anyone specifically concerned with overall corporate competitiveness. Nor do they seek relevant counsel and support. Advice may be sought in a whole range of areas but not about the factors that distinguish between winners and losers.

A necessary first step is to recognize that there is a gap between aspiration and achievement. Its existence may be concealed by another gap between perception and reality. The point was made in Chapter 1 that misperceptions are likely to occur when people have to confront new situations armed with memories, experiences, attitudes and prejudices derived from a different reality.

People seek meaning and predictability in order to cope with a confusing and challenging environment such as that found in transforming organizations. They tend to ignore, 'screen out' or rationalize evidence that does not accord with their deeply-held views of reality (Festinger, 1962). A battery of psychological devices are deployed by individuals to avoid recognition and acceptance of failure.

People who are 'in the thick of it' also fail to spot signs and signals that with hindsight, or to a third party, might appear obvious. The members of a transformation team may not be able to agree the meaning or source of what is observed. When success is a matter of changes of attitude, or the internalization of values, interpretation and assessment of what is happening is sometimes fraught with difficulties.

Not all of those involved in the management of change will agree on the extent to which there is a gap. Much will depend upon expectations. Corporate transformation is a process, and in a turbulent and ever-changing world it is one that is ongoing. Some will be more pleased than others with the rate at which progress is being made. One person's shortfall in achievement could be another's excuse for a celebration.

## AVOIDANCE AND CONCEALMENT

In the case of some gaps between programme objectives and actual outcomes, there will be those who do not know about the shortfalls. Others may be reluctant to tell them, or perhaps calculated concealment is taking place.

Bad news is generally regarded as a problem rather than as an opportunity to learn. In many companies, some managers will go to great lengths to conceal reality from others in the corporate organization. This is especially likely when they feel it is in their best interests to do so.

The extent of deception can range from an emphasis, a biased slant or selective reporting with a view to portraying an individual in a more favourable light, to outright distortion. People also report what they believe those above them might wish to hear. As anxiety mounts, executives long visibly for good news.

Appearances can often be deceptive. We see outcomes without understanding why they have occurred. Analyses from those seeking to sell particular approaches may only serve to distract and confuse.

Some disappointments such as the non-achievement of performance targets may be taken in their stride. Winners endeavour to accomplish what they set out to achieve, but for losers performance management becomes a game to be played. Other failings have more profound consequences. Hitting an overdraft or credit limit may trigger the appointment of a receiver or liquidator.

Lacklustre performance, stalled change programmes, lost customers and cash flow problems can all represent late steps in a long process. Frustration could simply be the result of unfortunate timing. Revenues often take longer than expected to arise. Had they come in earlier people might have been celebrating rather than commiserating.

Dissatisfaction can result from bad decisions. Maybe the venture, programme or offering was built upon foundations of sand, such as a rigid and inflexible model of operation, inadequate understanding of customer requirements or an unwillingness to change. Too many directors blame market conditions rather than critique their own actions. A relatively intimate relationship with a particular situation may be needed to cut through concealment, rationalization and excuse, and determine the root causes of a failure to achieve.

To find out what is really happening, a senior or programme manager may need to be astute and engage in subterfuge. Some chief executives operate informal intelligence networks to uncover a 'different' version of reality. Others have 'listening posts' scattered around the corporate organization, people who are pleased to have a degree of access to the CEO in return for 'telling it as it is'.

Avoidance and concealment involve risk. For example, when the 'truth is out', people may feel deceived and duped. No one other than the masochist likes to feel 'had'. A manager may feel bitter and angry at the betrayal of trust involved.

Given the risks and uncertainties, and the temptation to avoid, distort or conceal reality, it is not unreasonable to ask: why should anyone assume that a corporate transformation programme will succeed?

## APPEARANCE APPEAL

Appearance, rather than the reality of achievement, has great appeal for many managers. Dealing with symptoms can result in short-term payoffs, and may be less wearing than grappling with underlying problems.

In the case of some companies, appearance is the product. Disneyland does not have employees, but cast members. Image may be the essence of the appeal of the rock band, and may add millions to the value of a brand.

Appearance and image can be important, and in some sectors are the crucial differentiators. However, a management team should not become so 'wrapped up' with the world of appearance as to lose touch with reality. The cocktails and bow-ties of the agency reception, and the atmosphere on set when the commercial is shot may have greater appeal than the engineer's report, but the latter may focus on an issue that needs to be addressed.

## THE TEMPTATION OF THE VISIBLE

According to one managing director: 'The temptation is to stick or tie, rather than reach for the toolkit.' Activity, announcements, instant impacts, the quick fix and the new initiatives are immediate, visible and relatively easy to associate with individuals. They earn 'brownie points', they help people to become noticed, and they can build a reputation for being the 'right stuff'.

Advancement, reward and remuneration may all be influenced by appearance. How the manager looks, presents and behaves in social situations can be significant factors in promotion and selection decisions. When senior executives pride themselves on being able to judge a person in 30 seconds, or on the basis of a firm handshake, it is little wonder that image consultants are having a field day. Packaging is often all-important.

Activity and hype can also be fun. Rushing about gets the adrenalin flowing and makes you feel good. In contrast, some find that thinking can be hard work. Others get bored very quickly. They may be reluctant to spend the time needed to really get to the heart of an issue.

Appearance can be talked about. It can be used to impress, flatter and beguile. Individually and collectively it can give rise to self-deception and delusion. People may cling to appearance in order to avoid reality.

## REALITY RESISTANCE

Compared with appearance, reality is sometimes rather like the dull brother whom everyone wished had stayed at home. It can be uncomfortable, just as honesty may be unwelcome. The reality of achievement is hard work, and people may not wish to be reminded of this.

Achievement takes time, and may require the collective efforts of many people. It may not be easy for individuals to claim the credit when others are involved. Those who beaver away in unglamorous, but from a customer perspective important, activities may be hidden from view.

Some people will not want to commit to roles that are concerned with 'making it happen'. While they have their 'heads down' in the far reaches of the company close to the customer, they may be passed over in favour of the sly courtiers who are slinking and prowling head office corridors close to the centre of power.

Besides, reality is not so easy to 'fix' as appearances. What happens if it goes wrong? A focus upon reality, and a commitment to achievement, has been the graveyard of many careers. The achieving individual in a culture that does not encourage 'role model' behaviour, or reward achievement, may fail as a result of a lack of support from others. Favours may win over results.

The achievement of a significant change of attitudes and perspective within a management team tends to be associated with a change of leadership at the top (see Tushman, Newman and Nadler, 1988). Hence, people avoid radical approaches that might precipitate a change of roles and use their existing power to block them.

## APPEARANCE AS POLICY

There are occasions when managers set out consciously to build an image, erect a façade or create an appearance that does not accord with reality. They may not have any intention of translating a public vision into corporate reality, or of closing what may be perceived as a gap between aspiration and achievement. Rhetoric may not have represented true aspiration.

A company might perceive that it has a vested interest in rhetoric. By articulating strategies, issuing protestations of concern and generally cultivating an appearance of activity, a company may feel it might be able to stave off the introduction of costly regulation.

The challenge in such circumstances is to make people aware of the 'realities' without causing disillusion and despair, and to reconcile the desire to be honest with the requirement to maintain confidence and positive leadership. Winners are sometimes those who choose to overlook 'realities' that cause their competitors to give up.

There may be occasions when a management team has to address both rhetoric and reality, and respond in both arenas. For example, stakeholders may say one thing and do another, just as members of the public may vote one way through the ballot box, and behave differently when spending the money in their purses and pockets.

## JUDGING MANAGERS BY THEIR GAPS

A gap between aspiration and achievement is not something that is abnormal. Nor should it be a source of shame. The existence of gaps should not shock or be the cause of embarrassment. The likely existence of gaps should be assumed in the case of a wide-ranging and demanding change programme.

Deficiencies cannot be addressed unless they are first identified and their causes understood. Those without gaps may be the ignorant, those who have not set clear objectives or those who do not measure the extent of their achievement.

People who do not aspire do not have a gap between aspiration and achievement. In some competitive markets it may not be possible to achieve world-class performance without moving close to the limit of the capacity of the organization and its people to deliver.

Some people will not know they have a gap until their annual review of strategy takes place, or the annual results are announced. These events could be scheduled to take place some months in the future. By then it may be too late to take corrective action.

Managers can and should be judged by the gaps they have identified, their understanding of them and what action they propose to take to deal with them. What is the root cause of the gap which has developed, and who is responsible for delivering the agreed response?

To identify critical success factors for succeeding and winning we need evidence from surveys specifically designed to rank companies in terms of outcomes achieved, to distinguish winners and losers, and to isolate the principal causes of success or failure. A programme of such investigations has been undertaken by Policy Publications in association with the Centre for Competitiveness (see Appendix). They reveal a direct link between achievement and the number of key factors in place, and suggest practical steps that can be taken by virtually any business.

Many gaps occur as a result of external changes and developments. These may be beyond the control of the company. Things sometimes just happen, and may not be the fault of anyone in particular. 'Witch hunts' should be avoided if it is desired that people should be open about their mistakes, and prepared to learn from them and share what they have learnt.

## THE ROLE OF THE MANAGER

The role of the manager is to manage change. Once a direction has been set, objectives agreed and roles and responsibilities allocated, the manager should establish frameworks within which gaps between intentions and outcomes can be identified, and subsequently assessed as they emerge or monitored as they are closed.

People should be motivated to actively seek out and manage gaps. A company could build its philosophy of management upon the identification and closing of gaps between aspiration and achievement. A company that encourages every group to carry out regular 'gap', 'barrier' or 'helps and hinders' analyses is involving all of its people in a process of steering towards its corporate goals.

Many managers are reluctant to think through the implications of change programmes and the likely consequences of their own actions. Some company cultures actually discourage this sort of behaviour. Consider the following comments:

*If you see too many problems you get labelled as negative, a 'wet blanket' or a pain. You might be taken as someone who is not a team player, or perhaps you are too thick to understand.*

*People are reluctant to raise things in case they might have missed the point. People don't like to look stupid in front of others. There were many times when the obvious questions were not being asked.*

*It really was the chief executive's baby. I looked around the room. Everyone knew that it wasn't working, but no one was prepared to say anything.*

So pervasive are gaps between aspiration and achievement, and so determined are so many managers to move rather than solve problems, that there appears to be the managerial equivalent of the doctrine of original sin. Even where progress is made in closing some gaps, others seem to open up. Perhaps, like the poor, they will always be with us.

# ACCOUNTABILITY

Sometimes the gap between aspiration and achievement is so large that the question arises of whether individuals and organizations should be held accountable for claims made to raise expectations. At what point should hype be considered deception?

At the height of the Internet boom, leading financial services and consulting firms around the world were falling over themselves to promote e-business proposals and projects that stood little chance of success. The crash in Internet stocks has triggered legal claims. Credit Suisse First Boston has been cited in suits. The US Securities Exchange Commission has also investigated the bank's support of initial public offerings.

At what point should managers, directors and consultants be legally responsible for their words and deeds? When does covering tracks and avoidance behaviour become an offence? Ought a failure to address identified critical success factors for key areas of corporate performance be considered prima facie evidence of negligence? Should management fads carry health warnings?

Adaptation and the pursuit of flexibility are possible defences. First principles reviews and fundamental changes need to be undertaken ever more frequently. Windows of opportunity now quickly come and go while various barriers to entry are rapidly falling. Competitors may simply be the click of a mouse away. More businesses have to repeatedly reinvent themselves. Their strategies, processes and systems, and the minds of their people, need to be sensitive and supple, if not elastic, as well as versatile and resilient.

# MANAGING THE GAPS

More important than the scale of a gap, is the question: gap from what? A small gap may reveal a lack of ambition rather than limited management accomplishment. Those without visions, and those who do not dream, may be the satisfied and the content. It tends to be those who are restless and dissatisfied who move organizations forward.

A judgement may also need to be made (Figure 2.1) as to whether the source of a deficiency lies in the direction or speed of change:

- The gap that is perceived could be between a 'right' and a 'wrong' direction. A company could pursue the wrong (eg circuitous or tortuous) route towards an agreed goal or objective.
- Alternatively, the gap could exist between where a company thinks it is and where it is thought it ought to be. The movement could be in the right direction, and along the intended route, but at a slower speed than had been anticipated or hoped.

The route to be followed will depend upon the obstacles and barriers between where the company is and where it wishes to be. The desired speed of transformation will reflect the extent to which internal capability, attitudes and behaviour need to adapt to match the requirements for the achievement of corporate goals in the context of evolving opportunities and challenges in a changing external environment.

Sometimes the journey seems long and, like a traveller on a meandering river, you may appear to be heading in the wrong direction. However, knowing your destination makes it more likely that you will arrive. While effective leaders are alert to changing circumstances they also remain true to their core aspirations and strategic intentions. Jack

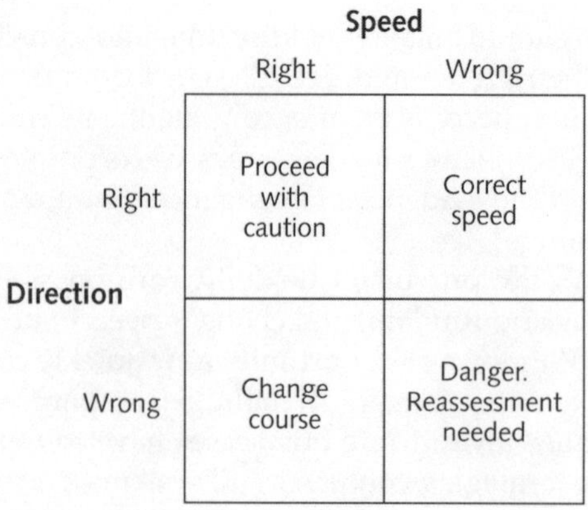

**Figure 2.1**   Speed and direction of change

Welch exuded determination and self-confidence during the 16 years he spent as chief executive of General Electric and achieved a significant turnaround in the company's fortunes.

## UNDERSTANDING THE SOURCE AND NATURE OF GAPS

There could be many reasons for the existence of a gap between aspiration and achievement. Here are some examples:

- The critical success factors for competing and winning may not be understood.
- The leadership of a company could be inadequate. There could be a lack of vision, will and unity at the top.
- The failure could be 'intellectual'. Corporate strategies could be inappropriate or wrong.
- What needs to be done, and what is necessary for its achievement, may not have been thought through.
- A company could be failing to understand and respond to the changing requirements of its customers.
- People may not be in a position as a result of the lack of skills, freedom to act, or resources, to do what they would like to do.
- They may be working on activities that do not add value for customers, or in ways that do not allow them to give of their best.
- They may lack clear priorities as a result of confused messages, or be perplexed by actions that do not match words.
- Initial expectations may have been unrealistic or overambitious.
- Some slippage might have occurred with 'follow-through' consequences, or perhaps the results have yet to work their way through.
- Too much faith may have been placed in panaceas, instant answers, particular and self-contained initiatives, or simplistic approaches.
- The necessary potential might well exist within the company, but it may be unrecognized, or it might not be tapped.
- The company may have the desired capability, but it might be in the wrong place and cannot be reached when needed.
- A reassessment might have led to the conclusion that it would now be too expensive to do what was originally desired.
- Progress may have been held up by internal disagreements, or sabotaged by opponents.
- The company may be receiving advice from those who do not see the 'whole picture', a possible case of 'the blind leading the blind'.
- Some areas of investment may have been counter-productive, leading to results other than those intended.
- Problem areas may have been tackled on a piecemeal or departmental basis, when a more holistic approach is needed.

- Some external party, perhaps a regulator or competitor, might have stepped in or acted in such a way as to prevent certain outcomes from occurring.

One could go on and speculate endlessly about the reasons for a gap between expectation and achievement. Perhaps there are a combination of reasons, the mix and their relative importance varying from situation to situation, and from company to company.

## CLOSING GAPS

A gap between expectation and achievement could be reduced by lowering aspiration or raising achievement (Figure 2.2):

- Aspiration could be reduced by a conscious effort to lower expectations. Rhetoric could be toned down and more modest claims made. A company could claim some credit for realism and honesty, and differentiate itself from the hype of others by stressing the responsible nature of its own statements.
- Achievement could be boosted by such means as clarifying objectives, increasing motivation, or by focusing on the key factors for competitive success. 'Helps and hinders' analysis could be used to identify strengths that could be built upon, and barriers and obstacles that could be tackled. The capability to deliver could be raised by a programme of improvements, and 'missing elements' could be put in place.

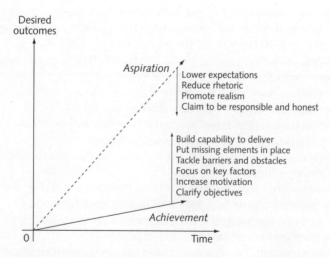

**Figure 2.2** The rhetoric/reality gap

In some situations it may not be easy to lower expectations. People may want to believe something else and may resist. If anything, raising achievement may be easier than reducing aspirations. Consider the following selection of views:

*Once people have tasted something, how can you take it away?*

*Not all the expectations arise from within. We are not alone in the marketplace, and there is a lot going on out there that is raising expectations.*

*If we reduce by one jot, a competitor will be in there like a shot.*

*It took a long time, much creativity and quite a bit of money to raise those expectations. You can't turn them off like a tap.*

A sophisticated management would understand the need to manage both expectation and achievement. Expectation has to be at a level to 'interest', while delivery needs to be sufficient to hold or retain allegiance. A healthy balance needs to be maintained between them. Any gap must be wide enough to stimulate greater achievement, but not so large as to disappoint and alienate.

## MISGUIDED ATTEMPTS

Some attempts by losers to bridge the gap between aspiration and achievement are misguided. For example:

- working harder may only mean sinking deeper into the mire, or moving further off course;
- spending more money may not be the answer if the activity in question is inconsistent with corporate objectives, or not adding value for customers;
- forcing dissent out of the boardroom may achieve unity at the cost of objectivity and balance;
- searching for a new panacea, or embracing an additional palliative, may result in the further postponement of necessary action;
- the use of common tools may help communication and integration, but if imposed in the face of cultural and other differences could achieve these benefits at the cost of a loss of diversity and involvement;
- relocating may demonstrate action, but may shift the site of the symptoms rather than deal with the underlying problems.

Often the source of unintended consequences will lie not in an individual change element itself, but in a lack of balance in its use. Some enthusiasts of particular tools and approaches do not know when to stop. As with

## Losers

Losers:

- are tempted and distracted by personalities and surface appearance;
- make the pursuit of the visible and the formulation of acceptable rhetoric a key element of policy;
- exaggerate achievements and talk up future prospects;
- conceal gaps between aspiration and achievement;
- often avoid grasping nettles and confronting harsh realities;
- close gaps between aspiration and achievement primarily by lowering expectations;
- rationalize their failure to deliver, for example by stressing how difficult it is to achieve a successful corporate transformation;
- are driven by insecurity to want and demand fast results;
- remain frustrated and vulnerable to probing questions by auditors, shareholders and investors.

## Winners

Winners:

- seek to penetrate surface appearance in order to understand the reality beneath;
- avoid rhetoric and focus policy upon the reality of actual achievement;
- give a balanced account of what has been accomplished and endeavour to make accurate and responsible forecasts;
- acknowledge and make explicit gaps between aspiration and achievement and assess, address and manage them;
- are not afraid to tackle difficult issues, take tough decisions and address realities;
- close gaps between aspiration and achievement by taking steps to raise the latter;
- survive and learn from setbacks and persist in striving to achieve what they have set out to accomplish;
- while recognizing that some customers and investors may be impatient are prepared to devote the time it may take to achieve a desired outcome;
- obtain the satisfaction and fulfilment of accomplishing much of what they set out to achieve.

most things, after a time, diminishing, and eventually negative, returns may result from additional use.

Also, some combinations of change elements may work better in certain circumstances than others. The art of change management is to know not just what to use, but also to consider such questions as: where, to what extent, how, with what, and by whom?

## THE TIME FOR DECISION

The crunch time has come. With economic 'daylight' around the corner it becomes more difficult to claim that the lack of visible results is the consequence of recession, or that benefits of change and quality programmes have been 'lost' among 'cutbacks' and other developments.

According to one chairman: 'The jury is still out. What will really show whether or not we are going to make it is the extent to which our business grows when the economy moves out of recession, and the global prospects for our industry improve.'

## THE LURE OF THE FAST RESULT

Doing the right thing may not be easy when there is pressure for change, and a pressing desire for some evidence of rapid results. For example, consider the bringing together of a cross-functional and multi-organizational team to consider a wider range of different aspects of a problem:

- Compared with just 'taking a view' on the basis of 'information to hand', this approach might appear to prolong decision making. Before any of the 'real work' is done the participants may need to be trained in how to operate effectively in such a team.
- However, as a result of the discussion, it may be both easier and faster to move through the subsequent delivery of what is required to an end customer. Potential pitfalls may be identified and thus avoided. Those involved in a 'first experience' may acquire skills that could be used in other groups to good effect. Thus wider benefits might accrue.

A desire for early and tangible results could lead to the avoidance of the team approach, but at the cost of later problems during the implementation phase. It sometimes takes a strong personality to remain underground while digging deeper foundations as others are already visibly piling the bricks on top of each other. For a time the risks inherent in shallow foundations may not be apparent.

# THE POTENTIAL FOR STRATEGIC MISUNDERSTANDING

A further reason for 'putting out' a strong warning signal is that companies often consider a change of strategic direction for the wrong reasons, and at the worst possible time:

- Not realizing the extent to which the failure to achieve corporate goals is the result of inadequate implementation, they assume an original strategy was at fault or, as one interviewee put it, they have been 'barking up the wrong tree'. With this perspective, and the need for change becoming daily more urgent, they engage in a frantic search for a new panacea or source of hope.
- Some companies move off in a new direction and abandon initiatives that in themselves may be valuable just at a time when the identification of the remaining elements required for successful transformation and the elimination of certain barriers could bring them within sight of their destination. They lose heart when so much of what needs to be done has already been accomplished.
- The desire to slim down and reduce overheads can lead to the negativism of cost cutting when the focus should be upon what additional steps should be taken to derive the latent benefits of past expenditure. Assembling the final pieces of the jigsaw puzzle may result in past costs turning out to have been strategic investments.

A fundamental reason for the gap between rhetoric and reality is the tendency to 'go automatic' on implementation. There is too often a reluctance to challenge basic assumptions and explore other alternatives. Too many managers cling like limpets to old ways. Accustomed to living for so long in a murky world of avoidance and rationalization, some find it difficult to adjust to the prospect of a reality that might consist of favourable outcomes.

Beyond focus upon customer value and critical success factors, little need be sacrosanct. Relevant core values, the determination and drive to succeed, and the confidence to change will be wasted if business fundamentals are not addressed.

The will to win is especially important. On occasion, people may have to be prepared to radically alter how they work and learn in order to remain current and viable in altered circumstances. They may have to throw away certain cherished assumptions and traditional building blocks of corporate capability. The trick is to do this without compromising the ability to cope with shocks and capitalize upon the unexpected. An organization and its people must remain awake, aware and adaptable.

# CHECKLIST

▶ Have the aspirations of your company's corporate change programme been clearly articulated?

▶ Have they been agreed by the board?

▶ Have they been expressed in operational and measurable terms?

▶ Who within your company shares these aspirations?

▶ How aware is the top management of your company of gaps between aspiration and achievement?

▶ How willing are they to confront reality?

▶ Is there agreement on the nature and extent of the gaps that have been identified?

▶ To what extent have any gaps between aspiration and achievement been publicly acknowledged and shared with the people of the company and other 'stakeholders'?

▶ Does the culture and reward system of the company encourage openness and trust, or avoidance and concealment?

▶ Are there areas in which the company has a conscious, if unstated, policy of rhetoric or concealment?

▶ Have the dangers and possible implications of such policies been thought through?

▶ Are the general and specific reasons for the existence of a gap between aspiration and achievement understood?

▶ How tolerant is your organization of mistakes?

▶ Has a 'helps and hinders' analysis been undertaken to identify the specific barriers and obstacles to progress, and what needs to be done about them?

▶ Has your company's management team thought through how it should divide its effort between managing expectations and managing achievement?

▶ Who balances the make-up of the various elements in your company's corporate transformation programme?

▶ Does your company fall prey to the lure of the fast result?

▶ Is your company considering a fundamental reassessment of its corporate transformation programme?

▶ Is this being undertaken for appropriate and valid reasons?

# REFERENCES

Coulson-Thomas, C (1992) *Transforming the Company: Bridging the gap between management myth and corporate reality*, Kogan Page, London

Coulson-Thomas, C and Coe, T (1991) *The Flat Organisation: Philosophy and Practice*, BIM, Corby

Festinger, L (1962) *A Theory of Cognitive Dissonance*, Stanford University Press, Stanford

Scase, R and Goffee, R (1989) *Reluctant Managers: Their work and lifestyles*, Unwin Hyman, London

Tushman, M L, Newman, W H and Nadler, D A (1988) Executive leadership and organisational evolution: managing incremental and discontinuous change, in *Corporate Transformation*, ed R Kilman and T J Covey, Jossey-Bass, San Francisco

# 3

# Transforming the Board

*'One sheep in the flock always manages to escape'*

## THE HIDDEN FACTOR

Read through the early bestselling 'guru books' and count the number of references to company directors and corporate boards. In some of the most popular management titles there was not a single reference to the board. It was as if the board did not exist.

Much of the management literature does not mention the group that should determine the purpose, vision, goals, values, objectives, strategy and policies of the company. What is the role of the board in relation to corporate transformation? Are boards catalysts, enablers, engineers and instigators of change? Or are they at best bystanders, and at worst obstacles to the change process, and a burden upon the body corporate?

## CORPORATE DRIVE AND PURPOSE

The board should provide the heart and soul of a company. It should be the source of its will, ambition and drive (Coulson-Thomas, 1993a). Without a sense of purpose, and the will to achieve, the most well-endowed corporation can wither and die.

Members of the senior management team are likely to take their cue from the attitudes, behaviour and commitment of the members of the board, both individually and collectively. The conduct of the directors as 'role models' can inspire and motivate, or stunt and sap the management spirit.

As one managing director put it: 'If we don't "walk the talk", why should we expect anyone else to?'.

A united directorial team that visibly displays a common and sustained commitment to corporate transformation can be a powerful force for change. A divided board can spread a canker of destructive forces throughout the corporate organization, undermining morale and resolve. Inconsistencies between words and deeds can result in a climate of cynicism, despair and distrust.

Successful corporate transformation is very dependent upon the quality of the board, and its commitment to the achievement of change (Coulson-Thomas, 1993b). It can thrive where there is an effective board composed of competent directors. So important is commitment at this level, that if it cannot be obtained, an executive team would be ill-advised to initiate a fundamental transformation.

## THE FUNCTION OF THE BOARD

Whether or not the board is perceived as an overhead cost or a source of focus and inspiration, and regarded as an obstacle or an enabler, will reflect its own view of its role. Too many boards concentrate upon 'staying alive', and responding to good or bad news, rather than proactively guiding their organizations towards the achievement of corporate goals.

Company chairmen describe the function of their boards in terms of establishing policy, objectives, strategy or vision, and monitoring and reviewing the extent of their achievement (Coulson-Thomas and Wakelam, 1991). The implementation of strategy is usually undertaken by a management team that is accountable to the board.

The focus of most boards is upon crafting strategy and monitoring the work of management. More effort is being devoted to providing strategic leadership, sponsoring entrepreneurship and mobilizing people and resources to better create customer and shareholder value. The term 'corporate governance' reflects the primary role of the board which is to govern. Governance generally involves:

- examining challenges and opportunities in the business environment;
- determining a purpose for the company, a reason for its continued existence, and articulating a vision that can be communicated;
- establishing achievable objectives derived from the vision;
- formulating a strategy for the achievement of the defined objectives;
- ensuring that the company has adequate finance, people, organization, supporting technology and management processes to implement the agreed strategy;

- in particular, appointing a management team and establishing the policies and values that define the framework within which management operates;
- agreeing and reviewing plans, and monitoring performance against agreed targets, taking corrective action where appropriate;
- reporting performance to the various stakeholders in the company, and particularly to those with 'ownership rights' and a legal entitlement to certain information.

## ANTICIPATING EVENTS

Events can develop at a frightening pace. The swift decline and closure of Independent Insurance and the rapid deterioration in the fortunes and share price of Marconi illustrate the requirement for independent directors who can spot warning signs, and the need for continual vigilance in boardrooms. Directors need to ensure they and their companies can monitor and react effectively to rapidly changing circumstances.

Apparently healthy situations can quickly crumble. Hence, directors need to think through the implications of their actions. In the 1990s, interest payments on debt were tax deductible but dividends were not. Some UK companies therefore sought to replace equity with debt. However, in less profitable times their boards found they had replaced a discretionary payment with a fixed obligation.

Corporate reputations can also erode rapidly. Directors must ensure that people throughout the organization act and behave to protect and build internal and external expectations and perceptions. Within the Bank of Scotland, reputation management is seen as the responsibility of all employees.

## THE BOARD AND THE MANAGEMENT TEAM

While assuming the ultimate responsibility for a company, directors usually delegate responsibility for operational implementation to members of the management team. The key members of the executive team may be appointed by the board. The organizational framework, including accountabilities, processes and values within which the executive team operates, is usually established by the board.

There is sometimes a stark separation between: (i) the role of the board in creating the vision; and (ii) the role of management in delivering the vision. As gaps emerge between aspiration and achievement, and management finds it difficult to deliver, some boards are recognizing that more effort needs to be devoted to motivating, empowering and equipping the people of the organization to 'make it happen'.

Successful transformation requires an interactive partnership of management and board. The focus of boards has shifted from command and control to empowerment, sharing, enabling, building trust and commitment, and the shaping of attitudes and values. Directors have been required to move into areas with which they are unfamiliar, and which many fear.

## THE ACCOUNTABILITY OF THE BOARD

To whom is the board accountable? There are various stakeholders in a company such as the owners or shareholders, the employees, customers, suppliers, the government and the community at large. The obligations of the board to certain stakeholders are covered by legal and other requirements. The prime 'legal' accountability of the board is to the owners of the company – the shareholders.

When the interests of certain stakeholders may be in conflict the role of the board is to arbitrate between them. In the more predictable world of the past, some boards approached this task as if 'dividing up the cake'. Dividends or pay increases were determined, and pricing decisions taken, on the basis of what could be afforded, or what the board thought it could 'get away with'.

In the world of emerging network organizations this 'static' view of the directors sitting around the boardroom table and allocating a determined pot needs to be replaced by a more flexible approach that focuses on flows and generating value. Various stakeholders provide inputs to, and receive outputs from, the process.

Boards need to be particularly sensitive to public concerns if they are to identify nascent trends and offer genuine alternatives. For example, in a world obsessed with speed, will growing reaction against the fast food culture symbolized by McDonald's favour those who offer a slower eating experience? With growing numbers of people using e-mail and text messaging in addition to 'word of mouth', the consequences of getting it right or wrong are more profound.

## SHAREHOLDER AND CUSTOMER INTERESTS: HARMONY OR CONFLICT?

Most boards emphasize their obligations to shareholders in speeches at AGMs and words in annual reports. However, actual shareholder returns in the form of the dividend cheque that arrives through the post are rarely the product of rhetoric. They are the net result of a number of factors, both 'helps' and 'hinders'.

Some boards that focus upon the process of delivering enhanced value to shareholders find that their priorities need to change. In particular, 'profit' may come to be seen as the consequence of initiating and undertaking a combination of activities that collectively result in satisfied consumers. Those who aim straight for 'profit', or 'return on net assets', without much thought as to the implications of their actions for customers, often find that what they are seeking turns out to be as elusive as the end of the rainbow. Hence companies like Xerox have put customer satisfaction at the top of their list of business objectives.

Dixons Group has practised 'value based strategic management' (VSM). The retailer consciously tackled 'value destroyers' and made long-term investments to create shareholder value.

The focus of the board should be upon the people who are ultimately the source of all value. Financial returns to shareholders should be seen as the product of satisfied customers, and the consequence of involved and fulfilled employees and partners who are empowered and equipped to deliver the value sought by customers.

The words and deeds of the board will reflect the depth and extent of its commitment to the customer. Table 3.1 identifies some of the positive and negative symptoms that may be evident in the boardroom agenda and the conduct of board business.

If the interests of customers are sacrificed to achieve a short-term accommodation with other stakeholders, the company in a competitive market

**Table 3.1**  The boardroom agenda: positive and negative symptoms

| Positive symptoms | Negative symptoms |
| --- | --- |
| Breakout/transformation | Spiral of descent to marginal commodity supplier status |
| Long-term focus | Short-term orientation |
| Redeploy to activities that add value for customers | Headcount reduction |
| Concern with creating customer and shareholder value | Concern with financial numbers |
| Investment approach to learning and IT | Preoccupation with costs of training, IT etc |
| Build added-value opportunities | Lower price/price competitively |
| Securing commitment | Wordsmithing |
| Speed up service to customers to increase customer satisfaction and generate cash | 'Screw customers' to increase margins and generate cash |
| Emphasis on building relationships | Bargaining and negotiation orientation |
| Enabling and sharing culture | Control culture |
| Focus on fact, reality and intention | Expressions of opinion, surmise and hope |
| Holistic approach | 'Line-by-line' approach |

may prejudice its longer-term capacity to serve all stakeholders. The wise investor prefers the reality of commitment to the customer to the rhetoric of 'investor relations'.

## CURRENT CONCERNS AND PUBLIC DEBATE

There has been much recent criticism of the performance and conduct of boards. In practice, in a world of 'strong chief executives' and dependence upon information supplied by management, boards are often not as powerful as the legal situation might suggest.

While some boards and institutional investors do flex their muscles, others seem powerless in the face of circumstances such as those surrounding the demise of the Bank of Credit and Commerce International or following the death of Robert Maxwell. In such cases, and there are many others, people ask: 'Where was the board?' Corporate governance, reports, codes of practice and initiatives over the past decade, including the author's own books *Developing Directors* (Coulson-Thomas, 1993b) and *Creating Excellence in the Boardroom* (Coulson-Thomas, 1993a), have sought to address various abuses and excesses.

## ASSESSING WHAT NEEDS TO BE DONE

To determine what still needs to be done to improve the effectiveness of boards it is necessary to understand the current situation. The companies in the news tend to be 'names' that are likely to be familiar to readers. The great majority of companies, however, are 'small businesses' and little known beyond the ranks of their employees, customers and suppliers. Their directors assume particular legal duties and responsibilities.

What constitutes a competent director and an effective board? How are directors selected? What do they consider the function of the board to be?

Over 800 individual directors participated in surveys undertaken by the author for the first edition of this book (Coulson-Thomas, 1992a), and over two-thirds of these were the chairman, CEO or managing director of their company. The boards covered by the survey programme were representative of the total population of companies.

## GAPS BETWEEN REQUIREMENTS AND REALITY

What emerged was that the reality of the boardroom was often very different from the requirements for successful corporate governance (Coulson-Thomas, 1992a, 1993a, 1993b). The very people who should be the fount of corporate drive and purpose are frequently plagued by insecurity and doubt.

The actual operation of boards is clouded by myth, uncertainty and misunderstanding. Here are some examples:

- Many directors are uncertain as to their directorial duties and responsibilities. Others experience a conflict between the different roles which they may have. An executive director could be a director, a manager and an owner, and in each role might be expected to have a distinct perspective on certain issues.
- In many companies, the allocation of responsibilities between the board and management is unclear. This can lead to confusion, both in the boardroom and throughout the senior management team.
- New members of a board are typically selected on account of being thought to possess directorial qualities. Once appointed, however, if executive directors are assessed at all, they are likely to be evaluated in terms of their managerial performance in running a department or activity rather than their directorial contributions to the business of the board.
- In few companies is there a clear path to the boardroom. The qualities sought in new directors are rarely made explicit. Hence, many managers with directorial ambitions find it very difficult to prepare for membership of the board.

When roles and responsibilities are unclear, the energy that is devoted to sorting out confusions and uncertainties in and around the boardroom is not available for the task of achieving corporate transformation.

## EXPECTATIONS REGARDING THE CONTRIBUTIONS OF DIRECTORS

There was little consensus among chairmen concerning the contribution that was expected from members of boards. Only one in eight companies operated any form of periodic and formal appraisal of personal effectiveness in the boardroom (Coulson-Thomas and Wakelam, 1991). As a result there was little to guide those seeking to improve the quality of directorial contributions:

- The evaluation of the effectiveness of individual members of boards was overwhelmingly informal, and little attempt was made to link performance assessments with the contributions sought from directors.
- When and where boards were assessed, this tended to be in terms of the overall performance of the business, rather than the dynamics of the boardroom and the distinct 'value-added' contribution of the board.

Perhaps because many chairmen find it difficult to define the 'outputs' of a board, their expectations regarding director contributions largely concern 'input' factors such as expertise and personal qualities.

## DIRECTOR EXPECTATIONS AND DIRECTORIAL FRUSTRATIONS

For the individual director, the gap between prior expectations and the realities of boardroom life can be a source of personal dissatisfaction. The following comments are representative of the disappointment with the directorial role felt by many directors:

> *I was originally selected because I had worked abroad and was thought to have an understanding of global issues. I'm now judged as a manager, by how I run my bit, not on the basis of my contribution to the whole.*

> *I had anticipated much more freedom, but the board is dominated by the CEO with the aid of a bunch of cronies.*

> *I should have known, but I expected more discretion. The tentacles of corporate bureaucracy reach across the sea into the boardroom. That's the penalty of being a subsidiary. To the head office bureaucrats we are local managers not directors.*

> *I sometimes wonder what value we really add. It is difficult to assess our contribution. Our role seems intangible.*

> *When you are struggling to keep your own end up, you don't have the time to go through everything with a fine-tooth comb. A lot of rubber stamping goes on.*

> *We are both judge and jury. As an executive director I decide on my own performance. We run the AGM on proxies. In a way I felt more under pressure as a manager.*

> *In law I am directly accountable. I feel I could be penalized for things I cannot really influence.*

Boards must focus on opportunities to make the greatest contribution to the achievement of strategic corporate goals. Too often there is an almost exclusive preoccupation with matters that could be described as 'nice to have'. While desirable in themselves they will not make the difference between winning and losing.

On occasion the penalties of disappointing corporate performance can be swift and severe. Mergers and acquisitions can also decimate boards, and the 'golden goodbye' will not always compensate for the damage done to a public reputation or to personal pride.

## THE GAPS BETWEEN ACTIONS AND WORDS

The board itself, in terms of its own role-model behaviour, may be partly to blame for the disillusionment that is found in many companies (Coulson-Thomas, 1993a) as a result of the growing gap between initial expectations of corporate change programmes and what is actually being achieved. The failure of 'actions to match words' is the source of much misunderstanding and distrust, as follows:

- Under pressure to perform and survive, the focus of many (particularly UK and US) boards has been visibly internal and short term, while the messages that have been communicated to managers have encouraged them to develop longer-term relationships with external customers.
- While directors advocate the transition to a team-based form of organization, the effectiveness of many boards has been limited by poor teamwork. Improved communication, open discussion, regular meetings and a shared or common purpose can help ensure that a board works effectively as a team.
- Many boards that call for a 'focus upon the customer' have not initiated activities to identify the key business processes that deliver customer satisfaction. Boards are defining goals without ensuring that the mechanisms are in place to achieve them.
- While the rhetoric of many boards stresses the need to put the customer first, their ordering of business objectives and the reward systems of their companies result in managers concentrating upon other priorities.
- Boards talk about 'continuous improvement' and the need to develop people, while failing to identify and address their own deficiencies. Many boards do not even recognize the need for improvement. Dissatisfaction is accepted simply because of an inability to determine how it might be addressed.
- Among those who advocate 'benchmarking' and the merits of the 'learning organization', there is little evidence of experimentation with new ways of organizing boards. Peer reviews by other boards, or the benchmarking of other boards, is rarely undertaken.

Many companies register high levels of employee satisfaction. They pride themselves on their internal communications and yet still find it hard to achieve corporate objectives in competitive markets. ICI and Pepsi Co are examples. General and across the board improvements are no substitute for action where it counts, namely on the critical success factors for competitive success.

# BRIDGING THE GAP BETWEEN REQUIREMENT AND PERFORMANCE

Reality suggests that one should not expect either directors to be competent or boards to be effective (Coulson-Thomas, 1993a, 1993b). In many companies:

- no one is consciously focusing upon the competence of the directors and the effectiveness of the board; and
- no initiatives are in place to bridge the significant gaps that often exist between directorial responsibilities, expectations and aspirations, and the capacity of the board to deliver.

Where action is taken, it is often inappropriate. For example:

- such 'development' as is provided may fail to take account of the distinction between direction and management;
- a new board structure might not match the situation and circumstances of the company, while the way the business of the board is conducted may frustrate contributions and inhibit the effectiveness of the team;
- new appointments may ignore the fact that every board is composed of a unique group of personalities. An 'impressive' individual who is effective on one board may be of little value on another. The contribution of individual directors can be very dependent upon the boardroom context.

So far as the implementation of corporate transformation is concerned, some boards do not acknowledge a role for themselves in closing the gaps that are emerging between expectations and achievement. In interview discussions, chairmen drew a distinction between formulating and implementing strategy. It is recognized that the 'right' strategies can be inadequately implemented. However, many boards do not apply 'output' measures to themselves when implementation is regarded as a managerial rather than a directorial responsibility.

# THE QUALITY OF BOARD DECISIONS

The obstacles and barriers that are giving rise to gaps between aspiration and achievement cannot be addressed without confronting reality. Many boards appear to operate upon the basis of opinion rather than fact. The information they receive, and the ways in which they conduct their business, does not allow them to penetrate the façade of appearance in order to identify root causes.

The pressure of events, and a concern with the lack of real progress, is resulting in an excessive focus upon 'the decision'. Many boards devote insufficient attention to understanding the true nature of the situation they are in. Having determined what it is that they wish to do, they give too little consideration to making it happen.

Many boards perceive their field of action in terms of discrete events rather than ongoing flows. Thus, a decision is taken to introduce a change programme or establish a strategic relationship. What happens thereafter is a matter for the management team.

Within the network organization, greater emphasis needs to be put upon the dynamics of situations, flows and processes. For example, relationships need to be nurtured and sustained. There are boards that establish relationships with aplomb, and subsequently devote far too little effort to consolidating them and learning from them.

Taking discrete decisions can demand a high level of analytical skill in the boardroom. The information is presented and a conclusion is reached. Once documented it becomes a matter of record. The building of relationships and the steering of processes that have the in-built capacity to learn and evolve may require greater sensitivity, and a heightened awareness of feelings and values.

In the case of corporate transformation, individual decisions of high quality may not add up to successful outcomes where crucial 'change element' building blocks are missing. It is the accumulation and sequencing of key decisions that closes the gap between aspiration and achievement (Figure 3.1). This requires a holistic approach.

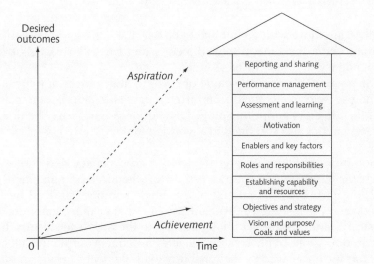

**Figure 3.1** Assembling the building blocks

# FOCUSING ON FACT RATHER THAN OPINION

Reference has already been made in Chapter 2 to the 'lure of appearance', and the tendency to focus on symptoms and cosmetics rather than causes and fundamentals. The following comments illustrate the frustration experienced by many chairmen:

*I respect their opinions, but would prefer some facts.*

*Everyone has views and opinions, and we are not short of background infor-mation. What we need is more understanding.*

*Too often I get played back something that was read or seen. This tells me something about the board members but very little about the problem.*

*We need a framework for structuring problems and sharing understanding.*

Structured discussion, the sharing of information and knowledge and the application of understanding does not just happen. The board and its members may need to be equipped with the processes and tools to focus upon fact and reality, in place of opinion and assumption.

# AVOIDING REALITY

Reality is not always welcomed with open arms into the boardroom. The failure of a key corporate programme to generate the hoped-for results can be painful to confront. People within a boardroom team may react to reality in different ways, as follows:

- There are those who do not like to be told there is a gap between aspi-ration and achievement. Some directors, and particularly CEOs, exhibit a tendency to 'shoot the messenger'.
- Others may 'play up' the value of encouraging sources of information and use 'selectively' the uncomfortable signals. When all, or a majority, of the directors adopt this ploy, the board as a whole may be not only deceived but also cocooned in a world of fantasy.

'Groupthink' and the collective denial by a group of key decision makers of what is happening in practice can distort their decision making (Janis, 1972). In particular, the pursuit of the single solution can lead to intro-version and the instinctive denial of any hint that so much emotional and physical commitment may not be leading to the hoped-for results. In the boardroom, 'groupthink' can have severe consequences from which many directors are only saved by their inability to implement. During a period of corporate transformation, the presence of non-executive or independent directors on a board can introduce a much-needed sense of objectivity, balance and perspective into a directorial team.

## PEOPLE AND NUMBERS

A board intent on changing attitudes and values needs itself to relate to them. It must be sensitive to feelings and values, and recognize the extent to which attitudes are healthy and supportive, and behaviour is appropriate. To do this the directors must look beyond the data.

It is easy to become mesmerized by numbers, especially after they have been carefully selected and packaged in the form of 'board papers'. Behind the ratings, the response rates and the involvement ratios, are real people. How do they feel? What do they believe or expect?

A board should carefully consider what 'the figures' mean. Here are two examples:

- 80 per cent of employees may be satisfied, and this might represent an increase over the previous quarter. But why are one in five not satisfied? How many people does this represent?
- An error rate may only be a fraction of one in a thousand components, but what might happen to an aeroplane in the event of just one failure? What are the 'worst-case' consequences, and are crisis processes in place to enable the company to respond in the event of a disaster?

Just relying upon numbers may enable a board to track some of the consequences of past decisions without necessarily being able to influence future events.

The very numbers used by a board can influence its own attitudes and perspective. For example, when investment decisions are made:

- the use of a measure such as return upon net assets can result in options being considered from the point of view of the company, and decisions could be taken that might, unwittingly, have adverse consequences upon customers;
- relating options to contribution to customer value may increase the prospect of them being assessed in relation to impact upon the customer.

The use of particular measures by the 'core' team to monitor and control the activities of a network organization can influence the thinking of all the members of the network. Others are likely to take a cue from, reflect or follow the approach of the board.

Changing the attitudes and values that make up the culture of a company can represent a major challenge. It also presents the board and senior management with a number of dilemmas. For example, certain of the attitudes and values that are not compatible with 'the vision' may need to be preserved for a while as others are changed. Some sense of continuity and shared values may be needed to hold the corporate team together.

## DECISION MAKING IN CRISIS SITUATIONS

Corporate transformations often occur in situations of crisis. Classic studies of crisis decision making have highlighted the tendency to focus on the short term, and to concentrate upon fewer options, when the 'going gets tough' (Allison, 1971; Steinbruner, 1974). There is a danger that a sense of balance and perspective might be lost just when it is most needed.

Members of boards can experience a tension between the requirement to become more deeply involved in order to demonstrate commitment, and the desirability of maintaining a distance in order to preserve a degree of independence and objectivity. A corporate change programme can increase this schizophrenic pressure upon the individual director.

One director summed up the dilemma:

*We are under tremendous pressure to maintain a façade of unity. People out there are beginning to question whether we will succeed. The views of analysts can't be ignored. They have a direct impact upon the share price. I'm being asked to 'bang the drum' and to go out there and 'sell the programme'. This puts off the day when we will have to 'grasp the nettle' and make some changes. To do this now could lead to a loss of confidence.*

In situations of crisis there is a tendency to cut out information and individuals who do not 'fit', and to concentrate power in the hands of a smaller group of people. This prospect can pose problems for directors who have genuine reservations which they feel duty bound to express.

A chairman should think twice before 'wielding the knife'. It is important to probe the reasons for hesitancy. Enthusiasm could be the product of sycophancy, and caution the result of thought. One chairman acknowledged: 'Team players are not those who just go along without thinking. Some of my colleagues are cautious. They are not obstructive. They are realistic.'

## LETTING GO

Given the many challenges facing companies which we considered in Chapter 1, and the pressures upon central decision makers, it makes sense for a board to delegate:

- In the bureaucratic company a very high proportion of significant decisions used to be taken by individual directors, if not the board as a whole. Corporate procedures existed to ensure this was the case.

- As bureaucracies transition to more flexible and responsive network organizations, boards are sharing rather than hoarding power. Decision-making discretion is being devolved closer to customers, many of whom increasingly demand tailored products and services, and to those managing networks of relationships with customers and suppliers.

One no longer needs to be a director in order to take significant decisions. Decision-making skills are now perceived by many as 'management' rather than 'directorial' competencies.

## INVOLVING AND EMPOWERING

A majority of boards meet on a monthly basis. Directorial duties tend to be intermittent. An executive director may spend a quarter of his or her time on directorial duties and devote the remainder to managerial responsibilities. Hence the need to involve managers in transformation roles that require continuous attention.

Executives are increasingly required to establish 'output' objectives for the business units and teams for which they are responsible and, subsequently, to monitor their achievement. Objectives of business units to which considerable discretion may have been devolved are negotiated with the board rather than imposed by the board.

Involvement does not just happen as a consequence of what is recorded in the minutes of a board meeting. The consequences of board decisions need to be thought through, as follows:

- Past attitudes can have a continuing impact. A board should not be surprised if some people have been reluctant to accept responsibility and risk. For many years a focus upon order and predictability discouraged initiative. One director commented in the context of a reluctance to 'accept empowerment': 'We used to decide everything. We didn't particularly want people around us to think. Their job was to implement and to do it "by the book".'
- People also need to be equipped to handle extra responsibilities and encouraged to prioritize and delegate if they are not to be swamped. As one director put it: 'We've cleared our plate, but out there they need help.' To become an operational reality, empowerment should go hand in hand with appropriate learning and development.

Involvement can have significant consequences for the board itself. In place of decisions concerning individual products, sales or investments, boards are considering framework issues such as whether the company has adequate processes for ongoing learning and change. The establishment and monitoring of frameworks, relationships, values and processes, and arbitrating and negotiating, have grown in importance as agenda items at the expense of 'one-off' or discrete considerations.

# LEADERSHIP FOR CORPORATE TRANSFORMATION

So how are boards performing as enablers and facilitators of corporate change? Many of them are not systematically assembling the building blocks shown in Figure 3.1. The board establishes the vision and wrings its hands as the gap between aspiration and achievement grows wider. According to one chairman: 'The role of the board is the formulation and implementation of strategy. We put our backs into the former, but when it comes to implementation we hand it over to management and hope for the best'.

Top management commitment continues to be a major barrier to change. It is essential in view of the complex nature of the change task in many organizations, and the number of individuals and groups that must be involved.

The widespread perception of a lack of commitment in the boardroom is understandable. As one director put it: 'How can they believe we are committed when we have not put in place all the actions that are necessary to make it happen?'.

Many boards are abdicating their responsibility for leading the process of corporate transformation. Determining vision, mission and strategy appears to be perceived as 'direction' rather than as an aspect of 'leadership'; while the term 'leadership' is applied to the 'management' process of motivating people to understand and achieve vision, mission and strategy, once these have been defined by the board.

'Leadership' appears to be seen by the chairmen of many boards as a management responsibility rather than a boardroom competence. It is not surprising that many management teams perceive a lack of commitment on the part of the boards of their companies.

# THE BOARDS OF WINNERS AND LOSERS

Directors of loser companies often fail to distinguish between operational and strategic matters. They get lost in the detail and are reluctant to delegate responsibilities to an effective management team. Such board meetings as are held tend to be rambling, unstructured and unfocused. Attendees may be largely unaware of their duties and responsibilities as directors and oblivious of significant developments and what is really important.

Winners establish an effective board. This gives them an edge in difficult circumstances. Competent directors are aware of their duties to the company itself and they endeavour to act in its best interests. Looking ahead enables them to identify obstacles and opportunities. For example, they may anticipate a drop in turnover and periods of peak borrowing requirements in time to take corrective action.

Regular meetings and accurate minutes enable specific responsibilities to be allocated and subsequent actions monitored. Losers avoid confrontations. Their meetings have a tendency to become polite rituals. Winners are much more willing to challenge, critique and probe. They question colleagues and hold people to account.

One means of introducing a form of peer review at a senior level is to appoint two or more independent directors to a properly constituted corporate board. Among smaller companies losers tend to avoid this step. Their reasons for caution are as varied as the extra costs involved and the risk of losing control. As a result, the principals of the business may confuse their respective roles as shareholder, manager and director.

People who are not subject to checks and balances sometimes 'go off the rails'. External parties may sense danger when they encounter a board consisting entirely of founder entrepreneurs who are still active in a business and who insist upon calling most of the shots. Those who initially established an enterprise may not be the best people to take it forward to the next stage of development.

Customers, employees, creditors, business partners and investors may all be reassured by the very existence of a balanced, confident, capable and committed board. The active involvement of effective directors may result in a premium being attached to share valuations, particularly when certain individuals have the skills and experience to encourage and support the further growth of a company.

Boards of losers undertake annual reviews of performance and competitiveness to identify problem areas. They concentrate upon the review of past performance and formulate general objectives that are imposed upon the people of the organization. When outcomes fail to match expectations results are fudged, concealed or rationalized, or spin is used to make them appear better than they really are.

In contrast, the directors of winners engage in regular reviews and continually monitor corporate performance. They focus upon resolving issues and taking steps to improve future competitiveness. They are also realists. They know that if there is a gap somewhere in the length of a hedge at least one sheep in the flock will find it. If there is a weak point, the cows will break through.

The direction and guidance that directors of winners give is simple, clear and specific, and they themselves act as role models. They operate as they expect others to behave. They assume accountability for their actions, conduct and decisions and they encourage accurate reporting and honest feedback.

Losers tend to regard observing the principles of good corporate governance as an end in itself. They think in terms of current structures rather than future opportunities. So long as the right committees are in place and their members turn up for meetings directors are thought to earn their fees.

Winners are more concerned with what the board and its committees actually do, for example to release talent and build and mobilize the capability to deliver greater value to more customers and hence achieve corporate objectives. They provide strategic leadership and support internal entrepreneurs. They ensure their companies remain vital and competitive.

## APPROACHES OF WINNERS AND LOSERS

Losers tend to follow others and be reactive. They also look over their shoulders, benchmark and copy. As a consequence they lose control of their destinies. They are insensitive, unaware and fail to anticipate events. Crises catch them unawares and they struggle to respond. Their lack of foresight puts them under time pressure and their inflexibility limits their options.

People in losing companies simply process items that fall into their in-trays. Business development teams respond to incoming invitations to tender. They wait for others to approach them. They reply to those who suggest deals, arrangements and joint venture or take-over proposals without first considering and clarifying their own objectives. Board meetings consider draft replies to the initiatives of others.

Losers can be a salesperson's dream. They agree to meet people who approach them with services to sell even though they may not have identified a requirement for what they are offered. They fall for sales patter and divert resources to distracting activities.

Smooth talkers can lead losers by the nose. Flattery can be used to persuade them to seek a listing. Yielding to pressure or going with the flow is felt by losers to be easier than weighing up the options. Better alternatives are not considered. Steps taken may not be in the best long-term interests of the people involved. Observers wonder whether the board or City advisers are calling the shots.

Winners are more pro-active. They set out to systematically identify the organizations they would most like to have as customers, suppliers or business partners. They analyse the aspirations, strategies, requirements and capabilities of their targets and make a direct or indirect approach to them. They initiate contacts, suggest discussion topics, craft tailored offerings and submit proposals with advantages for all the parties involved.

People in winning companies reflect, assess different courses of action, consider their implications and take decisions. They focus upon building

## Losers

Losers:

- lack will, drive and heart;
- mouth generalizations and have a relatively short-term perspective;
- avoid responsibility and blame others for the lack of corporate achievement;
- confuse the respective roles of director, manager and shareholder;
- are preoccupied with their status and uncertain about directorial duties and responsibilities;
- concentrate upon the internal, policing and stewardship aspect of corporate governance;
- engage in damage limitation and seek to protect their own positions and maximize their remuneration and compensation packages;
- do not provide a distinctive and compelling purpose or sustained and collective commitment;
- focus almost exclusively upon financial measures of performance and the control of costs;
- make little conscious effort to improve the competence of directors or the effectiveness of boards.

## Winners

Winners:

- have the will to win and are driven to succeed, while being able to show that they care;
- address specifics and take a medium to long-term view;
- assume responsibility and are prepared to be accountable for their actions;
- understand the different roles of director, manager and shareholder and the distinction between direction and management;
- are clear about directorial duties and responsibilities and preoccupied with enabling and supporting the achievements of others;
- concentrate upon the external, strategic and business development aspects of corporate governance;
- strive to 'build the business' and deliver additional value for customers and shareholders;
- provide clear direction, a distinctive purpose, and achievable goals that prove compelling to those working towards their achievement;
- manage performance by means of an appropriate range of indicators and concentrate upon developing new income streams, capabilities and intellectual capital;
- invest in director and board development and the professional selection, appointment and induction of new directors.

relationships, creating value and enhancing capabilities. They do not wait to be asked. They approach suppliers with specific objectives and procurement occurs on their terms. They then become demanding customers.

It is particularly important that processes and practices for winning business are proactive. Research has shown that establishing a relationship early on in the procurement process can significantly improve the prospects for success. Getting in before a requirement has crystallized can create opportunities to influence the scope of what is procured.

Winners ruthlessly weed out unsolicited approaches that do not satisfy their priority requirements. When they meet professional experts and advisers they do so on their own terms. They set the agenda. They sit in the driving seat and are seen to be in charge. At board meetings directors review corporate goals, prioritize objectives and review strategies, approaches and initiatives for attaining them.

## THE EFFECTIVE BOARD

A collection of outstanding individuals will not necessarily 'gel together' in the context of a particular boardroom. The effective board is composed of a united team of competent directors who are willing to assume responsibility for bringing about corporate transformation. The first step in formulating, communicating and sharing a vision of a different form of organization, and a transformation strategy, is for the chairman to ask the following questions:

- Do the members of the board share a common vision of a more flexible and responsive form of organization? If fundamental change is to occur there must be an agreed vision of a better way of operating and relating to various groups of stakeholders.
- Has the board identified critical success factors for competing and winning? What represents value for customers, and the processes that deliver this value? Are there hidden barriers that fall between responsibilities?
- Are the directors committed to an agreed change strategy? The directors should be committed to both a clear and compelling vision, and a common and realistic strategy for its achievement.
- How effective are members of the board at communicating with customers, employees and business partners? A clear and compelling vision has to be communicated and understood if it is to be shared, and if it is to motivate.

The board should be a facilitator of change, rather than its victim, and an active enabler of the transition towards the network organization. The views of the author on what boards need to do are set out in *Creating*

*Excellence in the Boardroom* (Coulson-Thomas, 1993a) and *Developing Directors* (Coulson-Thomas, 1993b).

## AVOIDING GENERALIZATION

Those who are intent on restructuring their board should bear in mind that there is no such thing as a standard board in terms of size and composition, and perceived roles and responsibilities (Coulson-Thomas and Wakelam, 1991). There is a variety of both boards and directors:

- The various types of board include unitary and supervisory boards, subsidiary and holding company boards, and boards of private and public companies.
- A board could contain different types of director, for example, executive and non-executive directors, and owner-directors or alternate directors.
- Corporate transformation is resulting in new portfolios and job titles. Within the boardroom team there could now be facilitating directors, or directors of change, transformation, involvement, empowerment, thinking or learning.

The right approach to adopt will depend upon the situation and circumstances of the individual company, and may need to evolve and adapt during the course of a transformation programme.

## BOARD SIZE AND COMPOSITION

The size and composition of a board should reflect what is necessary to develop a particular business and bring about a significant change from where a company is to where it aspires to be. To achieve corporate transformation a board will need to share, involve and enable.

Owner-directors of smaller companies are sometimes inhibited by the cost of bringing extra people on to a board. As company size increases directors may be given particular and exclusive responsibilities. Only in larger companies may there be a conscious search to appoint a director to a functional portfolio because of a 'vacancy'.

Board size and composition should not be taken for granted. The advantages and disadvantages of having more, or fewer, directors will depend upon a company's business opportunity and its transformation challenge.

## APPOINTING DIRECTORS

In corporate mythology there is tough competition for boardroom appointments. Every so often the chairman opens the door to the boardroom just long enough to let in some new blood before shutting it again in the faces of a jostling mass of ambitious managers. In reality, many chairmen find it difficult to identify individuals with directorial attributes.

Overwhelmingly, directors are appointed as a result of their personal qualities. Language skills and academic, professional and technical qualifications are only of secondary significance, and expert opinion tends to be treated with some caution and scepticism. Qualities sought include judgement, objectivity, balance, perspective and individuality.

Many chairmen are 'supply constrained' and would consider bringing extra directors on to their boards if individuals with the appropriate qualities could be found. When seeking additional members of the boardroom team:

- The key requirement is for individuals who are able to develop a perspective of the organization as a whole, and facilitate corporate development and change.
- There also needs to be an understanding of the distinguishing characteristics of the network organization, such as the relationships between its members, and the processes by which value is generated and delivered.

Above all, the attributes and qualities of new board members should complement and support those of the existing members of the directorial team. New appointments should be used to remedy deficiencies within the group and plug any awareness or perspective gaps that might emerge.

## ATTRACTING CONTRIBUTORS RATHER THAN COURTIERS

Many boards limit their search for potential directors to those who happen to be a member of a company's senior executive team, those holding senior management positions elsewhere or acquaintances of the chairman or chief executive. A more open approach would be to recognize that people with 'direction' qualities might well be found elsewhere:

- As greater numbers of managers focus on external customer requirements, acquire general facilitating competencies, and become involved in company-wide task forces and international projects, more of them may have an opportunity to acquire a sense of the 'company as a whole'.
- In contrast, a senior manager in a 'head office' environment may have little direct customer contact, and could well be immersed in the relatively narrow concerns of a particular unit. Such an individual may possess the qualities and characteristics of the bureaucratic past rather than the network future.

The people who reach the top of organizations are often those who have been adept at climbing the corporate bureaucracy, rather than those who can bring about change in the future. They are courtiers rather than contributors. Some of those who can influence, get along with others, create a good impression, and who appear to be team players, may lack the capability to deliver results.

Relationships with other organizations in supply chains, and individuals who are colleagues or partners rather than employees or subordinates, are assuming greater importance. Paying attention to both internal and external needs is a requirement for effective operation at all levels. The development paths of both directors and managers must now take account of this new reality. In the case of the 'network organization' the route to the boardroom is likely to consist of a journey around the network in order to gain some understanding of its various processes and components, rather than a series of steps up, or movement between, functional ladders (Figure 3.2).

Potential board members are increasingly aware of the legal liabilities which directors can incur. Some highly qualified and sought-after individuals prefer to avoid or limit board appointments in favour of working upon *ad hoc* projects for negotiated fees.

## DIRECTORIAL QUALITIES

The qualities that distinguish directors from managers derive from: (i) their different legal duties and responsibilities; and (ii) the role of the

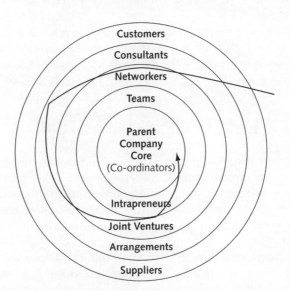

**Figure 3.2** The network organization

board. Directors require strategic awareness, the ability to see a company as a whole and understand the context within which it operates. Formulating a distinctive vision and a realistic strategy requires objectivity, the ability to look ahead and a willingness to assume individual and collective responsibility. At minimum, directors should be aware of their legal duties and responsibilities. A degree of self-discipline may also be needed to be an effective member of a boardroom team.

There are particular roles in the boardroom such as chairman, chief executive or non-executive director that may require 'additional' skills beyond those possessed by other directors. For example, independence and a willingness to probe and ask questions which executive directors may feel inhibited from raising, are desirable qualities in non-executive directors.

Directors from very different boards may face similar issues (Demb and Neubauer, 1992). Matters relating to the operation of the board itself of concern to many directors include:

- the need to balance delegation of responsibility to management with the maintenance of control;
- the need to reconcile involvement and commitment with the value of detachment and objectivity; and
- how to establish an effective team without inhibiting the contributions of individuals.
(Demb and Neubauer, 1992)

Many boards face a chicken-and-egg dilemma. Directors are expected to possess the attitudes and approaches associated with the flexible network organization if they are to bring it about, while acting within a more traditional context.

Many corporate organizations do not make explicit the qualities they are seeking in new directors or have open routes to the boardroom. This makes it difficult for those with 'different' qualities or characteristics to break in.

## DEVELOPING DIRECTORS

Companies and their chairmen may like to think they 'groom' their directors. In some larger companies there appears, at least on paper, to be a development and succession planning route from graduate recruit to the boardroom. So far as companies in general are concerned, however, there does not appear to be a generally practised path to a boardroom appointment.

Many companies operate an effective 'induction' process for newly-appointed directors. Unlike the effort devoted to briefing and inducting new members of staff, directors have been required to 'pick things up' as they go along.

Many companies do not acknowledge the need for investment in professional development in the boardroom. New directors should be made aware of their duties and responsibilities. Counsellors and mentors are required to guide the development of individual directors, and to work with boards to develop their skills as a team.

A chairman could use such opportunities as boardroom discussion for informal learning. Chairmen should act as catalysts in assessing boardroom development needs and ensuring that appropriate action is taken.

## FACILITATING DIRECTORS

A challenge for many boards is to bring about change, while keeping an existing 'show on the road'. Hence the appointment of facilitating directors to supplement or replace 'traditional' functional directors in order to enhance the ability of boards to cope with change. The 'end points' of this trend, so far as executive directors are concerned, are boards composed largely of the owners of 'horizontal' activities or cross-functional processes.

Many directors do not have the qualities, attitudes and perspectives, or the enabling and empowering skills, to undertake a facilitating role. Such places within the boardroom team will be occupied by those who can direct and manage change, and work with others, those who understand how to re-engineer and support key management and business processes, harness skills and build external relationships.

Facilitating directors with longer-term responsibilities relating to reshaping the organization to meet strategic business development opportunities may assist a company to achieve longer-term change, without losing a grip on the need to deliver current business objectives.

Individual members of a board may feel threatened by the prospect of fundamental change. The successful management of change may require the introduction of 'new blood' without loyalties, attachments and associations with the past. On the other hand, there is little point in importing new directorial or managerial talent if the circumstances are not created for it to be effective.

## HARMONY, UNITY AND EFFECTIVENESS

A long period of success can result in a complacent management team. Those who have known 'hard times' may be more flexible and resilient than those who have had it 'cushy'. Too often appointments to boards are made on the basis of a past record of success which may have done little to prepare those concerned for future challenges.

The chairman is the most appropriate person to monitor and evaluate how effectively the board works together as a team. Teamworking in a situation of collective responsibility in the boardroom can demand skills that are different from those required when working in a management group on an assigned task, either as a subordinate or project leader.

The danger of a comfortable group of people who are unwilling to challenge each other should be avoided. However, following full and frank discussion there needs to be some respect for a collective decision.

A group cannot effectively plan for change without assuming a degree of resistance and addressing how this should be tackled. It is arrogant of a board to assume that its decisions represent the end of the matter, and to automatically label any future dissent as a case of disloyalty or evidence that someone does not fit in.

## THE ROLE OF THE CHAIRMAN

During an era of corporate transformation it is especially important that the distinct roles of chairman and chief executive are both addressed. While all eyes are on the CEO, the role of the chairman tends to be overlooked. Ideally, and in most situations, the roles should be separated and two individuals should be involved:

- The CEO should have the prime responsibility for bringing about the transformation of the corporate organization and achieving business objectives.
- The chairman should ensure that the process of transformation is understood by the external stakeholders in the company, and that the board is effective in initiating, facilitating, supporting and sustaining it.

The chairman has a particularly important role to play in improving board effectiveness (Coulson-Thomas, 1993a). Reference has already been made to the need for company chairmen to ensure that all directors are properly prepared, and that their boards operate effectively as a team.

The chairman should:

- monitor the effectiveness of the board, and that of individual directors, on an ongoing basis;
- periodically review the size, composition and operation of the board;
- ensure that all candidates for boardroom appointments are made aware of the qualities sought in directors, and of the distinct legal duties and responsibilities of the company director;
- assess annually the personal effectiveness in the boardroom, and contribution to the board of all directors. Where appropriate, such an assessment of executive directors could draw upon the views of non-executive directors.

# SELF-ASSESSMENT

A chairman should encourage the board as a whole to take greater responsibility for its own effectiveness and performance. At least once a year all boards should carry out an objective assessment of their function and purpose, their individual and collective roles and responsibilities, and their overall effectiveness as a board. Few boards seek to compare themselves with and to learn from others. To ensure objectivity, some boards seek external assistance in facilitating their reviews. 'Non-competing' company boards could carry out a 'peer review' or audit of each other's performance.

Particular attention should be given to the appointment of non-executive directors, and whether the search for candidates for executive director appointments might be extended beyond the senior management team. Boardroom appointments could be rotated to give more members of a senior management team or network partners experience of board service.

# THE BOARD AND CORPORATE TRANSFORMATION

All boards tend to develop their own approach to corporate transformation. The role of a board in bringing about change could vary from a benign or hands-off approach, through encouragement by means of guidelines, more active planning, co-ordination and control, to active involvement in a number of initiatives to 'make it happen'.

If significant change is to occur, sustained and shared board and top management commitment is of crucial importance. Many boards would benefit from undertaking a review process along the lines of that shown in Figure 3.3. A systematic approach increases the prospects of identifying all the various 'change elements' that need to be brought together to achieve a successful transformation. To ensure that it fully confronts the transformation challenge a board must do the following.

## Determine what needs to be done

The board should determine a distinctive purpose for the company, a compelling reason for its continued existence and development and articulate a vision that can be communicated. It should establish achievable and measurable objectives derived from the vision, and formulate a strategy for the achievement of the defined objectives.

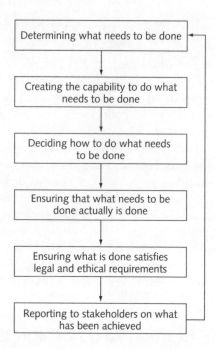

**Figure 3.3** Board review process

## Create the capability to do what needs to be done

The board should ensure that the company has adequate finance, people, organization, supporting know-how and technology, and management processes to implement the agreed strategy. In particular, it should appoint a management team, establish the policies and values within which management operates and put a performance management framework in place.

## Decide how to do what needs to be done

The board should agree and review plans, and allocate roles and responsibilities. In particular, it should identify the critical success factors for competing and winning, and the key processes that will deliver business objectives, and especially value to customers.

## Ensure that what needs to be done actually is done

The board should monitor performance against agreed targets, taking corrective action where appropriate. Gaps between expectation and achievement need to be identified and subjected to 'barrier', or 'helps' and 'hinders' analysis. Particular attention should be paid to the operation of processes, changes of attitudes and behaviour, and to ensuring that the necessary enablers are in place.

## Ensure that what is done satisfies legal and ethical requirements

The board should pay particular attention to its own conduct, and to ensuring that corporate codes of conduct and statements of corporate values thrive and are not regarded as 'nice sentiments' or 'words on paper'.

## Report to stakeholders on what has been achieved

Performance should be reported to the various stakeholders in the company in terms that reflect their interests and understanding.

The review process that links these responsibilities is that illustrated in Figure 3.3.

The board has to forge a balance between its vision, corporate capability and the demands of the external business environment and opportunities being pursued and created. Moving too far ahead of capability can disturb an established position and result in demoralization. Where corporate transformation is occurring, balance has to be maintained in a dynamic situation.

We have seen that a more customer-related and opportunity creating role is changing the priorities of many directors. Discussions with company chairmen suggest:

- Boards spend less time establishing and monitoring procedures, and devote more time to initiating and facilitating processes for entrepreneurship, delivering customer value, creating and exploiting know-how, and achieving ongoing adaptation and change.
- Boards devote significantly greater effort to corporate learning and performance management, ie 'making it happen', or ensuring that measurable objectives are both set and achieved. There is little point in crafting a superb strategy that remains as 'words on paper'.
- Boards pay more attention to attitudes, values and behaviour. Increasingly, companies are competing upon the extent to which their management and business processes enable them to cope with a changing business environment.

# INTERNATIONALIZING THE BOARD

The board of an international network organization requires a global perspective. There are various ways in which a board could be internationalized, as follows:

- Membership could be internationalized. ICL and Rank Xerox were early adopters of an international board composed of a mix of nationalities.
- Responsibilities, function or scope could be internationalized. Unilever established Lever Europe with a European board as part of its Europeanization strategy.
- Some companies such as Motorola and Xerox have held board meetings abroad which enable board members to meet local partners, government representatives and major customers.

When a main board is composed entirely of nationals of an ultimate holding company, and local operating company boards are largely made up of local nationals, a 'cultural divide' can arise.

# DIFFERENT NATIONAL PERSPECTIVES ON BOARDS

The author, brought up in a UK context, happens to believe that boards are important. However, a word of caution is needed (Coulson-Thomas, 1992b):

*A company negotiating with others should remember that the role and purpose of the board can vary greatly across countries. In some countries the board determines strategy and may act in a general supervisory capacity. In others its main purpose could be legal, to technically approve accounts or to appoint a chief executive to whom wide powers are delegated. Some boards exist to tap expert advice, to lend prestige or authority by drawing upon big names or to give the appearance that certain interests are represented.*

Those seeking to build international network organizations should remember that: 'The degree of influence exerted by a board and the importance of its individual members may not be easy to determine ... the main board may be but one decision making forum within a company (Coulson-Thomas, 1992b).

All sorts and conditions of boards may be encountered by those intent upon building international network organizations.

# CHECKLIST

▶ Who is responsible for ensuring that the board is effective and composed of directors that individually and collectively are competent?

▶ Does the board evaluate its own effectiveness at least once a year?

▶ What does the board do to benchmark itself against other boards?

▶ Is the nature of the board and how it conducts its operations appropriate to the situation and circumstances of the company?

▶ Is the board aware of its accountabilities to various stakeholders?

▶ Does the board fully understand the requirements of the various stakeholders in the company?

▶ Have the cross-functional and inter-organizational processes that deliver these requirements been identified?

▶ Are the individual members of the board aware of their legal duties and responsibilities as directors?

▶ Has the board identified a distinctive purpose for the company, and agreed and shared a compelling vision?

▶ Has the board agreed and shared clear goals and values, established measurable objectives and put a performance management framework in place?

▶ Have the 'vital few' actions that must be done been identified, and roles and responsibilities relating to their achievement been allocated?

▶ Does the board pay sufficient attention to the implementation of objectives and policies?

▶ Are the enablers, critical success factors and resource requirements for implementation in place?

▶ Are the people of the organization motivated, empowered and equipped with the necessary skills to make it happen?

# REFERENCES

Allison, G T (1971) *Essence of Decision*, Little Brown, Boston

Coulson-Thomas, C (1992a) *Transforming the Company: Bridging the gap between management myth and corporate reality*, Kogan Page, London

Coulson-Thomas, C (1992b) *Creating the Global Company: Successful internationalisation*, McGraw-Hill, London

Coulson-Thomas, C (1993a) *Creating Excellence in the Boardroom: A guide to shaping directorial competence and board effectiveness*, McGraw-Hill, London

Coulson-Thomas, C (1993b) *Developing Directors: Building an effective boardroom team*, McGraw-Hill, London

Coulson-Thomas, C and Wakelam, A (1991) *The Effective Board: Current practice, myths and realities*, an Institute of Directors Discussion Document, London

Demb, A and Neubauer, F-F (1992) *The Corporate Board: Confronting the paradoxes*, Oxford University Press, New York and Oxford

Janis, I L (1972) *Victims of Groupthink*, Houghton-Mifflin, Boston

Steinbruner, J D (1974) *The Cybernetic Theory of Decision*, Princeton University Press, Princeton, New Jersey

# 4

# Providing Strategic and Distinctive Leadership

*'Pike choose their hunting spots with care'*

## DOING THE VISION THING

Most executives assume the value of a compelling and distinctive corporate vision that 'grabs the attention' of customers and 'turns on' employees. The annual report is considered naked without its statement of vision, and helping companies to formulate visions and missions has been a lucrative area of practice for consultants.

A clear vision is of value internally and externally:

- Internally, it motivates people to achieve and focuses their efforts.
- Externally, the vision differentiates a company from its competitors.
- Internally and externally, the common and shared vision is a unifying factor in holding the network organization together and providing it with a sense of common purpose.

The people of some organizations are held together by a relatively simple shared intent such as the 'Kill Kodak' slogan of Fuji Film's enthusiasts. The Federal Express approach to the customer, 'absolutely, positively and overnight', and the Golden Corral mission of making pleasurable dining affordable both act as guides to what the organization is all about.

Chief executives consider themselves negligent if their companies are without a mission statement that is generally available to all employees. In the 1990s, companies devoted considerable effort to communicating corporate visions and missions throughout their corporate organizations. The evidence was all around, in the posters on the walls of corporate offices and the 'mission cards' carried by employees.

## VISION AND REALITY

Has all this activity been worthwhile? A vision can inspire, but it can also result in disillusionment if it is incomplete or incapable of achievement. Like an idea, it may have little value outside of an organization with the capability to give it a tangible reality.

Many attempts to formulate and implement visions and missions have been naïve, and in some cases destructive. A wide gulf has emerged between rhetoric and reality, and between aspiration and achievement. Instead of inspiration and motivation, there is disillusionment and distrust. In too many boardrooms the agreement of a vision is perceived as the 'output', rather than as an initial step on what may prove to be a long process of implementation.

This chapter examines what progress, if any, has been made in providing distinctive purposes and offerings, and the longer-term and sometimes hidden consequences of the short-term reactions of corporate boards to economic pressures. It emphasizes that changing attitudes and perspective generally takes longer than is first thought.

The lack of top management commitment and of communication skills are major barriers to change. To share a compelling vision requires new attitudes and approaches to communication. In this chapter we will also further examine the respective roles of the chairman and the CEO in relation to corporate transformation.

## THE NEED FOR CLEAR VISION AND STRATEGY

We saw in Chapter 1 that for a decade, and in the face of multiple challenges and opportunities, companies have sought to: (i) differentiate themselves from competitors; and (ii) become more flexible, responsive and adaptable (Coulson-Thomas and Brown, 1989, 1990).

The notion of the flexible and responsive network organization is far from being a quaint concept that 'sounds nice'. Hard-nosed chief executives are seeking to bring it about. A 1991 survey (Coulson-Thomas and Coe, 1991) reveals the extent to which changes were occurring within organizations: Approaching nine out of ten of the participating organizations are becoming slimmer and flatter, while in some eight out of ten more work is being undertaken in teams, and a more responsive network organization is being created.'

In such circumstances, involving change and uncertainty, a clear vision and strategy is essential. Without it, organizations can fragment during the transition from the bureaucratic to the emerging network organization. One CEO confessed: 'We almost lost control. People went off in all directions. I've had to put the old restrictions back on. They will have to stay until we can communicate or share the vision of what we are trying to do.'

## THE IMPORTANCE OF VISION

Survey evidence a decade ago emphasized the central importance of a clear vision:

- In the *Flat Organisation* survey (Coulson-Thomas and Coe, 1991): 'Every respondent believed clear vision and mission to be important, and about three-quarters of them considered it "very important"'.
- The *Quality: The Next Steps* survey (Coulson-Thomas and Coulson-Thomas, 1991a) concluded that: 'A clear and shared quality vision and top management commitment are essential.'
- In the *Communicating for Change* survey (Coulson-Thomas and Coulson-Thomas, 1991b), 'clear vision and strategy' and 'top management commitment' were jointly ranked as the most important requirements for the successful management of change.

The *Communicating for Change* survey concluded that: 'Clear vision and strategy, and top management commitment are of crucial importance in the management of change. The vision must be shared, the purpose of change communicated, and employee involvement and commitment secured.'

The board is primarily responsible for formulating and agreeing a company's strategic vision and ensuring its implementation. In some companies particular individuals have been given the specific task of ensuring that a corporate vision remains current and vital. These keepers of the vision attract various job titles. At USA.net someone known as the Chief Visionary undertakes the role.

A vision should capture the essence of what a company is all about. At the start of the new millennium, Steve Ballmer became CEO of Microsoft. His predecessor Bill Gates, a co-founder of the company, assumed the title of chairman and chief software architect. The latter role allows Gates to return to his roots and the activities he most enjoys. It also reflects the importance of a strategic vision in the development of new technologies.

## THE DISTINCTIVE VISION

A vision should be distinctive. It should differentiate, and answer the question: 'What's so special about your organization?' Consider the following typical comments:

*We have not given the company a distinctive purpose. We are in a commodity marketplace and are difficult to distinguish from our competitors.*

*Yes, like almost everyone else our vision is to be the best or number one – however it is phrased. But doesn't everyone want to be important? Wouldn't we all like to be number one?*

*Lop off the branches of a tree and it sprouts again, it has a sense of purpose, a drive for life. Too many companies give up at the first challenge, because their plans are not rooted in anything substantial.*

Sir John Harvey-Jones believes a vision should present 'an attractive and clear view of the future which can be shared. It must motivate, be ambitious, and should stretch people to achieve more than they might ever have thought possible' (Coulson-Thomas and Didacticus Video Productions Ltd, 1991).

The visions established by many boards fall short of this ideal. Quite simply, what is presented does not suggest any reason why a potential customer or possible employee should have any interest in whether or not the companies concerned live or die. No indication is given of what might be lost to the world in the event of their demise, or why anyone should care that they succeed.

## THE FAILURE OF IMPLEMENTATION

In the case of the vision of the flexible and responsive network organization, aspiration has not been translated into achievement. Many initiatives were doomed from the start. People were not equipped or motivated to change.

The BIM *Flat Organisation* report (Coulson-Thomas and Coe, 1991) concluded that: 'While clear vision and mission are thought to be essential, in many companies both are regarded as just words on paper and they do not act as a guide to action.' As one director put it, 'A document is dead'. A vision needs to live in the hearts and minds of all employees (Coulson-Thomas and Wakelam, 1991).

## THE FAILURE TO COMMUNICATE AND SHARE

The author's *Communicating for Change* survey (Coulson-Thomas and Coulson-Thomas, 1991b) found widespread awareness of the need to change. However, a commitment to significant change was rarely matched by a confident understanding of how to bring it about.

Simple and superficial changes, such as shifting priorities, or those involving the use of words, can and sometimes do occur overnight. Fundamental changes of attitudes, values, approach and perspective usually take a longer time to achieve. The timescale to bring about such changes may extend beyond the lifetime of the change requirement.

Recession increased the extent of cynicism and mistrust, as boards during the early 1990s felt it necessary to take short-term actions that conflicted with longer-term objectives. A managing director confided in despair, 'I know I'm doing things that will weaken us in the long term. What's worse, almost everyone else knows as well. I'm surviving, but one day when the recession is over what we have done will come back to haunt us'.

If a vision is to be shared by employees and understood by customers it must be seen by them as relevant. It must relate to their needs and interests. As one frustrated corporate communicator exclaimed: 'We have a vision and a strategy, but I don't see why anyone else should be interested. It is all about us.'

## CORPORATE TRANSFORMATION OR CORPORATE BUTCHERY?

The gap between vision and reality is particularly evident in the arena of corporate transformation. Many corporate transformation programmes are carried out with the subtlety of the crazed butcher wielding a chainsaw. The blind pursuit of 'flattening the hierarchy' or 'overhead reduction' can have unexpected consequences, as follows:

- The section that is cut out might hold valuable knowledge or be a vital component of a key cross-functional process. Many companies settle down to the task of amputation without first identifying the key processes that deliver the value sought by customers. These are the nerves and arteries without which the organization is dead meat.
- Areas and activities that 'lose money' may still generate a contribution. Cutting them out, without reducing activity elsewhere that does not add value for customers, could result in a heavier burden upon other units. Further activities may appear 'unprofitable' in the light of the reallocated costs.

Much of the damage results from the application of approaches that were accepted with some reluctance, practised and regarded as legitimate in the bureaucratic organization. In the network organization, however, they can be dangerous, and may also be in direct conflict with its articulated values.

## MOVING FROM MACHINE TO ORGANISM

The bureaucracy may have been perceived as a machine, with parts that can be replaced. But the network organization is a living organism made up of flows and relationships. Organisms are sensitive, and crude approaches to transformation can be as indiscriminate in their impact as the plague.

To set out with an objective defined in terms of cost savings, or head-count or management layer reduction, can be a recipe for disaster. Instead, the focus should be upon identifying and strengthening those areas, activities and processes that create opportunities, deliver value and satisfaction to customers, and contribute to corporate objectives, while eliminating those that do not.

Unwanted fat may be distributed throughout the corporate organism. Removing it can result in a leaner and fitter organization. However, many areas of fat lie close to vital organs, and uninformed and misguided butchery can result in a mutilated cripple that is left to die by its more nimble competitors.

## MECHANICAL AND INTUITIVE APPROACHES

Viewing the corporate organization as a machine can lead to a mechanical approach to planning. To implement a vision it may be necessary to reach and manage emotions and change attitudes, feelings and values. In a world in which establishing and sustaining relationships and partnerships with a range of stakeholders is of crucial importance, sensitivity to a diversity of values and cultures is becoming essential.

A living organism is in a continual state of flux as it evolves and adapts. Flexibility is a key requirement for successful change. The flexibility of execution may be as important as the appropriateness of the direction that has been established if success is to be achieved.

Flexibility requires the freedom to think and the empowerment, ability and will to act. The reality of the workplace is often far removed from the concept of the reflective feeling organization. As one manager put it: 'Stop to think about anything around here and you become a headcount reduction opportunity.'

## VISION AND THE NETWORK ORGANIZATION

The vision of an organization should represent a strategic intent to bring about a desired state of affairs. Many companies also have mission statements which set out the values, principles and priorities of the organization.

The compelling vision needs to secure the commitment of, and hold together, the diverse members of the network organization. To do this may require the skills of the politician in holding together a coalition of interests.

A global vision can bring about a degree of common focus and harmony of purpose, but at the same time care needs to be taken to ensure that responsiveness to local needs is encouraged. A transformation strategy may need to set out consciously to create both unity and diversity.

## TURNING VISION INTO REALITY

Many carefully crafted strategies of 'loser' companies remain on 'wish lists', or as 'monuments' in the form of dead documents gathering dust on shelves. They are not alive in the hearts and minds of people engaged in the task of implementation. Very often this is because of missing elements. For example:

- the strategy has not been converted into action programmes;
- roles and responsibilities relating to these programmes have not been allocated;
- critical success factors that distinguish winners from losers have not been identified; and
- target levels of achievement have not been set.

Goals need to be translated into objectives that can be measured in terms of tangible outputs. Otherwise they are not a basis for action. They will not pass the 'So what?' test.

Even when responsibilities have been allocated and targets set, the desired action may not occur where:

- the reward and remuneration system encourages people to do something else; and
- they are not empowered or equipped with the skills to do what is necessary.

Too many strategic activities are self-contained rather than carried on as an integral component of an overall management process. Very often visioning activities are hermetically-sealed exercises, that are carried on in isolation from the other elements of a corporate change programme. They happen at locations such as country house hotels that are as far removed as can be imagined from the world of work, and the little that is done afterwards to translate flip-chart scribblings into implementable initiatives ensures that they will never intrude upon it.

Both vision and strategy have to be communicated and shared. The results of communication should be monitored to ensure that it leads to understanding. One managerial interviewee pulled a mission statement out of his wallet: 'Here it is. They put it on a piece of card. I couldn't tell you what it says. It's one of those things that doesn't stick, but we've all got one.'

A board and its directors need to be persistent if barriers to full implementation are to be identified and overcome. We saw in the last chapter that many boards spend far too much time 'crafting strategy', and far too little time 'making it happen'.

## ROOTING THE VISION IN REALITY

In formulating change strategy, objectivity and a high degree of intuition and judgement is needed to identify and assess relevant developments in the social, economic, political, technological, physical and competitive environments. Carrying out an analysis of corporate strengths and weaknesses, and of external challenges and opportunities requires sensitivity, and the capacity to select and prioritize.

Not all developments can be foreseen, let alone quantified. Some tolerance of uncertainty and understanding of risk is required. In many cases it may be worth tracing through the impacts of alternative sets of assumption.

Some visions float. They do not appear to connect with reality. In the world of Orange's vision, speech is the primary means of communication. The mobile phone company has taken a series of practical steps to bring about a wire-free future. These range from the application of third generation telephony to the acquisition of companies with complementary capabilities. Additions to the Orange portfolio include Wildfire, a pioneer in the field of voice recognition and interaction, and Ananova, which can search for information on the World Wide Web and use speech synthesis to present the results in spoken form to whatever access device is being used.

## FOCUS AND HORIZON

A 'traditional' view has been that: 'directors [focus] on the external business environment... and are concerned with long-term questions of strategy and policy', while 'in comparison the great mass of employees are thought to concentrate upon short-term questions of implementation' (Coulson-Thomas and Wakelam, 1991). 'In reality' both directors and managers 'concentrate upon both the outside world and the company, and also the interrelationship between the two' (Figure 4.1), although the perspective of the manager may be that of a particular function or business unit.

Corporate visions and strategy have encouraged managers to 'think long term' and to develop more of an external focus. The efforts of companies to articulate and communicate a longer-term and customer-

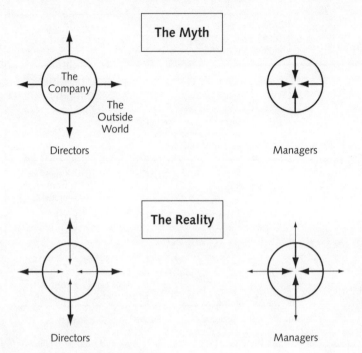

Source: *Coulson-Thomas and Wakelam (1991)*

**Figure 4.1**  The roles of directors and managers

focused vision has shifted the focus of many managers to the extent that distinctions of perspective between many directors and managers may have become a matter of emphasis or degree.

This should be a matter for celebration. Instead it has become a reason for concern. The following comments illustrate the dilemma:

> *For the first time people out there believe in all sorts of good things that we will have to ask them to stop doing for a while. We can't afford it.*

> *We've wound them up and now we've got to wind them down again. Due to a temporary blip, [some] things are going to be put on hold.*

> *They give us a hard time now. They have their own perspective and challenge us about impacts on their customers. In theory that's healthy. In practice it makes it tough for us.*

The efforts of many boards to 'share a vision' has increased the potential for conflict where vision and conduct are perceived to be incompatible.

Figure 4.2 illustrates the conflicting pressures at the heart of the relationship between directors and managers, head offices and business units,

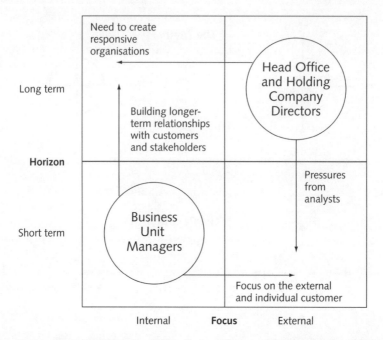

Source: Coulson-Thomas and Wakelam (1991), Coulson-Thomas and Coulson-Thomas (1991a)

**Figure 4.2**  Focus and horizon

and holding companies and their subsidiaries or national operating companies:

- Business unit managers and the directors of operating or subsidiary companies are striving: (i) to build longer-term relationships with customers and suppliers; and (ii) to focus externally on the customer and relationships within supply chains.
- At the same time, those occupying head office and main board positions feel under pressure from analysts to maintain short-term performance. They have put more emphasis upon internal headcount reductions, 'delayering', and corporate transformation, in order to contain operating costs, and create more flexible and responsive organizations.

## THE INTERNATIONAL DIMENSION

A significant justification of the largely location-independent network form of organization is its potential for internationalization. An international vision is relatively easy to articulate but difficult to achieve in practice. There are various cross-cultural issues, sensitivities and barriers.

The author's book on 'creating the global company' focuses upon the desire to serve the customer better, irrespective of barriers of place, time and national culture (Coulson-Thomas, 1992), but for some companies survival is the spur. For example, aerospace companies seek overseas partners in order to spread the costs of developing the next generation of technology and aircraft.

However, the international dimension may compound the problem of translating a corporate vision into a working reality:

- A proposed relationship based upon commercial logic between companies may trigger sensitivities, and the interests of regulators and other parties at local, regional and international level.
- An overseas market may prove difficult to penetrate, while an arrangement or joint venture is just as likely to fail as it is to succeed.
- It may take many years and sustained commitment both to penetrate a particular market such as that of Japan, and to develop the capability and forge the relationships needed to implement an internationalization strategy. In the meantime there will be frustrations and disappointments.

Access to resources will not shield a company from making costly mistakes. BT's internationalization strategy during the 1990s was built upon foundations of sand.

## VISIONING WINNERS AND LOSERS

Having considered some of the central issues involved in visioning let us turn now to how companies have fared over the past decade. What has been achieved?

The corporate visions of losers are often little more than words on paper. Most are instantly forgettable. A bland statement produced during an off-site 'planning day' is printed on a card and distributed to staff. Although it may make occasional appearances in corporate brochures it is rarely referred to. Whatever 'visioning exercise' was undertaken is viewed as a one-off event. The outputs may linger on in unchanged form long after they have ceased to reflect what is possible, current or desirable.

Loser companies often lack a distinctive or compelling reason for existing. They are one of a breed. They are not noticeably special or unique. People find it difficult to justify why they should join them, work with them, use their services or invest in them. Perhaps the initial underlying business concept lacked originality. Maybe it simply mirrored what competitors were already doing.

The wider world tends not to care when losers falter. External parties may have little interest in keeping such an enterprise alive. The corporate herd continues as individual stragglers fall by the wayside. Even failure may go largely unnoticed. While employees lose their jobs, customers may be able to obtain very similar products and services from other suppliers.

Many of the key players within loser companies are uncertain and insecure. They lack self-confidence and have little self-esteem. Other people have little interest or faith in them. They themselves are not really sure what they are about. In difficult circumstances they may not have sufficient inner conviction to do enough to keep the enterprise alive. They throw in the towel and are relieved when shot of onerous responsibilities.

Losers can appear dull, resigned and subdued. They drift. They seem to lack drive, personality, heart and soul. Senior managers in corporate losers become preoccupied with 'fitting in', 'hanging onto customers', 'papering over cracks' and surviving. After a time they lose sight of corporate objectives and lose touch with past dreams and their inner selves.

In contrast, winners are confident, vibrant and driven. They fizz. They are much more likely to have articulated a unique rationale. They endeavour to root their visions in real customer requirements. When their vision is described, people react. They usually understand it and they appreciate what is special about it.

Managers in winning companies feel important and wanted. They ensure that employees and business partners know what they have to do to bring a vision about. The vision lives and motivates because while it may be challenging it is also regarded as relevant and exciting. People are proud to be associated with it.

Winners stand out. They strive to be different. From the moment she first arrived in New York, Madonna endeavoured to meet the people who mattered. She registered and was remembered. Her single-minded determination to build her personal brand has made her a global icon. Richard Branson's ballooning exploits have helped to keep his name in front of the public and to entrench his reputation as a business leader who is different from the traditional 'suit'.

Winning businesses connect. They also contribute. Their people try to make them special and unique. Customers may find it difficult to obtain similar goods and services elsewhere. They would certainly notice and be inconvenienced if the enterprise failed. Like investors, they want it to do well.

When a winner stumbles, other people catch their breath. They are concerned and, because its role and contribution is important to them, a variety of 'interested parties' including customers, suppliers and business partners might be willing to provide temporary support during difficult times. Because business fundamentals and the critical success factors for competitiveness are in place, investors may be willing to provide additional funding to allow a winning company to ride out an occasional storm.

Winners never rest on their laurels or become complacent. Their people are restless. They search, test, learn and apply. Directors of winning companies are much more likely to regularly review their vision, purpose, key corporate goals and strategies during board meetings to ensure they are still current and relevant. If they are found wanting, people throughout the organization make whatever changes are necessary to reflect altered conditions and evolving requirements.

They are also much more confident, and less likely to 'cut and run' in crisis situations. Obstacles, difficulties and the unknown invariably confront those who venture ahead of the pack. People in winning companies derive self-worth and inner strength from the knowledge that their organization is valued and needed. Senior managers do not need to play games or pretend they know things. They trust their instincts and are not afraid to be themselves.

External parties who deal with winners know where they stand with them. While winners may be flexible and prepared to bend so far in the search for accommodation, they are unwilling to compromise cherished principles and core values. They also avoid promising more than they can deliver.

Winners are determined. Like a predator they play to their strengths and can also be patient when waiting for the right moment to go after an opportunity. They acknowledge and confront challenges. In difficult times they are open and honest with those whose support they seek. They tell it as it is and share rather than conceal reality as they understand it. As a consequence, they are more likely to receive help when they ask for it.

## BEGINNING IN THE BOARDROOM

So what needs to be done to make a distinctive corporate vision come about? The whole of this book sets out to address this question. But first, let us consider the articulation of, and commitment to, a common vision in the boardroom.

The board should be seen to be the source of the vision to be communicated (Coulson-Thomas, 1993a, 1993b). The board is in the best position to communicate with all the various stakeholders in the company. External, as well as internal, interests will be looking for evidence that a vision has the authority and support of the board behind it.

To formulate and agree an operational vision may require more than the board 'away-day':

- The vision should 'paint a picture' of a desired future that is preferable to the present, but rooted in marketplace reality. Underlying it should be an opportunity to generate and deliver value.
- The vision should be distinctive, and must command attention, and be both credible and memorable. It must create interest and be a catalyst of action. It should inspire and liberate. People must want to join the network and strive to bring it about.

- A vision should be succinct. It needs to be understood in a variety of contexts. To be shared and owned by a great many people, to live and spread across the barriers of culture, space and time the vision should stir the emotions, engender feelings and affect attitudes.
- The vision may be ambitious, but it should be achievable. It could stretch to, but not beyond, the limit. It must fuel an ambition to become better than the best.

In contrast to the compelling vision, many corporate mission statements are overly long, unfocused, too detailed and bland. They are pale, anaemic shadows, mere verbiage that stirs little interest. Few represent a guide to action, most are instantly forgettable. The vision should be not only agreed and shared, but should also ooze through every pore. Directors and managers should act as vision role models. Explanations should be provided for any departures from the vision.

There should be a clear link between vision, values, goals and objectives, and all the elements needed, from empowerments to processes, to implement the strategy for the achievement of the vision, must be seen to be in place. People must believe that it is going to happen. Each of them needs to know what they can and must do to help bring it about.

# ROLES AND RESPONSIBILITIES

Within the boardroom there are two distinct and key roles and responsibilities which will largely determine the extent to which a compelling vision is articulated, agreed, communicated and shared.

## The chairman

The chairman is generally the individual who is best equipped to form an overview of the board and its operations, and hence should be responsible for ensuring the board is equipped to play its part in formulating, agreeing, sharing and implementing the vision. In the last chapter it was suggested that the chairman should reflect upon the following questions:

- Are your directors committed to a common vision and an agreed strategy? Which of them are 'paying lip-service' or are 'just along for the ride'?
- How effective are the members of your board at sharing the vision, and communicating with customers, employees and business partners? Is anything happening out there?

The chairman should assume responsibility for ensuring that external stakeholders understand the vision.

## The chief executive

The chief executive should take a lead in: (i) securing the commitment of the people of the organization; and (ii) communicating and sharing the vision with them. The CEO can also play a key role in preventing the occurrence of 'perspective gaps' and 'arenas of confrontation'. Fellow directors and many senior managers tend to base their own level of commitment upon the priority being given to 'change' by the CEO.

One CEO summed up the dilemma of the 'fellow traveller' director: 'I lived for too long with directors who did not really believe in what we were trying to do. They didn't raise objections in the boardroom. What's worse, they sometimes said yes, and then went away and did nothing. They didn't implement the changes in their divisions, and everyone knew it.'

# EFFECTIVE COMMUNICATION

Once agreed by a competent and committed board, a vision has to be communicated and shared. Sir John Harvey-Jones believes that: 'effective communication requires effort, commitment, time and courage. Full commitment is the result of integrity, openness and real two-way communication' (Coulson-Thomas and Coe, 1991).

Visible commitment is crucial. For a decade CEOs have echoed the comments of Vern Zelmer, the former managing director of Rank Xerox (UK), that: 'the role of the manager must change from one of managing the *status quo* in a command and control environment to one of managing change through active teaching, coaching, and facilitating in a participative work group' (Coulson-Thomas and Coe, 1991).

Whatever their boards might think or hope is the case, in reality many companies have found it difficult to articulate and communicate a compelling vision. Words and slogans have been passed on without being fully understood.

# THE EFFECTIVE COMMUNICATOR

The effective communicator needs to think through what is being communicated, to whom and why, and demonstrate emotional commitment, trust and respect. Messages must be straightforward, and related to the needs and interests of the audience if they are to 'come alive' (Bartram and Coulson-Thomas, 1991). The communicator must be open, determined to build relationships and willing to learn. The communicator must share the vision, must feel the vision and must be visibly committed to it.

Customers and employees are attracted to those organizations whose principles they share. The 'vision message' must empathize with people's feelings and values, and it must be believed.

Honesty is even more important in an era of recession and retrenchment, when there is bad news to communicate. There are also, as we have seen, many gaps between rhetoric and reality, and aspiration and achievement, some of which strain patience and credibility. In some companies urgent action is needed to re-establish an atmosphere of trust.

## THE POTENTIAL FOR DIFFERENTIATION

Distinctive and compelling messages are usually easier to communicate. They may develop a life of their own and spread by word of mouth.

Copying, 'me-too' approaches, benchmarking and accessing and sharing commodity knowledge are not the route to market leadership. The superstars question, challenge, explore and discover. They use the 'know-how' of their superstars and corporate capabilities to craft distinctive offerings that provide customers with new options and genuine choices (Coulson-Thomas, 2001). They regard their knowledge, processes and ways of working as a source of competitive differentiation.

Creating and using knowledge to develop alternative approaches, services and enterprises is especially important for companies with growth ambitions. In a confusing and chaotic world in which consumers are assailed from all directions with a multitude of similar but conflicting messages, it is difficult to stand out. Being noticed is crucial for a business that needs to attract new customers in order to expand. Differentiation and tailoring to individual requirements can also enable the avoidance of commodity product traps and generate the higher margins needed to fund development.

Improvements in manufacturing, process and information technologies give us the potential to produce many more responses that reflect our individuality and particular interests and tastes. However, despite multifarious possibilities we find very often when we strip away the advertising claims that various suppliers offer essentially the same product. The packaging may be different but in essence competitive offerings are almost identical.

'Minimum differentiation' is all around us. Thus all cars within each price bracket seem to have the same aerodynamic shape. How many people would happily incur the fuel-mileage penalties of greater wind resistance if they could step into a more distinctive design? How many drivers would willingly pay for the self-expression experienced by the custom built vehicle owner?

Most businesses today have the potential to be unique and special. Yet we are enticed by standard offerings and lowest common denominator solutions. For example, software packages cause 'interface problems' and provide us with the same capabilities as everyone else when bespoke development would enable us to be different and might create additional intellectual capital.

## DIFFERENTIATING WINNERS AND LOSERS

In addition to having a distinctive purpose, successful companies strive to craft novel offerings and create memorable experiences. They also endeavour to work, learn and operate in imaginative ways that differentiate them from competitive suppliers.

Losers tend to become preoccupied with what others are doing. They imitate, copy and adopt 'me-too' approaches. They try to model their structure, management approaches and operations on how other organizations do things. If they make cosmetic changes during the implementation of what they adopt this may only be to avoid charges of plagiarism and infringement of intellectual capital.

Some losers are enthusiasts of benchmarking. Learning from others and applying relevant best practice can enable a company to catch up. However, at some point a business needs to create as well as consume if it is to successfully compete. Setting out to match what others have already done is hardly a recipe for innovation.

Losers are often modest and do not push themselves. They are cautious and tend to coast along. As a result of playing it safe they may not register with others. They fail to stand out. Their products and services tend to be perceived as commodities. The narrow margins they provide may be insufficient to improve products or fund the development of later generations of technology.

External parties tend to exploit losers. Consultants persuade them to undertake irrelevant or peripheral projects. Ruthless customers know they have the whip hand. They may provide losers with only just enough business to keep them alive as a captive supplier of standard products or services at cheap commodity prices.

Winners recognize they need to be innovative and distinctive to secure market leadership. They are not afraid to go out in front. They explore, discover and create. They exploit opportunities and pioneer new applications. When additional channels of communication such as those presented by the spread of e-business and use of the Internet become available they also use these to differentiate their offerings.

Winning companies recognize diversity and the need to differentiate according to the various distinctive requirements and individual expectations of the people their staff and business partners are seeking to build relationships with. What works for some may not do so for others. When, where, how and with whom they operate, work and learn will depend upon the preferences of the people who are important to them and what it is that they are setting out to achieve together.

There is little value in being different for its own sake. Winners recognize this and act accordingly. They ensure their distinctive features are recognizable and compelling in relation to customers' needs and requirements. They work hard and devote whatever time is required to create an arresting 'angle' or establish a 'differentiator' that proves irresistible.

A company has many ways of distinguishing itself from competitors. For each there could be a number of options. Its customer base might be unique. Its people may possess special knowledge or skills. Its products, trademarks and intellectual property could be protected. Its purpose might be special and it may pursue particular policies.

Ways of working and learning, corporate culture and values, management approaches and methodologies, and an image or reputation can all be distinctive. A company might operate, build relationships or form partnerships differently from other organizations. Winners put as many 'differentiators' in place as they can to ensure they stand out from any available alternatives and lock in their customers and business partners.

Winners find it easier to move up value chains, secure satisfactory and fair margins, and cross sell. A unique positioning and an appropriate image makes it easier for them to extend their range of services by developing new offerings based upon novel ways of exploiting their collective knowledge and expertise. They reap the benefits of being different.

# BREAKING OUT

Boards and management teams should strive to provide customers with additional options, genuine choices and better alternatives to those that are currently available. In order to make a mark and have an impact both people and organizations must look beyond the norm and escape from self-imposed constraints. Corporate culture, policies and processes should open, liberate and inspire rather than inhibit, imprison or trap.

Boards should seek alternatives to bland consensus and middle ways. They should champion reflection, debate and challenge; and instil a desire to innovate and an urge to discover in those for whom they are responsible. Some people may need to be helped to distinguish fundamentals from fads, substance from surface and reality from illusion. Checklists for doing this and questioning contemporary assumptions, and exercises for formulating new marketplace offerings are available (Coulson-Thomas and Coulson-Thomas, 1991a).

People can be equipped to challenge the relative importance of action and reaction, complexity and simplicity, activity and reflection and change and continuity (Coulson-Thomas and Coulson-Thomas, 1991a). Shifting the balance between them can produce genuine alternatives. Not everyone has the same preferences. Given options, many of us would make very different decisions from those determined on our behalf by suppliers. Thinking through where the herd is headed allows entrepreneurs to identify new opportunities.

## Losers

Losers:

- confuse direction and management and do not think strategically;
- do not have a shared and distinctive vision or sense of common purpose;
- fail to communicate, monitor and review what they are setting out to achieve;
- adopt mechanical approaches to management and corporate transformation;
- muddle and confuse roles and responsibilities;
- experience tensions and incompatibilities between functions, the roles of directors and managers, and head offices and operating units;
- are prepared to accommodate, rationalize or live with visions that remain little more than words on paper;
- do not secure the attention, commitment or respect of employees, customers or investors;
- drift, lose control and become hostages to fortune.

## Winners

Winners:

- understand the distinction between direction and management and develop competent directors and effective boards;
- share a common and distinctive vision and agree and communicate a realistic strategy for its achievement;
- effectively communicate, monitor and review what they are setting out to achieve;
- practise people-centred, organic and holistic approaches to management and corporate transformation;
- clarify roles and responsibilities and key relationships, such as that between chairman and chief executive;
- align complementary roles and achieve a high degree of compatibility and synergy;
- endeavour to achieve the realities and deliver the benefits of corporate visions;
- command the interest, respect and loyalty of employees, customers and investors;
- remain in control of their destiny and shape the future.

# DANGER AREAS

Many people, and various groups, may be responsible for delivering aspects of what is needed. Their commitment may be withheld until all the elements needed to achieve success are seen to be in place. Achievement then becomes a self-fulfilling prophecy. Because people believe it will happen, it actually does start to happen.

At the same time, a 'common vision' and 'shared values' should not be driven through the network organization to the extent that thinking is discouraged. The strength and vitality of the network may lie in the richness of its diversity. There will be differences of perspective and view-point, and these will need to be accommodated if co-operation is not to turn to conflict.

Thinking should not be regarded as an exceptional activity to be reserved for the occasional 'away-day' workshop or an annual corporate planning exercise. Nor is it something to be delegated to consultants or advisers. Thinking should be an essential component of daily management activity.

# VISION AND COMMUNICATION

Vision, differentiation and communication are like knife, fork and spoon. Each is of little use without the others. Vision without communication could be a private day-dream. Communication without vision or which does not register could be background noise. Vision, differentiation and communication together can 'move mountains'.

So far as corporate transformation is concerned, the vision of the flexible and responsive network organization must be compelling. It must be shared, the purpose of transformation communicated, and the involvement and commitment of stakeholders secured. The chief exec-utive should assume responsibility for communicating and sharing the transformation vision. Sharing can only be said to have taken place when people both understand and feel the vision.

The ability to change and communicate about change, in the context of change, is an essential directorial and management quality. The focus needs to be upon changing attitudes and approaches to communication. Significant change will not occur in many organizations, unless managers are equipped with the skills to bring it about.

# CHECKLIST

▶ Does the company have a distinctive vision that is rooted in the reality of customer requirements?

▶ Does it involve the development of new and distinctive marketplace offerings?

▶ Will customers be offered alternatives and genuine choices?

▶ Has the vision been agreed by the board, and communicated and shared with the people of the company, and with its customers, suppliers and business partners?

▶ Do people remember the vision? What does it mean to them?

▶ What would you do differently if you had not heard of the vision?

▶ Is there a clear, comprehensive and realistic strategy for implementing the vision?

▶ Is the strategy a document in a filing cabinet or a working process?

▶ Is it to be implemented through quantifiable objectives that are consistent with the goals and values of the company?

▶ Do all those with the responsibility for delivering each objective know what is expected of them?

▶ Have they the motivation, skills and necessary discretion to 'make it happen'?

▶ Have the resources and other implications of implementation been thought through?

▶ Have the implementation 'helps and hinders' been identified?

▶ In particular, have all the necessary management and business processes been established?

▶ What is being done to identify all those activities within the organization that are either not compatible with, or not contributing to, the objectives of the organization?

# REFERENCES

Bartram, P and Coulson-Thomas, C (1991) *The Complete Spokesperson*, Kogan Page, London

Coulson-Thomas, C (1992) *Creating the Global Company: Successful Internationalisation*, McGraw-Hill, London

Coulson-Thomas, C (1993a) *Creating Excellence in the Boardroom: A guide to shaping directorial competence and board effectiveness*, McGraw-Hill, London

Coulson-Thomas, C (1993b) *Developing Directors: Building an effective boardroom team*, McGraw-Hill, London

Coulson-Thomas, C (2001) *Shaping Things to Come: Strategies for creating alternative enterprises*, Blackhall Publishing, Dublin

Coulson-Thomas, C and Brown, R (1989) *The Responsive Organisation, People Management: The challenge of the 1990s*, BIM, Corby

Coulson-Thomas, C and Brown, R (1990) *Beyond Quality: Managing the relationship with the customer*, BIM, Corby

Coulson-Thomas, C and Coe, T (1991) *The Flat Organisation: Philosophy and practice*, BIM, Corby

Coulson-Thomas, C and Coulson-Thomas, S (1991a) *Quality: The next steps*, an Adaptation survey for ODI International, Adaptation, London and (Executive Summary) ODI, Wimbledon, London

Coulson-Thomas, C and Coulson-Thomas, S (1991b) *Communicating for Change*, an Adaptation Survey for Granada Business Services, London

Coulson-Thomas, C and Didacticus Video Productions Ltd (1991) *The Change Makers, Vision and Communication*, booklet to accompany integrated audio and video-tape training programme by Sir John Harvey-Jones. Distributed by Video Arts, London

Coulson-Thomas, C and Wakelam, A (1991) *The Effective Board: Current practice, myths and realities*, an Institute of Directors Discussion Document, London

# 5

# Winning Business and Building Customer Relationships

*'The thicker the morning mist the easier it is to feel'*

## CORPORATE TRANSFORMATION AND THE CUSTOMER

Corporate organizations are aspiring to become more flexible and responsive in order to better deliver value to customers. The vision is of networks of longer-term relationships embracing customers, suppliers and business partners. But, as we have already seen, the desire for change is not always matched by an awareness of how to bring it about.

Customers are the source of all value. In a market economy, the revenue of a company derives from its customers through voluntary exchanges in the marketplace. The first CEO of Xerox Corporation, Joseph Wilson, emphasized the importance of the customer: 'It is the customer and the customer alone who will ultimately determine whether we succeed or fail as a company.'

Ultimately the experiences of customers, clients and users will determine the rewards achieved by those who participate in the distribution of surplus value. Some companies like Johnson & Johnson devote management attention to them in proportion to their perceived contribution to success. The Johnson & Johnson 'Credo' or statement of values puts its consumers first, employees second, the community third and investors fourth on the grounds that returns to shareholders are a consequence of getting the other relationships right.

Virgin puts its own people first on the assumption that if they are not satisfied they are unlikely to give of their best when dealing with customers. The central focus of Virgin employees is the client. Xerox puts the customer at the heart of its management model and processes.

Many of the fundamental changes that are occurring within individual companies are driven by a desire to better serve the customer. Major corporations restructure to match their expectations regarding the future evolution of customer requirements. Major Japanese companies have moved R & D and market research activities into local communities in order to identify opportunities to adapt products to particular lifestyle trends. Ricoh and Sony encouraged managers, to put themselves in the shoes of local customers and employees. Matsushita established 'lifestyle centres' in major cities.

## STAYING CLOSE TO THE CUSTOMER

Successful pioneers motivate and inspire their customers. The smart ones may give a lead but they also travel with their clients rather than risk leaving them behind. Monsoon abandoned its first attempt at online trading and relaunched its Monsoon and Accessorize Web sites as information providers to promote its high street stores. It found visitors were reluctant to order fashion items via the Internet.

Being a first mover can sometimes be extremely risky if an enterprise loses sight of the critical success factors for competitive success. Boo.com, the Internet fashion retailer, failed as a stand-alone business venture because it lacked a complementary physical presence. Fashionmail.com uses a remodelled site to channel visitors to partner companies with premises.

Some traditional businesses have waited for 'dot.com' ventures financed by the naïve and greedy to flush out the major problem areas before they introduce their own e-business services. Winners may not copy others, but they endeavour to learn from their mistakes.

Supermarkets have also found that trusted brand names have a distinct advantage. Tesco's online activities built on an established reputation, allowed customers to specify their individual requirements and have been well received by them.

## THE CHALLENGE OF IMPLEMENTATION

Most companies claim to be dedicated to customer service. Customer focus is referred to in mission statements, on posters and handouts, in videos and house journals, and in speeches at annual general meetings.

However, in a growing number of organizations there is a considerable gulf between expectation and achievement. For example, in many companies the following can be observed:

- Visions, values, goals and objectives reflect the requirements of the company rather than those of its customers.
- People have not been equipped with the skills, or empowered and motivated to deliver bespoke services to customers.
- Cross-functional account teams and partnerships, and account management processes that give the customer a single point of contact, result in call centre queues and frustration. The customer is confused when trying to tap the potential and capability of the corporation.

## SOMETHING IS WRONG

The following selection of interview quotations illustrates the extent to which there is perceived to be a gap between rhetoric and reality:

*We still regard the customers as targets. We bombard them with direct mail.*

*Our approach to customers is a question of what we can get away with, not what we can do for them.*

*Our short-term requirements for survival are taking priority over the long-term interests of customers.*

*Every contact revolves around selling or persuading. There is not much listening or sharing going on.*

*Ask people about themselves at a party and you are surrounded in no time. When we meet customers we talk about ourselves and wonder why they are not interested.*

*Most of our products and services revolve around the things we can do, rather than customer requirements.*

Asea Brown Boveri is an example of a company that endeavoured to make a focus upon the needs of the customer more than rhetoric. According to Percy Barnevik, president and CEO: 'Our performance measures define success from the customer's point of view. … Customer satisfaction is not just another improvement programme, but an effort to permanently change our value system and to orient the entire [group] in the direction of the customer.'

# REACTIONS TO A CHANGING BUSINESS ENVIRONMENT

We saw in Chapter 1 that for a decade corporate transformation to a flexible network of relationships with customers, suppliers and business partners has been seen by many companies as a necessity rather than as a choice. There are environmental, social, economic and technological pressures to contend with. Markets have become more open, competitive and international; customers are more demanding.

Priority has been given to creating an organization that is adaptable and responsive to the changing needs of its customers. Those in the front line should be empowered and enabled to become facilitators, harnessing relevant expertise and resource by all available means, and irrespective of function and location, in order to add and deliver value for customers.

Where the transition is occurring, elation is replacing frustration as people find they can 'do things' for customers. According to one enthusiastic interviewee: 'Account teams are now where the action is. They're the fast jet jocks. What's left of the hierarchy is for the desk-bound who are past it.'

An ability to deliver can change the opinions of existing customers and attract new ones. Just as people are sometimes judged by the company they keep, so companies can be judged by how demanding their customers are. Without expectations they will not demand, and demanding customers keep companies on their toes.

# CARING

A lone jogger on a country path passes an entrance to a stone cottage and notices a hand painted message: 'plants for sale'. A few feet inside the drive is a table adorned with pots of young and lovingly cared for plants. During the summer such scenes are repeated throughout the countryside. Even the most remote of byways may boast a sign advertising plants, apples or honey for sale. Invariably someone has put them there who cares and who has something to sell and share.

The caring is immediately apparent. Every seedling is immaculate as if dressed for Sunday school. The effort is put in even if visitors are few and far between and the prospect of them stopping to look and buy might appear remote. The contrast of the indifference that greets many people who visit shops can be painful and dramatic. Of course many of those in the retail sector do care, but there are clearly many that do not. They appear to resent having to deal with customers in return for their salaries.

Caring pays. The returns from a continuing customer relationship may justify product sales at a minimal margin or even a loss. For many years

Xerox profits largely derived from sales of paper and other supplies, servicing installed machines and the financing of purchases rather than the sales of its smaller copiers. Manufacturers of aero-engines such as Rolls Royce undertake lucrative overhaul work and are able to sell spare parts at relatively high margins for the lifetime of their products. An initial sale can yield a 25-year income stream.

Considering companies that you are familiar with, how many people really care about them and their responsibilities within them? Are people mainly interested in their own prospects rather than those of their employers? Are they emotionally engaged? Do they really mind how well the company does or whether it has a future so long as they get paid? How many really care about what they do and take pride in their work? Do they do just enough to get by, or do they walk the extra mile?

## THE CUSTOMER IN RHETORIC

The customer appears to be king in thought if not in deed. A decade ago one report (Coulson-Thomas and Brown, 1990) found that building longer-term relationships with customers, and introducing a more customer-oriented culture were the most important management issues. Among those interviewed there was an overwhelming consensus on the following:

- The essence, purpose and vision of a company ought to derive from the customer. Initiatives, activities, organization and corporate culture should result from what is necessary to deliver value and satisfaction to customers.
- The customer needs to be better understood, and closer and longer-term relationships with customers forged. Mission, values, goals, objectives, strategy and processes should be defined and implemented in the context of customer understanding. Organizations need to be flexible, adaptable and responsive in learning from customers, and sustaining relationships with them as their requirements change.

## THE CUSTOMER IN REALITY

The customer should be seen as a partner and colleague, an integral and the central element of the network organization. The participation and contribution of customers should be encouraged and managed. Yet the reality is that many companies continue to treat customers as outsiders who should be 'kept at a distance'.

There is a fundamental 'mismatch' in the way different members of the network organization are treated. For example:

- The self-seeking head office manager who costs the company a great deal of money is trusted with access to 'privileged information', even while keeping in touch with headhunters just in case there may be opportunities to 'get more' from a competitor;
- In contrast, the customers who provide the company's revenues are treated with suspicion in case they might want or learn something. Without knowledge of corporate capability, how can the customer judge the potential benefits of a deeper relationship?

While the people of the company are asked to 'put the customer first', the organization itself, in terms of its business goals, and reward and remuneration practice, puts the priority upon 'share price', 'return on net assets' or 'market share'.

Short termism, and the perceived constraints upon directors and boards to focus excessively upon financial ratios, is killing many customer relationships. The pressures are particularly strong in the case of public or quoted companies, and tend to be more apparent during periods of economic slowdown and recession.

## HOW LOSERS TREAT THEIR CUSTOMERS

'Customer focus' is usually a core element of 'business excellence' approaches. Although most loser businesses use the rhetoric of putting consumers first they pay lip service to them. When responding to commercial opportunities their people are primarily driven by internal corporate needs. Sales staff concentrate almost exclusively upon what their employers wish to sell. For example, they may support a drive to clear stocks of a particular line. Customer requirements create opportunities rather than dictate outcomes. The aim is to sell not serve.

Managers in loser companies concentrate upon their individual performance goals. Overall, they devote too much effort to meeting their own personal objectives, and they put far too little emphasis upon understanding the motivations behind prospective purchases, and ensuring that what is offered is relevant to customer concerns and priorities.

Losers are reluctant to depart from standard procedures or involve colleagues in view of the extra costs that may be incurred. Bespoke responses are discouraged. They involve extra work. Departures from the norm, or 'variations', are viewed largely in terms of the process problems they create.

Within 'loser' enterprises customer management is viewed as an administrative chore and an area of business expenditure to be targeted for savings. Effort is made to reduce the cost of handling calls and servicing accounts. When processes are re-engineered customers are expected to do more themselves and corporate responses are depersonalized.

Pressure may be put upon customers and prospects to conform to whatever makes it easier to process transactions. Subtle at first, it becomes more overt if the responses sought are not achieved. Quantitative targets for the number of calls handled or visits made discourage people from spending too much time with particular clients. Hence opportunities to find out more about them and cross sell are missed.

Many people within corporate losers and associated with them genuinely believe they understand their customers. They believe their own and corporate rhetoric and are therefore surprised, even aggrieved when 'negative feedback' is received. They take it as a personal affront when their accounts look elsewhere. While they may have considered these relationships to be secure, their defecting clients may have felt taken for granted. They simply wanted out and walked.

Losers often have to work hard just to remain where they are. They have to win new accounts to replace lost customers. They miss out on opportunities to provide further services and secure the additional orders and the repeat business that could widen margins as a result of reduced selling costs. The churn that occurs is used as an argument for not 'wasting' money on supporting users who may well prove 'disloyal'. It also encourages sales staff to screw as much as they can out of customers while they have the chance.

# THE BUREAUCRATIC ORGANIZATION AND THE CUSTOMER

The bureaucratic, remote and uncaring organization is doomed. Giant corporations are wide open to plunder, and are being 'taken apart'. We saw in Chapter 1 that developments in the marketplace are increasing the bargaining power of customers *vis-à-vis* suppliers. The availability of the skills and technology of communication enables competitors to 'come from nowhere and walk off with the best customers'.

The 'new companies on the block' can afford to be selective, and the best advice in the world is generally available for a fee. As one jaundiced director emphasized: 'They are not interested in the rubbish. They target and work on the prizes, the ones that are keeping us alive.' Incisive competitors are like smart ticks feasting upon the blood of dumb beasts.

Established duopolies are not free of challenge, as the entry of Mars into the ice cream snack market demonstrated. The existence of Internet Communities and networks makes it easier for 'newcomers' to secure direct access to targeted groups. This can be done by avoiding channels and outlets that may be controlled or dominated by the 'established players'.

Operating units with market and customer responsibilities used to be organizationally separate from manufacturing units. Each reported upwards to a group board, with little lateral communication. Sales targets were given to marketing operations based upon what manufacturing could produce.

Manufacturing companies have put more emphasis upon meeting market needs and less on such considerations as available capacity. Flexibility and responsiveness is more important than optimization of aspects of the production process. A director of one manufacturing multinational expressed the view that: 'All parts of the organization will need to think from a marketing perspective.'

A company can be constrained by its past. The larger and more complex the bureaucracy, the greater the danger of being sucked into the internal operations of the company, the endless round of asset and headcount reduction programmes, as smaller and more nimble competitors 'cream' off the more lucrative business.

## SIZE AND RESPONSIVENESS

The desire of larger companies to focus on those things which they do well and hive off or subcontract non-core activities creates new opportunities for the smaller company. In the knowledge society there is more open access to insight, information, skill and funding. Scale is less significant as a source of competitive advantage compared with flexibility and responsiveness.

Opportunities that suddenly arise are new for all, large and small company alike. The rate of change erodes existing understanding and established capability. The small company does not need to develop large overheads if flexible access to appropriate skill and expertise is available as and when required. There is no reason why an alert and astute competitor should not tap the most relevant expertise and 'out-think' and out-perform a larger bureaucracy that feels compelled to make use of less relevant resources and procedures just because they happen to be 'on the books'.

Different parts of the corporation should be allowed to evolve distinct forms of organization and management processes that meet their own particular requirements. Tied together, all the business units may drown. Empowered, enabled and set free, some may survive.

## WHAT WINNERS DO DIFFERENTLY

Winners focus their actions and thoughts as well as their rhetoric upon customer requirements. During an initial contact they explore the motivations and rationale behind an expressed desire to buy. Instead of offering whatever is available, or mechanically churning out a standard proposal, a more bespoke approach is adopted. Staff, associates and business partners are happy to tailor a response to a particular culture, situation and context. Colleagues undertake peer reviews of complex and commercially significant proposals from a buyer perspective.

Sales staff endeavour to understand the situation a prospect is in, their aspirations and why a business opportunity has arisen. They explore the goals, the objectives and the commercial drivers involved. They examine the personalities involved in the purchasing process, those who take decisions and those who influence them and the criteria they employ. If they submit proposals they structure these so that recipients can easily determine that their requirements are met.

Losers sell. Many of them sell hard. Winners influence and support the buying process. From the moment an initial contact is made they take the first steps towards building a mutually rewarding relationship. By identifying and articulating the respective benefits the parties involved might expect and the costs of different options, they demonstrate that they care.

Winners do not assume their customers are satisfied. They do not take them for granted. They regularly check that what they are providing or offering is still meeting a need. They actively explore opportunities for improvements that would deliver more value from a client perspective. They consider additional and complementary services. They are flexible in negotiations and do not mind putting themselves out to 'get it right'.

Losers are reluctant to get too involved with their customers. They never think about them outside of office hours. While at work they are so distracted by immediate pressures that they rarely have time to reflect, sense and feel.

Losers also avoid online links in case viruses are imported. Winners link processes and systems. For example, customers may be able to dial up and find out how their order is progressing or view the availability of stock or the balance on their account. Because they are valued, such facilities and services lock customers in.

Winners view interaction with customers as an essentially creative and iterative process. They instinctively think about other people's problems and are always alert to ways of helping customers build their businesses. The emphasis is upon increasing understanding, adding value and sustaining intimate relationships.

In winning companies people devote the time it may take to fully assess a requirement and craft a considered response that is more likely to differentiate the company from alternative suppliers. They try to get into the heads of those they deal with. They become insiders. As a consequence, they may be able to judge future potential and identify further business opportunities.

Within corporate losers people are self-absorbed. They talk and present about themselves. They describe their organizations, their products, their achievements and their terms. Brochures and annual reports feature their offices and staff.

Winners define themselves and what they are about in terms of their major customers and what they do for them. Projects with particular clients and an indication of how they contributed to their objectives feature prominently in executive presentations. Staff and business

partners are increasingly likely to view their business as a portfolio of partnering relationships and a network of capabilities.

# PEOPLE AND THE NETWORK ORGANIZATION

The evolving company is becoming a network of those who share a
common vision and have compatible interests. We have seen that it is a
network including within its membership customers, suppliers and
business partners. It is also increasingly an international network that
matches the most relevant expertise to the greatest opportunities to add
value.

Networks need not be permanent, but may be called together to achieve
a particular task. The larger projects could be handled by a network
brought together for the specific purpose. People and organizations could
belong simultaneously to a number of networks. Networks could
resemble consortia of venturers coming together to stage an event or to
undertake a voyage.

People can also have more than one role within a network. For example,
most BT employees are also customers.

As companies focus upon core areas in which they have a strong
comparative advantage, a growing range of tasks will be subcontracted to
individuals and networks with specialist expertise in the activities
concerned. Another BIM study by the author (Coulson-Thomas, 1988)
predicted a greater distinction between those who commit themselves to a
managerial role within a single organization and 'new professionals' who
develop a distinct skill or competence which they are willing to make
available on a fee basis to multiple clients.

The people of the network organization facilitate the delivery of value to
its customers. Supporting communications technology needs to be flexible
and adaptable in allowing multifunctional, multilocation, multiorganiza-
tional and multinational teams to work together. Technology should allow
thoughts, insights and concepts to be captured, shared, refined and
amended. It should enable learning and development, and itself be
capable of learning and development.

Technology can create opportunities for new relationships with
customers. Purchasing can be located at a single point. Relevant expertise
around the world can be focused upon a particular opportunity.

Electronic links enable customers of courier companies to secure access
to their account details, check where their parcels are and initiate certain
activities and transactions.

More continuous intimate and intense relationships with customers
have become possible via the Internet. Developments in personal communications are allowing freer access to global networks. Converging technology enables 'multimedia' screens to be used for home banking, home
shopping, home working and home learning. Portable and disposable

technology options mean that individuals can work in a variety of locations, and use alternative technology environments, according to how appropriate they are felt to be to particular activities, tasks or projects.

## VALUES AND THE NETWORK ORGANIZATION

Networks have become global, bringing together all those who share certain values and goals, and who wish to contribute a proportion of their time to the pursuit of a particular vision. We saw in the last chapter that the vision, purpose and values of a network are key differentiators. Much effort needs to be put into articulating and propounding those that are distinct and compelling.

Values may need to be put up on hoardings in order to distinguish one network from another. When technology, information and knowledge become commodities, equally available to all, competition between networks may be on the basis of values, rather than such factors as price. Customers may choose between producers, all of which have access to state-of-the-art technology and up-to-date knowledge according to the underlying values of the producing or converting network. One value network, for example, may be chosen rather than another, because it is more environmentally conscious.

People who can learn and empathize with the changing values, emotions and desires of customers are of critical importance when competitors can copy more tangible products and services. Increasingly, intangibles are the basis of sustained competitive advantage.

## CREATING NEW RELATIONSHIPS

Within loser companies account development activities are focused upon existing customers. Those being supplied by competitors are not approached. As a consequence, areas of potential opportunity may be 'written off'. Little or no effort is devoted to assessing whether these other relationships are satisfactory from the perspective of the buyers. They may not be. From the outside an existing customer–supplier bond can appear more robust than it actually is.

As already mentioned, winners are proactive. They identify the organizations they would like to do business with. They know whether or not incumbent providers are already supplying some of the targets on their 'hit list'. They do not view these relationships as 'no go' areas. They establish contact, introduce themselves and endeavour to acquire certain accounts from direct competitors.

'Account capture' teams and plans should be drawn up for business prospects of commercial and strategic significance. Some winners develop a specific process for breaking into and converting competitor held accounts. They approach organizations they would like to have as clients with suggestions for collaborative activities that would help these target partners to achieve their objectives (Hurcomb, 1998).

Winners are reluctant to accept that certain areas and possibilities are off limits. They explore strategies for opening up new accounts, building trust and obtaining a physical or psychological presence. They might suggest ways of financing that would spread costs or make procurement easier. They could argue that splitting an order would allow a company to compare performance and reduce dependence upon a single supplier. While this might only involve a small proportion of a total order, it could severely damage a competitor's confidence and margins.

An incumbent provider may have moved or strayed beyond its area of competitive advantage. 'Unbundling' a requirement might yield benefits for the purchaser that would more than compensate for the extra relationship support costs of dealing with an additional supplier. Every proposal submitted should contain at least one specific service that a prospect ought to find irresistible irrespective of any other offerings that are in the frame.

## Losers

Losers:

- consider customers as outsiders;
- pursue short-term sales objectives and use their customers to achieve their own ends;
- leave customer relationships to sales staff;
- employ traditional 'hard sell' techniques;
- fail to distinguish between different categories of customer;
- make little effort to understand their customers' aspirations and businesses;
- avoid partnering commitments, online links and bespoke activities;
- use traditional sales techniques that do not recognize the growing bargaining power of customers;
- do not protect key account relationships;
- end up as suppliers of commodity products that are bought on price.

## Winners

Winners:

- regard customers as an integral part of the organization and learn with them;
- concentrate upon future potential and value their customers;

- involve multiple points of contact and senior management in building relationships with strategically significant customers;
- endeavour to understand and influence the buying process;
- differentiate, segment and prioritize customer relationships;
- understand their customers' businesses and look for ways in which their development could be supported;
- commit, integrate and actively encourage bespoke responses and seek to develop more intimate and mutually beneficial relationships with customers;
- influence buying rather than sell;
- take conscious steps to lock customers in and exclude competitors from key accounts;
- become long-term business partners sharing risks and rewards.

## LEARNING FROM THE CUSTOMER

Not all customers are prepared to wait. Some use their purchasing power to prise open a bureaucratic shell in order to get at what is within. The more confident and assertive customers are catalysts of corporate transformation.

The smart company actively learns from its customers. The awkward customers may be 'trying it on', or they may be useful sources of new product ideas. The demanding customer can be used as an agent of change to help shift internal attitudes and raise expectations.

Value is created by the customer. They must be not only understood but involved. They should be asked about their requirements.

Customer feedback does not automatically occur, it needs to be managed. Customers must be actively encouraged to give their views. As one interviewee put it: 'We've never listened. We always thought we knew best. Customers have never had any reason to be open with us.'

The learning loop process shown diagrammatically in Figure 5.1 illustrates how an organization's vision and capability should be matched to customer requirements. Distinct subprocesses are involved:

- An issue monitoring and management process, and customer satisfaction surveys should be used to review and refine the vision in order to ensure that the purpose of the company remains focused on the customer.
- The process used to deploy the vision and resulting values, goals and objectives must reach through to all the people and elements that collectively make up the capability of the company to deliver value to its customers.

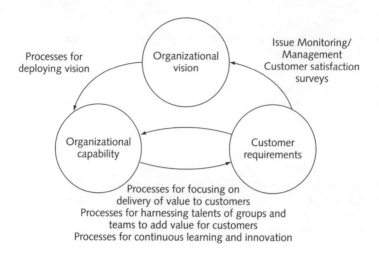

**Figure 5.1** The learning loop

- When matching organizational capability to customer requirements, particular attention should be paid to the processes that identify and deliver the value sought by customers, those that harness the potential and capability that this requires, and those that enable and facilitate continuous learning and innovation.

## BUILDING RELATIONSHIPS WITH CUSTOMERS

Some companies operating through intermediaries or channels of distribution may be surrounded by concentric rings of 'customer' until a final consumer is reached. In such cases relationships may need to be established with all of the concentric rings. Each will have its own concerns and requirements.

There appears to be growing awareness of the margin and profitability advantages of emphasizing higher added-value considerations and the wider benefits of products and services (Figure 5.2). A closer relationship with customers can enable a company to spring the commodity products trap. In some sectors this can involve working with customers to develop their understanding of what can be achieved and enhance their expectations. Customers have become collaborators and partners.

The growing heterogeneity of customer requirements suggests that if they are to be addressed, and a greater variety of relationships sustained, we will need to tap into and build upon the differences inherent in us. More attention should be paid to the recognition, identification and development of diversity. The need to ensure that the dogged drive for transformation does not destroy diversity is a recurring theme of this book.

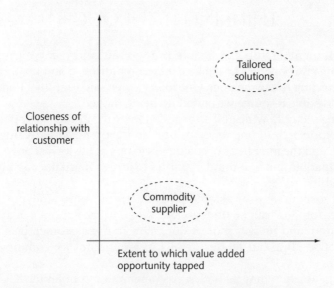

**Figure 5.2**  Breaking out of the commodity product trap

Relationships with groups of customers can be established by acquiring rather than competing with other companies that supply them. Such a strategy is particularly suited to sectors in which there are brand and other loyalties.

# RECONCILING INTEGRATION AND FOCUS

Traditionally companies have integrated forwards and backwards in order to control more of the opportunity to generate the ultimate value that is sought by customers. However, the desire to slim down and focus upon core strengths can run counter to an integration strategy.

The network organization that embraces a range of business partners is able to reconcile integration and focus. Integration may be achieved by bringing new members into the network, while the existing members concentrate upon those things which they do best.

Building relationships with customers may require a significant change of attitudes on the part of those involved. A career lifetime of bargaining and negotiation, and the 'zero-sum' perspective that regards the gain of one party as the loss of the other, needs to be replaced by different and co-operative patterns of behaviour.

Joint teams from the customer and supplier organizations need to work together in the 'positive-sum' search for outcomes that offer benefits to all players. This is often best achieved by encouraging those involved to focus upon an outcome to which all can aspire (Hurcomb, 1998).

# THINKING IT THROUGH

Network membership can enable individuals and companies both to contribute and benefit. The balance between putting in and taking out will vary according to the member. One interviewee said ruefully: 'Rather than access a flexible resource we ended up being milked.'

In some sectors a wide gulf appears between the desire of suppliers with their rhetoric of 'building relationships' and 'tapping added-value opportunities', and the intentions of customers to buy at the lowest price. It takes two compatible and like-minded parties to form a mutually advantageous relationship.

The consequences of establishing electronic links and putting the customer 'on line' can be unexpected. What, to the supplier, is a channel to 'broaden' and deliver more value, may, to the customer, be seen as a means of sending out tender details in an attempt to 'commoditize' a product.

An organization may be both a customer and a competitor. The people of the network organization need to be equipped to handle different and parallel sets of relationships with the same network partners.

# BARRIER ANALYSIS

In order to close the gap between where it is and where it would like to be, a company needs a realistic appreciation of its current situation and a detailed assessment of its desired state. Too often companies are unrealistic in their understanding of a current position, and a desired state is not translated into sufficient detail to allow important implications and requirements to be identified.

If corrective and appropriate action is to be taken, barriers and gaps between a current and desired state have to be identified. Out of this analysis of the situation will emerge a set of priorities for closing any gap between aspiration and achievement that exists or might emerge. These are the 'vital vitals' or 'vital few' that will determine the extent to which the company will 'make it'.

Figure 5.3 illustrates a summary of the barrier analysis undertaken by one company seeking to 'improve' its relationships with customers. In this case many of the 'hinders' represented outcomes that were perceived as desirable by customers. Hence, it was decided to stress the extent to which the 'helps' would benefit both customer and supplier.

Another message of the case illustrated in Figure 5.3 is that, in the absence of management action, the 'hinders' that 'are in the hands of external parties' may combine to widen the gap between aspiration and achievement. The company that treads water gets taken backwards by the current.

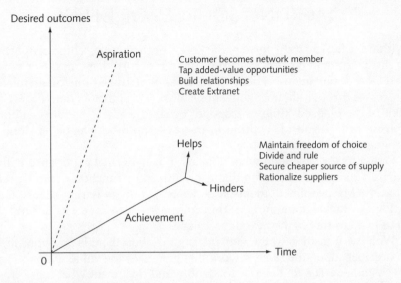

**Figure 5.3**  Helps and hinders

# SPEED OF RESPONSE

For many companies speed of response has been a major barrier and the focus of competition. For example:

- Many Japanese companies, such as Casio, based their competitive strategy upon the speed with which a new product concept could be turned into an offering in the hands of the customer.
- Hyundai of Korea moved the management of its worldwide personal computer operations to California in order to be closer to, and more responsive to, both customers and the creators of future generations of technology. Being closer to customers makes it easier for products to be tailored to individual requirements.
- Ford of Europe reduced its product range, giving greater discretion to those responsible for each product line, and introducing new project management techniques halved the time it took to develop new models.
- Sun Alliance considers intermediaries as integral elements of its organization. Sun Alliance International established e-mail links with members of its supply chain in order to build closer relationships with them.

Hewlett-Packard and Xerox achieved dramatic reductions in the time required to bring new products to the marketplace by asking 'first principles' questions about every aspect of activities and operations that had been taken for granted.

# TACKLING SOURCES OF DELAY

Within the bureaucratic form of the 'loser' organization, a high proportion of the delays and costs of non-conformance occurred at cross-over points between departments. Those companies that traced customer-related processes through their organizations often found that as much as 90 per cent of the elapsed 'time to respond' occured at these handover points. During this period of 'waiting in in-trays', nothing was being done to progress or add value.

One director described what appears to be a normal experience within the bureaucratic corporation that is organized by function rather than by process: 'My people kill themselves, working flat out with the latest technology to tackle something within minutes which then sits around for days in an in-tray in the next department.'

With the transition to the network organization there is an opportunity to organize along the flow of work that generates the value that is sought by customers. The first step is to identify and document what these cross-functional and inter-organizational processes are. The next stage is to simplify or re-engineer them. While this is being done, activities that do not add value may be discontinued and organizational boundaries redrawn.

In essence, process simplification involved putting a time stamp upon activities and cutting out those which did not deliver value to customers. It was sometimes possible to save three-quarters or more of waiting time by simple empowerment, giving people the discretion to act on their own initiative without seeking authority, unless in exceptional circumstances.

The boundary around what is exceptional can be drawn ever more tightly according to the extent to which people share corporate vision, goals and values and understand what they as individuals need to do to deliver value to customers or to contribute to specific corporate objectives.

There are those who thrive within corporate structures, who 'know their way around' and can work procedures to their own advantage. Those intent on change should examine how businesses operate in practice and how people get things done. Examining how the 'streetwise' salesperson uses an informal network to 'cut a path through' obstacles in order to meet a 'rush order' and win a place on the 'Performance Club' trip to Kenya may yield vital clues as to what might work. Looking at what shouldn't happen may be more useful than examining what should.

So impressive have been the improvements in speed of response achieved by one US financial services company, as a result of process re-engineering supported by the introduction of new technology, that delays were built back into the tail end of the delivery process. According to one manager:

*We were responding too quickly. Customers were saying 'You couldn't have spent much time thinking about it' or 'why should I pay that much when it only took you a couple of minutes?' By delaying, people feel happier, they imagine we must have at least spent a few days working on their problem.*

The speed with which new products can be introduced to the marketplace can result in product proliferation and confusion. Hitachi once sought to slow down the pace at which new models, types and varieties of product were introduced.

A company has to decide when enough is enough. Many Japanese companies pursued a policy of continuous innovation which resulted in a flow of new products to the marketplace. The result, in an era of economic slowdown, was an excessively wide range of products. Mass customizing now reconciles speed and flexibility with low inventory costs.

A company that does not properly understand customer requirements may devote a lot of effort to improvements which are not significant from the point of view of the consumer. In many companies people are not motivated to either learn from the customer or deliver what the customer wants.

Wherever possible, performance assessment and reward should be MACRO, (ie Measured According to Customer-Related Outputs) and not MICRO (or, Measured in Terms of Internal Company-Related Outputs). Barrier analysis can be used to identify the various 'helps' and 'hinders' relating to the achievement of output objectives.

## SEGMENTATION, PRIORITIZATION AND DIFFERENTIATION

A company, even the most extensive network, cannot be all things to all people. Segmentation, prioritization and differentiation are important, inter-related and interdependent (Figure 5.4). A segment could be a single customer, and all stages of the review process could be undertaken within an account team.

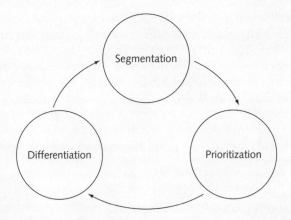

*Source: Coulson-Thomas and Brown (1990)*

**Figure 5.4**   The customer review process

Segmentation, prioritization and differentiation decisions increasingly require a knowledge of the customer and business environment, and of the company and its strategy beyond the product or business unit:

- Segmentation requires an awareness and understanding of the particular advantages an organization has *vis-à-vis* the alternatives available in satisfying decisive customer requirements. Such particular comparative advantages must be sustainable over the period of time necessary profitably to develop and supply whatever is needed to meet the selected needs.
- Prioritization of selected segments reflects current views of what the organization does best. Effective differentiation can require disciplined prioritization in order to focus effort and concentrate resources upon the requirements of particular sectors, segments and customers.
- Differentiation further sharpens those areas in which an organization can add the greatest value and this awareness is reflected in the further review of chosen segments. With each iteration of the review process groups and teams should have a sharper and more developed understanding of their comparative advantage.

Segmentation, prioritization and differentiation are ongoing processes that themselves need to be reviewed from time to time to ensure that they are capable of responding to significant and fundamental, as well as incremental, change. All those who deliver value sought by customers should be involved.

## WHO IS RESPONSIBLE FOR THE CUSTOMER?

We have seen that the vision of many CEOs is of a network that embraces both customers and suppliers. In many sectors an individual company cannot deliver the whole of the value-added sought by customers without working closely with other companies in the total supply chain.

Corporate focus has shifted from quality product to quality organization, and then on to quality network. Implementation within the network depends even more upon relationships, the agreement of equal partners rather than 'cascading from above'. Network quality is a mutual and joint responsibility.

Some companies find that the perceptions senior management have of relative worth and contribution bear little relationship with reality from a customer point of view:

- As many as one in four of those in a 'slimmed down' organization may not be generating value for customers.
- Whole groups of highly-paid staff may be preoccupied with tasks that have no direct link with customer satisfaction, while the activities of obscure and overlooked areas can suddenly assume considerable significance.

- In some cases up to one in five have been found to be engaged on activities that are directly counter to current business goals and priority objectives.

If the energies of a wider range of people, account groups and project teams are to be applied to co-operative and customer-related activities, greater empowerment will be needed.

## WHO SPEAKS FOR THE CUSTOMER IN THE BOARDROOM?

Departmentalism and professionalism are curses upon those trying to develop network organizations. We have seen that vertical departmental barriers are generally the prime source of delay in delivering the value sought by customers.

The consequences of departmentalism are painfully apparent in boardrooms. 'Specialist' directors in the boardroom are often obstacles to, rather than facilitators of, change:

- Many functional heads lack strategic perspective and other 'directorial' qualities. Their self-identity encourages them to think in a functional rather than holistic way.
- Many of those with 'director' job titles are technical specialists who lack 'people skills', and are unlikely to hold main board appointments. They cannot see the wood for the trees, and seek security by cultivating 'busyness' with technical matters.
- Many directors need to become more involved in the strategy of the business as a whole. Few of the key issues on the boardroom agenda can be neatly packaged into functional boxes. They are holistic business issues that frequently require a total response and absolute commitment.
- Functional heads and process owners are often excessively territorial and over-protective of their interests. One chairman grumbled: 'I get asked: whose budget will it go on? The question should be what can we do collectively for the customer?'

In the view of another chairman: 'Customers have been treated by our marketing people as cannon fodder for generalized ads and direct mail shots. Other people in the company, including personnel, are telling me we've got to start treating customers as individuals' (Coulson-Thomas and Brown, 1990).

## THE FATE OF THE FUNCTIONAL DIRECTOR

Customers are too important to be 'left' to one director; they are the responsibility of the whole board. Corporate transformation to a customer focused network requires the total commitment of all the people of the organization. There is a need for everyone to be involved in 'the change process'.

IT is regarded in many companies as an integral part of the subject matter of many disciplines, and of the processes of many functions. It cannot be left to technical specialists, and it must be in the hands of users, as the focus shifts from technology to its application. There is a requirement in many boardrooms for facilitating roles such as directors of learning or thinking. Companies are also allocating process owner roles at board level.

Ultimately the executive members of the board may consist of facilitators and key process owners (Coulson-Thomas, 1993). The cross-functional view will come to predominate and departmentalism will wither away. In the meantime, specialist directors will 'fight their corner'. The chairman or chief executive who genuinely wants to transform a company cannot afford to overlook their machinations.

# CHECKLIST

► Is the vision of the company, and are its goals and values, rooted in the customer?

► How differentiated is the company from its competitors in the marketplace?

► How bothered or inconvenienced would the company's customers be if the company ceased to exist?

► How customer-focused is the board? Where do the customers rank in relation to other stakeholders?

► What steps does the company take to identify customer requirements and measure customer satisfaction?

► How much of the value sought by the ultimate customer is delivered by your company, and how much by other members of the supply chain?

► What do the customers of your company really think about it?

► Is customer value at the top of the list of key management priorities?

► Is reward linked to the delivery of value and satisfaction to customers?

► Has the company identified those key management and business processes that deliver the value sought by customers?

► Are the critical success factors for building strategic and key account relationships understood?

► How effective is the company at harnessing and applying its resources to meet the needs of the individual customer?

► Who is, and who is not, adding value for customers?

► Are customers regarded as 'outsiders', or as colleagues and business partners?

► What processes are in place to learn from customers?

► How much effort is put into building close working relationships with customers, and other members of the supply chain?

## REFERENCES

Coulson-Thomas, C (1988) *The New Professionals*, BIM, Corby

Coulson-Thomas, C (1993) *Creating Excellence in the Boardroom*, McGraw-Hill, London

Coulson-Thomas, C and Brown, R (1990) *Beyond Quality: Managing the relationship with the customer*, BIM, Corby

Hurcomb, J (1998) *Developing Strategic Customers & Key Accounts: The critical success factors*, Policy Publications, Bedford

## FURTHER INFORMATION

A brochure describing the *Developing Strategic Customers & Key Accounts: The critical success factors* report and a series of 'Close to the Customer' briefings is available from Policy Publications, 4 The Crescent, Bedford MK40 2RU (tel: +44 (0) 1234 328448; fax: +44 (0) 1234 357231; e-mail: policypubs@kbnet.co.uk; Web site: www.ntwkfirm.com/bookshop).

# 6

# Transformation Intentions and Business Development Outcomes

*'Dragonflies evolve slowly'*

## ASPIRATION

Intention is not in doubt. Acceptance of the need for transformation is almost universal. In the 1990s downsizing, restructuring to focus on core activities and re-engineering became commonplace. Corporate organizations are now seeking to make the transition to more flexible, responsive and resilient networks embracing customers, suppliers and business partners that can create new opportunities and survive shocks. However, companies are finding the translation of intention into reality intractable and elusive. Expectations have not been fulfilled, and intentions have been 'blown off course' by the swirling winds of economic adversity.

## HOW MUCH TRANSFORMATION?

How much transformation is required, the form it should take, and its pace, will depend upon customer requirements, commercial opportunities, pressures of circumstances, and views and assumptions of what can be accomplished:

- Attempt too much and the programme may fail. People and resources may be stretched to breaking point. Companies, like individuals, can over-reach themselves by behaving recklessly, or with an excess of ambition.
- Move too slowly and the company may miss the strategic opportunity, or be 'beaten to the draw' and 'taken out' by a faster competitor. Move with speed but without sufficient weight and commitment, and the momentum may not be enough to 'break through'.
- The fleeting prospect may not be recognized by the self-centred or the preoccupied. On the other hand, while waiting for the 'main chance', necessary action may be postponed. A company can spend too much time looking over its shoulder at other corporations.

The transformation process involves a symbiotic matching of customer requirements, organizational vision and organizational capability (Figure 6.1). The aim is a perfect alignment of requirement, vision and capability.

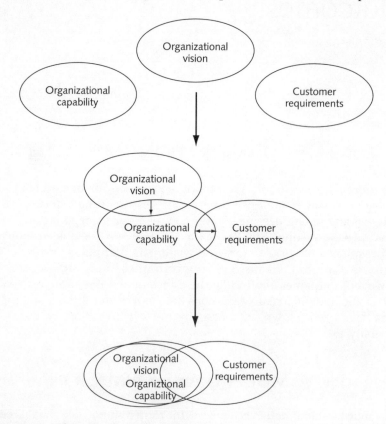

**Figure 6.1** The transformation process

When people have a choice, their attention and allegiance has to be won and retained. A balance should be kept between what is promised and what is delivered. Customers, employees and business partners are like the electorate in that they become bored, can take things for granted and may transfer their support elsewhere when they feel it is in their interests to do so.

## INCREMENTAL OR FUNDAMENTAL CHANGE

There is an evident and strong desire for corporate transformation. With all the smoke there has to be some fire. We saw in Chapter 1 that against the background of multiple and profound changes and challenges in the business environment, many managements accept that incremental change is no longer enough.

How fundamental the transformation should be will depend upon the situation and circumstances of the individual company. As one chairman put it: '*You don't transform for the hell of it.*' There are easier ways of getting directorial and managerial 'kicks'.

Circumstances might allow a gradual transition and incremental adjustment. For example:

- The pressure could be rather like the gentle but nagging pain that suggests some action now might avoid a toothache later.
- The penalty of failure could be mild, perhaps a marginal loss of market share.

Alternatively, a crisis situation might require radical, even revolutionary change. For example:

- The crisis could be more like a heart attack that demands an immediate change of lifestyle.
- The penalty of failure could be severe, even receivership or liquidation.

Managers need to understand the profound nature of the distinction between evolutionary and revolutionary change, and the requirements for bringing about a revolution in thought. They must learn from radicals rather than administrators.

## TRANSFORMING THE LEVIATHAN

The past experiences of many companies and managers has not equipped them to cope with a transformed market environment. They face the twin tasks of dismantling a past structure and pattern of operation they can no longer afford, while at the same time creating a new form of organization to cope with a world they do not understand.

Large companies can be more, rather than less, vulnerable than smaller rivals. Protected from reality by a flow of profit resulting from past decisions, they may be slow to recognize and react to changing circumstances.

Restructuring a big but inflexible company is rather like stopping an oil tanker. It takes a long time: like dragonflies they evolve slowly. Restructuring can also be expensive.

The experience of IBM during the 1990s illustrates the range of responses required to transform a bureaucratic corporation in the face of various challenges in the business environment. The search for flexibility and responsiveness involved many elements:

- the monolithic corporation set out to become a federated network of increasingly independent businesses;
- business units were encouraged to focus upon particular market segments;
- the corporation assumed greater responsibility and risk in broadening and deepening its relationship with the customer;
- the focus shifted from products to services in order to tap greater added-value opportunities;
- a growing number of joint ventures and arrangements were concluded to create a comprehensive global network of relationships;
- a uniform corporate culture was replaced by greater diversity;
- the culture became less paternalistic, and managers were required to assume extra responsibilities;
- certain central and service functions became separate businesses;
- a programme of disposals spun off businesses that did not fit the new direction;
- worldwide units were formed to pull together certain areas of expertise and capability;
- new co-ordinating mechanisms and processes were established to manage the evolving organization;
- the internal bureaucracy was sharply cut back;
- layers were taken out of the corporate organization and spans of control widened;
- new independent but wholly-owned subsidiaries were set up to compete with the mainstream business.

The transformation war against complacency and inertia needs to be waged simultaneously on a number of fronts. However, some companies restructure or re-engineer just about every area of corporate activity except the process for winning business. This is where transformation should start. Determining what needs to be done to establish and build more intimate relationships with customers reveals the nature, scale and extent of the changes that need to be introduced.

Many approaches to corporate transformation and business development are unnecessarily complex. Asda and Sainsbury's built new picking centres to support their moves into online retailing. Tesco, a rival supermarket chain, moved more quickly by adopting a simpler strategy. Existing stores would fulfil local orders. Although the initial take up of home shopping was slower than expected, Tesco soon covered the direct costs involved. Asda and Sainsbury's would take much longer to secure a return on their higher start-up investment.

# RHETORIC AND ASPIRATIONS

A decade ago, approaching nine out of ten of the organizations participating in the *Flat Organisation* survey (Coulson-Thomasand Coe, 1991) were becoming slimmer and flatter. In some eight out of ten participating organizations, more work was being undertaken in teams, and a more responsive network organization was being created. Functions and organizations were becoming more interdependent, and procedures and permanency were giving way to flexibility and temporary arrangements.

The first edition of this book (Coulson-Thomas, 1992) mentioned companies that were either transitioning to a network form or had successfully transformed to a network model of operation. Examples were given of marketing co-operatives, collaborative purchasing and new electronic networks, markets and communities that were allowing 24-hour-a-day trading independent of particular locations.

The US company Lewis Galoob Toys had subcontracted to a network of suppliers a range of management activities that had been traditionally undertaken in-house. Only such key tasks as strategy formulation and co-ordination of the network were performed by the core team. Apple had used an international network of subcontract and temporary staff to speed up the introduction of tailored products. Sherwood Computer Services operated a flexible network form of organization based upon client service teams and market co-ordination groups. All the staff were involved in the process of reviewing the form of organization and method of operation which would best enable the company to meet the requirements of its customers.

Aspects of the network organization were being introduced into large and mature companies. Within BP, networking across national borders was encouraged to bring together groups and teams to handle particular tasks. The global network of Daiwa Securities allowed management responsibilities to be reallocated to different locations around the network according to the pattern of trading that developed. The organization never slept, as some markets came on stream while others closed down as the earth spun relentlessly on its axis.

Computer-based networks for individuals with common interests and characteristics were springing into existence. Members of SeniorNet secured access to a range of services, and its system supported the establishment of subnetworks of those with particular interests in common.

Transformation can be done. In some knowledge-based sectors, and in certain types of start-up situation a decade ago, the network form of organization became a norm. However, many major corporations have found their people and customers remain frustrated as their expectations have grown, while the flexibility to cope with economic downturn without the dramas of cut backs and lay-offs still eludes them. As the suffering herd tramps through the bleak desert of trial and tribulation, only a few are 'sensing the presence of water'.

A major reason that investor, customer and management frustration, and work-life balance debates continue is that people are working hard to improve or transform activities that are not critical to competitive success. Processes are re-engineered and new technology is introduced – both at a high financial and human cost – but the results do not make a significant, positive and distinctive impact upon customers and prospects. Senior management barks up the wrong trees.

## SENIOR MANAGEMENT PREOCCUPATIONS

There are many claims upon the time of senior staff. How they use it is extremely revealing. In 'loser' companies they are usually busy attending meetings, taking calls and reading e-mails. Although overloaded, many of them are reluctant to share, prioritize and delegate. When they do hand over tasks to subordinates they often retain the trivia and take their eye off more critical activities.

Paint schemes are reviewed and Christmas cards are selected. Expense claims that have already been approved are countersigned. The directors may attend lunches for past employees but they may not be involved in the preparation and presentation of major bids or meeting strategically important customers.

Many senior managers seem all too ready and willing to hand over the business development role. They set ambitious growth targets, recruit new sales staff and select key account managers. When appointments are made they visibly relax. They then stand back and wait for additional business to flow in.

Invariably losers are disappointed. Before they can become effective new staff must settle in, understand the company's offerings, make appointments and build relationships. The lead-time to acquire new orders can be very protracted. In the meantime there is a significant extra salary bill to cover every month.

Winners do not make such mistakes. They focus upon the areas of greatest opportunity and are ready to engage. For example, they understand that involving senior managers in a bid presentation can be extremely helpful (Kennedy and O'Connor, 1997). It is a visual and personal demonstration that a particular opportunity is being taken seriously. The contributions made are also directly related to the project in question and demonstrate an awareness of the purchaser's aspirations and requirements.

Senior managers should act as ambassadors and take a lead in relationship building. Important existing and potential customers and business partners may expect to meet one or more directors of a company at some point during the year or while negotiations are in progress (Hurcomb, 1998). They may feel slighted if they do not. This is particularly true of prospects in many overseas markets.

Of course, key people cannot be in two places at once and there are many claims upon their time. Much will depend upon the nature of the market, the types of products and services on offer, and the sums of money involved. If there are a large number of customers and a relatively small proportion of turnover and profit is accounted for by individual contracts, it may be difficult for directors to become involved in individual responses.

However, winners are sensitive to what is at stake. They look ahead at the future implications of obtaining or losing a particular order. They endeavour to get involved in opportunities of strategic significance. The teams fielded for visits and presentations reflect their importance to the various parties involved.

Managers in winning companies are cautious when taking new people on board. They spend money on additional staff as if it is coming from their own pockets, and they think through the overhead and cash flow implications of additional hires.

Senior managers also understand that new members of a team might take some time getting up to speed. Fresh recruits, and any staff transferred from other projects, may need to acquire particular skills and tools before they can perform at the levels of more experienced colleagues. The practices of high performing sales staff are captured in ways that allow them to be shared with new hires.

## THE IMPLICATIONS OF CHANGE

Rationalization, uncertainty, concealment, perceived self-interest and deception can so muddy the waters that it is not easy to uncover the reality of what people are feeling and thinking. Comparing winners and losers reveals certain telltale successful and unsuccessful change symptoms, such as those shown in Table 6.1.

Change is not neutral in its impact and may adversely affect certain senior staff and many middle managers, thus encouraging them to block initiatives. In order to contain the intrigue and infighting that can result, mechanisms and processes that are perceived as objective and neutral may be required. An 'internal market' is one example. Some companies retain only those staff functions which business units are prepared to fund.

**Table 6.1** Achieving the transition

| Unsuccessful symptoms | Successful symptoms |
| --- | --- |
| Working harder for longer hours | Working smarter in a more focused way |
| Change seen as headcount reduction and cost cutting | Change seen as improving service to customers, innovation and entrepreneurship |
| Insecurity and uncertainty | Confidence and commitment |
| Internal politics, competition and power struggles | Common customer focus |
| Complaints about information provision | Active creation of knowledge and intellectual capital |
| Keeping head down and playing it safe | Assuming responsibility and getting it right |
| Frantic search for instant and final solution | Frank discussion to build understanding of what is required |
| Repetition of slogans and production of motherhood videos and brochures | Each group responding according to context |
| Directed or instructed change | Shared desire to change |

When people are required to do more with less and assume extra responsibility, not all will react in the same way. While some may thrive, others may experience stress. Process and technique may appear a poor substitute for 'love and kindness'. Support such as help with shopping, child-minding and relocation can take the heat off people.

## MOVING FROM THE PARTICULAR TO THE GENERAL

Having got some movement in the right direction, the next problem may be to hang on. Transformation has a tendency to get out of control. When momentum appears to be building, the wagon may suddenly slip off the rails. Here are some examples:

- Initial transformation projects may focus upon carefully chosen topics and where there is a reasonable prospect of success. As enthusiasm spreads and greater numbers of people acquire the desire 'to be seen to be doing something' groups may be set up all over the place. Chaos can result, with teams tackling everything bar the key priorities of the business.
- The first change project may be carefully selected, and all available expertise and a fair amount of senior management time may be devoted to it. These conditions may not apply to follow-on projects, and when

processes under examination appear to overlap, or be in conflict, confusion can reign.
- A prototype micro-business unit, entrepreneurial venture or self-managed workgroup may require and receive extensive support from a number of central centres of competence. Once the pilot is up and running, subsequent groups may be left to fend for themselves. Senior managers may assume that later groups will learn from the pioneers, without putting in place a process to enable this to happen.

Once a number of cross-functional or 'horizontal' processes are in place, process owners need to negotiate the boundaries between processes. In some companies process owners enter into contracts to provide each other with services.

## THE TIMING OF CHANGE

A corporate change programme may need to cope with a variety of economic situations from boom to bust. Both the extremes present problems:

- At the peaks the people may be running flat out to meet orders and unwilling to be distracted from 'making hay while the good weather lasts'. The most typical response may be: 'Let's talk about it later.'
- During the troughs there is pressure on budgets, and a preoccupation with cutbacks, laying people off and 'keeping the creditors at bay'. This is not the best time to interest people in long-term commitments that may be perceived as requiring up-front investments.

For some it will never be the right time to initiate a transformation programme. Sooner or later the nettle needs to be grasped if a transition is to be voluntary, rather than an imposed consequence of adversity and crisis.

## THE NEED FOR NEW ATTITUDES

Transformation is not a state, but a combination of changing attitudes and expectations. People's perspectives should extend to the total process with which they are concerned so that they can assess their own priorities in terms of the purpose of the process and their own role in it.

The network organization is an organism rather than a machine. The extent of the need for new attitudes is illustrated by comparative features of the bureaucratic machine organization and the organic network identified by the author over 20 years ago (Coulson-Thomas, 1981). These are shown in Table 6.2.

The network is dynamic, and an organic whole. The 'health of an individual department or "organ" will influence the general health of the

**Table 6.2** The bureaucratic machine v the organic network

| Company as machine | Company as organism |
| --- | --- |
| Self-contained and independent | Interdependent |
| Hard shell | Porous skin |
| Separate departments | Communicative groups and communities |
| Objectives to maximize sales and profits | Objectives reflect society and interests of stakeholders and customers |
| Focus on maximization | Focus on satisfaction and the creation of value |
| Efficiency | Adaptation |
| Insider/outsider distinction | Information and knowledge flows |
| Assemble resources | Establish and build relationships |
| Closed organization | Open, flexible and receptive |
| Directive | Negotiative |
| Ideas judged by source | Ideas judged by quality and relevance |
| Innovation seen as a threat | Ideas considered important |
| Avoids risks | Encourages innovation and entrepreneurship |
| Fosters myths | Frank and honest |
| Conceals weaknesses | Tackles deficiencies |
| Hidebound by tradition | Dynamic |
| Competitive | Co-operative |
| Deals | Obligations |
| Orders and instructions | Bargaining and negotiation |
| Authority and direction | Debate, consensus and respect |
| Vertical communication | All channel communication |
| Task centred | People centred |
| Understand through parts | Understand through the whole |

| Machine manager | Network member |
| --- | --- |
| Technician or driver | Communicator, expert or entrepreneur |
| Defined skills | Intuition and sensitivity |
| Functional specialization | Holistic perspective |
| Keeps machine running effectively | Organism lives and spreads |
| Conscious of position/status/authority | Aware of when adding value |
| Talks | Listens |
| Administers | Creates |

whole organization and vice versa… the communications system is rather like its nervous system'. If flows and processes are blocked, 'organs will go to sleep and then gangrene will set in' (Coulson-Thomas, 1981).

The author concluded as follows (Coulson-Thomas, 1981):

*Organic management is concerned with flows rather than stocks, dynamic rather than static situations, change and development rather than order, effectiveness and adaptability rather than efficiency… Organic growth is evolutionary. Survival is a question of balance between capacity and capability, and problems and opportunities… Success is a matter of coping with change and uncertainty… an ability to objectively assess relative strengths and weaknesses and to learn and keep on learning. 'Organic' managers are sensitive, subtle and aware.*

A move away from the bureaucratic organization undermines those who are dependent upon situational power. Within the network organization power can ebb and flow around the network as new relationships are formed and situations change. This can be disturbing for those who like to know where they stand.

In the arena of co-operation and partnering, power is shared, rather than exercised, and the focus is upon common interests and mutual strengths that can be built upon, rather than individual weaknesses that should be exploited.

## FORMAL AND INFORMAL ORGANIZATION

Plodding through the existing organization in terms of seeking to determine what happens next can be a soul-destroying occupation. Reading the reports is rather like listening to a confessional. In many companies a high proportion of document flows still terminate in dead ends. The individual trying to create value, opportunities and new ventures may find the corporate game has many snakes and few ladders.

The organization to 'work on' is the one which operates in practice as opposed to what ought to or is thought to happen. The official or formal view, as set out in the organizational chart, may not reflect what happens on the ground. In view of the inefficiences of the bureaucracy, various people find 'informal' ways to cut corners.

One quick and crude way of determining what the flow of work ought to be is to create a series of open environments, in which there is relatively free access to information and most departmental constraints are removed, and then watch and wait. When left to themselves, people that have been focused upon the customer are likely to establish whatever network linkages and relationships, and to follow whatever paths, best enable them to respond to customer requirements. The informal organization that emerges could become the basis for redesigning the formal organization.

# WINNING BUSINESS

Sustaining success is extremely difficult. Human nature works against you. Once people feel they have 'got it cracked' or have hit upon a 'winning formula' they tend to become complacent. They stop reviewing, questioning and learning. When it all seems too good to be true it probably is. A consequence of competitive markets and economic cycles is that what is discovered or given can also be lost or taken away.

Until a slowdown in expenditure on IT and 'telecoms' occurred, it seemed that the rapid growth of Cisco Systems would continue without interruption. Few foresaw retrenchment and layoffs around the corner. Likewise, not many commentators expected Polaroid to experience a cash flow crisis. The assumption was that these business-generating wonders would go from strength to strength.

People often focus upon cutting costs rather than increasing revenues because they feel the financial results are likely to be more certain. However, the most direct impact upon corporate performance can usually be obtained by transforming processes and practices for winning business. It is precisely when times are hard or complacency has set in that the payoff can be the greatest.

Evidence from the 'winning business' series of reports (Kennedy and O'Connor, 1997; James, 1999, 2000, 2001; Kennedy, 1999, 2000; Hally, 2000; Harris, 2000) produced by Policy Publications in association with the University of Luton, suggests the differences between consistent winners and regular losers are stark. They could almost be considered separate species. Their bid teams have distinct attitudes and contrasting approaches. When visiting them it is possible to tell very quickly which is which.

# BUSINESS DEVELOPMENT LOSERS

Losers are undisciplined, unimaginative and reactive. They keep their heads down and work alone and in standard ways. They rarely leave their offices and avoid networking with their colleagues. Many have not seen or experienced the services they are endeavouring to sell. They pursue far too many opportunities, and focus primarily upon their employers' concerns, objectives and priorities.

Members of 'loser' bid teams 'go automatic'. They respond mechanically to incoming invitations to tender. Internal information is collected and documentation processed. If they think at all it is about adherence to procedures and whether something similar has been encountered before.

They also tend to be cold and unemotional. They 'hold back'. They may only commit significant effort when a prospect is judged to be 'seriously interested'. By the time they become really engaged it may be too late to make a difference.

Losers tend to meet deadlines. They will get something in on time. They become preoccupied with the practicalities of producing proposals such as obtaining up to date costs and CVs. When colleagues are slow in responding they become anxious and find themselves under pressure to meet submission deadlines. Yet they ignore tools that could speed up their basic activities and free up time for differentiation, tailoring and polishing.

Winning business specialists in 'loser' companies describe their jobs in terms of 'writing and submitting bids'. They actually spend their days losing potential business, as most of the proposals they send in are rejected.

Bid team members in companies with below average success rates are left to 'get on with it' by their colleagues. Senior managers loftily describe them as 'techies' or 'engineers' and find the details of what they do uninteresting and the repetitive nature of how they work boring. Key people, and even colleagues with relevant specialist experience, are only very rarely involved in individual opportunities.

Companies that lose measure success by the number of proposals submitted. They make little effort to learn from their experience or 'best practice'. They don't find out why some bids are accepted and others fail. Rejection letters enable them to 'close the file' and move onto the next proposal. Above all, they don't actually mind losing. Failure is accepted as the norm. Phrases such as 'someone has to lose' or 'you can't win them all' are used.

## LETTING CUSTOMERS GO

Losers also lose out on repeat business. They use rather than value their existing customers. They haggle over prices and margins, and discourage 'variations' from standard offerings that might create 'extra work' and cause 'systems problems'. They do just enough to fulfil any contracts that are won. They don't really care about their customers' businesses and keep 'outsiders' at a distance to protect their 'know-how'.

Losers do little to lock their customers in. They are reluctant to establish online links because of worries about importing viruses. Open book accounting and partnering relationships are also avoided. Not surprisingly, clients seeking a deeper and more intimate relationship look elsewhere.

## BUSINESS DEVELOPMENT WINNERS

Winning bid teams are very different from losers. Their members are far more confident and creative. They evaluate and understand their company's offerings. They also visit customers and end users to assess their reactions, experiences and suggestions.

Some companies find that sales of their products are held back by consumer insecurity or lack of knowledge. Homebase found that many people did not understand how to undertake simple DIY tasks in the home but were too embarrassed to seek help from family and friends. The company provides basic information, DIY guides and practical advice on the Homebase Web site which visitors can access and study while online. As a result, better-informed customers turn up at Homebase stores.

Winners are also proactive. They identify and approach prospects with growth potential that would make good business partners. They take the initiative in contacting the people they would most like to work with.

Winners are very selective. They ruthlessly prioritize available opportunities. If a request for a proposal does not match their business development aspirations and qualification criteria it is rejected. Turning down some invitations to tender allows more effort to be devoted to those bids that are retained.

Winners also set out to succeed as a consequence of the performance of their customers. Hence they really want their consumers, users and prospects to do well. They become absorbed in their problems and opportunities. They focus upon and think about their needs and priorities. They come up with new ideas for achieving client and partner objectives. They suggest, advocate and champion. They warn, share insights and provide tip-offs.

## MAKING THE COMMITMENT

People in winning company bid teams only work upon opportunities that are considered important. Hence when they do respond it is with commitment, passion and clear objectives. They think through, articulate and strive to achieve the outcomes and relationships they would like to secure.

Winners do not hold back or 'wait and see'. They set out to win. They hit the ground running. They also allocate sufficient resources early on to build up an unassailable lead. If anything, they become more confident and continue to refine and improve their offering as deadlines approach. Colleagues willingly support them. Their contributions are sought, received and valued.

Key players in the more successful companies willingly participate in important sales pitches. They attach a high priority to winning business and building strategic customer relationships. They understand that visible and active support of senior management can be decisive in close contests, and they may not wait to be asked.

From the moment of first contact winners also try to understand how buying decisions are made and the criteria likely to be used to narrow the possibilities and make the final selection of a supplier. They consider the personalities involved and their particular requirements. Proposals are structured to reflect these, and section and executive summaries are drafted to allow the people evaluating proposals to quickly determine if their prerequisites are met.

When asked to present, losers tend to summarize submitted proposals. They refight battles that they have already won. Winners remain sensitive to changing buyer concerns throughout the purchasing process and the issues that are known, or are most likely to arise, at each stage. During face-to-face meetings they work hard to establish empathy, build trust, and match the culture of prospects.

Where possible, winners automate the more mechanical aspects of bid production. Eyretel supplies multimedia recording and analysis services for call centres, and is one of the UK's fastest growing companies. Its international expansion was constrained by the time taken to train new sales staff to sell complex products. Members of the Eyretel sales force now use a laptop-based tool to give presentations, configure and price solutions, and generate cost justifications and proposals. The rule-based system was developed by Cotoco, which specializes in improving sales force productivity. Time saved from assembling information and performing calculations is used to tailor responses, differentiate offerings and build relationships.

## LOCKING CUSTOMERS IN

Winners care about their clients' businesses. They take specific steps to become more intimately involved. They share information and knowledge and pass on leads. They are always on the look out for ways of 'adding value' or helping customers to solve their problems.

They lock out competitors by integrating their own systems and processes with those of their customers. They may become involved in joint planning and the development of their client's services. Relationships they forge grow into formal partnerships with joint and mutual objectives, shared rewards and savings, commitments to specific and measurable performance improvements, open book accounting and simple, quick, low-level dispute resolution procedures.

## WANTING TO WIN

At the end of the day, winners actually want to win. They see their names written all over the opportunities they pursue. They are gutted when they lose. On occasion, they may refuse to accept 'no' as an answer and press for a review of decisions that go against them or negotiate a role for themselves.

Winners strive to do even better. After their customers and prospects have announced their purchase decisions they hold debriefs to learn from both successes and failures. Win or lose, they regularly review their processes and practices for winning business, and periodically submit them to an external audit or health check.

## Losers

Losers:

- assume change is beneficial and pursue changes almost for the sake of change;
- introduce change programmes without thinking through their implications;
- disrupt customer relationships to achieve internal objectives;
- do not ensure that all the elements needed for a successful transformation are in place;
- subject people to changes without first preparing them or equipping them to cope;
- fail to anticipate obstacles and barriers to change;
- introduce change programmes that are at odds with other objectives, policies and messages;
- delegate change management responsibilities to contractors, consultants and external experts;
- enforce common corporate standards and approaches during the process of transformation.

## Winners

Winners:

- recognize the downsides, risks and costs of change and endeavour to limit changes to the critical success factors for delivering greater value to customers and achieving key corporate objectives;
- carefully consider how much change is needed, where, when and for what purpose;
- protect customer relationships while achieving other objectives;
- assemble the various pieces of the jigsaw puzzle that may be required to bring about a desired transformation;
- involve people in the planning and implementation of changes that affect them and equip them with the knowledge, skills and tools needed to achieve successful transitions;
- anticipate and address likely obstacles and barriers to change;
- ensure that corporate communications, rewards and management behaviour are consistent with and support desired changes;
- ensure internal ownership and senior management leadership of strategically important changes;
- advocate diversity and encourage bespoke responses where various parts of the organization may need to operate quite distinctly if the individual requirements of different customers are to be accommodated.

# NEW PROBLEMS FOR OLD

Change for the right reasons, but with the wrong attitudes and values, can create new problems as rapidly as older ones are tackled. While passionate advocates of change may view central units as a burden, some of those who are squeezed or eased out may have added value. New models of organizations also have their problems. For example, the following views were expressed by a few of the early exponents of process re-engineering:

> While the processes have changed, the people remain the same. The process owners cling to their processes – they see them as their processes, and they talk about their group – and run them as if they were running another department.

> The first was a sweat, but now we have overlapping processes, even boundary problems between processes. It's becoming a bit of a mess.

> How do you explain an organization that's all processes? The whole becomes too complex. People put their heads down and tend to just concentrate upon a bit of one process – they are already compartmentalizing.

> Try to draw our processes and it comes out like a ball of wool that the cat has been at.

> I worry that we may replace a set of 'vertical' problems with another set of 'horizontal' problems. We've turned the organization around, but not ourselves.

Roles and responsibilities have to be created anew in the very different operating context of the network organization. A transformation vision of a 'new world' needs to give some idea of the sorts of beings that inhabit it. How will they operate and interrelate? What constitutes acceptable and exemplary conduct? Without knowledge of what may be encountered, it is difficult to prepare for the journey.

Another common question is: 'Where is this new world?' Is it just around the corner, or separated from present reality by what may appear to be an unbridgeable chasm? Some transformation visions appear to 'float in space'. Others are rather like a negative. As one director explained: 'We are not too sure what it will be like. At times we are more conscious of what is missing.'

A diagrammatic vision of the journey from bureaucratic to network organization is set out in Figure 6.2. The first stage is to obtain a realistic appreciation of the nature of the challenge by ensuring that the attitudes, values and behaviours of both are understood. During the transition stage, the attitudes, values and behaviour of the network organization will

**Stage 1: The Challenge**

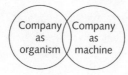

**Stage 2: Risk of Confusion**

**Stage 3: Changed Attitudes and Behaviour**

**Figure 6.2** The organic eclipse

slowly replace those of the bureaucratic machine. This will occur more rapidly and painlessly for some than for others. During this stage there is the ever-present risk of confusion, if not chaos.

Eventually when, and if, the transition is achieved, a new set of attitudes, values and behaviours will emerge. The outcome is likely to be a fusion or synthesis rather than a replacement. Some aspects, particularly distinctive strengths and relevant qualities, will live on through the organic network.

## THE TRANSFORMATION JIGSAW PUZZLE

The efforts of many companies to achieve transformational change have been counter-productive. Some of those who 'believed', or who 'tried', now feel betrayed. There is insecurity, widespread disbelief and cynicism in many companies.

One of the reasons why so many people question either the commitment of senior management to change, or the feasibility of transformation, is that they perceive that all the change elements that are necessary for successful transformation are not in place. Consider the following selection of comments:

*For many years not much happened. Then we stumbled upon a few things we hadn't done. It broke the log jam.*

*For far too long we just assumed it had to come good because of the amount of money we were spending and the amount of talking we were doing. We didn't deem it necessary to identify and address the few things that were getting in the way.*

*It's what you are not doing that tends to be the problem, not the things that you are doing. We overlooked a couple of things that were absolutely crucial to making it happen.*

*We asked people to do one thing, and then we paid them for doing something else.*

*There is no point asking or expecting people to work in new ways if you do not give them the skills, resources or discretion to succeed.*

As well as critical success factors, some obvious areas are being overlooked. The document, whether physical or electronic, is the currency of a business, the signals that pass through the nerves of the organic network and trigger intelligent reactions. It is the means by which most activities happen. Yet many organizations are unaware of how much time and resource are devoted to this unrecognized area of business, the production and distribution of documents.

## LEADERSHIP FOR CORPORATE TRANSFORMATION

There is some consensus among winners concerning what is important, and what needs to be done, to bridge the gap between transformation expectation and transformation achievement that is found in many companies:

- A clear and compelling vision and strategy is essential for both differentiation and transformation. The vision should embrace both the transformation 'end state' and the transformation process.
- Top management commitment is of crucial importance in the management of change. It needs to be communicated and sustained. A practical and necessary demonstration of commitment is to ensure that all the pieces of the transformation jigsaw puzzle and the critical factors for competitive success are in place (Coulson-Thomas, 1997 & 1998).
- People need to be empowered and equipped to manage change, and to handle the extra responsibilities that are being placed upon them. This

requires a holistic perspective, new attitudes, fresh approaches and additional techniques. In particular, there is a need for the qualities associated with the 'organic manager'.

- Within corporations there are hidden businesses. Management and business processes should focus energies and resources upon those people and activities that make the greatest contribution to business development and competitive success.

Champions and guardians of corporate transformation are needed. All forms of organization attract the adventurers and the opportunists. The organic network is unlikely to be an exception. New breeds of people will emerge that are especially adept at 'playing' the network organization. Temperamentally, they may be very different from the traditional organizational bureaucrat. Rather than 'toadie' upwards, there will be horizontal relationships for the network politician to forge.

---

# CHECKLIST

▶ Does your company have a vision of a flatter and more flexible form of organization?

▶ Is there a corporate-wide transformation programme in place to bring it about?

▶ Does it address winning business and the creation of value, 'know-how', opportunities and new ventures?

▶ Does the programme embrace facilitating skills, enabling processes and supporting technology?

▶ Is it designed to influence attitudes by changing behaviour?

▶ How disruptive will it be of short-term customer relationships?

▶ What will be done to retain the commitment of those who may be disadvantaged at a particular stage in the change process?

▶ How committed is top management to achieving the transformation?

▶ Has this commitment been communicated?

▶ Do the managers of the organization, and particularly the senior managers, behave as role models?

▶ Have all the requirements for a successful transformation been identified?

▶ What 'building blocks' or 'pieces of the jigsaw puzzle' might be missing?

▶ In particular, are the necessary enablers in place, and have skill requirements been addressed?

▶ Is it clear to the people of the organization that the programme has been thought through?

▶ Is the reward system compatible with the changes that are being sought?

▶ Have likely obstacles and barriers been identified, and are programmes in place to deal with them?

# REFERENCES

Coulson-Thomas, C (1981) *Public Relations in Your Business: A guide for every manager*, Business Books, London

Coulson-Thomas, C (1992) *Transforming the Company: Bridging the gap between management myth and corporate reality*, Kogan Page, London

Coulson-Thomas, C (1997 & 1998) *The Future of the Organization: Achieving excellence through business transformation*, Kogan Page, London

Coulson-Thomas, C and Coe, T (1991) *The Flat Organisation: Philosophy and practice*, BIM, Corby

Hally, M (2000) *Winning New Business in the Legal Profession*, Policy Publications, Bedford

Harris, N (2000) *Winning New Business in Engineering Consultancy*, Policy Publications, Bedford

Hurcomb, J (1998) *Developing Strategic Customers & Key Accounts: The critical success factors*, Policy Publications, Bedford

James, M (1999) *Winning New Business in Management Consultancy and Advertising*, Policy Publications, Bedford

James, M (2000) *Winning New Business in Accountancy and PR & Marketing Consultancy*, Policy Publications, Bedford

James, M (2001) *Winning New Business in IT and Telecoms Consultancy*, Policy Publications, Bedford

Kennedy, C (1999) *Winning New Business in Construction*, Policy Publications, Bedford

Kennedy, C (2000) *Winning New Business in Information Technology and Telecoms and Engineering and Manufacturing*, Policy Publications, Bedford

Kennedy, C and O'Connor, M (1997) *Winning Major Bids: The critical success factors*, Policy Publications, Bedford

# FURTHER INFORMATION

A brochure describing the 'Winning Business' series of reports is available from Policy Publications, 4 The Crescent, Bedford MK40 2RU (tel: +44 (0) 1234 328448; fax: +44 (0) 1234 357231; e-mail: policypubs@kbnet.co.uk; Web site: www.ntwkfirm.com/bookshop).

# 7

# Replacing Rhetoric with Communication

*'Get into trouble in a lock and a crowd always seems to appear'*

## COMMUNICATIONS ACTIVITY

Communication is regarded as an integral element of management. In many companies it is almost impossible to find a manager who has not been on a communication skills course. Corporate speeches extol the importance and virtues of communication, and statements of corporate values highlight the need for openness, integrity and trust.

Never before has so much been invested in the technology of communications. Companies are spending large amounts on intranets and other channels of internal communications. They are advised by some of the brightest minds of the younger generation, who have flocked to join corporate communications consultancies.

## COMMUNICATIONS RESULTS

Yet, what is the result of all this communications activity? Too often energy and resources appear to have been consumed to little beneficial effect:

- Executives struggle to cope with the volume of e-mails and corporate bumpf and to keep up to date with new media. Many are worn down, swamped or rendered ineffective by the flow.
- Where there should be understanding there is confusion. As one chief executive who was interviewed explained in frustration: 'I am the target of a hundred and one presentations, and half the world seems to be trying to impress me. But whenever I want an answer [to] something I'm really interested in, no one seems to know.'
- In place of trust and motivation there is suspicion and insincerity. One director confided during a discussion of his company's approach to internal communications: 'Given our track record, if anyone believed this they would be either naïve or a bunch of crawlers'.
- People are lured into complacency just when they need to be alert and on guard. Spending on hype is best avoided as it can make it more difficult to get people to confront reality.

## TRANSFORMATION AND COMMUNICATION

Communication is especially important in a revolutionary context. The first move of any insurgent group is to control the means of communication. The presses and the airwaves are used to encourage dissatisfaction with what is, and support for a suggested alternative.

According to Vern Zelmer when he was managing director of Rank Xerox UK: 'People move in the way they think and believe. This determines what happens, not what you say and want, which may or may not lead to changes in perception and behaviour. The management of change is all about influencing the way people think and believe.'

The legitimacy of change and the extent to which the network organization is accepted, will largely depend upon the process of communication, and the extent to which it is supportive or undermining of the values and ethos of the network. Communicators in a situation of change may be 'playing with fire'.

Chester Barnard recognized in the 1930s that the extent to which people accept organization depends upon their understanding and participation in the communication process (Barnard, 1938). Barnard saw the essence of the managerial role in terms of building cooperative activity through communication, motivation and sharing of values.

We have already seen that there is a widespread failure to communicate and share a clear transformation vision and strategy. In many companies, a perceived lack of director and top management unity and commitment is the most significant barrier to change management.

In this chapter we will examine internal communications. We will see that the prevailing pattern of communications is that of the bureaucratic rather than the network organization, and that many managers are deficient in their approaches and attitudes to communication.

The author has argued for 20 years that those appointed to the key positions within companies should be selected according to their communication skills rather than their professional or technical understanding of the field in question (Coulson-Thomas, 1981). For example, the best financial director may be the individual best equipped to share financial understanding, rather than the person most familiar with the intricacies of the latest recommended accounting practice; similarly, the best person on the marketing side may be the individual most attuned to the requirements of customers, and sensitive to what needs to be done to build relationships with them.

## THE NEED FOR EFFECTIVE COMMUNICATION

Those at the core of the network organization must create a culture of openness and trust, within which there is a willingness to obtain and share relevant information about the world as it is, rather than as it ought to be. Reality must be confronted if change is to occur. This requires listening, feedback and all-channel communication.

According to the author, following a comparison of open and closed approaches to communication:

*Management is about information, communication. Without adequate information an organization cannot adapt. Without any information the organization becomes a corpse.*

*Receptiveness is the key to organic management. The healthy organism needs internal information about its own state of health and acute senses to detect and evaluate what is happening in the environment. A company needs to know what is going on around it, at many points of contact, and in good time if it is to cope... The closed organization can filter out a message that does not fit in with the conventional wisdom or which might rock the boat. The open organization lives while the closed organization rusts on the scrap heap.*

*(Coulson-Thomas, 1981)*

Barriers and obstacles need to be actively sought out. If they are concealed, the 'helps' and 'hinders' type of analysis cannot be brought to bear on them. 'The grapevine may be more valuable as an information source than the formal information and reporting system. A pocket of information can represent a time bomb ticking away at the heart of an organization' (Coulson-Thomas, 1981).

# THE REALITY OF CORPORATE COMMUNICATION

Corporate life is often far removed from the sharing, trusting and cross-functional communication of change programme rhetoric. The *Communicating for Change* survey (Coulson-Thomas and Coulson-Thomas, 1991a) revealed that 'reality does not always match our aspirations and intentions'.

- The approaches adopted tended to be those of the bureaucratic 'loser' rather than network organization:

    *The priority channels of communication are vertical flows, or a cascade, down the hierarchy of the corporate organization. Cross-functional and horizontal communications have yet to become... widespread... While there is often a desire to create flatter and more flexible and responsive organizations, the patterns of communication being used to bring about major change are typically those which characterize the bureaucratic hierarchy, ie predominantly 'top down' and with inadequate 'feed-back'.*

- There was a fundamental incompatibility between communication preferences and communication channels:

    *Face to face meetings with teams and groups are the preferred channel of communication, but there is little confidence that middle and junior managers can communicate effectively with the employees as a whole. As a consequence the vision, strategy and commitment of the board is not reaching the 'coal-face' employee in a form which can be understood.*

- Companies were uncertain about how to address the evident deficiencies:

    *Many companies acknowledge that their middle and line managers are not able to communicate effectively, but do not know how to remedy the situation. The traditional 'technique-oriented' communication skills courses are thought to be inadequate when changes of attitude and approach are called for, and the insecurity of many managers has to be addressed.*

The lack of 'role-model' behaviour, and the perceived gap between rhetoric and reality, was a cause of disillusionment and despair. 'In many companies there is a feeling that visions and missions are just words on paper. ... The recession has increased the extent of cynicism and mistrust as boards have felt it necessary to take short-term actions that conflict with longer-term objectives.' 'Communications technology was not perceived as a significant barrier to communication.' The problem lies in its use and application. People are reaching for the video of the company broadcast rather than talking and listening.

# THE COMMUNICATIONS PARADOX

Of particular concern was the suggestion that the desire to achieve corporate transformation could actually give a new meaning and purpose to bureaucratic channels of communication.

According to the *Communicating for Change* survey:

*Companies face a paradox. Many are seeking to delegate, and to encourage greater co-operation across departmental barriers. There is a real desire to undertake more work in cross-functional and multi-location teams. The objective is often to replace 'top down' vertical communication with horizontal communication. However, in order to achieve the significant change of attitude and approach that is required, companies are using 'top down' cascade processes to drive change through their organizations.*

*Care should be taken to ensure that 'top down' approaches to communicating the need for, and nature of, change do not entrench the existing hierarchy and make it more difficult to bring change about.*

*Many boards face a communications dilemma when particular layers of management are perceived as a communications barrier between themselves and employees. Communicating direct with employees cuts through this barrier at the expense of reducing the authority of managers, many of whom are already feeling insecure. On the other hand, building the role of managers as communicators and investing in the development of their communication skills may take some time to be effective.*

*(Coulson-Thomas and Coulson-Thomas, 1991a)*

A decade later the tension between leadership and involvement is still evident in the use of intranets and computer- and video-conferencing. Concerns are still expressed in many companies about the limited impact being achieved upon attitudes and behaviour.

# COMMUNICATING QUALITY

In the early 1990s, as technical quality was assumed, the competitive focus shifted to quality of process, quality of attitude, quality of understanding, quality of behaviour and quality of relationships. A 'quality' survey (Coulson-Thomas and Coulson-Thomas, 1991b) concluded that 'Quality needs to influence attitudes, feelings and values.' It must 'go deep' and reach the 'core' or 'essence' of all employees. The quality priorities were the 'quality of management' and the 'quality of behaviour, attitudes and values'.

The desire to change made the inability to 'make it happen' all the more frustrating. Consider the following two comments which highlight some of the frustrations that were encountered:

> *This time it's for real, but we have been trying to appear committed for years to whatever was the flavour of the month. By now the immunity factor is quite high.*

> *We have all been trained in public speaking, and spend a fortune on the videos. The problem is no one believes a word, even though we mean it. The packaging seems to get in the way.*

Winners are sensitive to the feelings of others. They feel the vibes. However, many companies engaged in competitive struggles to survive do not specifically monitor and manage the morale of their people. Sento, a US high-tech company, has appointed a Chief Morale Officer.

## COMMUNICATIONS AND THE NETWORK ORGANIZATION

In order to bring about change, corporate leaders have to be able to communicate effectively with a variety of groups that have an interest in a company:

> *The modern company is not a machine to be run or driven by its board but rather is a complex organism, a network of interests co-operating in some areas and conflicting in others. One of the jobs of the board is to arbitrate between the various interests in the company... In essence this is a political activity. Its critical component is communication.*

> (Coulson-Thomas, 1981)

In the case of the network organization, the communications network is the organization. However, in many cases the approaches to communication still being adopted appear to be closer to the bureaucratic past than the network future.

The members of the network organization of the 'vision' are participants, collaborators and colleagues. Yet the reality is that members are too often treated as targets. Rather than use the technology of the network to involve, learn and encourage participation, it is being used to 'blast' people with the corporate message.

For the network organization, communication with customers, suppliers and business partners could be said to be 'internal'. Customers with a choice may place their business with the supplier that responds the quickest. Communications technology sustains relationships among and between network members, blurring the distinction between 'internal' and 'external' communication.

Communications need to reflect the dispersed and increasingly international nature of network enterprises. Overseas employees, associates and partners are sometimes overlooked when announcements are made. Marks & Spencer's staff in Paris learnt from the broadcast media of their impending layoff as a result of announced store closures.

Significant stakeholders expect to be kept informed of major developments. The rapid decline in the fortunes of Marconi led to accusations that chairman Sir Roger Hurn and chief executive Lord Simpson had kept investors in the dark. Their resignations quickly followed.

## INVOLVING OR INHIBITING THROUGH TECHNOLOGY

Satellite, broadcast and mobile technologies allow almost instantaneous communication across a network organization. One interviewee summed up an area of concern for change managers: 'You can directly reach your people all over the world. What we haven't done is thought through what the broadcast approach, and the simplification and packaging means for involvement and participation. Should we be listening more, and broadcasting less?'

The *Communicating for Change* survey uncovered some anxiety that the technology of communication can discourage two-way communication:

*Electronic communication encourages people to 'hide behind the technology'. Electronic messages are passed on without being interpreted. Managers can become lazy, and may not add value to information or test if it has been understood.*

*In contrast, face-to-face communication can allow a manager to explain or tailor a general message to the needs of a specific audience. The message can be put into a particular context, instant feedback can be obtained, and managers can demonstrate personal commitment to what is being communicated.*

(Coulson-Thomas and Coulson-Thomas, 1991a)

Enthusiasts of transformation need to take care that they do not run over those they want to empower and 'build' with a technological juggernaut, or seduce them into blind acceptance.

Brave leaders allow views to be expressed by means of 'electronic voting'. Alternative courses of action and assessments of their consequences can be 'put' to the people and members of a network.

A network's technology can be used, perhaps informally or unofficially, to organize opposition or to canvas support. Groupware and intranets allow significantly more open access to information and have eroded the position of 'gatekeepers'.

## COUNTER-PRODUCTIVE COMMUNICATIONS

An approach to communications can itself be counter-productive. In many companies there is still a basic incompatibility between the means of communication used to increase awareness of corporate goals and objectives, and the communications requirements for translating these into relevant activities and resulting outcomes:

- The aspiration, or what needs to be done, is generally communicated by means of a 'vertical' or 'top down' approach to communication. This 'one-way' approach views communication as a series of discrete activities (see Figure 7.1). As one managing director put it: 'When we have something to say, we tell them.'
- Managers adopting the discrete approach decide, inform, allocate, arrange, provide and determine according to their status, and what is

Communication as discrete activities

Communication as ongoing responsibilities

**Figure 7.1**  Changing approaches to communication

set out in their job description. The techniques and channels of communication adopted are those which 'get the message across'.

- Achievement, or 'making it happen', depends upon 'horizontal' communication across departmental and functional boundaries. The cross-functional and inter-organizational pattern of communication makes the flexible network organization a working reality.
- Within the organic network, communication is seen as an ongoing responsibility (Figure 7.1). The emphasis is upon 'involvement' through visioning, sharing, empowering, enabling, facilitating and supporting. Attitude is important rather than technique. Managers need to be sensitive, intuitive and patient in order to learn, build relationships and establish mutual trust.

Likert's various studies from the early 1960s suggest that a participative style of management and a free flow of communications, up, down and across organizations are more likely to achieve results than more authoritarian approaches that involve top down communication (Likert, 1961, 1967). This is especially true of the network organization.

Losers tend to play their cards close to their chest. Disclosures are often forced or too late. Winners are more open. They take other people into their confidence. They discriminate between occasional items that might harm or be subject to legal or regulatory constraints and the information and knowledge that they willingly share.

People should communicate not because they have to but because they want to. Only by communicating might we benefit from the reactions and comments of others. Those who keep their aspirations to themselves may inadvertently pass by many others who would share and empathize with them. They miss opportunities to work with those who could help make their dreams a reality.

# DIVIDING BY COMMUNICATION

Paradoxically, the very investments in the technology of communications, for example ever-slicker videos, that result from a desire to spread the 'change message' are making it more difficult to change. They are reinforcing the 'top down' approach, and are distancing top management from the rest of the organization.

The slickness of the packaging results in the passive and disinterested acceptance of what is sought as a *fait accompli*, rather than as an aspiration that will only become a reality with the active participation of the people of the organization. Little hint is given of the desire for involvement and the need for thinking, elaboration and refinement during the implementation process.

Too many communication professionals initiate activities without first analysing the situation, and thinking through what they need to communicate and to whom. There is often little attempt to encourage two-way communication, or establish a dialogue or relationship. There is also little correlation between how much is spent on communication and the success of a campaign. In fact, the reverse is often the case. A little thought about objectives, and what people might be interested in, can go a long way.

Overall, far too high a proportion of time is spent upon 'doing things', and too little attention is paid to analysis, thinking and planning. Being more focused early on in terms of objectives, and selective in respect of publics, can allow time to be saved, and a better use made of resources, later on. Many professional communicators apply their technical skills to individual jobs and are not an integral element of a multifunctional team at the heart of a co-ordinated set of change processes that make up a comprehensive transformation programme.

## COMMUNICATIONS WITHIN LOSERS

Within 'loser' companies managers still have offices and take decisions without consulting those directly involved. They alone may hold the information needed. Besides because they prefer to focus upon 'hard' systems and process issues the feelings of others are not necessarily taken into account.

People with responsibilities over others like to feel they are in charge. Requests for approval and documents requiring a countersignature are channelled upwards. Seniority within the management hierarchy rather than the possession of relevant knowledge and expertise gives particular individuals the right to be involved.

Corporate guidelines reserve an extensive range of decisions for the board and senior management. Policies are formulated to cover various eventualities. Responses to less significant matters are prescribed in manuals and procedures. When a situation or requirement is encountered that has not been covered, the debate is about who should be involved rather than what should be done.

More junior staff usually have little discretion or freedom to act. The rhetoric of empowerment may be used, but in practice they are rarely consulted and they keep their own counsel. When they do have individual concerns their line managers are not that interested in them.

## COMMUNICATIONS WITHIN WINNERS

Directors and senior managers of winners operate differently. They are more open and welcome the opinions of colleagues. They seek out those with relevant expertise. They test reactions and discuss alternatives. Because they share information and knowledge, other people are better qualified to contribute.

Status and empowerment are not issues. Corporate leaders ensure their people have the discretion to act and make decisions whenever and wherever it is practical and beneficial for them to do so. Judgements relating to customers are made as close to them as possible.

Because people desire the best possible outcomes they consult to the extent required and justified by the nature and importance of each decision. They avoid interrupting others unnecessarily or involving them for cosmetic reasons or to cover their tracks. If they think they need help or someone else's counsel would be of value, they seek it.

When they feel they can handle a situation, people in winning companies do what they feel is necessary or appropriate. Senior managers recognize that unless they encourage and support internal initiatives and ventures they run the risk of losing their most capable people and their most valuable clients. With customers requiring more imaginative and bespoke responses, businesses need to become enterprise colonies that tap, build and realize the entrepreneurial potential within their people (Coulson-Thomas, 1999).

Senior managers in winning companies no longer assume they have relevant knowledge and experience, let alone expect to have all the answers, or the best ideas. Managers are sensitive to 'softer' people issues and are concerned about how their colleagues, customers and business partners feel. They seek their views and opinions and enlist their support. Exploration and innovation in the marketplace is preceded by careful preparation.

Within winning companies individuals and groups come forward with new business proposals. Directors invite requests for venture capital support, and they offer promising prospects access to central accounting, legal, personnel and other services. Later on the company may provide development and marketing assistance. Increasingly, the rewards for successful entrepreneurship are shared among the people who are primarily responsible for its achievement.

Within 'loser' companies remuneration is closely linked to seniority and status in the management hierarchy. This is not necessarily the case among winners, as other factors such as contribution to the creation of value for customers or intellectual capital assume greater significance. Rewards are the result of 'doing' rather than 'being', achieving outcomes rather than simply occupying a role.

# COMMUNICATING CORPORATE CAPABILITIES

Corporate reputation can be very significant when purchasers visit Web sites, investors place their funds, and invitations to tender are issued. From the perspective of a potential customer or partner, the longer the term of the relationship that is sought, the greater the importance likely to be placed upon a company's general standing in the marketplace.

Similarly, as requirements become more complex and bespoke, the technologies, methodologies, know-how and experience a company can access and deploy assume greater significance.

Losers in search of short-term sales spend heavily on product-related advertisements, but devote comparatively little effort to preparing corporate credentials. When a presentation is required a set of slides may be quickly produced the night before.

Winners are more concerned with building longer-term relationships. Hence they invest in credentials that clarify their purpose, intentions and capabilities and emphasize what is distinctive about their approach, qualities and offerings.

Potential customers – particularly in relation to business-to-business products and services – may prefer interactive presentations that enable them to take their own individual route through the available material, and assess different options by themselves and in their own time. Such facilities can be provided on laptop or palm-top computers or via a corporate extranet.

Within many 'loser' companies business development staff work in complete isolation from their colleagues. Bid team members may have little or no contact with marketing professionals. In contrast, winners ensure that corporate communications, public relations and general marketing expenditures contribute directly to the winning of business in competitive situations and building customer relationships.

BT created a specific budget to support a successful pitch to win a major contract in the United States (Kennedy and O'Connor, 1997). Corporate advertisements were placed in certain golf club magazines, and selective direct-mail shots were undertaken, to reach particular individuals likely to be involved in the decision-making process.

Share price too can depend on communication of the essence of what a company is about. Certain high-tech companies may find that few of their staff understand what they actually do. Dana Corporation has used animation and graphics to explain how the properties of its bearings depend upon the structure and composition of the materials used in their manufacture.

The perceptions and expectations of customers, employees, associates, suppliers, business partners and investors can all depend on how a company communicates its aims, capabilities and prospects. In a communications vacuum people may apply general assumptions rather than understand the particular case. They may not appreciate, for example, that low margins at Rolls Royce reflect new business wins that should result in lucrative follow-on work for many years to come. What is perceived as a problem might actually be an indicator of success.

Concealment rarely works. Life seems to conspire against it. Our mistakes become apparent and our embarrassment public. Run a boat aground or get into trouble in a lock and a crowd always seems to appear.

# COMMUNICATION AND CORPORATE TRANSFORMATION

There is little point in communications activity that does not contribute to business goals and objectives. Figure 7.2 sets out a systematic approach to communication which has been developed by the author (Coulson-Thomas, 1979), and identifies where the various steps relate to other vital corporate processes.

The communication process should be integrated with the other activities that are being used to bring about corporate transformation. Here are some examples:

- A first step is to understand the situation in order to ensure that underlying or root causes are identified. Use should be made of relevant outputs from a SWOT (strengths, weaknesses, opportunities, threats), analysis or issue monitoring and management process.

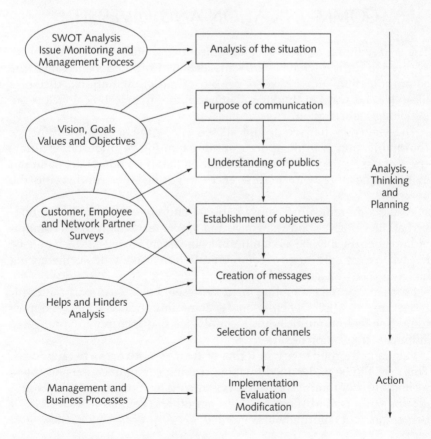

**Figure 7.2** Communication process

- The analysis of the situation, establishing both the purpose of communication and specific communication objectives, and the creation of messages should all reflect the vision, goals, values and objectives of a company.
- The results of customer, employee and network partner surveys could be used to better understand those with whom it is desired to communicate. They could also be used when messages are crafted.
- Communications objectives and messages should also take account of the results of relevant 'helps' and 'hinders' analysis, if communications activity is to be focused upon specific barriers and obstacles to change.
- The selection of communication channels should take account of any work that is under way to identify, document and simplify or re-engineer business processes. If communication is undertaken along cross-functional and inter-organizational processes, communications activity will support the transformation process.

## COMMUNICATION AND DIVERSITY

The cross-cultural aspects of communications should not be overlooked. We need to address what Nobuo Kanoi of Sony Corporation has called 'the communication gap between people of different nations, different lifestyles and ways of thinking'. Human rather than technical factors are inhibiting globalization.

The reality is that we do not all see things the same way. Effective communication is built upon an understanding of underlying differences of perception, while communication that does not reflect them can make people more aware of differences and bring latent conflicts into the open.

When communicating across national and cultural boundaries, non-verbal clues, such as body language and the context within which communication occurs, may be as significant as the language used. Much may be lost when electronic forms of communication are used. Video-conferencing has certain advantages in this respect.

Problems for the grumbling many represent business opportunities for the astute few. NEC saw cross-border communication as a market opportunity for telecommunications technologies that incorporate a range of automatic translation facilities.

People and groups vary in terms of their receptiveness to new ideas. This needs to be understood by those driving communication and transformation programmes through organizations. Some individuals and groups will respond more quickly than others, and varying degrees of persistence and tailoring will be needed.

# COMMUNICATION BY ROLE-MODEL EXAMPLE

One of the most potent channels of communication is the role-model behaviour of senior managers, and the extent to which they 'walk the talk'. Do managers themselves 'practise what they preach', or are their actions at variance with the carefully crafted messages that seep or blare from the official channels of communication?

Role-model behaviour does not just happen. In the case of the 'hard nosed', conditions may need to be created within which they understand what 'role-model' behaviour is, and believe it is in their best interest to exude and practise it. In particular, the following should be noted:

- Role-model behaviour should embrace focus and orientation; attitudes, values and behaviour; and contribution to business goals and objectives.
- Those seen to be rewarded should be the people who 'take on board' and practise role-model attitudes and values, while those who consistently and quite naturally act as role models and achieve results could be 'fast-tracked' for promotion.
- Some companies encourage people to assess each other in terms of role-model behaviour. Subordinates could be given an opportunity to assess their managers, or teams could carry out peer reviews.

Role-model behaviour should be demanded at all levels and, in terms of example, can be especially important at the senior level. There are those who believe the use of particular 'role-model' techniques is 'for the little people'. Not so, they can be used at the micro level by a work group or at the macro level by the board.

Changing the role of the manager from command and control to that of counsellor, mentor, coach and facilitator has important consequences for communications. It is difficult for those who are incapable of listening to counsel and coach.

The following selection of quotes sums up the sense of frustration felt by those at the top of organizations:

*Passing something on is not communicating. Too many of our managers see the corporate message as an in-tray item. They get it out the other side without adding value to it.*

*Communicating has become a substitute for thinking and understanding. There is a lot of traffic on the line, but what does it all mean?*

Insecure people are still hoarding information and knowledge. They need to be given the confidence, perspective and skills to achieve rapport, openness and trust, and share what they know with colleagues.

# THE EFFECTIVE COMMUNICATOR

Messages must be straightforward, honest and related to the needs and interests of the audience if they are to 'come alive'. The communicator must be open and willing to learn. The communicator must share the vision, must feel the vision and must be visibly committed to it.

Communication must be seen as an ongoing and key element of the role of the manager, and not as a discrete and intermittent activity (Figure 7.1). The ability to communicate is an essential management quality. Companies cannot afford to continue to acknowledge the deficiencies of their managers as communicators without taking concrete steps to improve their attitudes and approaches to communication.

More emphasis needs to be given to the role of the manager as a communicator within groups. Significant change will not occur in many organizations unless managers are equipped with the awareness and skills to bring it about and understand better the concerns, perspectives and terminologies of a wider range of colleagues. If fundamental shifts of attitude and perspective are to occur, managers cannot abdicate their responsibility for communicating with people and allocate it to professional specialists.

Changing attitudes can take many years. Establishing the extent to which attitude changes are occurring is not easy when managers rapidly assimilate what they perceive to be the words that are in vogue, while retaining their previous views, opinions and perspective. This eagerness to agree and conform, and to appear supportive and a 'team player', can make it difficult to judge the extent of internalization or 'real understanding'.

Attitudes will not change if observed conduct, as opposed to the words, reinforces them. In many companies, there is considerable cynicism and not a little distrust. Flexibility and responsiveness are perceived by many as a cover for overhead savings and headcount reductions. According to one divisional director: 'Corporate vision and top management commitment has been tested, and has been found wanting.' Honesty and openness in communication is even more important in an era of recession, retrenchment, and terrorist threats.

# COMMUNICATION AND CARING

Companies need to focus upon the reality of managerial attitudes, not wishful thinking. In many companies there is an overwhelming sense of personal insecurity. Individuals doubt that their efforts will result in more than temporary recognition and reward. People feel a loss of loyalty and mutual commitment when their value and relevance has to be demonstrated on an almost continuous basis, and they must fight daily for their jobs.

Economic recession and corporate change sap morale and commitment at a time when greater flexibility is required. The battle for 'hearts and minds' is being lost in many companies.

A little caring and sympathy would go a long way. One chairman admitted: 'All too often, when heads are taken out of organizations, priorities are not reassessed and achievable objectives are not rematched to available resources. This comes across as callous, unfeeling... as if we don't care.'

'Delayering' can cast a shadow over many lives. 'Flattening hierarchies' sends a chill up many spines. In contrast to the rhetoric of 'widening opportunities', the actual experience is too often of previous workloads and responsibilities being just reallocated to those that remain. People are required to do more with less, and are rarely equipped or helped to cope with the extra pressure. After a time people can feel that they are on a treadmill, where the harder they work the more they attract extra tasks.

## Losers

Losers:

- are preoccupied with their own objectives and the messages they would like to get across;
- use rhetoric and spin to distract, exaggerate or conceal;
- concentrate upon the form and style of communications;
- engage mainly in one-way communications;
- feel and display little emotion, distance themselves from issues, and endeavour not to become emotionally involved;
- devote little effort to encouraging feedback or monitoring effectiveness;
- have little commitment or confidence in many of the messages they are putting across;
- view communications as a distinct activity to be undertaken by dedicated specialists;
- find it very difficult to explain technical matters to non-specialists;
- struggle to articulate what is special or distinctive about them and their organization.

## Winners

Winners:

- are preoccupied with the interests and concerns of those they would like to establish, build and sustain relationships with;

- address communication requirements and endeavour to increase understanding;
- concentrate upon content and its relevance;
- engage wherever possible in two-way communications;
- care about the subject matter of communications and the interests and well-being of many of those with whom they are communicating;
- put great emphasis upon encouraging and responding to feedback in order to improve the effectiveness of communications from the perspective of all the parties involved;
- genuinely want to build mutually beneficial relationships and increase understanding;
- build feedback and the sharing of information, knowledge and understanding into processes and the role of the manager;
- use visual images and relevant technologies to enable non-specialists to understand complex issues and technical matters;
- are able with conviction to explain the essence of what they are about.

# SYMBOLS

When the reality, whether an actual situation, hidden motives or the thinking behind communication is hidden, people judge on the basis of appearance. Symbols can be of great importance in shaping behaviour. People do take account of what they see, and this visible evidence is still the source of credibility gaps in many companies. Substantial pay increases and pay-offs for directors at a time of cutbacks, happen, are noticed and get talked about. Events and images that do not appear to match stated priorities and objectives can result in a breakdown of trust.

Management decisions communicate unintended messages. The video and Web site may stress the need for satisfied customers and investment in training, while managers are rewarded for achieving short-term cost-savings which may have adverse longer-term consequences.

One of the most potent sets of symbols in any company derives from the factors that lead some people to visible success. Among the senior ranks of many companies are the 'whiz-kids' who move quickly around the corporate organization, dazzling people with short-term activity and rhetoric. When the longer-term consequences of their incumbency of various roles catch up with their successors, these often seem to make their previous performance even more impressive.

If changes of attitude and behaviour are to occur, and cynicism is to give way to a focus upon the delivery of measurable objectives that create value and opportunities, reward and advancement must be seen to be related to achievement, to outcomes rather than to activity. The bias towards activity must be replaced with a focus upon results. Activity that does not contribute to desired outcomes must be driven out.

People are not fools, but perceptive and astute. A lack of commitment among one or two directors who are 'going along' with colleagues can seriously undermine a change programme. People notice when directors and senior managers say one thing and do another.

The 'tone' is set by those at the top. Their deeds must match their words. They must exude visible commitment and consistent action, although consistency may need to be tempered with flexibility if it is not to constrict and constrain.

Divisions within the boardroom are usually difficult to hide. Time spent agreeing and sharing a transformation vision and a change strategy is rarely wasted. The same words may mean different things to various people. Understanding should be tested to ensure a shared appreciation of the meanings of key words.

## CHECKLIST

▶ Is communication activity in your company an integral part of its management and business processes?

▶ Is communication regarded as a number of specialized activities, or is it the responsibility of every manager?

▶ Does communication activity follow an analysis of the situation?

▶ Do people think through why they are communicating, and what needs to be communicated to whom?

▶ Have surveys been undertaken to determine the requirements and interests of those with whom the company wishes to communicate?

▶ Are the messages used compatible with the vision, goals and values of the organization?

▶ Is the prevailing pattern of communication one way or two way?

▶ How genuine is the desire to involve, listen and learn?

▶ What is really happening out there? What do people think and feel?

▶ Have the barriers to communication been identified, and are action programmes in place to deal with them?

▶ What is done to monitor and assess the result of communication activity?

> ▶ Do the signs and symbols support or undercut change messages?
>
> ▶ Do key people in the organization exhibit role-model behaviour?
>
> ▶ What incentive is there, in terms of reward and recognition, for people to act as role models and positive symbols?

# REFERENCES

Barnard, C (1938) *The Functions of the Executive*, Harvard University Press, Cambridge, MA

Coulson-Thomas, C (1979) *Public Relations: A practical guide*, Macdonald and Evans, Plymouth

Coulson-Thomas, C (1981) *Public Relations is Your Business: A guide for every manager*, Business Books, London

Coulson-Thomas, C (1999) *Individuals and Enterprise: Creating entrepreneurs for the new millennium through personal transformation*, Blackhall Publishing, Dublin

Coulson-Thomas, C and Coulson-Thomas, S (1991a) *Communicating for Change: Communications and the management of change*, an Adaptation Survey for Granada Business Services, London

Coulson-Thomas, C and Coulson-Thomas, S (1991b) *Quality: The Next Steps*, an Adaptation Ltd Survey for ODI International, Adaptation, London and (Executive Summary) ODI, Wimbledon, London

Kennedy, C and O'Connor, M (1997) *Winning Major Bids: The critical success factors*, Policy Publications, Bedford

Likert, R (1961) *New Patterns of Management*, McGraw-Hill, New York

Likert, R (1967) *The Human Organisation: Its management and value*, McGraw-Hill, New York

# 8

# Introducing More Flexible Patterns of Work and Knowledge Management

*'Boats of all shapes and sizes succeed in making the journey'*

## WORK, FLEXIBILITY AND THE NETWORK ORGANIZATION

The essence of business success lies in establishing and maintaining effective relationships with various groups of people; and harnessing the talents and potential of people in order to create value and opportunities:

- Individuals with skills that are in demand know that they have a greater choice than any generation in history in terms of how, where, when, with whom and for whom they can work. A long-term trend for over a decade, concealed by the insecurities of economic recession, is a greater desire for fulfilment, satisfaction and personal identification with outputs.
- Organizations have to be more adaptable and responsive in order to cope with change, seek more flexible access to skills and expect people to assume more responsibility. Particular attention is given to harnessing contributions from 'superstars'.

On the face of it, during an age when technology facilitates a wide range of patterns of work, the interests and requirements of both individuals and organizations appear to coincide. Given the availability of practical approaches, methodologies and tools for introducing new ways of working (Coulson-Thomas, 1995), one might expect an explosion of innovation and experimentation. Yet there is often despair and disappointment when there should be fulfilment.

Some progress has been made in undertaking the transition from bureaucracy to network organization (Figure 8.1):

- The transformation process begins with the functional bureaucracy. Within the 'hard-shelled' command and control corporation, compartmentalized by vertical functional divisions, early efforts are devoted to establishing cross-functional groups to undertake certain tasks.

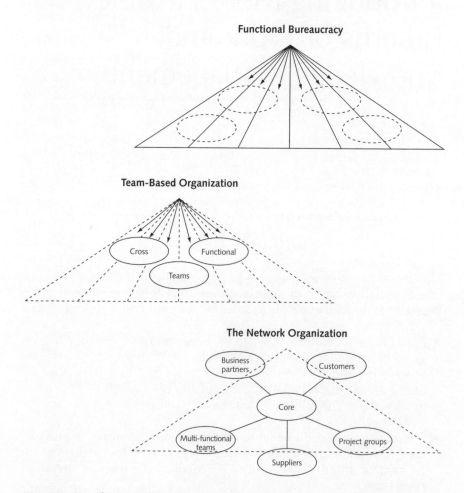

**Figure 8.1** The transitioning organization

- As the cross-functional teams become more established, the functional barriers begin to fade. The team-based organization's shell is more porous, as it is willing to learn from others and establishes a network of external relationships. During this transition phase a central but loosening grip may be kept upon the change process.
- Eventually, a network of empowered groups and project teams – including inter-organizational teams – that share a common purpose is created. The network organization has arrived. The co-ordinating core concentrates upon the review and refinement of vision, values, goals, objectives, relationships and processes.

## SO WHAT'S NEW?

The transition to the network organization tends to be 'sold' to its people in terms of the wider and richer range of opportunities it provides. However, in terms of how organizations treat people and vice versa, there has always been a wide gap between actions and words:

- Individuals pledge loyalty and commitment, but 'head hunters' would be out of business within weeks if most people did not perk up at the thought of obtaining something better. People 'play the corporate game', in between reading the situations vacant columns. Most will readily 'jump ship' and switch organizations, given the right opportunity for 'me plc'.
- Company media stress the commitment of organizations to their people. Yet, most larger organizations have implemented corporate initiatives to 'delayer', 'slim down', 'reduce headcount' or 'tackle the cost base'. Bonds of trust have been broken.

People forget that career change and advancement for many plateaued managers was a dream rather than a practical reality:

- Towards the top of the pyramid, the corporate structure became too narrow for more than a few to achieve any significant advancement.
- Occupying a particular slot, or moving up the ladder, depended heavily upon the views of a handful of people. Many individuals became blocked for a variety of personal reasons, while others greased and slimed.
- Remuneration was tied to position in the bureaucratic hierarchy, so for the plateaued manager a substantial real increase in remuneration was also an unrealistic prospect.
- It was difficult for people to 'be themselves', as progress depended upon displaying the characteristics associated with the occupation of particular slots in the organization structure.

In reality, the bureaucracy constrained rather than liberated enthusiasm, energy and initiative. It forced people to put up with a great many inhibitors of the ways in which they would naturally work, think and learn, in return for illusory rewards, fancy job titles and other trappings of status. When the curt 'early retirement' note arrived, many of those who lived a dream were pole-axed by reality.

## THE NETWORK ORGANIZATION

In theory, the flatter team-based network organization should satisfy desires for personal responsibility, growth, development and fulfilment. It should offer a rich environment of continuing opportunities and future challenges for those who wish to learn and be themselves:

- As projects are completed, groups are formed to undertake new ones.
- The individual with particular strengths, who stays up to date and delivers, should receive invitations to join a number of project teams. A relatively open market for skills should result.
- Remuneration tends to be tied more to output, so there are prospects of varying rewards, according to individual and group contribution to corporate objectives. People rather than the organization establish ceilings and limits.
- As those with the responsibility for leading individual projects seek to assemble teams made up of people with complementary skills, so there is every advantage in focusing upon those things one is good at and does best.

Within the network organization there are roles in relation to business objectives rather than job descriptions. Getting on is a question of growing, changing and enriching roles rather than 'climbing ladders'.

A decade ago the author observed (Coulson-Thomas, 1992) that UK and US managers may persist in seeing life in terms of a series of steps up a career ladder to an eventual goal that will justify the hard work and commitment of the intervening years. The company, however, may be intent on replacing functional chains of command with a flatter organization composed of teams and taskforces working on various projects. This may match the aspirations of those in other cultures who see life as a journey between situations, each of which should be handled and even enjoyed, but that do not inevitably lead to a certain destination.

## TECHNOLOGY AND NETWORKING

Many people perceive and describe the 'new organization' as an IT network, embracing internal and external project groups, customers, suppliers and business partners. The network runs along supply chains, and is blurring the distinction between locations and, in some organizations, executive and consultant.

Once people start to work electronically, and in groups, it soon becomes clear that the source of valued added often bears little relationship to position in the formal hierarchy. People go direct to those who can help.

The work of the network organization can be undertaken from wherever it is possible to access the network. The log cabin in the hills or retreat in the forest might be the best location for a group engaged in a 'thought-intensive task'. Locations in India and Caribbean islands such as Barbados, Jamaica and St Lucia have become 'offshore' centres for a variety of information and transaction processing activities. Supporting technology can facilitate the creation of working and lifestyle environments to support particular individuals.

Over a decade ago IBM, ICL and Rank Xerox operated telecommuting networks. 'Telecoms' companies such as BT and Cable and Wireless and the European Commission have introduced various initiatives to promote more flexible patterns of work such as teleworking. Yet their adoption has been much slower than champions and early enthusiasts predicted. At the end of the last millennium and 30 years after today's 'baby boomer' chief executives read Toffler's (1970) expectations, only 1 in 20 of the US labour force were telecommuting. While corporate structures have undergone significant change, traditional ways of working persist.

New patterns of work are often perceived as matters for those concerned, and not as issues for the boardroom agenda. The focus of boards has been more on whether or not whole functions and activities should be contracted out or hived off. The preoccupation continues to be with the organization rather than its people.

Many 'loser' organizations make little attempt to assess the quality of working life from the perspective of their employees. If their concerns, preferences and priorities are not known, they cannot be addressed.

Overwhelmingly, changes in the way people work and their implications are considered in terms of impacts upon the ability of companies to survive, rather than consequences for those who work within them. Consider, for example, how the transition from bureaucratic to flexible network organization could affect lifestyles and prospects.

## THE POTENTIAL FOR FULFILMENT

Many young professionals do not want to be pieces on someone else's chess board (Coulson-Thomas, 1988). They are seeking greater control of their lives and opportunities to build a portfolio of particular skills and competencies. Individuals with the sought-after expertise would prefer to make it available to those who are sufficiently responsive to offer a form of relationship that matches the way they would like to work.

There are many situations that affect millions of people, from the desire to start a family, through safeguarding school prospects, to supporting a partner's career and remaining active later in life, which can be addressed by more flexible patterns of working (Coulson-Thomas, 1989). Too often, however, the solutions that would mean so much remain as pipe-dreams because of 'ageism' and blinkered attitudes towards patterns of work. The frustration of those with a sense of what is possible is particularly intense.

## FRUSTRATION RATHER THAN FULFILMENT

In many companies frustration is more widespread than fulfilment. The reasons for this range from duplicity, through naïvety, to a failure to 'think things through'. Consider the following comments:

*Helping people to realize their full potential is a credo of the company. That is so long as they are prepared to work in a way, and at a time or place that is compatible with our procedures, systems ... and just about every other impediment you could think of.*

*We focused so much upon the customer that we forgot our own people. When we started measuring their satisfaction we got a shock. External improvements in satisfaction had been achieved at a cost in terms of internal morale.*

*It used to be simple, people followed the procedures and did what they were told. Now they are self-managed, managing projects, participating in processes, building relationships, practising quality – you name it and we are asking them to do it.*

*We had a working party on the 'demographic time bomb'. After a year of economic recession it was disbanded. The long-term problem is still there, but it is not today's priority.*

## GROUPS, TEAMS AND PROJECTS

Team work has been championed for a couple of decades. It is not brought about by talking about it, but by recognizing its distinct requirements as an approach to harnessing the talents of people within organizations.

The concept of teamwork is inseparable from the notion of the network organization. Yet, in many companies there is still a wide gulf between what is and what should be:

- Too frequently, groups and teams are departmental and semi-permanent rather than inter-organizational and ad hoc.

- Many companies that champion teamwork are not equipping their people to work in groups and teams.
- Many groups and teams are not being given objectives that are expressed clearly in terms of measurable outputs.
- Teams are set up to undertake tasks that could be accomplished by a competent individual.
- Those at the top of organizations who 'play politics' or 'defend their turf' are frequently perceived as poor role models of teamwork.
- Even where groups have clear objectives and are motivated, the necessary empowerments and supporting technology may not be in place to 'make it happen'.

Many groups and teams are MICRO managed, that is according to internal company-related objectives, rather than MACRO managed, that is according to customer-related objectives. The preoccupation tends to be with internal quantitative measures rather than external requirements and opportunities.

As network organizations become portfolios of projects, competent project managers are in demand. The good project manager is used to being accountable for delivering a defined output within a set timescale, and to agreed levels of performance.

However, some companies still fail to understand the distinct nature of project management competency (Coulson-Thomas, 1990). Also a smooth transition from one project to another may not be easy to achieve when both parties have differing views on the appropriateness of different project opportunities.

A traditional drawback of project management is the prospect of periods of down-time between assignments. Against this risk, may be set factors such as discretion, accountability, relative freedom in terms of 'how to do the work' and more of a chance to be oneself. According to one interviewee: 'Project management is empowerment for real. If people are to feel a part of something it needs to be on a human scale.' In terms of harnessing commitment and encouraging entrepreneurship, the self-managed workgroup can evolve into an enterprise within an enterprise.

# THE CURSE OF AGEISM

'Ageism' is a good example of a widespread set of prejudices based upon myth and misunderstanding (Coulson-Thomas, 1989). The population of the EU is ageing. In many respects, age and the experience that comes with it can be positively beneficial. And yet age discrimination can prevent victims of 'rightsizing' and women who have left the labour market in order to raise families from returning.

Companies that are strong on people rhetoric are as singleminded as a terminator in weeding out 'over-aged' or 'plateaued' managers. Whose fault is it that the contributions of these people are not being fully tapped in the first place? When were they last equipped to undertake new challenges?

As some are forced into early retirement, others are encouraged to seek it. Those remaining may miss colleagues that have retired, and can feel left behind. As younger generations move into positions of power, older employees can experience a sense of 'isolation'.

Older people bear disproportionately the unemployment costs of economic change and structural adjustment. They tend to be over-represented in the long-established and declining industries, while in start-up and rapidly growing sectors there is a tendency to recruit younger employees. The motto for many 'caring companies' should perhaps be: 'Stay smart, keep in, play the game, give your all, but don't grow old.'

## THE TERROR OF TERMINATION

Sudden retirement can have traumatic consequences for the physical, psychological and social health of an individual. For a company it can lead to a loss of access to knowledge and expertise that has been accumulated over a number of years. A more gradual transition for both parties, involving part-time or temporary work, could be less disruptive and increase the chances of successful adjustment.

The use of more flexible patterns of work could smooth the burden of adaptation to changing economic circumstances. An alternative to compulsory redundancy would be to phase in retirement for volunteers by offering a reduction of, say, one day in the working week each year for a period of five years.

Given the great range of motivation, energy and capabilities among older generations, it is not easy to identify an optimum or standard age of retirement. A more flexible approach would be to link the payment of levels of benefit to the number of years in which contributions have been paid. Individuals could be given the choice of opting to receive a higher level of payment, commencing at a later date.

## AGE AND TRAINING

Many employers are still reluctant to invest in the training of those over 45. One manager observed: 'The promises about developing you... appear to have a "cut-off" point. One day you are a non-person... something that is not worth investing in any more... You just give up.'

The argument that older employees are not worth training, as there will be inadequate opportunity to secure 'a return upon the investment', has less force in a turbulent business environment:

● Innovation and change continually erode existing skills and demand new ones. Ongoing development and updating becomes a requirement for all. In this respect, the 'window of opportunity' to benefit from newly acquired technical or professional understanding may last no longer for the younger employee than for an older person.

- Also, companies such as B&Q that have gone out actively to recruit older staff find that very often they change employers less often than their younger colleagues. They tend to stay, customers have confidence in them and the enlightened employer benefits.

# FLEXIBLE COMPANIES

Innovation and experimentation in terms of new patterns of work was occurring over a decade ago:

- Not only did the Brazilian manufacturing company Semco become flatter and more flexible in structure, but employees determined their own salaries and hours of work. Mutual respect and trust, and shared goals and commitment, replaced traditional hierarchical authority.
- IBM introduced a 'Space, Morale and Remote Technology' or 'Smart' initiative. Staff were equipped with mobile telephones and laptop computers, and were able to work at various locations, including at home and on client premises, accessing information from the IBM corporate network as required.
- Rank Xerox introduced 'self-managed work groups'. These were given business objectives and planned themselves how to achieve them, monitoring and assessing their own performance, and determining matters such as hours of work, holidays and the rewards and remuneration of individual members of the group.

# FLEXIBILITY AND BUSINESS DEVELOPMENT

Flexible operation is the key to the success of some entrepreneurial companies. Hazell Carr offers the services of professional actuaries who work from home. Training services are provided to the freelance knowledge workers, and checks are in place to monitor the quality of calculations resulting from the company's virtual model of operation. Working at night enables RS Communication Services staff to install phone lines in City Offices while their users are asleep or clubbing.

Virgin and easyJet have based their business strategies upon doing things differently. Small companies sometimes give a lead when it comes to adopting alternative ways of working. Although operating in a traditional sector, Swift Construction allows its people to work flexible hours and to job-share.

Cisco Systems grew rapidly by providing products that allowed others to use the Internet and embrace e-business. New ways of working also create business opportunities for those who help to make it happen.

Telework Systems' products include software for tracking, monitoring and managing mobile and remote workers.

All too often the workplace is a constraint, an overhead cost and the cause of 'sick building syndrome' rather than an enabler of creativity and flexibility. Arthur Andersen has designed offices to support particular relationships, behaviours and patterns of interaction and encourage imaginative thinking. There are quiet spaces for personal reflection and activity areas that teams can use for brainstorming and other group sessions.

## WORK AND CORPORATE TRANSFORMATION

Innovation excites some and worries others. As change programmes are cascaded through an organization, not all those likely to be affected may consider what is sought to be desirable from their point of view. For example, consider the case of the company that is operating internationally:

- The introduction of a greater number of multilocation and international project groups and teams can bring people into contact with each other who may be paid very different amounts in various parts of the world for work of a similar nature, and give rise to comparability complaints.
- The vision of the flexible organization may be received very differently according to local labour market conditions. According to one MNC manager with the responsibility for introducing changes into a German company: 'They are cynical and distrustful. There is such a large gap between what we say and what we do. Every move is seen by our social partners as a way of cutting costs.'

## HOW LOSERS OPERATE

Losers tend to stick with a particular and hierarchical model of operation. The structure is set out in organization charts. There are probably job descriptions for most positions, and how the organization operates is set out in a physical or electronic manual. Preparing these and understanding them takes time. Hence people are reluctant to make changes that might involve altering diagrams, updating files and reprinting documents. Some people become complacent. They believe they have discovered or created a formula for continuing business success. They also swear by particular approaches and enshrine them in standard processes and procedures. The framework solidifies.

Many losers have a weakness for single solutions, panaceas and fads. They believe that this management approach, that technology or a particular consultant's methodology will provide an answer and solve their problems. While struggling to make a chosen course of action work they fail to consider alternative options. They lock themselves in.

Employees who can be trusted to operate in approved ways and observe standard practice are promoted. After some time corporate structures, processes, systems and mindsets become rigid and inflexible. Subject them to increasing stress and they first creak and groan, and then snap. Increase workloads and transaction flows and people in 'loser' organizations struggle to cope. Rather than operate in new ways or change processes they endeavour to work harder, faster and for longer hours. They quickly become overloaded and break down. Work–life balance is an issue in these companies because staff suffer the pressures without enjoying any of the compensating benefits.

There are often alternative ways of achieving the same objective. Boats of many types and sizes may be capable of making the same journey, although imposing very different demands upon their crews. The craft chosen will reflect their preferences and aspirations. There may also be alternative routes to the same destination. James Brindley adopted meandering routes for the canals he built. They follow the natural contours of the landscape, whereas later engineers such as Thomas Telford used cuttings, tunnels and embankments to achieve straighter routes. Which is best depends on whether one is a commercial carrier or leisure boater and the relative costs of maintenance and water supply.

## CHANGE AND SATISFACTION

Organizational change can be protracted and costly. For example, termination payments to people and penalties relating to changed property arrangements can both be expensive. In some companies it would appear that decisions regarding who should be kept or made redundant are governed more by accumulated rights in the event of termination than managerial merit or quality. Some assets are also difficult to dispose of in a recession.

Occasionally, companies become carried away with concepts and push their application to the extreme. Judgement is needed to decide how far to go in relation to the current situation and context of a company. Trade-offs may still exist. For example, Saab found that giving groups of people greater added-value responsibilities improvedtheir 'employee satisfaction', but at the cost of longer car production cycles.

For a period, and until the benefits appear to come through, corporate transformation may be accompanied by a slide in the employee satisfaction ratings. The trends need to be monitored, the causes identified and, where appropriate, remedial programmes put in place. Opinion surveys can be used to track attitudes to change in various parts of the corporate organization.

Understanding the reasons for dissatisfaction could lead to a change in transformation priorities, if not in direction. Japanese companies such as

Honda encourage their staff to be dissatisfied with whatever has been achieved in order that they will aspire to do even better.

# WINNING WAYS

Winning corporate cultures are more tolerant of uncertainty and diversity. Their people think in terms of flows rather than structures. They reflect. They are willing to question, review and consider alternatives. Fluid roles, flexible systems and adaptable processes enable these organizations to move in new directions as situations and circumstances change.

Winners avoid blind allies and dead ends. They do not take continuing success for granted and are always open to alternative ways of operating. They are less wedded to precedent and more likely to treat each case on its own merits. They are also willing to reinvent themselves and to learn to work in new ways as the occasion demands. Innovative responses and novel approaches are recognized and rewarded. Bespoke products and services are offered. Processes and their supporting systems exist to support developing relationships with customers. Learning is built into them. They are updated as required, and individual tasks are handled in whatever ways are thought to be most appropriate. People endeavour to improve and build upon what has gone before rather than merely replicate previous responses.

On the whole, winners are pragmatic, catholic and wary of 'single solutions'. They assemble creative and practical combinations of whatever ways of working and learning and change elements they feel will enable them to achieve their purposes. They are always alert to the possibility of better alternatives and vary the factors selected to improve outcomes and cope with changing circumstances. Their attitudes, processes, systems and ways of working and learning are relatively robust and resistant to stress. Because they flex to accommodate changing conditions and circumstances, they do not fall over when the going gets tough. Winners handle new challenges and opportunities by prioritizing, adapting and securing flexible access to whatever additional resources are required.

# ENCOURAGING DIVERSITY

Organizations composed primarily of knowledge workers have tended to assume a community of people of similar competence, working as individuals rather than in teams. In early network organizations, the focus was upon teams, developing variety and facilitating change, and there was more emphasis upon the management of groups. Awareness has grown of the value of diversity within teams, and the extent to which professionals vary widely in their competence and attitudes, their market value, and their work, lifestyle and learning preferences (Coulson-Thomas, 1988).

The imposition of standard approaches, and an appreciation of the value of common tools, should not be allowed to result in an organization losing sight of the value of diversity. The recognition of individual differences can be important when roles are allocated.

Harmony does not mean that we all have to be the same. The achievement of balance implies that differing forces are at work, and a degree of reconciliation or accommodation within a relationship has been achieved. People, whether employees, network members, colleagues or business partners, should be encouraged to play to their strengths. The Xerox approach to diversity is only to discriminate on ability.

# KNOWLEDGE MANAGEMENT

Is the critical knowledge and essential understanding of the people of your company captured in a form that enables it to be shared and exploited? Or does it simply walk out of the door each evening in the memories of key employees – those most likely to be poached by competitors?

Is your company's core capability succinctly summarized in a format that can easily be presented, accessed and understood by employees, customers, suppliers and business partners? Or do you, and your colleagues, struggle to explain what is special or distinctive about its technology, products and services?

Is your company's know-how expressed in the form of badged approaches, copyrighted methodologies and patented technologies that can be licensed to others? Or is it scattered around the organization, unprotected and largely unrecognized?

If the former questions are true, the foundations are in place for developing your people, winning new business, and creating value. If the latter situations are the case, then you could be in serious trouble. The full potential of new ways of working will not be achieved until knowledge management practices match and support them.

Know-how accounts for an increasing proportion of the value delivered to end-users. Customers themselves expect ever more imaginative and tailored applications of relevant knowledge and understanding in the development of bespoke products and services that meet their individual requirements. There are endless possibilities for knowledge entrepreneurship (Coulson-Thomas, 2000), while professionals and knowledge workers have never had so many opportunities to derive additional incomes from what they know and can do.

Investigations undertaken by the Centre for Competitiveness (see Appendix) in key areas such as (1) winning business, (2) building relationships with customers, suppliers and business partners, (3) taking full advantage of e-business technologies, and (4) learning more effectively than competitors, reveal that some individuals and organizations are much more effective than others at managing their knowledge. They know what they know and how best to exploit it. They lever their particular insights, unique qualities and distinctive strengths.

The creation, capture, sharing, packaging, application, valuation and exploitation of information, knowledge, understanding and intellectual capital has become a critical success factor of strategic significance. And some companies are getting it right. Cotoco Ltd, a knowledge management specialist (www.cotoco.com), reports the following client experiences:

- The captured expertise of a group of skilled craftsmen is used to induct and train new entrants into an exciting and fast-moving industry. The 'solution' has been so well received by companies in the industry that the sponsoring trade association is deriving an income from selling it as a training programme.
- One company has used a CD ROM-based compendium and represen- tation of its capability to support sales activity in the field with impressive results. One user was so impressed that his parent corpo- ration bought the business. Another company has captured the process steps, knowledge and understanding required for configuring and pricing its offering and preparing proposals.
- A group of professional firms have captured their basic expertise in a form that allows others to understand the situation they are in and to identify areas in which they need more specialist advice. The profes- sionals concerned are finding that people come to them better prepared and with more structured requests for assistance. The time saved enables them to devote more hours to higher-margin work.

Knowledge management should be so much more than a fad. It requires appropriate attitudes, a systematic approach, and the right combination of enabling technologies. There are knowledge creation, sharing and exploitation processes to be identified, established and supported. There could be intellectual property to protect and 'knowledge assets' to value for sales or balance-sheet purposes. US companies are appointing Chief Knowledge Officers or Chief Learning Officers. Should European companies appoint Directors of Learning or Directors of Intellectual Capital?

We have a choice of approaches, tools, technologies and supporting services. Learning, knowledge sharing and intellectual capital management processes can be introduced or re-engineered. The scope of initiatives can be extended to embrace supply-chains partners. When used effectively, knowledge management enables corporate renewal, learning and transformation. More value can be created for the various stake- holders in a contemporary enterprise.

## PROBLEM AREAS

People need to select their approaches and partners with care, however. Along with undoubted opportunities there are also pitfalls. Intercompany communications create fresh challenges, from 'security of the network' to the 'protection of intellectual property'. Some people join collaborative networks to suck them dry of intellectual capital. Many boards are aware of risks to financial and physical capital, but naïve when it comes to safeguarding knowledge assets.

Certain management practices can actually reduce corporate capability:

- Restructuring and cost-cutting can disrupt relationships and destroy knowledge.
- Valuable understanding may leave with delayered employees and prematurely retired older workers.
- Re-engineering and 'multi-skilling' often replaces experts with generalists who lack the knowledge needed for bespoke responses.
- Mobile high fliers may change jobs too often to obtain any in-depth understanding.
- Outsourcing can 'hand over' capabilities relevant to future strategic opportunities.

Many companies lack awareness of the risks and a balanced understanding of what needs to be done. Some introduce 'virtual' operations without considering the competencies required for leading and managing them. Others focus excessively upon knowledge that is easy to collect, such as financial or production data, while 'softer' areas such as an understanding of attitudes, values and relationships, or motivation and learning, are overlooked.

Widespread interest in knowledge management is accompanied by considerable confusion. Few companies understand what is available. Suppliers unashamedly push their particular technology-based offerings. Their staff may not understand how these might be combined with complementary products and services. As a result there is an unhealthy reliance upon 'single solutions' such as a corporate intranet.

## ESTABLISHING THE FUNDAMENTALS

A newly appointed Chief Knowledge Officer should establish where a company is and where it should be. Corporate knowledge may relate to the past rather than tomorrow's opportunities. People can drown in irrelevant information, while lacking crucial knowledge for current roles and future priorities.

Many companies do not know what they know, what they do not know, or what they need to know. There are many factors to consider. For example:

- Internal knowledge might be exaggerated or undervalued in comparison with that elsewhere.

- Knowledge can exist in many forms, for example facts, theories, opinions, values, issues, priorities, risks, probabilities, attitudes and assumptions.
- It may also occur in varying formats from electronic databases, animations and visual images to print, audio and video material.
- People may differ in their understanding of cases, requirements, rules, policies, processes, tools and relationships.
- Knowledge requirements may vary at individual, group and corporate levels; and between different departments, projects, business units, network partners or customers.
- The significance and value of knowledge can depend on use, application, time and context.
- Perspectives also vary. While professionals stress practical understanding born of experience, an academic may put more value upon theoretical knowledge.

Understanding and expertise are relevant only if they relate to business goals. Access to information is one thing, its beneficial use quite another. Professionals whose social positions are eroded as the emphasis switches from knowing to creating value for customers may hoard knowledge and develop protective strategies.

Considerable judgement is required to determine: what knowledge to capture, develop and share; the value to place upon existing knowledge; and the likely benefits of further knowledge in relation to the additional cost of creating or acquiring it. Some companies focus excessively upon capturing and managing a current stock of commodity knowledge (Coulson-Thomas, 1997 and 1998).

## KNOWLEDGE CREATION AND CONSUMPTION

There are far too many passive consumers of other people's knowledge, and unimaginative users of standard tools. To ensure relevance, individuals and teams should be encouraged to develop their own approaches and understanding. Innovators and market leaders move beyond what is generally known or assumed. They voyage into the unknown, discover new knowledge and create additional competencies relevant to the achievement of their entrepreneurial visions.

Learning is dynamic. It is concerned with flows, processes for creating new knowledge. In many companies there is an imbalance between the consumption and development of knowledge. People simply draw down an existing supply without replenishing the well (Coulson-Thomas, 1997 and 1998). The value of knowledge can rapidly diminish if it is not developed and kept current and relevant.

Winners champion knowledge building and sharing. Their balanced scorecard assessments embrace learning, intellectual capital issues, and whether knowledge is being appropriately valued and effectively exploited.

Ultimately, a company and its people must outlearn competitors. Effective and collaborative learning can require creative combinations of complementary approaches, environments, processes and technologies. We will see in Chapters 13 and 14 that focus, relevance and the support of appropriate learning partners are essential and strategic requirements.

# NETWORK ACCESS TO KNOWLEDGE AND SKILLS

Citizens of the network organization are reluctant to 'make do' with average professionals when a world expert may be a phone call or electronic mail message away. Access to knowledge and skills is becoming more important than the particular means by which these are secured. The network organization is a knowledge and skills network.

The globalization of business has given rise to a requirement to access and focus relevant expertise on an international basis (Coulson-Thomas, 1992). Too many management teams began with an existing organization and looked for new ways of keeping it alive. This 'old approach' tended to regard the structure of the organization as a given. How one worked depended upon a standard contract of employment. In some cases, work would only be packaged when it was felt necessary to seek some external advice on a consultancy basis.

Under one approach that has been suggested (see Figure 8.2) a company should undertake the following steps:

1 It should begin by setting out a vision of what might be achieved to encourage people to offer or contribute their skills to 'make it happen'. The vision needs to be compelling – bearing in mind that both customers and employees have a 'choice'. How far it is communicated and shared will depend upon the ambition and reach of the company.
2 The company should next determine what needs to be done in order to achieve the vision. Values and goals should be determined, and a strategy formulated to achieve the vision. Measurable objectives will need to be established. A roles and responsibilities exercise could also be undertaken.
3 The outcome of all this activity should be a list of specific tasks to be performed, and a set of project group and team requirements. These are the 'vital few' programmes that need to be undertaken to deliver value, create opportunities and achieve corporate objectives.
4 Relevant knowledge and skills have now to be identified. People, whether as individuals or in groups, will need to be 'profiled' to help locate those who have the capability necessary for the accomplishment

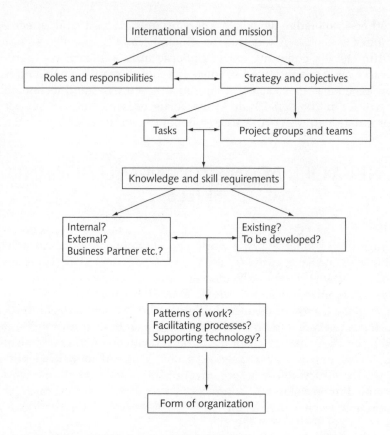

*Source: Coulson-Thomas (1992), Creating the Global Company*

**Figure 8.2** International skill management strategy

of the identified tasks. Complementary sets of skills will need to be assembled. Where key cross-functional and inter-organizational processes that deliver value to customers are known, these will also have an influence upon skill requirements – but customers, not processes, should come first.

5 Sources of knowledge and skill will need next to be identified. The aim should be to find the most appropriate source, whether 'internal' to, or employed by, the organization, or 'external', eg an independent contractor. Where particular capabilities do not exist, they will have to be developed.

6 The identified sources of knowledge and skills will now need to be contracted to provide the services that are required. Process and technology support requirements will also need to be identified and agreed. The contracted arrangements will need to suit both the organization and the individuals whose contributions are sought.

7 Various patterns of work will emerge, according to what is required to meet the needs of, and suit the preferences of, knowledge and skill suppliers. They will also need to reflect the requirements of customers. A form of organization will evolve that best allows the co-ordination of the various network 'partners' in the achievement of the vision. Their talents and contributions will be harnessed and focused upon that which delivers value to customers and exploits opportunities.

## HOW LOSERS DEFINE CAPABILITIES

Corporate losers define their capabilities in terms of the physical and financial resources they own and control and the individuals whom they employ and can manage. Their markets are places. Their people are more comfortable with tangible assets that can be seen, smelt and touched, and easily counted, measured and valued.

Because their activities depend on the availability of physical resources some losers can operate only in certain geographical areas. It may be difficult for people living elsewhere to access them and work with them. Buildings become prisons and those excluded from participation become outsiders.

In general, losers prefer more rather than less. Some consider the accumulation of resources as an end in itself. Recruiting more staff and moving to a larger property is viewed as evidence of progress. Losers focus upon the individual items of capital rather than their relevance and use, and the flow of benefits that they provide. The more losers succeed in accumulating fixed overheads, the more vulnerable they become to economic forces, commercial constraints and financial pressures.

## WINNING CONCERNS

Winners are more concerned with feelings, values and relationships. In competitive situations such intangibles are often the critical differentiators. Quality and commitment are regarded as more significant than quantity. Flexible access to resources and capabilities rather than their ownership is the key issue. What they are able to do and who they can or might be able to work with are more important than what they have.

As we saw in Chapter 1, the organization is perceived as an inclusive community or network of people with shared values and common objectives. Its boundaries are limited only by the availability of access devices. Its markets are wherever and whenever buyers and sellers come together, whether in cyberspace or on the ground. The corporate 'family' includes contractors, business partners and the staff of customers and suppliers, as well as employees.

People in winning companies endeavour to avoid being locked into inflexible ways of working and rigid commercial arrangements. They take a longer-term view and like to keep their options open. Their focus is upon returns, margins and revenue generation, and they create value and develop categories of intellectual property such as customer databases, documented ways of doing things and management methodologies that can be easily exploited.

# THE REQUIREMENT FOR FLEXIBLE IMPLEMENTATION

Needs can change while transition occurs. In some cases, a major change such as a relocation can take longer to achieve than the likely timescale of an operational requirement. Hence the interest in the more flexible forms of network organization that can enable groups and teams to work together for particular purposes independently of location.

People should be allowed to work in whatever ways best allow them to achieve the objectives they have been set, particularly in terms of satisfying customers. Paying on a flexible basis for tangible and agreed outputs can allow an organization to secure access to a higher calibre of staff than would otherwise be the case.

The effective network is sufficiently flexible to make use of whatever pattern of work is most appropriate for the task in hand. Individuals are able to work in a mode and at a location that best taps their competence and expertise. The response to those who wish to be different is 'No sweat' rather than 'No way'.

By operating as a flexible network, accessing a range of relevant knowledge and skills, as and when required, organizations have become learning networks that devote a higher proportion of their resources to working and the facilitation of learning, and a lower proportion to 'overheads' such as land, buildings and permanent staff costs. We will consider learning networks in Chapter 17.

## Losers

Losers:

- have strong views regarding the best ways of operating and seek to impose standard ways of working;
- give priority to the achievement of corporate objectives when structuring organizations;
- enjoy status and believe they know best regarding what should be done and how to do it;
- become involved in the details of implementation and interfere in how others go about doing tasks that have been allocated to them;
- recruit and promote those who conform to characteristics that they define;
- tend only to trust those whom they employ or feel they can control;
- favour employees to the extent that associates and business partners feel second-class citizens;
- hoard and consume existing knowledge.

## Winners

Winners:

- are tolerant of different ways of working and allow people to work in whatever ways enable them to give of their best;
- work with others to build a form of organization and introduce ways of working that are acceptable and beneficial to those involved;
- are concerned with ends and concentrate on the formulation and agreement of goals, values, objectives and priorities;
- leave the best way of achieving whatever is desired to those who are closest to what needs to be done;
- consciously seek to attract, encourage and reward a diversity of talents;
- are willing to trust those who share their values, common goals and shared objectives;
- involve associates and business partners, who feel part of the organization;
- create, share and apply new knowledge.

# INTRODUCING NEW PATTERNS OF WORK

If a new pattern of work, such as a telecommuting programme, is to be successfully introduced (Coulson-Thomas, 1995):

- it must be appropriate for both the tasks to be performed and the people concerned;
- tasks should be defined in terms of supplying a specified 'output' with fixed parameters of cost and time;
- the people selected should be inner-directed, and able to apply their knowledge and skill independent of a particular location;
- those likely to be affected should be both prepared and involved;
- not only the programme participants, but those who work with them and manage them, should also be prepared;
- employees, or network members, should participate in the design and implementation of the programme;
- top management commitment should be secured and retained, and clear objectives and targets set;
- a respected member of staff should be appointed to lead the implementation programme;
- the programme itself should be voluntary, and allowed to evolve naturally;
- every effort should be made to communicate regularly with the programme participants during both the implementation and operational stages.

If the implementation requires compulsion and needs to be forced, one should question whether it meets the needs and objectives of those concerned.

# MORALITY AND CHANGE

On occasion, moral and other arguments are deployed against transformation programmes on account of their impacts upon jobs, and the disruption and stress which they can cause. Such concern is certainly valid in respect of reorganizations that move problems rather than solve them, and deal with symptoms rather than underlying causes.

In reality, work on activities that do not deliver value, or which are incompatible with the objectives of a company, is not ethical. When, in their hearts, people either cannot perceive their contribution or doubt its value, they become prey to temptations to 'look busy' or to exaggerate the importance of their role. The uncertain may become 'easy meat' for the corporate butcher, even though their contribution may be real.

Knowing or believing that one does not contribute saps the management spirit. It can lead to deception and protectionism. Much of the communication and visible activity within the bureaucratic organization consisted of internal self-promotion and role justification. Bureaucracies breed corruption.

When roles and responsibilities relate to the achievement of corporate goals, and objectives are established in terms of measurable outputs, a transparent honesty is introduced into working relationships. People know that they and others are working on activities of importance and value, and they can measure the extent of their achievements. The scope for concealment and sophism that favours the smart rather than the sound is reduced.

The scope for discrimination on such grounds as sex, colour, religion, age or nationality is reduced when the focus is put upon the generation of agreed outputs, rather than subjective 'input' considerations such as 'appearance' or 'commitment'. Reward and recognition can be more easily related to achievements. In the absence of measurable outputs, rewards and status tend to drift to those who possess certain characteristics, irrespective of what they actually do.

Network organizations with appropriate values, processes and policies have the potential to become honest corporations. Expectations relating to role-model behaviour, shared values and a rigorous focus upon the generation of value, and customer and employee fulfilment, can represent the moral cement that holds the network together.

## CHECKLIST

▶ What importance does your company place upon employee involvement and participation?

▶ Does it measure employee fulfilment and views?

▶ Is there a business objective to achieve measurable contributions to employee fulfilment?

▶ What does your company actually do to empower employees?

▶ Do members of the management team understand what empowerment means?

▶ Are the processes that deliver value for customers identified and documented in order that opportunities can be found to speed them up through the empowerment of people?

▶ Do all the people of your organization know what they are expected to contribute to corporate objectives?

▶ Does each person have a 'vital few' list of things to do?

> ▶ What use does your company make of self-managed workgroups?
>
> ▶ Does the knowledge and skill management strategy of your company match the needs of its situation and circumstances?
>
> ▶ How flexible is your organization in terms of access to knowledge and skills?
>
> ▶ How tolerant is it of diversity in terms of both people and patterns of work?
>
> ▶ How moral is your company, and how might it be made more honest?

## REFERENCES

Coulson-Thomas, C (1988) *The New Professionals*, BIM, Corby

Coulson-Thomas, C (1989) *Too Old at 40?*, BIM, Corby

Coulson-Thomas, C (1990) *The Role and Status of Project Management*, an Adaptation Survey for the Association of Project Managers, London

Coulson-Thomas, C (1992) *Creating the Global Company: Successful Internationalism*, McGraw-Hill, London

Coulson-Thomas, C (1995) *The Responsive Organisation: Re-engineering new patterns of work*, Policy Publications, Bedford

Coulson-Thomas, C (1997 and 1998) *The Future of the Organization: Achieving excellence through business transformation*, Kogan Page, London

Coulson-Thomas, C (2000) *The Information Entrepreneur*, 3Com Active Business Unit, Winnersh

Toffler, A (1970) Future Stock, The Bodley Head, London

## FURTHER INFORMATION

The Information Entrepreneur by Colin Coulson-Thomas can be ordered by telephoning UK freephone 0800 222 222, via Web site www.ntwkfirm.com/bookshop/or by visiting the 3Com Web site at www.3Com.co.uk/active-business.

A brochure describing 'The Responsive Organisation' report, methodology and toolkit for introducing new ways of working is available from Policy Publications, 4 The Crescent, Bedford MK40 2RU (tel: +44 (0) 1234 328448; fax: +44 (0) 1234 357231, e-mail: policypubs@kbnet.co.uk; Web site: www.ntwkfirm.com/bookshop).

# 9

# From Quality through Business Excellence to Entrepreneurship

*'When the water is clear you can see the bottom'*

## PANACEA OR PLACEBO?

The first edition of this book contained a chapter on the prospects and priorities for the quality programmes then being driven through organizations (Coulson-Thomas, 1992). Quality gurus were jet-setting around the world and performing to packed houses at corporate conferences. Hardly a company of any significance was without its brochures and videos calling upon staff to 'get it right first time'. In larger companies there were hundreds, if not thousands, of quality improvement projects under way. For many companies, total quality was *the* route to corporate transformation.

As technical quality was increasingly assumed, the competitive focus shifted to quality of process, quality of attitude, quality of understanding, quality of behaviour and quality of relationships. Experience was bringing about a change of quality perspective (Table 9.1). In particular, customers and suppliers were increasingly regarded as a part of the quality network. They are colleagues and business partners rather than outsiders.

Network quality is a mutual and joint responsibility. Preoccupation with internal transformation should not be allowed to obscure the importance of network relationships.

As electronic and other collaborative links were established forward into customers, backwards to suppliers and sideways into business

**Table 9.1** Changing quality perspective

| Old focus | New focus |
| --- | --- |
| Product quality | Quality attitudes and values |
| Quality as distinct programme | Quality as integral process |
| Use of statistical tools | Focus on relationships |
| Quality as a cost | Quality as an investment |
| Quality a choice | Quality essential |
| Achieve quality standard | Move beyond quality to business excellence |
| Corporate focus | Supply chain focus |

partners, the quality organization was becoming the quality network. General progress towards the creation of the network organization, and its associated attitudes and relationships, can be a powerful enabler of the development of quality along supply chains.

Customers increasingly assumed quality and reliability. In some sectors all competitors had quality programmes. As one CEO put it, 'Those who didn't supply quality are no longer trading.' Technical or product quality of itself no longer differentiated between alternative suppliers. Many CEOs were looking beyond 'traditional' or 'internal' quality, that is concerned with products, and towards attitudes and values, less tangible factors such as 'look' or 'feel', and the quality of external supply chain relationships.

Many quality programmes were running out of steam. After some initial improvements 'diminishing returns' set in. One chairman used the analogy with a drug: 'At first it works, but then the effect wears off. You get used to it, and have to take extra doses, or take something else to make an impact.' Consider the following comments:

> We have a quality standard for documenting and operating our processes. I can't tell you whether they are the processes that deliver the value that is sought by customers.

> You can't afford to be without quality – it's become the norm in our business. However, you would be naïve to think a standard approach to quality is of itself going to make you world class.

> All our customers now assume quality. Their expectations are rising faster than our ability to deliver.

> Basic attitudes have not changed. Something is missing.

> However good we are, we cannot deliver more than a proportion of the value sought by customers. And yet each of our major customers and suppliers, all components in a supply chain, have their own quality programme.

In general, companies were initiating quality programmes without thinking through what they were trying to achieve, or anticipating the various change elements that needed to be lined up to achieve a successful implementation. Over the past decade many companies have moved beyond quality and re-engineering to achieve excellence through business transformation and their experiences are discussed in my book *The Future of the Organization* (Coulson-Thomas, 1997 and 1998). This chapter considers what companies need to do to encourage and support enterprise and entrepreneurship.

## THE RELEVANCE OF QUALITY

When quality was born, the business environment, or context, within which managers operated was less turbulent, and in many ways less demanding. It had many of the characteristics associated with the 'old' environment examined in Chapter 1 (Table 1.1).

The business world has subsequently experienced profound change. There are the environmental, social, economic and technological pressures of the 'new' environment. Markets have become more open, competitive and international, and customers are more demanding.

Companies that track, learn from and respond to fundamental market changes can adapt and prosper. Jardine Matheson has coped with a succession of challenges in China and Hong Kong from the Opium Wars of the 19th century to the Cultural Revolution instigated by Chairman Mao. The trading house has remained true and committed to its geographical roots, while periodically renewing its capability and updating its operations and tactics in the light of new conditions and opportunities. It has done this quietly, in its own way and without drama or the fashionable fads adopted by so many other companies.

Action to increase value to customers needs to be matched by regular strategy reviews. While committed to improving the life experiences of those who use its products, Johnson & Johnson moves in and out of different lines of business. Thus in the area of disposable products, nappies were dropped and higher-margin contact lens introduced. While product quality is the concern of all employees, the strategic quality of the company's portfolio of offerings is a central concern of senior management.

The quality of life within suppliers as well as that of employees and customers needs to be considered. Both Nike and Reebok suffered from media reports that manufacturers of their products in developing countries were employing under-age workers. As a result and in reaction, some customers pointedly opted to buy from other suppliers.

For the network organization, the priorities a decade ago of securing competitive advantage and the quality of values, relationships and contributions (Coulson-Thomas and Coulson-Thomas, 1991) are still both relevant and important. Dispersed individuals and scattered teams need to be inspired to excel. Integrity and quality of performance can transcend death. Eva Cassidy refused to compromise as an artist during her life. Sales of her recordings took off after her death from cancer at the age of 33, her album Songbird topping the UK charts two-and-a-half years after it was first released.

# UNDERSTANDING WHY COMMITMENT IS LACKING

Why do so many senior people appear hesitant and 'half-hearted'? Why are the communications concerning change programmes so anaemic, especially when coming from those who have little difficulty in putting their points across in other contexts?

We have to get at the roots of ambivalence. The reasons for concern, quiet dissent, and a reluctance to commit need to be probed:

- Apparent support may only mean that those concerned are crawlers, bootlickers and toadies. There is often a reluctance to accept the reality that all manner of loathsome and self-serving creatures inhabit the corridors of corporate bureaucracy. Their wiles, and the games they play, which are so transparent to outsiders, and destructive of external relationships built upon mutual trust and respect, go unnoticed or are ignored within.
- Those who appear 'difficult' may be the individuals with intellectual reservations. These could relate to the application of a programme in a particular area, or to an initiative as a whole. The 'objectors' could be the ones who have thought it through and uncovered missing elements. An implementation process needs to incorporate a means of listening to, and learning from, those who have valid objections.
- Also, not all customers have the same preferences. What is added value for one person may be regarded as an expensive luxury by another.

Bland 'motherhood' statements suggest people have not thought through what needs to be done. As one manager put it: 'If they knew what to do, I wouldn't be fed a diet of slogans... unless they think I'm a fool, which I don't think I am.'

People judge by what they see rather than on the basis of what is said. We saw in Chapter 7 that the informal messages, the examples and the symbols, can undercut formal communications.

Too often, the changes of attitudes that are sought are not reflected in the language used by managers, the anecdotes and 'war stories' that make up the mythology of a company, in symbols such as the allocation of parking spaces or use of exercise facilities, and in how a myriad of day-to-day matters are handled. Changing structures and processes may not be followed by attitudes where managers themselves, and particularly senior managers, refuse to act as role models.

## INDIVIDUALISM AND COLLECTIVISM

British Aerospace could have gone the way of the UK's indigenous car industry. With a falling share price and facing a dramatic scaling down of military aircraft purchases as a result of the end of the cold war, its survival as an independent player seemed in doubt. And yet the company bounced back, repositioned itself and, following acquisitions in the United States and Europe, became the world's largest supplier of defence electronics. CEO Dick Evans and his management colleagues managed to persuade the company's people that individually and collectively they could make the transition.

Expect people to do too much or what they perceive as unobtainable and they are likely to give up. Individuals may commit to doing whatever is required only if they believe a 'critical mass' of other people are likely to do the same. The BAe Systems transformation programme encouraged questioning and challenge and introduced the new ideas, technologies and ways of working needed to secure competitive advantage. The sheer scale of its major projects means that collective action is required. Many individuals would find it difficult to operate outside of the corporation.

In other contexts, such as a wide range of professions and knowledge-based service businesses, independent operation by individual contractors and small and specialist practices is possible. People may remain part of a larger group only if they feel it is in their best interests to do so. For example, as an employee of a larger organization, it may be easier to secure the portfolio of projects needed to construct an impressive CV and to have access to leading-edge technologies.

In relation to companies that you are involved with or familiar with, consider the advantages and disadvantages from an individual perspective of remaining within the corporate embrace. What are the advantages of being and remaining part of a larger group? How easy would it be for people to operate on their own or in smaller groups? What form of relationship could be offered to those who decide to leave?

## LOSING ATTITUDES AND PRACTICES

Successful innovation requires individual initiative and creative collaboration within an entrepreneurial culture. The people of loser companies tend to be cautious 'loners'. They work in relative isolation and cling to the familiar. They settle into their role and associated lifestyle and endeavour to avoid significant changes. They 'stick to the brief' and try to resolve issues by themselves. When reviews are held individuals become defensive and protective of departmental interests.

Knowledge workers take pride in their educational qualifications and membership of qualifying bodies. Their professional status is important to them. They tend to resent being 'second guessed' by others and may interpret requests for a second opinion as a questioning of their integrity and competence.

Groups within loser companies keep to themselves and departmental colleagues. They assume they know best and jealously guard their autonomy. Major bids, especially when time pressures are involved, may be dispatched without being subjected to any form of peer review.

People within loser companies play their cards close to their chest and are reluctant to invite external comment. Some avoid networking opportunities. They worry about cost and confidentiality. Paradoxically, they also imagine that 'outsiders' would find it difficult to master the peculiarities of their businesses.

When occasional independent reviews are held of the processes and activities of 'loser' companies, little tends to happen. The pressure of work and preoccupation with non-critical or even trivial matters militates against the adoption of any suggestions or recommendations made.

Proposal quality is critical (Kennedy and O'Connor, 1997). Business development teams find the sheer grind of assembling and submitting a large number of bids limits the time available to refine and tailor any particular document. The aim becomes getting them out the door before a deadline arrives. Yet considerable value can often be added at a final stage. Thus a draft could be reworked to focus on prospect requirements or to emphasize and summarize key 'differentiators'.

## HOW WINNERS THINK AND BEHAVE

Winners are more open, self-assured and willing to change. Current contribution and future relevance rather than past achievements define personal standing. Teamwork, interaction and the sharing of information and knowledge are widespread and an integral element of working practices.

Individuals are sufficiently secure to seek the opinions of their colleagues and peers. Drafts may be circulated to other departments and external parties for comment. In general, the interventions and contributions of colleagues are regarded as helpful and they are actively encouraged.

Business development teams seek whatever inputs will increase their chances of success. They submit significant proposals to a 'red team' review and listen carefully to any comments and reactions. People who have not been directly involved in preparing a bid response may find it easier to adopt an objective and customer perspective. Hence, their views can be of considerable value.

Winners are more likely to seek and use independent evaluations. They subject critical business processes to external reviews and 'health checks'. Winners also circulate among their peers and look for opportunities to make new contacts and forge additional relationships. Their best defence against others copying them and catching up is to innovate and thus stay out in front.

As we saw in Chapter 6, winners are more selective and enter fewer competitive races. They are not risk averse, but they navigate shallow rivers only when they can see the bottom. Their people have more time to develop, critique and refine the proposals they do submit. Automating the more routine aspects of document preparation, for example calculating prices, also helps to free up the resources needed to improve, add value to and tailor individual responses. Winners are also on the look out for ways of becoming even better. Successful companies are more likely to subject their processes and practices for winning business to critical peer review. Inaction cannot be excused. There are invariably practical steps that can be taken based on critical success factors that have been identified. The more of these that are put in place, the more successful a business is likely to be (Kennedy and O'Connor, 1997).

# BEWARE OF AWARDS

Don't be fooled, or seduced into complacency, by external recognition. It may be possible for a company to acquire a recognized quality standard by demonstrating that various processes are in place, documented and observed. But these may not be those most appropriate, or even relevant, to delivering value or achieving business objectives.

Having obtained a 'standard' and documented everything, managers may be reluctant to introduce changes, even when these may be desirable or necessary. The achievement of a standard can result in the 'freezing' of an organization when it needs to be fluid. It can lead to denial of the requirement for diversity. Supporting technology and mechanical approaches to the management of change can lead to an organization becoming muscle bound when it needs to be flexible.

Increasingly, companies are competing not so much on the basis of their products and services, as on their processes for: continuing learning, adaptation and change; and attracting, retaining, motivating and developing human talent. Scale can be a burden when it does not allow a flexible and rapid response to changing requirements.

Imposing a standard approach to business etiquette can defeat one of the main purposes of seeking a network form of organization, namely to achieve the flexibility to handle diversity, and respond differently to changing requirements and varying local circumstances.

According to one interviewee: 'Manuals and procedures smack of bureaucracy.' In a world of changing relationships people should not be tied down with the shackles of restrictive procedures and the dead weight of dating manuals. Once they know what they are about, they should be encouraged to be loose and free.

A degree of concern and dissatisfaction is encouraging. Complacency can lead to stagnation. The need for improvement, refinement and change is easier to communicate when there is dissatisfaction with a current situation. A critical, questioning corporate environment appears to be generally regarded by those interviewed as healthy, and as a challenge, rather than as a threat.

## INDIVIDUALS AND ENTERPRISE

Does your company's culture encourage enterprise and intrapreneurship? Is latent entrepreneurial talent identified and released? In most organizations little is done to stimulate enterprise or encourage entrepreneurship. Much more effort should be devoted to creating value, developing new ventures, and generating additional sources of revenue.

Senior executives should be worried. The contemporary requirements for business success are very different from those experienced by today's corporate leaders at the outset of their career. Those who felt they 'knew best' ran the monolithic corporation, with its set procedures and standard products. Subordinates did what they were told. They worked upon prescribed tasks. They implemented rather than created.

As we saw in Chapter 1, conditions and requirements have dramatically changed. Customers are demanding bespoke services and imaginative responses to their individual requirements. Increasingly, people in the front line need to think and act like entrepreneurs.

People at all levels are also fed up with restructuring, retrenchment and re-engineering. 'Taking out' and 'cutting back' are essentially negative activities, and there are too many visible losers. While victims of redundancy struggle to assemble the income streams that will maintain their lifestyle, those still employed toil ever harder and for longer hours. Employees are feeling the heat. A growing number want a more balanced lifestyle.

The 'shake-outs' of the 1990s shattered many illusions about continuity of employment and the endless benevolence of big business. Many individuals resent being a piece upon someone else's chessboard, to be picked up, moved or sacrificed according to whatever their managers need to do to remain in the game of corporate survival. They are looking to change direction, reduce dependency and become more fulfilled.

If companies fail to respond, they will lose their most capable people and their most valuable customers. The pendulum is swinging away from de-layering and downsizing in favour of business development and value creation for individual customers. As it picks up speed, there is likely to be an explosion of interest in innovation and enterprise. Companies must turn passive, resigned and cynical employees into motivated entrepreneurs and committed business partners who actively develop new income streams (Coulson-Thomas, 1999).

# OPPORTUNITIES FOR ENTREPRENEURSHIP

There has never been a better time for personal entrepreneurship or for aspiring corporate intrapreneurs (Coulson-Thomas, 2001). While the rapid growth in Internet usage erodes the livelihoods of dealers and middlemen, the greater ease with which buyers and sellers can be brought together creates unprecedented opportunities for entrepreneurs to establish new electronic markets. Moreover, these can be in areas of special interest to those launching new services. Making a business out of a hobby enables people to achieve both financial success and personal fulfilment.

There are a host of opportunities for business and social entrepreneurs in health, leisure and learning that will open up the boundary between the public and the private sectors. Concerns and anxieties represent business opportunities. The imaginative and innovative can respond to 'worries about the environment' with recyclable products and more sustainable developments. A widespread fear of crime can be addressed by more secure ways of working and living, and services that can assist prevention, detection and conviction. Entrepreneurs could create model communities within which people with complementary aspirations could share facilities and provide a degree of mutual care and cover.

Information and knowledge about emerging requirements are accessible at the touch of a button. People can search the far corners of the globe for good ideas from their mobile office or living room. Knowledge entrepreneurs are helping people to assemble the particular information, knowledge and understanding that they need to create value for their customers (Coulson-Thomas, 2000).

Individual, corporate and collective interests can be reconciled. Just as people aspire to greater control over their own destiny, so more corporations expect their employees to manage their own work, careers and development, while governments – concerned about future obligations in an ageing society – require citizens to assume greater responsibility for their own financial security.

Individuals and organizations also have interests in common. Companies do not want to lose their 'brightest and best'. Corporations like Xerox would be substantially more profitable if they had managed to secure even a minority stake in the many new business ventures set up by former employees and business associates. Similarly, people should not have to 'jump ship', and turn their back on colleagues and corporate opportunities, in order to establish new enterprises. All too often they are forced to walk away from valued relationships with people who know them 'warts and all'.

# TRANSFORMATION INTO AN ENTERPRISE COLONY

Modern corporations need to transform themselves into enterprise colonies that can tap, build and realize the entrepreneurial potential within their people (Coulson-Thomas, 1999). The Post Office invites individuals and teams with innovative ideas to come forward and request funding and support. Companies should provide venture teams with development capital, marketing assistance and central services in return for an appropriate equity stake in new initiatives.

Empowerment and delegation are being championed in many companies. But empowerment to do what, and delegation for what purpose? General drives need to be matched with specific steps to promote enterprise and build entrepreneurial qualities.

Confident companies encourage people to better understand their inner selves, and take advantage of their unique qualities and distinctive strengths (Coulson-Thomas, 1999):

- They invite suggestions for new ways of exploiting corporate capabilities, and building and delivering value to consumers.
- They stimulate diversity, establish working environments that are conducive of reflection, and introduce ways of working and learning that raise spirits and fire the imagination.
- They encourage the creation, packaging, sharing, application and exploitation of new knowledge and understanding.
- They are also prepared to share rewards with those primarily responsible for successful entrepreneurship.

Personal and corporate transformation must go hand in hand. Increasingly, people need to think for themselves and make choices. Many intending entrepreneurs require new skills and knowledge, and specialist support. Many traditional management tools and techniques are simply not appropriate for those who seek both business success and personal fulfilment.

Small- and medium-sized enterprises (SMEs) and new corporate ventures are the primary source of tomorrow's work opportunities. In recent years governments and corporate leaders around the world have put a higher priority upon enterprise and entrepreneurship. The aspiration is clear. However, many people lack the competence and experience either to become entrepreneurs, or to manage corporate relationships with them.

Relevant help and suitable development programmes are now available. For example, my own book *Individuals and Enterprise* (Coulson-Thomas, 1999) contains 28 exercises which people can use to better understand the situation they are in, review their aspirations, assess their capabilities, and determine what they need to do to create and launch new ventures. Practical issues addressed include: securing family support; assembling the right team; overcoming inhibitions, pitfalls and constraints; getting started; and winning business.

Another book, *Shaping Things to Come* (Coulson-Thomas, 2001), contains strategies and directors' and entrepreneurs' checklists for developing alternative and distinctive offerings, while *The Information Entrepreneur* (Coulson-Thomas, 2000) contains checklists for entrepreneurs, investors, directors and various members of the management team relating to the establishment of new information and knowledge-based ventures.

Enterprise needs its own entrepreneurs. Slimmed-down organizations require the services of counsellors with the experience, sensitivity and intuition to help others to become successful entrepreneurs, while the resulting ventures will need learning and enterprise support services at various points in the enterprise life cycle.

# INFORMATION- AND KNOWLEDGE-BASED OFFERINGS

As the 'know-how' proportion of goods and services continues to rise, the economy is increasingly knowledge-based. Have you and your colleagues fully considered the opportunities open to you to make money by packaging and selling information and knowledge? Entrepreneurs need to understand how to access, share, work with and exploit information. Its use should result in the development and application of knowledge and understanding that creates intellectual capital and value for customers.

So much information is available in a variety of formats that busy people are overloaded. Much of it is dated and not relevant to contemporary priorities and concerns. There are therefore unprecedented opportunities to help people cope with the flow. Information needs to be sifted, screened and sorted – to be presented in ways that make it easier to absorb and understand. Increasingly, people demand tailored selections of information relevant to particular requirements, issues or decisions.

Emerging technologies represent additional channels of communication that can be very effective at reaching tightly defined target groups whose members are widely scattered (Coulson-Thomas, 2001). Enterprising individuals have already successfully launched many information- and knowledge-based services (Coulson-Thomas, 2000):

- Virtual stores sell goods ranging from books and compact discs to Scottish salmon and cakes. Auction, fan, sales and swap sites cover a wide variety of special interests. Experts, specialists, craft workers and creative artists can promote their offerings and services. They need no longer be hidden or obscure. Niche groups of enthusiasts and collectors can be catered for. Search engines and facilities allow them to track down those who can help.

- 'One-stop shop' and support services for professionals and knowledge workers include call forwarding and response services, research assistance, analysing and categorizing e-mail, and the provision of cover during illness and holidays or periods of peak workload.
- Virtual departments provide capabilities that organizations are reluctant to establish internally, perhaps because a requirement would not fully employ a 'whole person', or appropriate people cannot be recruited. Network partnerships overcome barriers of distance and time to bring together individuals who would not otherwise be able to work together.
- Activities such as writing software, designing Web pages, developing and implementing initiatives, programmes and campaigns, auditing or diagnosis, testing and monitoring can be undertaken remotely in almost any location.
- Electronic publishing offers many opportunities to provide customized information services. Those who assemble particular packages of information, knowledge and understanding can license them for the internal use of client networks and organizations.
- There is a large and growing market for distance learning. Having access to an electronic tutor, coach, adviser or counsellor willing to act as a sounding board can be immensely valuable.
- Discussion and focus groups and opinion and other surveys can be held online. Lobbying campaigns can be initiated and managed by e-mail. Views, arguments and cases can be assembled and presented to political and corporate decision-makers.
- Various sales, marketing, public relations and 'help desk' services can be undertaken by electronic means. Online catalogues, bulletin boards, newsletters and discussion groups can be initiated and supported with or without related advertising. Subscriber and advertisement fees can amount to a significant source of income.

Packages of processes, technologies and services are available that cover almost every aspect of setting up an electronic business. Trading and brokering services were among the earliest forms of business to be established. They are also particularly suited to electronic operation. Individuals can trade for others, and for themselves, for example investing on their own account.

## MANAGING INTELLECTUAL CAPITAL

The more effective creation and exploitation of intellectual assets can boost share valuations. According to the report 'Managing Intellectual Capital to Grow Shareholder Value' (Perrin, 2000), 51 companies that currently derive gross income of around £9.3 billion from their 'know-how' expect revenues from 19 out of 20 key categories of intellectual capital to increase over a five-year period.

There were stark differences between the 'leaders' who expect intellectual capital revenues to grow substantially and the 'laggards' who are expecting small or no growth during the same five years. The 'leaders' are twice as likely to believe that paying more attention to intellectual capital will improve shareholder value, and that they have not explored enough opportunities for doing so. The 'leaders' are around four times as likely as the 'laggards' to be under 'pressure from investors to do more to exploit intellectual capital'.

## INFORMATION AND KNOWLEDGE ENTREPRENEURS

Much depends on the energy and imagination of information and knowledge entrepreneurs. They need to identify specific opportunities being created by the greater availability and accessibility of information and knowledge, and craft distinctive information- and knowledge-based products and services.

All entrepreneurs have to identify opportunities to add value by meeting requirements that are not being addressed, and they must be focused and tenacious and possess a clear sense of direction. Most entrepreneurs need also to be tough, pragmatic and resilient. In addition, information and knowledge entrepreneurs need the following qualities (Coulson-Thomas, 2000):

- They must know how to acquire, develop, share, manage, exploit and capitalize on information, knowledge and understanding, and be able to help and enable others to use and apply them effectively. This may require combinations of emerging technologies to connect relevant people and organizations together, and the competencies to network with others, work and learn in new ways in order to create value, lead and manage virtual teams, and establish and manage knowledge businesses.
- They need curiosity and drive to undertake intelligent searches and to be able to judge or determine the significance, relevance and value of what they uncover. Many more people can access information than assess it or use it effectively. Understanding where information has come from, the underlying assumptions and how it has been compiled can prevent an enterprise or a course of action from being built upon foundations of sand.
- They require enough understanding of systems to be able to use an appropriate range of technologies to identify and access relevant sources

of information, knowledge and understanding. However, technical expertise is unlikely to be enough. Communication and relationship-building skills are also required to interact with information providers and bring together the combination of experience and knowledge needed to assemble a package that has market value.

*The Information Entrepreneur* (Coulson-Thomas, 2000) provides practical help and guidance. It is designed to stimulate a more proactive approach to the development of information- and knowledge-based businesses.

People should be proactive in assessing, developing and applying their personal knowledge and experience and thinking through the implications of 'the information and knowledge society'. Assessing its impacts upon others may enable business opportunities to be identified.

# INFORMATION AND KNOWLEDGE ENTREPRENEURSHIP

Losers are risk averse. They are 'talkers', not 'doers', passive followers rather than active leaders. If they do act, they blunder about. The silt they stir up prevents them from seeing the bottom. Aimless and rudderless, they run aground on the sands of distraction.

Entrepreneurs take risks. They initiate rather than copy. They have the qualities and will to succeed and win. They are calm, confident and can reflect. They look below the surface of people and events and steer purposefully towards the shores of opportunity.

Winners carefully assess opportunities. Gaps in existing provision in terms of content, format, access and reliability should be reviewed. Users might be prepared to pay for specific changes to be made. There might be flows of information, or specific expertise, that could form a commercial package that would meet the needs of particular communities of people in the external marketplace.

There might be alternative and better sources that could be used. Perhaps availability, responsiveness or cover could be improved, the flow speeded up, or 'on demand' access or 'help desk' support provided. Discontinuing services that are no longer required could yield savings.

There should be clear potential to 'add value' by providing a distinct information service to an identifiable group of people who would be willing to pay for it. Costs involved need to be recovered from subsequent user fees or subscriptions. External 'start up' finance may be required to launch a service, and there could be opportunities for collaborative ventures with other entities.

The further work that may need to be undertaken to put information into a form required by end-users should be assessed, and those who could undertake this identified. Business colleagues should have sound judgement of requirements, situations, people and opportunities. Shared values, goals, commitment, information and knowledge can greatly increase the chances of success.

Winners act while windows of opportunity still exist. They prioritize, focus and tackle the most important matters first. They also build winning teams, networks of people to whom they can turn for independent and objective advice. Particular deficiencies can be balanced by the complementary qualities of others.

Successful e-business and entrepreneurship requires more than simply putting appropriate technology in place (Coulson-Thomas, 2000). Investors and management teams need to assess the potential for information- and knowledge-based ventures:

- Are information, knowledge and understanding accounting for an increasing proportion of the value being generated for customers?
- Does the company have any information and knowledge entrepreneurs?
- Are people encouraged to come forward with ideas for information- and knowledge-based businesses?
- Do they create, share, package and apply new knowledge and understanding?
- Are relevant information, knowledge, tools, techniques and support made available and used?
- Have the various forms of intellectual capital been identified and protected?
- Are they fully exploited and is their revenue contribution monitored?
- Is an appropriate framework used to capture and store intellectual capital in a variety of formats?

Reward strategy should support the creation and exploitation of intellectual capital. Processes and procedures should be in place to monitor and measure learning, information and knowledge sharing; and intellectual capital creation and exploitation.

As we saw in the last chapter, knowledge exists in many forms. K-Frame (www.K-frame.com), a knowledge management framework which won the international e-Business Innovations Award for Knowledge Management, can handle intellectual property in a wide range of print, presentation, audio, animation and video formats.

## NEW MARKETS FOR INTELLECTUAL PROPERTY

Information- and knowledge-based businesses have been well represented among finalists for the e-Business Innovations awards (see www.ecommerce-awards.com). In some cases, new markets for certain forms of intellectual capital have been created. Thus Photodisc offers an image library of over 75,000 high-resolution images and personalized information services, while Music Now allows music tracks to be purchased and downloaded via its Web site.

The overall winner of the 2000 e-Business Innovations Awards for SMEs and the recipient of the 3Com Active Business Award was Atom Films of Seattle, in the United States (www.atomfilms.com). The company has created a Web-based market for animated films, with over 2 million movies being streamed in a month and another 500,000 films being downloaded.

## Losers

Losers:

- are preoccupied with competing for today's customer;
- focus almost exclusively upon physical assets and tangible aspects of quality and performance;
- have a narrow and dated view of what constitutes intellectual capital;
- apply management initiatives to people they employ and within corporate premises;
- limit quality, re-engineering and transformation projects to the company;
- seek to acquire and impose standard management solutions;
- work hard to satisfy the requirements for obtaining certain kite-marks;
- end up with relatively bureaucratic and costly processes for retaining kite-mark registration;
- encourage conformity rather than initiative;
- struggle to make existing operations more effective;
- are laggards when it comes to recognizing and managing intellectual capital.

## Winners

Winners:

- strive to learn, adapt and change more effectively than their competitors and to attract, retain, motivate and develop better people;
- address and endeavour to influence intangibles such as attitudes, behaviour, values and relationships;
- recognize the wide variety of forms in which intellectual property assets can exist;
- extend management initiatives to customers and supply-chain partners;

- work with business partners to apply quality, re-engineering and transformation projects to the whole value chain;
- develop a variety of approaches to meet the needs of different contexts and circumstances;
- work hard to create additional options and extra value for customers;
- employ flexible and cost-effective approaches that remain current and relevant;
- encourage and support entrepreneurship;
- establish new information and knowledge-based ventures;
- are leaders in the creation and exploitation of intellectual capital.

## Think through the implementation requirements

While 'rushing into activity' may be thought to demonstrate commitment, the people of the organization might be more impressed with evidence that implementation requirements have been thought through and there is a degree of programme flexibility:

- Activity is no substitute for thought. Voluminous information does not necessarily lead to better understanding. Processes at a premium are those that achieve output objectives which both add value for customers, and develop the individuals and groups involved.
- A company should determine what it needs to do, and whether it has adequate resources to do what it wants to do, before rushing into change projects. Otherwise, people may work harder to do more effectively activities that they shouldn't be doing in the first place. This is the difference between doing the right thing and doing things right.
- Off-the-shelf solutions and the generalizations of gurus should be taken with a pinch of salt. Each organization needs to formulate, and refine in the light of experience and changes of circumstance, its own approach to change. This will reflect many considerations, such as marketplace factors, leadership style, corporate culture, and the contributions of suppliers and customers.

The commitment to change needs to be sustained if barriers to full implementation are to be identified and overcome. Change may need to be driven through internal organizational barriers. Everyone needs to be involved in the change process.

Innovations can be copied. In a turbulent marketplace continuing vigilance and processes for ongoing adaptation, learning and change are needed. At all stages there should be openness and a willingness to challenge cherished views and existing practices.

# CHECKLIST

▶ Does your company have a business excellence, transformation or entrepreneurship programme?

▶ Is it taking root or running out of steam?

▶ How does the programme relate to the central purpose of your company, and to its vision, goals and values?

▶ Are all the members of the board and the senior management team committed to it?

▶ Who is responsible for the programme?

▶ Is everyone involved?

▶ Is your company's approach tailored to its own particular situation and circumstances?

▶ Is the encouragement and support of new ventures an integral part of your company's management and business processes and practices?

▶ Does the programme embrace other members of the supply chain, whether customers, suppliers or business partners?

▶ Is there a gap between internal and external expectations, and what has been delivered?

▶ How much emphasis is attached to the 'softer' elements of management and entrepreneurship, such as the building of quality relationships?

▶ Is the programme influencing attitudes and behaviour?

▶ Is know-how being created, packaged, protected and exploited?

▶ Is top management behaviour, and are board decisions, consistent with the vision?

▶ Is the output of improvement, change and new venture teams focused upon key customer-related activities?

▶ Is the reward and performance management system supportive of corporate and stakeholder goals?

▶ From time to time does your company reassess its approach to business excellence, transformation and entrepreneurship?

# REFERENCES

Coulson-Thomas, C (1992) *Transforming the Company: Bridging the gap between management myth and corporate reality*, Kogan Page, London

Coulson-Thomas, C (1997 and 1998) *The Future of the Organization: Achieving excellence through business transformation*, Kogan Page, London

Coulson-Thomas, C (1999) *Individuals and Enterprise: Creating entrepreneurs for the new millennium through personal transformation*, Blackhall Publishing, Dublin

Coulson-Thomas, C (2000) *The Information Entrepreneur*, 3Com Active Business Unit, Winnersh

Coulson-Thomas, C (2001) *Shaping Things to Come: Strategies for creating alternative enterprises*, Blackhall Publishing, Dublin

Coulson-Thomas, C and Coulson-Thomas, S (1991) *Quality: The next steps*, an Adaptation Survey for ODI International, Adaptation, London and (Executive Summary) ODI, Wimbledon, London

Kennedy, C and O'Connor, M (1997) *Winning Major Bids: The critical success factors*, Policy Publications, Bedford

Perrin, S (2000) *Managing Intellectual Capital to Grow Shareholder Value*, Policy Publications, Bedford

# FURTHER INFORMATION

Details of Individuals and Enterprise, which contains checklists and exercises for those interested in creating new ventures and more entrepreneurial corporate cultures, and Shaping Things to Come: Strategies for creating alternative enterprises can be obtained from Blackhall Publishing (tel: +353 1278 50 90; fax: +353 1278 44 46; e-mail: blackhall@eircom.net). Details of The Future of the Organization can be obtained from Littlehampton Book Distributors (tel: +44 (0) 1903 828 800; fax: +44 (0) 1903 828 801; e-mail. kpsales@kogan-page.co.uk). These books can also be ordered via www.ntwkfirm.com/bookshop.

# 10

# Understanding the Business Environment

*'Weed growth fouls propellers'*

## THE PHYSICAL DIMENSION

Environmental problems are not new. Early Spanish explorers found the basin of what is now Los Angeles polluted with the smoke of Indian camp fires. What has changed is 'attitudes towards' and 'tolerance of'.

## THE ENVIRONMENT AND THE NETWORK ORGANIZATION

In June 1992 over 100 world leaders, and some 30,000 experts, advisers, advocates, activists and other interested parties assembled in Rio de Janeiro for an Earth Summit concerning the environment. This unprecedented public expression of concern revealed the extent to which the international network organization needed to confront the environment as an issue:

- Attitudes and behaviour concerning the environment were of growing significance for the internal and external relationships between the network and its various members, such as employees, customers, suppliers and business partners; and the different stakeholders in a company.

- Just as at the Earth Summit differences emerged between the approaches and priorities of various groups, so within the network the views of different members may differ. For example, network members from underdeveloped countries may have different views from those from the developed world, and this could introduce an element of strain into relationships.
- The international spread of the network organizations brings it into contact with the regulatory activities of governments, and numerous governmental and non-governmental bodies with interests and activities relating to the environment.

# THE QUESTIONS

The visible attention being devoted to environmental issues raised a number of questions, as follows:

- How much of the concern expressed is deeply rooted, or is likely to prove transitory? How much is empty rhetoric and hype?
- How real are corporate concerns? Are environmental issues assuming greater importance on boardroom agendas, just as in public debates?
- How aware are companies of the likely impacts of environmental issues upon their own activities and operations? What are the implications for different functions in public and private organizations?
- How well thought out are corporate reactions? Have clear goals been set and measurable objectives established?
- Who is, or should be, responsible for environmental policy, and what environmental policies are organizations planning to have?
- What are companies actually doing, and what should they do, to achieve their goals, objectives and policies? Are there gaps between rhetoric and reality? Are they making it happen?

# THE EVIDENCE

To answer these and other questions a *Managing the Relationship with the Environment* survey (Coulson-Thomas and Coulson-Thomas (1990)) was undertaken for the first edition of this book (Coulson-Thomas, 1992). Respondents exhibited high levels of concern, while discriminating between issues:

- Significantly greater importance was attached to the 'external' physical environment rather than to the 'internal' working environment. Some companies appeared to be overlooking internal opportunities directly

to improve working conditions as a result of a new-found, and less tangible, preoccupation with the external environment.
- 'Direct' impacts of organizations' own activities upon the physical environment appeared to rank ahead of the 'indirect' issue of pressures from consumer lobbies. As one manager put it: 'We used to feel hassled by external critics [and] we were very defensive. Now the pressure is internal... we want to do something.'

People can think something is important without being overly concerned about it. There is also the 'groupthink factor' to consider. One US chairman confided: 'No one would dare say global warming is a good thing, but I love it. The garden grows and we save on heating costs.'

## THREATS AND OPPORTUNITIES

The *Managing the Relationship with the Environment* survey (Coulson-Thomas and Coulson-Thomas, 1990) revealed an overwhelming consensus that quality of life was a key issue of the 1990s, that environmental issues should be seen as opportunities rather than problems, and that all organizations should have an environmental policy. If companies translated environmental rhetoric into operational action, suppliers that did not satisfy the environmental criteria being established by their customers faced the prospect of going out of business.

In the arena of environmental concerns, the large corporation can appear remarkably vulnerable. If a company is to respond to threats and seize opportunities, it needs to monitor environmental issues in the business environment, think through their implications, and determine appropriate responses. One chairman pointed out: 'Once an environmental issue passes to the business decision maker it tends to become general. We are in danger of becoming so general and unfocused that I cannot see any practical or workable solutions emerging.'

The National Westminster and other banks examine the environmental policies and achievements of business customers prior to making loans. Loan applicants have been asked to undertake an environmental audit in order to provide the information needed to make a decision for or against providing financial support.

The more open network organization might view a challenge as an opportunity to enter into a new form of relationship. The macro problem can also be a macro opportunity. For example, additional regulatory controls on manufacturers represent new opportunities for suppliers of components and materials that allow the new requirements to be satisfied. One managing director was emphatic: 'There are things we have to do... the regulators will see to it. The fastest with the solution will get the business. We're not interested in how wonderful the products are, [we] just want it fixed.'

Speed and flexibility of response may be needed to react to sudden changes in consumer sensitivity to environmental issues. A change in the general climate of opinion which results in the independent decisions of thousands of consumers not to buy aerosols with CFCs, or goods with excessive packaging, can have a devastating impact upon the company which is unprepared. If a company is to secure commercial benefit from environmental concern, it needs to be aware of the environmental issues, and priorities of actual and potential customers. As one director pointed out: 'Why should the environment be any different or any more difficult? The technologies we use every day are complex enough. It's a question of listening, learning and flexible response'.

Discussions about whether the United States should sign the Kyoto treaty on climate change and the implications for companies of its adoption by other countries has ensured that environmental issues remain on the corporate agenda. Ten years on there is still a diversity of views and practice:

- Increasingly companies seek direct contact with customers in their social environment in order to shape their experiences and build brand associations. Thus Lever Fabergé has sponsored an annual dance music event and set up a chain of barbershops under its Lynx brand.
- Not all companies want their operations to blend into the natural environment. Premises of the Big Yellow Self Storage Company sited close to main roads are painted bright yellow to stand out. Customers can access storage units throughout the 24-hour day and coffee machines, modems, fax lines and insurance services are available.
- Many companies find that recycling waste saves disposal costs and can provide a cheaper supply of materials than an original source. USG, a manufacturer of wallboards, buys gypsum from operators of coal-fired power stations under pressure to reduce sulphur-dioxide omissions. The price of gypsum produced as a by-product of chimney spraying is less than half of that obtained from a quarry.
- Making products that do not become quickly outdated with interchangeable parts that can be easily taken apart and replaced may allow them to be recycled. Remanufacturing has expanded steadily since the Ford Motor Company started rebuilding car engines in the 1930s. Xerox has sold reconditioned copiers for many years. A Kodak single-use camera may be recycled up to ten times after the initial film has been developed.

Positive and negative issues need to be continuously managed. If left unchecked, even minority interests can grow like weeds in a waterway and block navigation. Proactive approaches can generate considerable goodwill. BP-Amoco acknowledged the risks of global warming ahead of other oil companies and announced its intention of securing specific reductions in carbon dioxide emissions over a defined period.

# UNDERSTANDING THE BUSINESS ENVIRONMENT AND CONTEXT

Environmental changes affect us in different ways. Global warming means lower heating bills for some and inundation from rising sea levels for others. Future predictions are fraught with difficulty. Forests are being cut down for agricultural purposes, while higher rainfall, raised carbon dioxide levels and increased temperatures should encourage vegetation growth. At some point one effect might be counterbalanced by the other, just as companies like Xerox that have examined recycling options have found the impact of some remedial actions can create more problems than they solve.

Losers are often unaware of impending challenges and pressing requirements to change. They simply do not see them. They tend to be largely oblivious to developments in the marketplaces in which they operate. They also do not anticipate or look ahead, and they are not alert to threats and opportunities. Hence, when they do wake up to what is at stake, they may have little time in which to adapt even if they had the will and means of doing so.

Losers just hunker down. They make cosmetic references to environmental and social concerns in annual reports and accounts. They stick to what they know and feel comfortable with and plough ahead regardless, hoping that any problems they encounter will blow over. If they do stop and take stock of where they are, it is generally infrequently. Whatever changes are made tend quickly to become permanent features.

Opportunities can also be resisted if responding to them would require changed practices and behaviour. New requirements may be perceived as distractions until such time as they become so pressing and potentially lucrative that they can no longer be avoided. Some only act when legislators or competitive activity requires them to do so.

In contrast, winners have more acute and sensitive antennae. They look out for the weeds that can foul propellers. They are aware of what is happening around them and in the business context. They are also entrepreneurial. They view problems as arenas of potential opportunity (Coulson-Thomas, 1999) and take the initiative in shaping the future (Coulson-Thomas, 2001).

Winners identify and monitor economic, political and technological trends, and assess their likely impact both upon themselves and upon their customers. They then consider what, if anything, they should do in response. Such exercises are undertaken on a regular basis, and at least once a year. Resulting actions are subsequently reviewed and if need be challenged and amended as events unfold.

Because they read the road ahead, winners generally give themselves sufficient time to register, react and adapt. Changes are made quickly as and when they are needed. They are often implemented before they are imposed or otherwise formally required.

People in winning companies address problems rather than conceal, ignore or avoid them. Hence, problems do not build up to the point where they are either insurmountable or appear to be so. Steps are taken one at a time. A series of adjustments over time – some small, others more fundamental – may allow winners to cope with radically altered circumstances.

# ENVIRONMENTAL SCHIZOPHRENIA

People do not necessarily want to implement all aspects of corporate policies, just as there are laws which are not always enforced. They look good on the books. They may be fine, but 'not for us, here and now'. Many senior executives still appear to be schizophrenic in relation to many issues. For example:

- As citizens they may be generally concerned about what they perceive as major threats to the world environment. They may be aware of the damage done by their own industry, and of the extent to which pollution can transcend national borders to become a global problem.
- However, as managers, their responsibilities may be limited to a particular operation within one country. While the external impact of any action they might take may be uncertain, and the benefits diffuse and shared, the internal costs can be real and particular to the individual company.

The existence of schizophrenia makes it difficult for some boards and management teams to portray a united front that is positively committed to the achievement of carefully thought-out and clearly-defined objectives. There are also some dangers in driving a common approach to particular issues throughout an international corporate organization to the extent that local differences are overlooked. Attitudes and governmental policies on an individual issue can vary greatly between countries.

In general, some companies appear to be in favour of commercial activities that are consistent with sustainable development, but opposed to specific regulatory measures, or the imposition of an implementation timetable. The extent to which appropriate responses can be left to the free interplay of market forces will depend upon whether a critical mass of companies are able to translate aspiration into achievement.

To respond to particular public proposals, a company needs to identify its own 'hot spots', and assess the impacts of proposed measures upon its operations and activities. Likely obstacles and barriers to implementation should be identified and examined. The preference of many legislators and regulators for 'workable solutions' means that corporate factors can sometimes be taken account of in the drafting of regulations, if they are notified early enough.

In the background lurks the prospect of public intervention. Within the market environment, individual companies that are genuinely concerned about environmental and social issues can respond quickly and flexibly, tailoring their policies and actions to their particular situation. In comparison, action by government can be tardy, cumbersome and indiscriminate.

More convincing corporate performance could enable governments to establish broader frameworks, supplemented by specific action only where it is needed. Rather than be subjected to detailed regulation and intervention across the board, companies would be left to respond to the changing needs of their environmentally and socially aware customers. Progress towards the flexible network organization can result in the framework and attitudes that are likely to increase the prospects of corporate success.

## Losers

Losers:

- are attracted by panaceas and simple solutions;
- desire the speedy resolution of issues and tend to adopt the first acceptable solution;
- consider environmental and social concerns as a threat;
- endeavour to 'pass the buck' and avoid responsibility;
- keep a low profile, avoid publicity and limit discussion of environmental issues and related communications to the boardroom;
- react to external pressures and work in isolation to protect their internal and corporate interests;
- develop cosmetic responses and resort to spin in difficult situations;
- behave in a defensive way when challenged by politicians and the media.

## Winners

Winners:

- are aware of the complexity of certain issues and endeavour to address root causes by whatever combinations of measures are appropriate;
- endeavour to understand the situation and explore options before selecting a course of action that is likely to stand the test of time;

- regard responding to environmental threats and social concerns as a major business opportunity;
- assume responsibility for making a positive contribution to the environment;
- involve others in planning, communicating and implementing positive strategies;
- are proactive and work with collaborating partners to further their customers' interests;
- develop new and alternative approaches that generate goodwill and incremental income streams;
- work with politicians and the media to achieve both corporate and social objectives.

# THE LURE OF THE SIMPLE

The action team, competing on speed, and focusing upon the 'vital few' priorities, loves simplicity. Objectives that are complicated and inter-related may be difficult to express as a few bullets points on a slide. Yet, many environmental and social issues are comparatively complex. Rapid progress may be difficult to measure in terms of quantifiable outputs.

The following views are typical of others which suggest that, in common with quality and general transformation initiatives, a 'wall' or 'hump' is often reached with the onset of the realization that the issue may be more complex than was first thought:

*The initial enthusiasm turned to disinterest when we became aware of some of the practical problems. Recycling can actually be more damaging environmentally than disposal. Do you react to today's clamour, or tomorrow's realization?*

*We were looking for something to report on in the next annual report. There are initiatives to demonstrate concern that we could publicize. But as for results, you can't change an industrial process overnight. We don't want to be accused of staging stunts.*

*I'm being pressured for results, but we are only a link in the chain. The public associates us strongly with the product, but the real environmental damage is done upstream. It takes time to build the relationships to tackle the problem, and when other companies are involved that's not something I can do at my level.*

In order to ensure that the complexity of what needs to be done is fully understood, a company should identify both the cross-functional and inter-organizational processes that deliver the company's negative environmental impacts, and those which will be needed to achieve significant improvements.

## THE DRIVE FOR SPEED

The 'time culture' can impose unrealistic deadlines upon those who are charged with the responsibility for delivering improvements. When a supply chain is involved, the single company may be no more able to achieve a tangible impact upon the external environment than it can deliver all the value that is sought by a final customer. When others are involved, there is likely to be bargaining and negotiation.

Environmental initiatives should not result in the pressure for speed or 'response' driving out the long-term thinking that is required. Assuming 'results' are required, these might best be achieved as a result of flexibility within the framework of a longer-term relationship.

Today's craze can be tomorrow's memory. Too many managers assume that trends will continue longer than subsequently turns out to be the case. With many environmental and social policies taking many years to have a significant impact, companies face a dilemma similar to that encountered by those seeking to change attitudes and behaviour. By the time the outcomes initially sought have been achieved, the requirement may have changed. Will there be a backlash when people count the costs? Will they become bored? Will certain lobbies go the way of the skateboard and the Rubik's cube as people become more aware of the lack of achievement in relation to fundamental problems?

Attempts to deal with 'isms' can open a Pandora's box of dashed hopes and unfulfilled expectations, especially when initiatives are not thought through. Enough noise may be raised to alarm some, while not enough is done to appease or deliver to others. Companies should beware of cosmetic programmes.

Winners assemble a comprehensive, complementary and co-ordinated set of initiatives, embracing all the parties involved, that are likely to have a significant impact upon an environmental or social issue. They achieve significant changes of attitude or behaviour, because all the various change elements that are necessary have been put in place.

# CHECKLIST

▶ Does your company monitor quality of life and environmental and social issues in the business environment continuously?

▶ Does it have a quality of life or environmental vision, and related goals and values?

▶ Has the vision been communicated and shared?

▶ Is your company aware of the views of customers, employees, suppliers, business partners and other 'stakeholders' on key quality of life and environmental and social issues?

▶ Has your company carried out any form of SWOT analysis to examine strengths, weaknesses, opportunities and threats?

▶ Has it determined how these will impact upon its operations and activities?

▶ What does your company plan to do in response?

▶ Have clear and measurable objectives been derived from the quality of life or environmental and social vision, goals and values, and is there an agreed strategy for their implementation?

▶ Are there clear quality of life or environmental and social roles and responsibilities?

▶ Have 'vital few' priorities been established, and have likely barriers and obstacles been identified?

▶ Have people been equipped and empowered to take the necessary actions?

▶ Are they motivated to respond and deliver?

▶ Have the cross-functional processes and the inter-departmental linkages necessary to deliver appropriate corporate responses been identified?

# REFERENCES

Coulson-Thomas, C (1992) *Transforming the Company: Bridging the gap between management myth and corporate reality*, Kogan Page, London

Coulson-Thomas, C (1999) *Individuals and Enterprise: Creating entrepreneurs for the new millennium through personal transformation*, Blackhall Publishing, Dublin

Coulson-Thomas, C (2001) *Shaping Things to Come: Strategies for creating alternative enterprises*, Blackhall Publishing, Dublin

Coulson-Thomas, C and Coulson-Thomas, S (1990) *Managing the Relationship with the Environment*, a survey sponsored by Rank Xerox (UK) Ltd, Adaptation Ltd, London

## FURTHER INFORMATION

Details of *Individuals and Enterprise*, which contains checklists and exercises for those interested in creating new ventures and more entrepreneurial corporate cultures, and *Shaping Things to Come: Strategies for creating alternative enterprises* can be obtained from Blackhall Publishing (tel: +353 1278 50 90; fax: +353 1278 44 46; e-mail: blackhall@eircom.net). Details of *The Future of the Organization* can be obtained from Littlehampton Book Distributors (tel: +44 (0) 1903 828 800; fax: +44 (0) 1903 828 801; e-mail: kpsales@kogan-page.co.uk). These books can also be ordered via www.ntwkfirm.com/bookshop.

# 11

# Operating in the International Marketplace

*'On the bank the swan is vulnerable'*

## THE OPPORTUNITY

International opportunities abound for the network organization with a global ambition. Companies have widened their perspectives to encompass the globe. The spread of privatization, and the impact of a general slowdown in growth and particular national economic recessions presents the acquisitive with a flow of new opportunities, while barriers continue to fall as a result of deregulation and market forces. The global integration of manufacturing and other activities within international companies means that 'internal' trade within international network organizations accounts for a significant proportion of cross-border trade.

## THE GLOBAL PERSPECTIVE

People are developing a global perspective. Thinking global is the first step towards acting global. All over the world, attitudes and perceptions are being influenced by the pervasiveness of certain media. While a younger generation may share a similar taste in popular music via MTV, their professional and executive parents may turn to Cable News Network (CNN). People all over the world could share the same images of unfolding events in New York and Washington on 11 September 2001 through global news networks.

Scratch what is perceived as a national institution, and an international organization may be found underneath. For example, the Compagnie de Saint-Gobain may appear to be quintessentially French. It was established on the initiative of Louis XIV in an age of mirrors and chandeliers, when glass-making was regarded as a strategic industry. Yet two-thirds of the company's 100,000 employees are non-French.

## THE CHALLENGE

While the opportunities are alluring, internationalization is also bringing companies into contact with new areas of challenge, risk and uncertainty. Here are some examples:

- Wars, disorders, revolutions, disasters and crises are a distressingly frequent feature of the international business environment. From a global perspective, they are no longer 'somewhere else', and as one director put it: 'When they happen they are big. They affect us'.
- There are various states, and a variety of governmental and non-governmental organizations to contend with. Companies in the international arena cannot assume that 'the institutions' are 'on their side', or even on their wavelength.
- There are forces of both regionalization and fragmentation at work. While western Europe attempted to unite, eastern Europe disintegrated into nationalism.
- In addition to customer and supplier risks, there are cultural and currency risks. New arenas of confrontation can arise for those unable to cope with a greater diversity of interests and perspectives.
- A network of cross-border links and relationships may need to be formed in order to meet the needs of global customers and markets. Communication within the network has to overcome barriers of distance, culture and time.
- The globalization of the marketplace has given rise to a growing requirement for the internationalization of management, and the capacity to access and harness relevant skill, regardless of location and nationality.

To operate effectively in the international business environment, a company needs to be open and receptive. There are relevant political, economic, social, technological and market developments at national, regional (eg EC) and international levels, to be monitored. Without the nourishment that comes from awareness, openness and external relationships, the closed corporation finds it difficult to develop the capability to respond appropriately.

Information on national and market differences needs to be up to date. As with customers, it is important to listen to people on the ground. Learning is a necessity, not a luxury.

Dealing with foreign governments, as well as overseas customers, may be a new experience for some companies. The multinational company (MNC), at both the local and the strategic level, may have to reconcile the competing demands of responding to global competitive threats and opportunities, and 'host' government and stakeholder requirements.

## THE GAP BETWEEN ASPIRATION AND ACHIEVEMENT

A decade ago research undertaken for Surrey European Management School (SEMS) (Coulson-Thomas, 1990), and my book, *Creating the Global Company* (Coulson-Thomas, 1992) revealed that for many companies 'internationalization' remained an elusive goal. For some, reality extended no further than the paragraphs in the annual report which referred to international ambitions. A typical view was: 'Internationalization sounds nice, but what does it actually mean?'.

At all levels, there appeared to be problems in internationalizing the people of those companies with international visions and ambitions. To take some examples:

- The membership of the main boards of most companies was made up exclusively of directors having the nationality of the 'home country'.
- Efforts to build a more balanced international management team were frustrated by the fact that managers of different countries varied greatly in the extent to which they were prepared to be mobile.

Too often, groups of people of a particular nationality were locked into territorial and departmental ghettos. The bureaucratic limits that have been placed upon their ambitions and prospects make them slaves rather than citizens of the MNC.

## THE ROOTS OF FRUSTRATION

The internationalization of management teams was more talked about than practised. Intention was not being translated into achievement for a variety of reasons, as follows:

- Many organizations were not thinking through what internationalization means for them. In some sectors, such as shipbuilding, it may be possible to generate a high proportion of overseas turnover, while employing few foreign nationals. In services industries the reverse may be the case.

- While there are surface manifestations of internationalism, such as international travel and the ability to speak foreign languages, few managers appeared to have developed an international perspective.
- While articulating the need for international managers, many companies did little to develop and retain their local managers, who were being lured away by local competitors.
- At a time when some companies were seeking to develop a cadre of mobile international managers, a growing proportion of their managers appeared to be reluctant to move abroad. The 'dual-career' family, and the desire to allow children to complete their education without interruption, become location anchors.
- Few people were being equipped with international project management skills or to work in international teams. People need to be aware of the impact of their own culture and those of colleagues upon attitudes and behaviour within a multicultural group.
- Activities were rooted territorially, rather than spread around the network. Thus, many companies talked internationalization while retaining all the key decision-making capacity and core activities such as R & D in the 'home' country.

A decade ago internationalization and globalization were critical issues for many large companies (Coulson-Thomas, 1990). In a world of network operation, the Internet and e-business, any business – even a one-person operation – can be quickly accessible from almost any location. It is increasingly difficult to avoid international operation. Columbia and other business schools have discontinued separate MBA programme modules in favour of an appropriate international element in all courses.

National economies appear ever more interdependent. A slowdown in the United States makes it more difficult for other countries to achieve greater growth. Pain as well as gain is quickly spread. When major corporations experience a shortfall of expected orders or start to make losses, job cuts may occur throughout the world. Daimler-Chrysler's plan envisaged shedding 20 per cent of the global workforce, by any standards a substantial reduction.

# ADDRESSING REALITY

Because some markets are becoming global, it does not follow that all are. Assumption should never be allowed to take the place of observation. Every company needs to think through what internationalization means for its own activities and prospects. Honda came unstuck with its vision of the global car. For a period, the lure of the economies of scale of global production blinded the company to the realities of local market differences and a desire for customization.

There is much misunderstanding concerning the requirements for, and indicators of, successful internationalization. Big companies like Siemens are not necessarily the most international in terms of the geographical distribution of their activities, while in some sectors it is possible to develop a significant international business while employing relatively few people abroad.

Even when a company's employees are 'spread around the globe', it does not follow that more than a small minority of them may have an international perspective. As one interviewee pointed out: 'Having offices around the world does not make you international. Most of our people are imprisoned in national operating companies. We can't use them to satisfy a customer anywhere else'.

Success formulae in one context may need to be adapted to work in another. Wal-Mart has not found it easy to replicate its US retailing performance in overseas markets like Germany and the United Kingdom. Ultimately it hopes its purchasing power and dedication to cost reduction will allow it to undercut local rivals sufficiently to attract their customers.

Concerns in one part of the world have implications elsewhere. In Europe there has been a reaction against the accelerating pace of modern life. Activists are calling for slower work and 'slow food' to reduce tension and the incidence of burnout. Municipalities are declaring themselves 'slow cities'. Fast food chains such as Burger King and Kentucky Fried Chicken may find it difficult to sustain their rate of growth if eating patterns change.

# NATIONALITY AND THE NETWORK ORGANIZATION

In many companies, few managers are being equipped to build working relationships with network partners.

There are areas of the world in which the transition from bureaucratic to network organization may be seen as a move 'with the grain'. In parts of Asia the issuing of commands in the hierarchical organization represented an unfamiliar and 'western' form of behaviour for many new MNC recruits. These people may instantly empathize with the network approach, and breathe passion and life into it. Outsiders can suddenly become insiders.

When multinational groups are formed, or people are introduced into international teams, account should be taken of distinct national approaches. For example:

- A German may be inclined to be more formal, and such formality should not be mistaken for a lack of 'team spirit' or commitment to the group.

- Whereas a Japanese manager may feel bound to observe a consensus outcome because of the 'legitimacy of the process', a French colleague may not feel obligated to implement a decision with which he or she personally disagrees.

Within the network organization the attitudes of certain members or partners may reflect national characteristics:

- A US or UK company may pursue short-term self-interest. Equity ownership by institutions that compare and trade stocks according to changes in relative performance may encourage such behaviour.
- In contrast, much of the equity of a Japanese company may be held by other companies with which it trades, or by supply chain partners. The Japanese company could well be a loyal member of a network, and may exhibit concern for the good of the network as a whole.

## INTERNATIONAL AWARENESS

Winners recognize that true internationalization is of attitude, awareness, approach and perspective. It is evidenced by openness, tolerance and active encouragement of cultural and national diversity. For many years Asea Brown Boveri, British Gas, The Netherlands company DSM, ICL and Nissan have all recognized the need for managers to have an international awareness and perspective.

According to one director: 'You don't have to fill airport lounges to be international, or train everyone in foreign languages. That may enrich their lives. You probably do need to broaden their perspective, and to focus them on understanding... customers wherever they may be.' Mobility and travel *per se* may reinforce prejudices, and build bigots.

People can be internationalized in many ways, from visits, exchanges, job swaps to joining international project groups, task forces and teams. Moving roles around the organization and managers through various international projects and teams helps to build a multiple perspective. Opportunities to come together across traditional divides expose many individuals to a diversity of viewpoints.

Companies that have thought it through use a combination of approaches, rather than the 'single solution'. Internationalization is also integrated into mainstream processes, rather than regarded as a 'bolt-on for those who need it'.

## MOBILITY AND INTERNATIONALIZATION

Losers use measures such as trips of staff abroad. Mobility may, or may not, be an indicator of internationalization, according to its purpose. The appearance of internationalization in the form of the jet-setting executive could conceal the reality of a lack of localization. More local involvement, not to mention computer- and video-conferencing, might obviate the need for so much travel. The acid test should be the extent to which customer requirements are met.

The flexibility of the network organization can allow major corporations to create internal labour and information markets to overcome the imperfections of external markets. The network can grow or contract organically, according to market opportunities and economic circumstances, without the dramas of starting up or closing local operations associated with the bureaucratic form of organization.

Mobility has its costs. For example, after an initial 'honeymoon period', an adverse reaction may set in, with 'the vision of mountains, sea and sand being replaced by the reality of crime, disease and telephones that do not work (Coulson-Thomas, 1992). Mobility can be expensive, and may create tensions between expatriates and local managers. On the other hand, staff travelling overseas may obtain opportunities to work with and learn from customers.

Mobility is widely perceived as a means of equipping managers with an international perspective. In reality, it may provide them with some insight into particular countries and cultures, without developing a broader international awareness. Ford has taken the view than an international perspective should precede the assumption of international responsibilities, rather than be left to arise as a consequence of them.

The qualities being developed by many companies appear not to be specifically related to internationalization. One human resource director explained: 'We have not really thought through what becoming an international company means. … We go for the obvious qualities that are always valuable. … But [with internationalization] we are back to changing attitudes… and also preferences in terms of who you work with. … It's not easy to do.'

## THE GOAL OF THE NETWORK ORGANIZATION

Over time, as the volume of 'overseas', 'foreign' or 'international' business grew, companies used to evolve through a series of identifiable stages (Coulson-Thomas, 1992). Initially, foreign orders were treated as exceptions. Then, as more of them were received, an export department was set up. This might grow into an international division, as arrangements for various 'territories' have to be established and managed.

In time, the establishment of local operating companies could be justified, and the multinational company came into existence. This could evolve into a complex, if not confused, matrix of internal functional and geographic reporting relationships. The final stage in the process of evolution was to move from multinational matrix to international network.

In the knowledge society, e-business, modern telecoms and the Internet allow companies to go straight to the network organization that is particularly suited to internationalization:

- The resources of traditional multinational companies were imprisoned in the 'mini bureaucracies' of self-contained national operating companies.
- The global network offers the prospect of being able to overcome the barriers of nationality, distance and time in order to bring together teams composed of the best people in order to address the needs of individual customers, wherever they may be.

As one chairman put it: 'The international network organization must be the end point of corporate transformation.' For many years NCR, Procter and Gamble and Unilever have operated as transnationals. International headquarters functions, relating to significant areas of the business, are located outside of the country of ultimate incorporation. Global responsibilities may be spread between a network of locations in different countries, rather than concentrated at a single point.

## THE NETWORK SOLUTION

We have seen that the company has become a network, as 'electronic' links are developed with customers, suppliers and business partners. Experts and specialists become facilitators, harnessing relevant expertise by all available means in such a way that it can be applied to add value for customers. As networks become global, effort is put into articulating or propounding a distinct and compelling mission that can transcend national boundaries.

Whether the customer is becoming European or international, or both European and international, a company intent on supplying its requirements will need to find a means of communicating rapidly across national boundaries. The network organization must itself become European and international.

The corporate network should be sufficiently flexible to allow resources to be accessed and activity undertaken at local, regional or global level according to requirements and comparative advantage. The aim of management should be to minimize the costs of co-ordination or barriers to communication and interaction that might otherwise distort the location or focus of activity.

## UNDERSTANDING THE PROCUREMENT PROCESS

A challenge and opportunity for many companies is the internationalization and centralization of purchasing (Coulson-Thomas, 1992). During sales activities 'losers' focus upon themselves and their internal requirements. They endeavour to impress selection panels with the scale of their operations, their customer base and product range, and generally emphasize how good they are. During negotiations they concentrate almost exclusively on their own corporate objectives.

Losers can be insensitive to their audiences. In particular, many people who operate in business-to-business markets should devote much more effort to understanding the procurement processes of their prospects. For example, who is involved in what roles when purchase decisions are made? What are their concerns, priorities and hot buttons.

Winners endeavour to understand the purchasing arrangements of customers and prospects so that they can address their selection criteria and any known concerns. They endeavour to make procurement decisions as easy as possible for buyers (FitzGerald, 2000).

There are many ways of simplifying procedures and reducing the complexity and cost of procurement. Prospects can fill in templates and place orders online. Configuration or design tools might allow them to assess alternatives when formulating their requirements. Software upgrades can be delivered over the Internet. Online progress chasing, automatic reordering and budgetary control facilities can all be provided.

Different people could be involved, and discrete considerations might apply, at each stage of a complex procurement process. Knowing the personalities and interests of key players enables them to be taken into account at preliminary meetings, in formal proposals and during presentations and subsequent negotiations. Winners structure their documentation and pitches around the priority requirements of prospective customers and whatever significant influencing factors and decision criteria they identify.

Proposals and presentations should be easy to assimilate and assess from a 'user perspective'. Too often, losers bury their key points within a sea of text, and devote far too much attention to their own track record. Conversely, too little emphasis is given to the contribution of what is offered to achieving the prospect's objectives. If they feel insecure, they fudge or try to avoid sensitive issues and difficult questions.

Winners allocate available space and time according to the requirements of the recipients and audiences they are seeking to build a relationship with. Some use storyboarding to help to ensure a better balance of content, and executive and section summaries to help prevent important messages from being lost. Visual images can also be used to break up intimidating blocks of text and communicate complex messages.

Winners come clean. They aim at clarity and transparency. If they have the choice, they select venues for meetings that give them the edge. Like swans taking to the water when their position is vulnerable, they endeavour to operate at locations and in ways that play to their strengths.

# CUSTOMERS – THE PURPOSE OF INTERNATIONALIZATION

Customers should determine the nature of the 'international' responses that are required. For example, as MNCs increasingly demand 'European' and 'international' solutions to regional or global problems, so their suppliers are having to establish European and international project groups, teams and task forces in order to respond. The teams that result are likely to be increasingly multifunctional, multilocation and multinational. Team members will need to be able to work with those of other cultures and nationalities.

Prior to establishing a mission, objectives, strategy, organization and management processes, a basic question needs to be asked – who is the customer? Can the customer be defined and understood in terms of attitudes and values, location, age, sex, nationality or other attributes?

Values and lifestyle preferences have become more significant in customer categorization. Organizations increasingly define themselves in terms of their customers. The interaction of supplier and customer may help to shape the attitudes and values of each, according to the depth of the relationship.

# MATCHING CORPORATE AND CUSTOMER CULTURE

A conscious effort should be made to match international corporate and customer cultures (Figure 11.1). Here are two examples:

- Where both corporate and customer culture is differentiated, diversity should result as efforts are made to tailor and match at the local level. When both are undifferentiated, a common global approach can be adopted. A matching of cultures allows the company to build upon its strengths.
- When corporate and customer culture do not match, help may be needed to achieve cultural adaptation. Where customer culture is differentiated, while that of the company is undifferentiated, local partners may be needed to tailor locally. When the customer culture is undifferentiated, while that of the company is differentiated, help may be needed to build global brand image and awareness.

The long-term customer could be a more significant 'network member' than the peripheral or marginal employee. Some network companies list their major customers and collaborators alongside or, in some cases,

**International Corporate Culture**

|  | Differentiated | Undifferentiated/ Common |
|---|---|---|
| **International Customer Culture** — Differentiated | Encourage diversity, tailoring and matching at the local level<br><br>[Build on 'strength'] | Build links with local partners able to tailor locally<br><br>[Need help] |
| **International Customer Culture** — Undifferentiated/ Common | Build global awareness/brand through use of international agencies<br><br>[Need help] | Encourage common global approach<br><br>[Build on 'strength'] |

**Figure 11.1** Matching corporate and customer culture

instead of their key employees in their profiles, brochures and annual reports. The portfolio of customers represents the essence, purpose and drive of the flexible network organization.

In a global, and increasingly interdependent, marketplace, a company should view the world in terms of concentrations of actual and potential customers. These may or may not match state borders. In different locations, there will be cores of greatest opportunity surrounded by concentric rings of prioritized prospects.

Suppliers and customers should work together to meet customer requirements (Bartram, 1996). Joint teams could be set up with agreed objectives. The 'sale' may become a project to be managed. Awareness is growing of the margin and profitability benefits of emphasizing higher added-value considerations and breaking out of the 'commodity products trap'. In some sectors, this can involve working with customers to develop their understanding of what can be achieved and enhance their expectations.

International networks of alliances, consortia, cooperative ventures and other arrangements have been forged as companies have come together in various forms of cooperative activity to cope with the scale of international challenges and opportunities. Many companies have still not adequately addressed the need for network venture and relationship management skills. As one director put it: 'We are back to throwing people in at the deep end, and there are more drownings than there should be.'

# NAÏVE EXPECTATIONS

Many 'loser' companies have not thought through the consequences of their drive for internationalization. Table 11.1 sets out selected enablers of the transition from multinational to international network organization. The attitudes that help the transition are those associated with the open and organic network, while the 'hinders' are likely to be the closed attitudes and debilitating prejudices associated with the self-contained, bureaucratic form of organization.

Each form of organization presents its own management problems, as follows:

- The transition from multinational to international network organization may result in the potential for controllable travel costs being replaced by the reality of uncontrollable telecommunications costs.
- Along with an enhanced capability, may come a greater vulnerability to sabotage or commercial espionage on a global scale.
- Interface, funding and management problems may follow in the wake of technologies that are developed more rapidly than they can be applied.

**Table 11.1**   The transition from multinational to international network organization

| | |
|---|---|
| Encourage international networking and cross-border all channel communication | Involve international participation in planning and issue monitoring, and management exercises |
| Create opportunities for informal international contact | Encourage shared and joint use of resources and facilities on a regional or international basis |
| Recruit to secure most relevant skills on an international basis | Build interfaces between national IT networks, and develop a global computing and telecommunications network |
| Replace national procedures with international project groups, task forces and teams | Encourage organic growth and the shift of power and resources away from historic centres of bureaucratic influence and strength, and to areas of greatest customer opportunity |
| Strengthen functional, business and sector units, and customer account groups, at the expense of national geographic units | |
| Create mutual respect for, and build understanding of, cultural differences and variety | |

*Source*: Coulson-Thomas (1992)

- Insufficient thought may be given to the behavioural aspects. An interviewee commented: 'Just assume that... behavioural problems will be there.'
- It may not be easy to establish a basis for allocating the cost of the network between its various members. Inevitably, costs will be compared with the benefits.

The people in the spotlight may be the gung-ho managers who are rushing about the world, signing up international joint ventures and arrangements. Those whose commitment to internationalization appears to be in doubt may actually be the cooler heads, addressing such questions as: 'Who is going to manage this?' or 'What about the infrastructure requirements?'

One director of business development raised a telling point: 'How many of these [arrangements] can we handle without confusing the customers, ourselves and just about everyone else?' Some companies ought to pose the question: 'What would we look like if it all actually happened?' Again, one encounters the phenomenon of companies being saved from chaos by their own inability to implement.

## JOINT VENTURE MANAGEMENT

The winner has every reason to be cautious as well as ambitious. A high proportion of joint ventures fail. While strategists assess the relative merits of different options for arrangements and joint ventures, their management colleagues 'bite their nails':

- Those in human resources worry about where the people will come from to run a joint venture, when few, if any, existing managers may have had experience of operating within a joint venture framework.
- The marketing team may worry about whether proposed 'partners' share assumptions, and have a similar understanding regarding customer attitudes, values and motivations. Will there be empathy between a prospective 'partner' and existing customers?
- The engineers will be concerned about the extent to which there could be a mismatch between the technologies of partner organizations. Their IT colleagues may have similar concerns about the compatibility of systems where IT may have been acquired from different suppliers, and 'the boxes may not talk to each other'.
- A range of people from general managers to corporate communicators may face the challenge of accommodating and sharing visions, values, goals and objectives that have derived from different cultural contexts with those of further nationalities and cultures.

The gap between aspiration and reality could be the result of external political factors rather than commercial logic. Arrangement negotiations may be stopped or reviewed as a result of national political considerations. Awareness and sensitivity can be especially important in the international dimension.

Too many advocates of 'relationship management' appear to believe in the inherent 'goodness' of relationships, independently of degree of commitment or shared vision and values. In a significant proportion of joint ventures, one party 'rips off' the other.

Traditionally, if anything is retained in the host country it is research and development. Companies and nations jealously guard their intellectual capital. Yet international cooperation in research and development can yield benefits and result in partnership relationships.

Partners should be chosen with care. One director warned: 'You need to keep your wits about you.' In view of the relatively high number of strategic alliances and joint ventures that fail, a more flexible approach is to establish links and relationships on a project-by-project basis.

# CORPORATE TRANSFORMATION – THE BENEFITS

Shared goals, common values, a distinct corporate culture and pervasive tools, techniques and approaches can help to hold an international network together. There are operational advantages. For example:

- Those who are internationally mobile, or who work with others across national borders, may 'know what to expect' when they join a new group or team, and find it easier to become integrated.
- Similarly, mobile customers, or those in segments that transcend national borders, or who buy at the regional (eg European) or international level, may be able to develop certain consistent expectations as to the standards of quality they may receive at various locations.
- The creation of a distinct and international corporate culture makes it easier for people to come together in *ad hoc* groups and teams. They will have certain expectations concerning the way colleagues think and the tools, techniques and approaches they are likely to adopt to tackle problems.

At the same time, there needs to be a degree of local flexibility. Different elements of a business should be allowed to organize and operate in a way that is most appropriate in terms of their own situation and circumstances.

# CORPORATE TRANSFORMATION –
# THE DANGERS

Corporate transformation can cut across internationalization. When international initiatives cascade or spread one or more change programmes throughout a corporate organization, problems can arise:

- Exposing corporate initiatives to those from a different national and cultural background sometimes reveals the extent to which they are 'culture bound'. The universal panacea may turn out to be very much the product of a 'home country' or 'head office' culture, and unintended consequences can arise at the local level.
- The imposition of norms and standards may be in conflict with the desire to build greater tolerance for cultural diversity. The international organization may wish to accommodate a mixture of cultures in order that some do not feel excluded, and all are encouraged to give of their best.
- An international company may need to establish working relations with many governments and interests. This requires the flexibility to respond to a range of industrial policies, quite different approaches to the regulation of business, and attitudes to what are perceived as non-national companies that vary from the inviting to the paranoiac.

Multicultural awareness should not be sacrificed upon an altar of monolithic corporate culture. Closer 'positive sum' relationships with 'international' customers require effective cross-cultural communication. International segmentation, prioritization and differentiation require an understanding of the relevance and significance of similarities and differences across national boundaries.

# INTERNATIONAL EMPOWERMENT

An important element of a corporate transformation programme may encounter unexpected problems when applied internationally. Consider, for example, empowerment:

- An empowerment strategy may present particular difficulties for the company that has traditionally been reluctant to devolve management discretion to the locally recruited and foreign employees who run overseas subsidiaries. These may be little more than distribution outlets, with the key decisions regarding what is sold, and at what price, being taken many thousands of miles away at a head office.

- The company that is relatively self-contained at home may have local joint venture partners in overseas operations. The implementation of an empowerment strategy overseas might be perceived as a new departure, the sharing of power with other enterprises.

One manager cautioned: 'Some concepts travel better than others. The "OK" guy from the country you met at business school knows the score… back home people think differently.' Something that seems second nature to one culture can bewilder or appear meaningless in a different cultural context.

# DIVERSITY

In spite of the hype of advertisers and their cronies, all the trends are not pointing in the direction of the undifferentiated global brand. There are people out there who think, feel and dream in a billion different ways. They are individual human beings, not a line on a graph.

More demanding customers may switch their attention to tailoring to particular circumstances, or less tangible factors, as they seek to become comfortable with what is offered. As a consequence, national differences may become more, rather than less, significant.

Tailoring and the satisfaction of softer requirements are likely to require a closer relationship between customer and supplier. In some cases the boundary between the two may become more difficult to discern. Again, joint teams or project groups, involving both customer and supplier staff, may be set up to explore and meet particular requirements (Bartram, 1996). Members of such teams will be out there with the people. They will need sensitivity, intuition and cross-cultural awareness rather than media schedules.

The open company understands incoming messages. Language training should reflect the requirements of customers, and the need for effective communication with them. Switchboard operators, receptionists and Web sites may be the first point of contact with customers.

Which languages should be learnt will depend upon the requirements of existing customers, and which markets are being targeted. For example:

- If the aim is to become an international rather than a European company, Spanish and Portuguese may need to assume a higher priority.
- Even in fields such as computing and electronics, where a high proportion of the documentation may be in English, service and retail staff in direct contact with customers may need local language skills.

A language audit should be undertaken of the availability of language skills, and the language requirements of establishing relationships with customers and delivering value to them. A distinction should be made between reading, writing, listening and speaking skills.

# RECONCILING UNITY WITH DIVERSITY

While propagating the rhetoric of internationalization, the head offices of many companies with extensive international operations appear to be largely the preserve of nationals from the 'home country'. This need not be so. For one director: 'Our vision is international, that is the important thing. Our people and resources can be almost anywhere so long as you can get hold of them.'

Matsushita responded to the need to increase international awareness and mutual understanding between operating units and the centre, by bringing 200 foreign managers into its head office in Osaka. The company also ensures that there is an input from subsidiary companies into its key management processes.

The imposition of a standard corporate culture can prevent a company from obtaining the full benefits of diversity within international teams. A coming together of distinct values, viewpoints and approaches within a group can be a source of creativity. Xerox has recognized the importance and positive benefits of diversity in both a domestic and international context:

> [Building] and sustaining a healthy, empowered work team necessitates the recognition and optimization of diversity within the team. Each team is characterized by a unique array of talents, experiences and backgrounds. These individual qualities should be blended harmoniously, rather than toned down and homogenized.

> Managing diversity is one of our greatest potential advantages over [competitors who] are unified in their culture, history, and race. As superb as they are, this is a limiting factor. By contrast, we represent a cross-section of the richest mix of ethnic groups and races. The richer the mix, the broader the perspectives and the greater the creativity. Each… manager is faced with the challenge of developing the real potential of our fantastic mix of people, thus capitalizing on the competitive opportunities offered by employee diversity.

Corporate transformation can be compatible with both the desire for a global unity of purpose in terms of vision and goals, and diversity in response to local market conditions. Thus the technology of the organization could be used to link people together, while empowerment could be a means of achieving local diversity. Winners recognize that these distinct change elements must be in harmony rather than in conflict.

## Losers

Losers:

- prefer common approaches, standard solutions and global products;
- allocate resources, define roles and manage relationships across national borders;
- attempt to define and impose a corporate culture independently of their customers and people;
- have naïve expectations of international developments, new management initiatives and organizational changes;
- keep to themselves, trust no one and operate alone;
- do not think through the consequences of their actions;
- do not equip their people to manage effectively those joint ventures that they enter into;
- mouth the rhetoric of internationalization, while ensuring that all key positions are in the hands of nationals of the 'home country'.

## Winners

Winners:

- endeavour to tailor to local circumstances and requirements;
- allow people to network and forge whatever cross-border relationships will best enable them to achieve their objectives;
- strive to match corporate culture to the cultures of customers and suppliers at local level in order to develop closer relationships;
- think through the implications of whatever it is they are endeavouring to do and anticipate and address likely problem areas;
- form networks of relationships with various collaborators;
- are realistic and think through likely consequences, outcomes and reactions before they act;
- act to reap the benefits of joint ventures and to ensure that they are properly managed;
- recruit a diverse and multinational cadre of managers where appropriate and ensure that management positions go to those who are most qualified for each role.

# EVOLUTIONARY EXPLORATION

While other corporate initiatives 'proceed at the gallop', some 'winner' companies cautiously 'feel their way' with 'internationalization'.

Internationalization is not sought for its own sake, but only in so far as it relates to building more satisfactory long-term relationships with customers. The key human resource priority is creating a more flexible and responsive organization. Such companies recognize that their approach to 'internationalization' must take into account a multiplicity of different requirements. There is a requirement for flexibility and tailoring rather than the imposition of standard corporate programmes.

On the other hand, losers are slow to think through the people consequences and requirements of becoming a genuinely international organization. A leisurely pace of implementation, and a relatively low priority in relation to other corporate initiatives, can result in a failure to adjust in time to cope with the full rigours of a more competitive international marketplace.

## LEARNING FROM OTHERS

Companies should be more prepared to learn from others, including network partners. The board and senior management team might benefit from a greater range of international experience. Perhaps more non-nationals should be brought on to the board as non-executive directors.

Many companies devote much time and effort to external benchmarking, while doing little to learn from other parts of the same organization. In an international context, different national subsidiaries or joint venture partners could learn from each other. A company could also actively learn from its international customers, suppliers and business partners.

The full benefits of diversity may not be found within a single region. An organization based in the EC might feel that corporations in the United States or Japan might be more complementary business partners than companies in Europe with similar strengths and weaknesses.

The desire for flexibility may need to be tempered with accommodation to national restrictions relating to recruitment and new patterns of work. This may inhibit what would otherwise allow each business unit or account group to respond best to customer needs and opportunities.

National operating companies and local units, like individual employees, are seeking greater discretion. Aware of local preferences and needs, eager to generate local added value in meeting local customer requirements, they demand greater freedom from central control. Many are no longer content just to be local distributors of a product designed and produced overseas within a strategy set by a board whose view of the world is limited to that of a group of similar people largely drawn from one company.

'Loser' companies advocate diversity while seeking to export panaceas, slogans, standard solutions and simplistic models in their eager search for corporate transformation. Their efforts are resisted. Some programmes are foundering upon the rocks of the very diversity that is being heralded.

The natives, whipped up by the talk of involvement, empowerment and customer focus, become restive. Gaps between actions and words make them fidgety. They have waited too long for achievements to come through. When the damp night of recession gives way to the dawn of recovery, they may rise up and challenge the centre.

---

# CHECKLIST

► Does your company have an international vision?

► How international is the perspective of the 'key players'?

► How tolerant are they of cultural diversity?

► Is the membership of the board drawn from a mix of nationalities?

► What does your company do to understand, and respond to, developments in the international business environment?

► Who are the key global competitors?

► Does it have a nationality, or is it an international actor?

► Whose cultural values predominate throughout the organization?

► Are the resources of the organization equally accessible from any point?

► What is done to allow the total resources of your company to be harnessed to deliver value to the individual customer?

► How is it responding to centralized purchasing?

► How easy is it for the people of the company to work together in groups and teams across the barriers of function, distance, nationality and time?

► Is it realistic for staff at various locations around the world to aspire to senior management positions?

► Are 'head office functions concentrated at a single point, or dispersed around the international corporate network?

---

# REFERENCES

Bartram, P (1996) *The Competitive Network*, Policy Publications, Bedford

Coulson-Thomas, C (1990) *Human Resource Development for International Operation*, a Survey sponsored by Surrey European Management School, Adaptation, London

Coulson-Thomas, C (1992) *Creating the Global Company: Successful Internationalisation*, McGraw-Hill, London
FitzGerald, P (2000) *Effective Purchasing: The critical success factors*, Policy Publications, Bedford

## FURTHER INFORMATION

Brochures describing Effective Purchasing: The critical success factors and The Competitive Network with its methodology for using electronic commerce to re-engineer supply chains are available from Policy Publications, 4 The Crescent, Bedford MK40 2RU (tel: +44 (0) 1234 328448; fax: +44 (0) 1234 357231, e-mail: policypubs@kbnet.co.uk; Web site: www.ntwkfirm.com/bookshop).

# 12

# From Confrontation to Collaboration

*'Go too fast and the bow wave erodes the bank'*

Fundamental change can open a Pandora's box of problems and conflicts. Just as the Soviet Union fragmented into the Commonwealth of Independent States once the fetters were loosened, so enterprises can fragment also. The process of disintegration might be encouraged and helped by the lure of 'hiving off', the temptation to stage a management buy-out, or the attractions of de-mergers.

When the rate of change speeds up, new ways may need to be found to handle disagreement and confrontation. Where these enable latent and hidden conflicts to be brought to the surface and resolved, pent-up frustration may turn to advocacy of the change process. Even some dissidents may be willing to move ahead in the confidence that a means exists by which concerns can be raised and subsequently addressed. If they are not handled, when the 'going gets rough' group promotion may turn to self-protection.

## SCOPE FOR CONFLICT

Changes may be resisted where people do not see their relevance to familiar situations. The redesign of an organization could even be seen as a distraction from more important tasks.

Many individual components of a corporate transformation may give a new impetus to old debates. For example, the need for training could initiate a fresh round of discussion on the relative benefits which the company and the individual derive from expenditure on training and development.

It would be naïve to assume a company could ever be peopled by those who are entirely satisfied. As expectations change, the satisfied employee, like the satisfied customer, can become a moving target.

There is more scope for conflict in some organizations than in others. Within the diversified conglomerate some units may have little in common with others. Those initiating corporate change programmes should reflect upon the extent of diversity within a large business or group context (Figure 12.1):

● In the case of relatively homogeneous business units, it may be possible to use a standard transformation plan, subject to a modest amount of refinement and tailoring of the implementation to suit each unit.
● Where business units are relatively diverse, it may not be possible to use a transformation plan without some review and modification of the plan itself. Initiatives may need to be undertaken on a unit-by-unit basis.

Within a diversified business, there may be some entities that need to be run quite differently from others. De-mergers can release latent shareholder value.

Some management teams seem intent upon confrontation with one or more groups of stakeholders. Marconi alienated investors by wishing to

|  | Degree of Diversity | |
|  | Homogeneous Units | Diverse Units |
| --- | --- | --- |
| Universal approach | Little modification of transformation plan. Corporate process simplification | Review applicability of transformation plan |
| Particular approach | Tailor implementation of transformation plan | Process re-engineering on unit basis |

**Degree of Applicability of Corporate Programmes**

**Figure 12.1** Transforming the diversified business

reprice its share option scheme at a lower level following dramatic reductions in share values as a direct result of the company's policy of concentrating its activities in the recession-hit telecoms sector. The National Association of Pension Funds advised its members to vote against the proposal. Within months the company's shares had plummeted still further and both the chairman and chief executive had resigned.

## ASPIRATION AND ACHIEVEMENT

When there is a gap between rhetoric and reality, a change programme may annoy all the interests involved:

- The 'haves' with a vested interest in the *status quo* may feel threatened by the prospect of change.
- The 'have nots', the 'revisionists' who hope to benefit from change, may in return be disappointed by the lack of achievement.
- When the rhetoric continues, those in favour of the *'status quo'* may view the lack of results as no more than a 'temporary relief', or a 'calm before the storm'.
- The disappointment of the 'have nots' can turn to disillusion, despair and even a sense of betrayal, where the rhetoric has raised expectations beyond the prospects of delivery.

Managers have a tendency to follow their beliefs rather than the words. Burying your head in the sand may enable you, for a time, to avoid contemplating awkward realities. Understanding what people really believe gives you some idea of what you may be in for. Some managers may just not believe that it is going to happen.

## ACKNOWLEDGING CONFLICT

Too many managers conceal problems rather than solve them. A range of tensions and conflicts sometimes exist within organizations. The variety of these is illustrated by the following selection of comments:

*We just accept the differences of viewpoint and perspective without trying to do much about them.*

*Our chairman has solved the internal differences problem. When people ask about our differences, the latest line is to claim our cultural style is to encourage debate and internal competition as this benefits our customers.*

*A pyramid which narrows at the top encourages confrontation. Managers have a vested interest in rubbishing colleagues if they want to get ahead.*

*There was so much focus upon getting it right for the customer that we drove our people into the ground.*

*I can read and hear. I see their reports and I can hear what they are saying… It is what they are thinking that I would really like to know.*

The realities underlying confrontation need to be addressed. Beneath the symptoms, a latent conflict may be lurking. The drive to impose a change of culture, or a standard approach throughout a corporation, can bring issues to the surface. Under the pressures and demands of corporate transformation, the cracks may widen until the organizational structure blows apart.

## TENSIONS BETWEEN DIRECTORS AND MANAGERS

Let us examine some examples of potential arenas of confrontation. In Chapter 4 we challenged a 'traditional' view that directors focus on the external business environment, and are concerned with long-term questions of strategy and policy, while the great mass of employees just concentrate upon short-term questions of implementation (Figure 4.1).

Many boards still describe their function in terms of the company and its activities, rather than the business context within which it operates. Even when establishing strategies, objectives and policies, the main consideration is the survival and development of the company, rather than the nature of external challenges and opportunities, and how the business might respond.

In practice, and at a time of economic downturn, the focus of many directors is internal, while horizons have become noticeably short term (Figure 4.2):

- Directors recognize that, in order to respond effectively to challenges and opportunities in the business environment, their organizations need to be more flexible and responsive. Many have sought to create a slimmer, flatter and more adaptable organization.
- At the same time, boards of public companies feel under increased pressure from analysts to increase performance. They focus on short-term actions to improve financial ratios and the impact of corporate activities and policies upon share price.

Once chairman confided: 'We are in a bind… we really are.' The dilemma, while exacerbated by recent circumstances, is not new. Back in the 1940s Drucker recognized the challenge of maintaining a balance between a long-term strategy focused upon the core purpose and capability of a corporation, and the maintenance of satisfactory levels of short-term performance (Drucker, 1946).

Managers have been focusing externally and thinking longer term (Coulson-Thomas and Coe, 1991). They have been asked to devote more attention to external customers and supply chain relationships.

The shift of emphasis makes people question board and senior management decisions that appear to be in conflict with stated long-term aims. Pragmatism and 'accommodating' may appear out of step with corporate values. When short-term actions impact upon customer and employee satisfaction, unease can develop into annoyance and hostility. As one manager puts it: 'Screwing up our relationships with customers goes against everything we have been expected to believe in.'

We saw in Chapter 7 that actions and symbols can communicate more than words. Table 12.1 lists a few of the areas in which there is sometimes a difference between what the board says and what the board does.

The view that actions can often lead to consequences that are different from those intended is not new. Chris Argyris recognized that managers are frequently faced with contradictory pressures, and are in receipt of messages that may appear to be in conflict. In response they may adopt 'defensive routines', which may best be tackled by matching the speed of change to the rate at which people and groups can learn, and the benefits of incremental developments become apparent (Argyris, 1985).

# APPORTIONING THE BLAME

When things go well, everyone wants to take the credit. Unintended consequences, however, are always someone else's fault. When things do not work out as planned, people start to point the finger. As one CEO put it, too many managers, 'assess changes in terms of the impacts upon their own roles and standing in the corporate bureaucracy'.

Interviews with CEOs suggest they associate 'vested interests', 'organizational politics' and 'cynicism' with people who are thought to have the

**Table 12.1** The board as a role model

| The board says | The board does |
| --- | --- |
| Satisfy customers | Set RONA* targets |
| Build relationships | Reorganizes and disrupts relationships |
| Encourage teamwork | Divides and rules |
| Exercise restraint | Awards itself large increase in remuneration |
| Invest in people | Reduces training budget |
| Delegate and empower | Still takes the decisions |
| Calls for long-term commitment | Overreacts to short-term pressures |

*Return on net assets

greatest stake in the *'status quo'*, or to have most to gain from it. According to one CEO:

> *Looking back I realize some of my colleagues in the boardroom were just playing with words. They would nod agreement, and then do nothing in their divisions. When people say things like 'If you say so' or 'You're the boss', you know you are in trouble. We should have kept at it until they were all committed... If I had my time over again, I would have been tougher on one or two of them.*

## THE HEAD OFFICE–BUSINESS UNIT DIVIDE

An expectation gap, or the failure of the main board to deliver, can poison the relationship between head office and business unit. Head offices and business units may also have conflicting views and perspectives on the steps needed to implement a vision.

In the rhetoric, the management teams of business units may have been encouraged to act as 'independent businesses'. However, the reality of a 'different viewpoint' can be the cause of resentment. Often, the 'thinking teams' are labelled as troublemakers, rather than listened to. They may be avoided just when there is the greatest need for dialogue.

The use of financial measures to assess business unit performance, when corporate goals stress 'customer satisfaction', appears to be the source of much frustration at the business unit level. One divisional director complained: 'I bought into quality, and the vision, as did my team. Everyone talks about quality, but I'm measured by the same old ratios... The ratios decide my next move, not how many quality improvement projects I've got.'

The criteria used to recover central or overhead costs are also a 'bone of contention'. One business unit general manager complained: 'I get memos from head office to reduce headcount and cut costs, while my reallocated overheads have increased.' In many companies, the most that can be learnt from the relative bottom line performance of business units is something about the basis of group, or head office, overhead allocation.

## RELATIONSHIPS BETWEEN HOLDING, SUBSIDIARY AND OPERATING COMPANIES

Differences of perspective and emphasis are particularly evident in the relationships between holding companies, and their subsidiary and operating companies. Relations between group boards and those of national operating companies may be distorted by misunderstandings that might result from differences of nationality and culture. A desire for consistency of implementation can result in the imposition of approaches that may not be appropriate in particular contexts.

According to one international director with personnel responsibilities for Central and South America: 'Many of my colleagues never think about how much our strategic vision is bound up with our own culture. [People] don't relate to it in South America. … It's not their vision – it's our vision. We're telling them about it, not sharing it with them.'

Delayering and headcount reduction programmes appear to have exacerbated tensions. Many operating companies appear resigned to the prospect of 'absorbing' an unfair proportion of 'cutbacks', as corporate organizations are slimmed down. According to one subsidiary director: 'You always cut someone else. … When group [makes] cuts, it's us [who feel the impact]'.

Perhaps corporate power should be redefined in terms of the ability to reduce someone else's headcount. A subsidiary managing director explained: 'Who gets the misery depends upon power, and there's still a lot of it at the centre.'

Many of those at the corporate centre appear adept at protecting their own interests. In some companies, new staff positions and specialist roles appear to spring up as rapidly as others are cut out. One frustrated CEO exclaimed: 'It's like wrestling with a multiheaded beast. We cut off heads, but new ones spring up. … [Because of this] we have to resort to crude tactics like imposing headcount reductions. … This drives out the good with the bad.'

## CONFLICT WITHIN THE NETWORK

In the case of the network organization, the scope for internal conflict or 'family quarrels' extends to the relationships between the core team and various project groups, and those with the customer, supplier and business partner members of the network. Some internal pressures may need to be generated to keep network members on their toes. The degree of dissent could be an indicator of the extent to which progress is being made. It is difficult to envisage situations that could lead to a revolt breaking out in the midst of the bureaucratic corporation. This is not so in the case of the network organization in which all share common values and an understanding of what needs to be done.

One can imagine circumstances in which a province might rebel against the empire, a new venture team accusing a head office of breaking faith with the vision and values, and appealing to stakeholders for support. Insecure senior executives of the future may need to put down the 'quick reads' on how to achieve harmony and light in five easy stages, and dust off some tomes on why people rebel and revolt (Gurr, 1970; Davies, 1971).

# DIFFERING NATIONAL PERSPECTIVES

Within the international network there is further potential for misunderstanding and conflict:

- A UK manager may retain attachment to financial measures of performance, and focus upon profitability.
- A German colleague might stress turnover growth, and attach more importance to the employees or 'social partners'.
- The Japanese equivalent might be more receptive to corporate values concerning the customer that are portrayed as a 'philosophy of business'.

When an attempt is made to reconcile these distinct perspectives through discussion there could well be scope for protracted debate. If a particular priority is imposed, then not all are likely to be equally committed.

Clashes of corporate culture can also arise in the cases of joint ventures and acquisitions. Cultural differences should not be 'swept under the carpet'. Winners find that bringing problem areas into the open and discussing them leads to a better understanding of the differences of culture and perspective between members of workgroups drawn from different national backgrounds.

# CULTURE AND CORPORATE TRANSFORMATION

The implementation of elements of a corporate transformation programme can also be affected by national and cultural differences. For example, there are significant differences in national approaches to involvement:

- Senior executives in US companies tend to decide first and then seek involvement in implementation. There is often a reluctance to trust people with major decisions. These are seen as the prerogative of corporate leaders. Many senior managers consider they would be earning their salary by fraud if they spent too long listening to other people, as opposed to taking decisions.
- In Japanese companies it is not unusual for initiatives for change to arise at a number of points and levels within the corporate organization. Suggestions travel around and through the organization, gaining support and being refined according to various contributions from those likely to be affected. By the time a proposal reaches a senior management level many of the implementation issues will have been addressed, and a favourable consensus may already have been assembled.

Clearly, how a change programme is implemented would need to reflect these and other differences. Over-generalization should be avoided, and it may be necessary to strip away a cloak of mythology. We saw in Chapter 11 that diversity can be a source of corporate creativity and strength.

## THE DESIRABILITY OF CONFLICT

Invisible or hidden barriers cannot be tackled. Opposition, particularly when self-interested or malevolent, is better out in the open than concealed where it can carp and corrupt. Without moving the stone it may not be possible to disturb the reptiles and creepy-crawlies lurking beneath it.

Change tends to impose strains and can exacerbate differences. Role-model behaviour must include a tolerance for uncertainty and diversity, and the ability to recognize, confront and resolve differences. A common vision or a shared focus on, or commitment to, the customer can act as a reference point, or a kind of cement that holds the corporate organization together.

Some of those who are sceptical may be opinion formers. Their very caution, and a reputation for thoughtfulness, may cause them to be respected by various people across a corporate network. Their attitudes and responses to change may be watched by others. Their views need to be obtained and considered, and their concerns addressed. Because of their informal or political influence, they should not be ignored on the grounds of their role in the formal hierarchy.

Many managers draw the wrong conclusions from their analyses of situations. For example, because top management commitment is important it does not follow that there should be an excessive, if not exclusive, focus upon the driving and cascading of a change programme through an organization. Commitment at other levels is important as well, and this may be reduced rather than encouraged by the 'top down' approach. Imposition tends to result in compliance rather than commitment, and discourages people from questioning and learning.

## MECHANISMS FOR AVOIDING CONFLICTS

Some companies have recognized the potential for arenas of conflict to arise, and have created mechanisms to deal with them. Given goodwill and trust, latent conflicts can be brought into the open. Specific means of diffusing potential conflict areas include the following:

- Giving local operating units greater autonomy and staff greater discretion to respond to local circumstances.
- A 'ring fence' could be put around a newly acquired company to reduce the risk of culture clash, and maintain valued cultural characteristics.

Fujitsu sought to maintain the European identity and special character of ICL following its acquisition.

- Allowing greater involvement of operating and business units in corporate issue monitoring and management exercises.
- Representatives of operating and business units could be invited to attend board and management meetings for those items that directly concern them, and in respect of which they are known to have strong views.
- At the cost of some delay, every attempt should be made to secure operating and business unit involvement in the formulation of corporate visions, values and missions. This may allow early identification of issues that might arise in respect of certain countries and cultures.
- Local operating companies should be involved in the formulation and implementation of the various host country strategies developed by an international company. In cases where there is a clear conflict between global and national interest, at least local management will be made aware of the global viewpoint.

Winners learn from how others avoid conflicts. Confrontation and disputes have long been the norm in the building industry. Contracts have traditionally ended in claim and counter claim. Willmott Dixon has pioneered partnering as a way of forging win-win collaborative relationships with customers. United House Group, another construction company, requires its building workers to sign a code of conduct to support the relationships it negotiates.

## HANDLING CONFLICTS

A company may need to establish fora in which debate and the exchange of views can take place. To take two examples:

- General Electric of the United States established a corporate executive council to bring together board members and those heading the corporation's various business units. This created a forum for the discussion of issues of concern.
- L M Ericsson has used subsidiary boards and inter-unit teams to resolve differences. Participants build up their understanding of the distinct perspectives of various parts of the organization by spending periods on assignment and working in cross-functional and multinational teams.

While implementing significant change there must be a means of authoritatively handling differences of opinion that might arise in such a way that outcomes are accepted as legitimate by those involved. People are more likely to regard a change process as legitimate if their concerns can be developed and openly expressed, and they are subsequently evaluated and assessed.

Critiques that arise within the corporate organization should be well informed, and criticisms should be justified. In the absence of argument and appropriate data, differences of opinion can be difficult to reconcile. Xerox encourages 'fact-based management', while Intel expects its managers to question, but on the basis of rigorous analysis and supporting information.

Conflict can be functional or dysfunctional. A culture that encourages challenge and debate may stimulate an excess of negative criticism. People should be encouraged to relate their points to the achievement of corporate goals.

The commitment of various groups may be better harnessed by encouraging them to focus upon customer problems that are significant to their particular business units or areas of activity. People should discover for themselves what the key barriers to delivering value to customers are. Top management should concentrate upon helping them with whatever tools and approaches are relevant to the solution of these problems.

## IDENTIFYING COMMON GROUND

In order to reconcile conflicts, it is necessary to determine the extent of agreement, and the source of disagreement. For example, it would be advisable to assess whether the conflict concerns any of the following:

- The factors influencing the change requirement. According to perspective, the pressures could be seen as motivating or overwhelming. Very different views could be taken of strengths, weaknesses, opportunities and threats.
- The need for change. Opinions might vary on how much freedom of action a company has. Even where a storm strikes, some may suggest seeking temporary shelter, while others favour riding it out.
- The timing of change. Does it need to be rushed, or could it be carefully planned and introduced at a leisurely pace?
- The nature or extent of change. Is a fundamental transformation required, or some incremental adjustment to what is? Does the need extend to the whole company, or is it confined to particular divisions?
- The process of change. One person might favour a more democratic route of involving and sharing in order to 'win hearts and minds', while another individual could view such an approach as 'a luxury that cannot be afforded'. In the time available, it may be felt that changes should be forced through.
- The use of change techniques. Even though agreement may have been reached to re-engineer a process, views may vary on how this should be done.

- The desired or achievable speed of change. Some members of a transformation team are likely to have more faith than others concerning the capacity of people, processes, organizations and systems to cope with the speed of change.
- The impacts or implications of change. Views may differ on how to assess and weight consequences. Change can be unequal in its impacts and the burdens of readjustment it imposes.
- What has been achieved in terms of change. While some may be concerned at the lack of progress, others may argue that enough has been done, or even that some aspects of change have gone too far.
- Why change is occurring. Some way into a change programme, people can lose sight of the original reasons for change. A case could be put for reassessment in the light of altered circumstances and what has been achieved, while others might stress the need to 'stay true and see it through'.

To achieve a successful transition, a mixture of consensus and coercion may be needed, and the nature and extent of each will vary from company to company according to circumstances, the required speed of change and the make-up of individual elements of the network organization.

## THE INVISIBLE DIMENSION

What needs to be changed may not be visible. The people hard at work, the activity you see, and all the procedures and technology that support it may not be the problem. They may not be perfect, but rather than squeeze small incremental improvements out of what is already relatively effective, you should probably look elsewhere.

From the customer's point of view, the major sources of delay may lie in the invisible dimension for which no one is responsible (Table 12.2). Having been worked upon with diligence and speed, e-mails and documents processed in minutes may wait for hours or days in mailboxes and

**Table 12.2** Visible and invisible dimensions

| Visible | Invisible |
| --- | --- |
| Activity | Delay |
| Work time | Waiting time |
| 'In play' | 'Off the court' |
| Departmental responsibility | Lack of overall responsibility |
| Formal structure | Informal consultation |
| Processing cost | Cost of delay |
| Investment in information technology | Lack of investment in document management |
| Problem of justification | Customer dissatisfaction |

in-trays as they pass through the limbo land between work groups. And at each cross-over point they may be ranked differently in priority. At certain stages in the journey the priority may be low indeed.

As much as 90 per cent or more of the elapsed time through an order to delivery cycle may be spent 'waiting' at cross-over points that fall between accountabilities. This invisible dimension does not appear on lists of roles and responsibilities.

When the consequences of delay result in investigations and enquiries, blame and recrimination may have a field day. Different individuals and groups may be at each other's throats as they try to pass the buck. The unit boundary is the source of many of the most virulent and debilitating conflicts that can arise within corporate organizations.

## FROM VERTICAL TO HORIZONTAL VIEW

In the bureaucratic corporation, the 'vertical' divisions between functions and departments, such as those shown in Figure 12.2, acted as a series of barriers between customer requirement and customer satisfaction. Well-meaning people struggled to resolve the inevitable consequences of inherent defects in the organization.

Conflicts that arose at the 'hot spots' between departments often ended up as disputes that were taken to the board by the heads of the functions concerned. When not brought into the open, the simmering issue can poison the atmosphere in the boardroom.

The transforming organization reviews and simplifies or re-engineers its cross-functional business processes. These are the 'horizontal' processes that deliver the value that is sought by customers. When directors are given process, as opposed to departmental, responsibilities they tend to take a more holistic and customer-focused view of the enterprise.

## INTEGRATING THROUGH PROCESSES

After a decade of experience, winners approach process re-engineering with caution (Coulson-Thomas, 1994, 1997 and 1998). Cross-functional processes, such as those shown diagrammatically in Figure 12.2, can encourage cooperation and act as an 'integrator', creating a lattice work of horizontal and diagonal linkages, and shared purpose in place of former rivalries.

At the same time, there is a risk that processes might be identified and re-engineered more quickly than the attitudes to operate them effectively can be firmly established. Processes need to be managed to deliver the value sought by customers. Herein lay the source of potential new arenas of conflict:

- Process owners needed to be identified to take responsibility for the people, assets and information associated with each process, and to

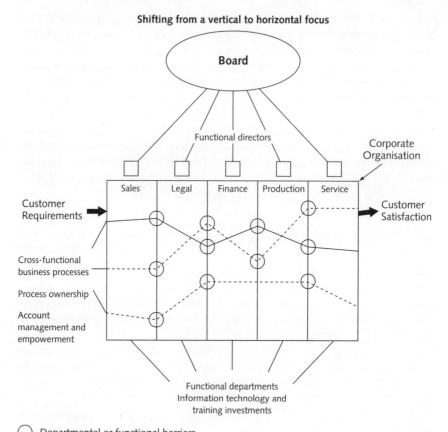

**Figure 12.2** The board and cross-functional business processes

ensure they operated effectively and evolved to meet changing requirements. These people are sometimes possessive and territorial.

- While eventually a company might become organized on the basis of 'horizontal' processes rather than 'vertical' departments, during a long interim period a mixture, or matrix, of joint responsibilities may exist. This can result in a level of confusion, and some individuals might experience conflict between their roles as process owners and departmental managers.

- Identifying and re-engineering a first process such as the 'customer order to product delivery lifecycle' may be greeted as a novelty. When a number of processes are tackled simultaneously, the task can become overwhelmingly complicated.

- Displaying a complex process diagrammatically can be a major challenge. When further processes are identified, a degree of overlapping and crossover is almost inevitable. The diagrammatic representation of the processes of the network organization can appear like a plate of spaghetti.

Ultimately, the process organization can become as confusing and political as the bureaucracy, with 'boundary problems', and conflicts of view and priority between processes and those responsible for them replacing those between departments (Coulson-Thomas, 1997 and 1998).

## COLLABORATION WITH OTHERS

People associated with 'loser' companies are cautious collaborators. They stress the time and expense required to establish and build relationships, and they conclude that the likely results are not worth the investment required. In making such a choice they act as though working with others is an option rather than a necessity. At heart they prefer to operate alone.

Some prize their independence so much that they pass up opportunities to grow that would require them to work with other suppliers. Collaboration is seen as a constraint upon freedom. They settle into familiar ways of operating. If existing arrangements and practices appear to work reasonably well, they are reluctant to consider alternatives that might offer additional benefits.

Bill Gates, the ultimate achiever, pursued a compelling vision to become the richest person in the world. Gates and Microsoft, the company he founded, aimed at winning rather than cooperation. They turned their back on collaboration with other technology vendors in favour of achieving sole dominance in their marketplace. Not surprisingly, when subject to an anti-trust investigation, the company found it had few friends within its industry.

Winners are more ready and willing to cooperate with complementary suppliers. They see and seek the advantages of collaboration. It might enable them to better learn and develop, offer a wider range of services to their customers, and pursue a broader range of opportunities. They are always open to approaches. They welcome suggestions for doing things in new and better ways. They actively search for potential business partners and explore possibilities for joint initiatives or collective action.

As companies outsource and focus on core competencies, they may hive off or transfer various activities to specialist suppliers. As a consequence, combinations of organizations working together in supply chains rather than single entities are delivering ever more value. A company that endeavours to do everything itself may become a jack of all trades and master of none.

Consortium responses to invitations to tender for complex and large-scale projects are also increasingly common in certain sectors. Only by working together may the respondents be able to assemble the capabilities required. Companies that collaborate may significantly improve their prospects for winning business.

## SELECTING COLLABORATORS

When they do need to work with others, losers tend to seek out potential collaborators similar to themselves. As a consequence, they sometimes find in crisis situations that the whole is not necessarily greater than the sum of its parts. Like drunks endeavouring to prop each other up they compound each other's weaknesses.

If the parties endeavouring to cooperate are very different, they may not have enough in common to cement a relationship. On the other hand, if they are so alike as to add little to each other's capabilities, collaboration may not be justified. Winners are more likely to understand that lasting relationships often involve dissimilar but complementary partners that allocate roles and responsibilities according to comparative advantage.

## BUILDING RELATIONSHIPS

Losers tend to be essentially selfish where relationships are concerned. They want them on their terms and they often put the bare minimum of effort into maintaining them. They hold back and endeavour not to become too deeply involved. They may even undertake cost–benefit assessments, seek to 'score points' and adopt win-lose approaches to negotiations.

Collaborative 'partnerships' can take various forms. Whether informal arrangements or formal joint ventures, such relationships can be of considerable importance. Opportunities can be addressed and significant amounts of new business won as a result of cooperative action. The consortium bid for a major contract, with each member focusing upon an area of core expertise, is increasingly acceptable and may be encouraged.

Winners work hard at reaping the benefits of cooperation. They commit the effort required to establish and regularly review collaborative processes and practices for winning business. They put practical arrangements in place to clarify the ownership of customers, prevent poaching and protect intellectual property.

Winners also recognize that if relationships are to grow and deepen they should be mutually beneficial to all the parties involved. Instinctively, when engaged in negotiations they look for win-win outcomes. They also endeavour to avoid rushing. Like a boater, they know that if they are making waves, they are probably travelling too fast. Some parties take longer to adjust and integrate than others.

Winners understand the dynamic nature of associations and arrangements. They cannot be taken for granted. Time, effort and care may need to be devoted to them if they are to become closer and more intimate.

The goodwill of others is of particular importance to professional services firms that derive many of their assignments from referrals and 'repeat business'. The more successful practitioners assiduously network and attend a wide range of local events. Professional 'superstars' actively manage their contacts and are regularly in touch with them, passing on news and leads likely to be of value (James, 1999, 2000, 2001; Kennedy, 1999, 2000; Hally, 2000; Harris, 2000).

Winners willingly commit. They become involved. They are flexible and understanding, and prepared to do things differently to accommodate a particular customer. They are also not 'fair weather friends'. They can be relied upon in a crisis situation. Many are genuinely interested in their client's businesses and will readily pass on ideas and suggestions they feel might benefit them. They are always on the look out for ways of helping them.

Relationships should not be pursued at all costs. They should also not become a distraction. They need to deliver in relation to what a board is setting out to do. Some losers devote great effort to achieving 'teamwork'. They conceal or sideline differences and gloss over concerns in order to achieve a bland consensus.

Winners adopt a more entrepreneurial approach. They identify and reward individual contributions. They encourage open and frank discussion. They become demanding partners who do not tolerate under-achievement. On occasion they create waves in order to make faster progress. If need be, they end a relationship.

---

## Losers

Losers:

- pursue divisive and zero-sum strategies for promoting their own interests;
- are divided by arenas of confrontation between internal departments and other groupings, including between head offices and operating units;
- confuse roles and relationships, and experience responsibility gaps and areas of overlap;
- do not understand the differences between ownership, managerial roles and directorial roles, as a result of which there are tensions between directors and managers;
- foment conflicts to achieve sectional interests;
- miss root causes, latent issues and 'hidden' areas at the handover points between departments and processes;
- adopt an unthinking approach to benchmarking and tend to uncritically accept and replicate what other organizations are doing;

- are reluctant collaborators and devote minimal effort to building relationships.

## *Winners*

Winners:

- seek win-win outcomes that meet the legitimate interests of all significant parties;
- believe in diversity, healthy challenge and active debate, but different parts of the organization endeavour to support each other;
- clarify roles and responsibilities and take care to avoid overlaps and responsibility gaps;
- understand the respective duties and responsibilities of owners, managers and directors;
- endeavour to find common ground, resolve conflicts and promote shared interests and goals;
- identify root causes, bring latent issues to the surface and adopt an end-to-end view of processes to avoid handover problems;
- adopt a critical approach to learning from others and are not afraid to go out in front and innovate;
- proactively seek relevant collaborators and work at building mutually beneficial relationships.

# SHARED LEARNING

Shared learning can be a potent tool for focusing people externally, and distracting them from debilitating internal squabbles. The subject of analysis is how others have coped with similar situations. People can identify what needs to be changed and why, without their own sensitivities and defensiveness being involved.

Speculation and assumption concerning what might be is replaced by the consideration of what is, and what can be learnt from it. Awareness of the scale of an external challenge can act as a catalyst in bringing about the internal unity and resolve to confront it.

Shared learning also enables a company to identify what needs to be done. It allows an assessment to be made of the scale and pace of change, and it may also be possible to estimate resource requirements, and identify drawbacks and 'side effects'.

Securing internal support is helped by the fact that people are being asked to match or better something that is being done or has already been achieved. This tends to be less divisive than a change or cutback for a vague or undisclosed reason which can appear arbitrary, uncertain and obscure.

# CHECKLIST

▶ Have the supporters and opponents of change been identified in your company?

▶ What is being done to understand the viewpoints of those who appear to be opposed to change?

▶ Do members of the board and senior management team have the capacity to listen?

▶ How tolerant are they of diversity?

▶ Is open and vigorous debate encouraged?

▶ Do the company's key players have the respect of people throughout the organization?

▶ Do they themselves always behave as role models?

▶ Why should anyone believe the company's messages?

▶ Who cares if they are believed?

▶ What will be lost if they are not believed?

▶ Is the business and change strategy of your company credible?

▶ What evidence is there of senior management commitment to it?

▶ Where does it rank in the list of their priorities?

▶ Is day-to-day action consistent with the 'words'?

▶ What can be learnt from those who appear to lack commitment?

▶ Are managers able to distinguish between a healthy level of questioning and disruptive opposition?

▶ Do they encourage collaborative activity and shared learning?

# REFERENCES

Argyris, C (1985) *Strategy, Change and Defensive Routines*, Pitman, London

Coulson-Thomas, C (ed) (1994) *Business Process Re-engineering: Myth and reality*, Kogan Page, London

Coulson-Thomas, C (1997 and 1998) *The Future of the Organization: Achieving excellence through business transformation*, Kogan Page, London

Coulson-Thomas, C and Coe, T (1991) *The Flat Organisation: Philosophy and practice*, BIM, Corby

Davies, J C (ed) (1971) When Men Revolt and Why, The Free Press, New York

Drucker, P F (1946) *Concept of the Corporation*, John Day, New York

Gurr, T R (1970) *Why Men Rebel*, Princeton University Press, Princeton, NJ

Hally, M (2000) *Winning New Business in the Legal Profession*, Policy Publications, Bedford

Harris, N (2000) *Winning New Business in Engineering Consultancy: The critical success factors*, Policy Publications, Bedford

James, M (1999) *Winning New Business in Management Consultancy: The critical success factors and Winning New Business in Advertising: The critical success factors*, Policy Publications, Bedford

James, M (2000) *Winning New Business in Engineering: The critical success factors, Winning New Business in Accountancy: The critical success factors and Winning New Business in PR and Marketing Consultancy: The critical success factors*, Policy Publications, Bedford

James, M (2001) *Winning New Business in IT and Telecoms Consultancy: The critical success factors*, Policy Publications, Bedford

Kennedy, C (1999) *Winning New Business in Construction*, Policy Publications, Bedford

Kennedy, C (2000) *Winning New Business in Information Technology and Telecoms and Winning New Business in Engineering and Manufacturing*, Policy Publications, Bedford

# FURTHER INFORMATION

Brochures describing the 'Winning Business' series of reports are available from Policy Publications, 4 The Crescent, Bedford MK40 2RU (tel: +44 (0) 1234 328448; fax: + 44 (0) 1234 357231; e-mail: policypubs@kbnet.co.uk; Web site: www.ntwkfirm.com/bookshop).

# 13

# Integrating Learning and Working

*'Darkness hovers around low-burning candles'*

## DESTROYING THE DRIVE TO LEARN

All of us are born with an innate desire and drive to learn. We come into the world restless and curious to explore, and to experience. We search and investigate, open and receptive, eager for the stimuli that will expand our awareness and understanding. At the same time, we are fed, winded and largely left to our own devices.

Later in life, as children, we are confined for several hours a day, during many of our most receptive years, in institutions of education. Ostensibly, a central purpose of schools is the pursuit of learning. And yet, for most people, the efforts of many thousands of well-meaning and committed teachers over a period of years destroys this desire to learn.

The educational system fails most people. They learn what they are not good at according to one approach to the development of understanding. As the 21st century unfolds, most of us will approach the grave bereft of any real appreciation of our individual learning capability. We can peer into space and speculate about the origins of the universe while much of what happens within our own heads is unexplored territory. The 'non-academic' majority go through life without ever knowing how they might most effectively learn.

# THE HIGH COST OF LIMITING POTENTIAL

To achieve this is expensive. State expenditure on education produces a majority who are functionally illiterate in maths and science. Much of corporate training is devoted to remedying the deficiencies of the educational system.

In the United States one in four people are receiving or delivering some form of education or training. And yet, most young Americans lack a range of basic competences. Why? Because the US educational system, like others, is based upon an inadequate understanding of the learning process. While our understanding is so limited, further investments in education could be said to be building upon foundations of sand.

We will return to the question of learning in Chapter 17. Without it, the corporation acts like a zombie. Education, training and development should light the touch-paper, not suffocate the spark.

# THE CORPORATE CHALLENGE

In a global marketplace in which the knowledge worker is becoming the critical and limiting resource, the corporation or society that first and wholeheartedly adopts new approaches to learning that allow individuals to tap more of their potential will reap an enormous competitive advantage.

Is training and development a 'help' or a 'hinder'? How does one build a learning company that must operate within countries which are not learning societies?

Over a decade ago a survey (Coulson-Thomas, 1990) was undertaken by Adaptation Ltd for Surrey European Management School (SEMS). It revealed a clear preference for the integration of learning and working. The place of work was the preferred location of learning, and the most relevant approaches were thought to be tailored company-specific programmes with a project component. Human resources were perceived as a critical success factor, and there was an evident desire for more work to be undertaken by project groups and teams with clear output objectives. Yet a more recent investigation (Coulson-Thomas, 1999) suggests that despite much rhetoric, little progress has been made in creating learning cultures.

# RHETORIC AND REALITY

A commitment to the development of people has long been a core element of the business philosophy of many companies. According to Hiroshi

Hamada, when president of the Japanese company Ricoh: 'Realizing the full potential of every company member is the company's most important aim.'

As more people become aware of the extent to which their companies are competing on the basis of their ability to learn and apply what has been learnt, greater interest has been shown in the concept of the 'learning organization'. Yet while the critical importance of identifying, attracting, developing, motivating, tapping and retaining human talent appears to have become an article of faith, many training and related budgets are cut back when the going gets tough. In many organizations training and development activity is not focused upon the activities and processes that win business or add value for customers, and the skills being imparted are not specifically relevant to the achievement of corporate goals and objectives (Coulson-Thomas, 1999).

Whether training is a 'help' or a 'hinder' depends upon its nature and purpose. Many companies find it difficult to decide how much to spend on training. The 'heart' wants to believe that training is a 'good thing', while the 'head' suggests that the results of training efforts are difficult to determine. The reality of 'what is' often differs greatly from the vision of 'what ought to be'. The intention may have been to 'invest', but the results of training can be disappointing.

According to one chairman: 'We are turning the organization upside down... [and]... assuming people will be able to cope. ... So much of it is new to them... [yet] most of our training continues as before.'

Paradoxically, because of a failure to implement, some of those companies that have 'taken a lead' in trying to equip people for team work in the context of a flexible organization have developed skills that cannot be effectively practised. Management qualities such as flexibility and adaptability need to be matched by a similar development in corporate capability.

## CHALLENGING THE CONVENTIONAL WISDOM

Have companies 'invested' wisely in training, or have they just spent money preparing people for a world they are now turning their backs on? Consider the following selection of comments:

*Lots of people have gone on courses, but attitudes and behaviour have not changed.*

*We think it is nice for people to learn things, whether or not they are of any relevance. We do not relate training to specific tasks.*

*Most training is departmental. People train with their function. Yet most of the key processes that generate value for customers are cross-functional.*

*If you are into debates about measuring the effectiveness of training, you are probably into the wrong training... or consider it as a cost. If you know what adds value for customers [and] have clear customer objectives... expressed in output terms, you just do what is necessary.*

Overall training and development should no longer be automatically assumed to be a 'good thing'. In many companies, including those in sectors that have made major investments in training, managerial productivity fell during the late 1980s and early 1990s. As the author concluded at the time (Coulson-Thomas, 1992):

> Training is not necessarily desirable; it depends both upon the training and the trainer. Many trainers continue to teach out-of-date ideas or jump aboard the latest bandwagon without thinking through the consequences for an individual company. Many of the notions that can appear the most compelling on the trainer's slide, and are delivered with the panache and confidence that come from frequent repetition, have limited application in the work context.

A key question is the extent to which the skills that are developed, and the process of development itself, encourage the attitudes and approaches required by the network organization. For example, does the Japanese emphasis upon rote learning and team work inhibit individual creativity?

## UNINTENDED CONSEQUENCES

Management education and development should reflect the requirements of the emerging network organization. Initiatives such as the UK's Management Charter Initiative, with its succession of stages from supervisory, through junior and middle, to senior management, may have helped to entrench the hierarchical view of organizations, just at a time when within network organizations the need is to equip people to move between project teams and roles, rather than to climb functional ladders.

So many people appear to be working so hard to frustrate those CEOs who are trying to break free of past practices. They are sometimes imprisoned by their own prejudices and misunderstood preferences.

Many general trends in management education and development during the 1990s had unintended consequences, as people in 'loser' companies uncritically applied whatever happened to be the latest craze. To take two examples:

- The definition of standard competences can result in great effort being devoted to the development of qualities that may not be relevant to the situation and circumstances of a particular company. Rather than think through what is required in a particular context, the trainer 'plays safe'

and builds some general competence which may not relate to key priorities, or quite specific current transformation requirements.

- The transferability of skills can be dangerous when people move
  between organizations that are very different in structure or culture, or
  at different stages in the process of transformation. Whereas the
  practice might have been to address a requirement in a way that met the
  needs of the company, instead a tick is made in the 'skill checklist' that it
  was obtained elsewhere.

When unique people and particular companies are involved, and the
requirement may change during a transition process, trainers who 'go
automatic' can be dangerous. Too many glib experts appear to have
answers up their sleeves that turn out to achieve little:

- One director complained: 'Even before I've finished speaking they've
  reached for the jargon. We may not have done it before… [but] out come
  the words.'
- Another interviewee questioned: 'Why can't they just go away and
  think about it for a few days? I hope I'll still be here.'

We encountered in Chapter 4 the dangers of allowing rationality and
prescription to drive out sensitivity and intuition. There are atmospheres
to experience, relationships to understand, considerations to digest, situations to sense and feel, and people to listen to, before recommendations are
put together.

Technique and the mechanical are no substitute for inspiration and flair.
While Sir Paul McCartney could not read or write a word of music, he
created a succession of hit songs, and regularly collected gold and
platinum records.

## LEARNING ABOUT LEARNING

That we have such a limited understanding of how people learn should
not come as a surprise. The root of today's skills crises lies in past over-
sights. The Institute for Research on Learning (IRL) calculated that in the
United States R&D on learning was 0.025 per cent of expenditure on
education during the late 1980s (Institute for Research on Learning, c1988).
This compared with health and business R&D of 1.5 per cent and 1.6 per
cent respectively of expenditure, while high-tech businesses could spend
10 per cent or more of their turnover on R&D.

The IRL concluded:

… any business that spent such a minuscule portion of total expenditure on fundamental research as education is spending, particularly at a time of rapid increase in demand and a revolutionary

change in available technology, would inevitably be facing just the sort of monumental crisis that education is now perceived to be in.

Institute for Research on Learning (*c*1988)

Until recently, far too few educationalists bothered to ask fundamental questions about how people learn. The teachers and advocates of learning have themselves been reluctant to observe, reflect and learn.

For many people, the traditional classroom is among the least effective of learning environments. The IRL suggests they feel 'cut off' and do not relate to the abstract symbols that are used in such subjects as maths and science. Relevance and purpose are often not perceived when learning is artificially separated from living and working (Coulson-Thomas, 1990).

## DEVELOPMENT AND CORPORATE OBJECTIVES

Development activities ought to reflect the situation and circumstances of a company, its business objectives and its key priorities. For example, there is little point in a company building hypothetical 'team skills' without addressing the following:

- The purpose of the team. For example, a bid team might require specific bidding skills such as defining value in customer terms.
- Where team members are located. People in virtual teams may be widely scattered and they may need special training.
- The role of groups and teams in the management of change. The management culture and management style must be supportive.
- The clarity of the goals given to teams, and the relevance of their priorities to business objectives. People need to understand the broad boundaries within which they operate in terms of goals and priorities.
- The discretion given to teams, and the extent to which people are given the required freedom to act.
- The commitment of senior management to team work, and especially cross-functional and inter-organizational team work. They must be dedicated to ensuring that decisions are taken as close to the customer as possible, and people are enabled to do what is necessary to add value for customers.
- Prevailing attitudes, such as the extent to which people feel part of teams. Empowered team work should be pervasive, rather than the isolated experiment.
- The management cadre. Managers should counsel and coach, value diversity, and foster and encourage teamwork, collaborative activities, self-development and group learning.
- How open people are, and the degree of trust and confidence they have. People need to feel they are able to take initiatives without being paralysed by fear of the consequences.

- Existing performance within teams, the tools shared within teams, and the approaches and support in terms of technology and process available to them. For example, there should be relatively open access to relevant information.
- Rewards and performance management. This should be supportive of, and should recognize, team work, the acquisition of team skills and the exhibiting of role-model behaviour.

## SUPPORTING CORPORATE TRANSFORMATION

When other transformation building blocks, such as specific and measurable objectives, are in place, the contribution of training to 'making it happen' can become apparent. As one personnel director put it: 'Training is not something you have to believe in any more. It doesn't have to work hard to justify itself. Either there is a place for it, or there isn't… people now know what they have to do. … They come forward with specific development requirements.'

Changes of behaviour do not occur just because the board believes it is a good idea. For example, managers do not become coaches and facilitators without themselves receiving coaching and facilitation. As one manager put it: 'It took the board five years to understand what a process is, and they have been talking about facilitation for three years. When they finally get there, why should they expect us to do it overnight?'

Transformation and learning ought to be natural bedfellows. Both should be a continuing process. Companies such as General Foods, ICL and Motorola gave the training role a central place in their corporate change programmes. 'Winner' companies relate management development activity to the achievement of specific business objectives, but losers appear slow or reluctant to learn from their experience.

A shared belief that a company has found a magic formula for success can greatly reduce the desire of its people to learn. In competitive markets, complacency can kill. Marks and Spencer became so satisfied with its regular appearance at the top of lists of the UK's most respected companies that it failed to take account of changes that were blatantly obvious to other retailers, such as the desire of customers to use their credit cards. The company assumed it could impose its own terms and preferred ways of working upon visitors to its stores.

Sometimes the lack of awareness of particular companies appears staggering. Had it not happened it would seem inconceivable that IBM, the dominant force in the IT sector, would fail to grasp the significance of the personal computer. The corporation's loss was Microsoft's gain. More recently IBM has managed to learn new skills required for operating in the computer services and project management marketplace.

# LEARNING IN A DYNAMIC ENVIRONMENT

Corporate transformation is a process of transition from one form of orga-nization and associated activities, attitudes and values, to another. It is not a discrete event that just happens. It cannot be obtained 'off the shelf'.

It is particularly important that managers think in dynamic terms, and focus upon trends rather than static pictures. Reality is dynamic. The world is changing while we think about it. As we describe what we have seen, or what we feel is happening, events and circumstances are making our description more or less valid.

People without prior experience will need to be equipped to operate in unfamiliar ways, for example in a self-managed workgroup or new-venture team. The process of preparation may continue over a period of time, as new areas of responsibility are phased in or a business develops.

Fundamental transformation changes do not occur 'on the first of the month'. Independence may come at midnight when one flag is lowered and another run up, but instilling an enterprise culture may be a gradual process. Those who claim there is a gap between rhetoric and reality could be describing the particular stage that has been reached, with the expec-tation that further progress ought to have been made.

Some will be satisfied earlier than others. For example, many advocates of empowerment are reluctant to allow groups of people to allocate their own remuneration. At a certain point they decide 'enough is enough', and draw a line in the sand.

Within the transforming organization, learning should be related partic-ularly to the gaps which emerge between expectations and outcomes. How have they come about, and what can be done to put transformation back on track?

If appropriate action is to be taken, the issue to focus upon may not be that a gap exists between aspiration and achievement, but whether it is closing or widening. Is the company on track, or are matters getting out of control? If the existence or direction of a trend is not identified, corrective action may make matters worse rather than better.

People need to probe and question. Reporting a trend does not allow appropriate action to be taken, if the reasons for it are not understood. Why has it occurred? Why is the gap wider in some areas and locations than in others? There are lessons in gaps and trends, and these need to be teased out.

Learning how to operate more cheaply should be a continuing preoccu-pation, not a periodic and crude response to the impact of an economic downturn and pressure to meet the expectations of analysts. Small and start-up companies grow by winning new customers. Low costs and keen pricing can give them the edge. At Waymade Healthcare, a distributor of pharmaceuticals, all members of staff are encouraged to think about ways of cutting costs. Euro Packaging attributes its success in penetrating the market for carrier bags to an obsession with cost reduction.

Of course, alternative strategies can be pursued if learning is applied to critical success factors. Zara, the clothing retailer, incurs a cost penalty by manufacturing its garments in Europe rather than cheaper Third World countries, such as China. However, its greater speed in bringing new designs into its stores allows it to respond to fashion trends more quickly and to have lower stock-holding costs. Overall, the company has been more profitable than rivals such as GAP and H&M.

## THE PROCESS VIEW

A focus upon processes is unlikely to lead to a process view of an organization, still less to seamless processes that speed actions and requirements through and between organizations, without a degree of development. Empowerment does not just happen. Processes need to be put in place to enable power and authority to be delegated, and people need to be equipped to deliver what is required. The rate at which actual authority is devolved and delegated should match the rate at which the capability is developed to use the additional discretion in the desired ways.

A number of the requirements for successful corporate transformation are inter-dependent. For example, the implementation of process re-engineering is critically dependent upon the empowerment of people (Coulson-Thomas, 1994). Without the discretion to act, the time that has traditionally been spent seeking authorization cannot be saved.

Whereas much of the benefit of process simplification can be obtained through empowerment, process re-engineering is more radical, involving fundamental or 'frame-breaking' change (Coulson-Thomas, 1994). Successful execution requires an examination of the interaction of people, process and technology. Management development is but one element; the development of compatible and mutually supportive processes and technology is also required.

## THE LEARNING PROCESS

Learning itself should be a process of exploration and discovery. It should continue throughout life, as capabilities are developed and matched to changing opportunities and requirements.

The traditional approach to education tends to assume that we all learn in a similar way. In fact people learn in a variety of ways. Those who perform best in approaches that require logic and structure may not be so effective in approaches that require sensitivity to links and patterns. The former may lead to academic honours. The latter may be what is needed to exploit the full potential of an artificial intelligence environment.

Our approach to learning is deep-rooted. Since the 12th century, logic has held sway with its emphasis upon categorization and procedure, moving forward in incremental steps from current positions. There has been little emphasis upon the more process-based relational approach, which has been the source of many 'scientific revolutions'. This is more concerned with links, patterns and relationships involving things which have not been logically related.

What is needed is self-awareness and self-confidence, communication and team working skills, adaptability and flexibility and a commitment to lifetime learning. All of these are qualities which can be built by new approaches to learning, and yet are too often stifled by existing approaches.

# DESTRUCTIVE TENDENCIES

Some disturbing aspects of many corporate transformation programmes are inhibiting the development of the required attitudes and approaches:

- The pressure of work, compounded by the reallocation of the tasks of those who have 'left' the flattening and slimming organization, has squeezed out what little time many managers have for thinking.
- The effort to communicate goals and values, and the desire of many employees during an era of 'headcount reduction programmes' to demonstrate their allegiance and commitment, is discouraging critical comment.
- The concentration on a 'vital few' programmes, and the allocation of ever more specific responsibilities and objectives is causing many people to narrow their focus at a time when coping with internal change and a turbulent business environment, and the desire to tap greater value-added opportunities in relationships with customers is demanding a 'broader view'.
- The lives of many managers, as a consequence of long hours and heavy workloads, have become more unbalanced at a time when handling competing pressures and the uncertainties of transformation require a sense of proportion.

While listening to talk of empowerment, release and liberation, people have been labelled, confined and crushed. Too many are still treated like pawns in the game of corporate reorganization. Having been given an overview of the whole board they find themselves stuck fast to one square. To think and learn, people need the emotional space to 'breathe'.

The categorization of people into levels can impede rather than assist progress towards the network organization. To create the network, the challenge is to change attitudes and share values. The training implications of corporate transformation can extend through and beyond the ranks of management.

In today's turbulent and changing world (see Table 1.1) we need people who can think. Decisions can no longer be left to 'the few'. Having established the framework, they are likely to be too far away and uninvolved to know what needs to be done in particular cases.

Customers increasingly require tailored products and services. They, and not the organization, are the centre of their worlds, and they are demanding personal attention. Processes for continual adaptation and learning, and individualized responses, are replacing standard procedures. Everyone needs to be involved in the development and delivery of added value.

Empowerment happens not when people are trained, but when customers feel that those they meet from the company can do things for them. It is alive when the people of the organization believe they can 'make it happen' for their customer.

## ESTABLISHING LINKS AND RELATIONSHIPS

Creating opportunities to add value is often a question of establishing links and relationships. Within the network organization, there is a need to develop relational approaches to problem solving.

Learning foundations and a commitment to continual learning ought to be established in school. If more people could themselves adapt to changing situations and opportunities, billions spent by industry and commerce on 'inducting', 'relearning' etc, could be saved. In the meantime, companies must act.

So what is needed? Essential first steps are as follows:

- A commitment to helping every individual to become aware of how he or she can learn most effectively. Everyone is good at something. Let us help people to discover what they can do best and most enjoy doing.
- Whatever is available for a person's education or development should first be used to help them uncover something of their own potential. A person requires self-awareness and self-knowledge to know how best to contribute to a group or team. There are too many people in companies who 'play back' slogans and 'go along with things' without really knowing who they are.
- To recognize that knowledge itself is becoming a commodity. It is increasingly there on the database, accessible by a terminal at home or on the manager's desk. While information sits in a data warehouse, customers may be going elsewhere, and the company may be folding.
- The value of data arises when it helps to improve understanding, and this is used to add value for a customer or further a specific objective. Machines store data. People use information and understanding for useful purposes. Working with it, discussing it, refining it and applying it are important, not just knowing it.

- Teachers and trainers, rather than pouring facts into the heads of people, should become facilitators of learning, able to guide, assist, counsel and complement each individual. The skill set required is that of the coach and partner, rather than the instructional approach of the traditional educator.

How people are approached and developed should reflect the values of the corporation. If the rhetoric refers to them as 'partners' and 'colleagues', they should not be treated as an 'audience' or as 'development fodder'. People can, and do, recognize inconsistencies between corporate words and training deeds.

Companies such as Apple, Ford, McDonald's, Motorola, Johnson & Johnson, SAS and TRW have run their own corporate colleges for many years and many of these have evolved into corporate universities (Coulson-Thomas, 1999). This enables them to ensure that development activity matches their particular requirements, and can give them greater freedom to use the services of those individuals with skills that are especially relevant.

Development and awareness-building activity should be opened to customers and business partners. This enables a company to build more intimate and mutually beneficial relationships. According to David Thompson, when Xerox opened its learning centre at Wokefield Park:

> The customer is not an outsider, but a colleague and a partner in training. Customers should be directly involved in training and other activities that add value for them. The customer is part of the business. Suppliers should share their understanding with customers, work with them and learn from them. This is what joint, relationship, or supply chain training is all about.

> The perspective and vision of trainers needs to be broadened beyond the company. It needs to embrace all those who add value for customers. These include suppliers, business partners and the customers themselves.

Effective learning comes from doing things and observing the outcomes. Group and team learning can be particularly beneficial in this respect. Learning and working should be integrated. Learning is more successful when its purpose and relevance to the work context are perceived.

The nature of the workplace has changed. The fixation of much of management education with competing and negotiating has meant that many managers have had to discover for themselves that companies have common interests, and while rivals in some areas, they may usefully cooperate in others.

## Transforming the workplace

We considered in Chapter 8 the reality for far too many companies that the workplace is an overhead cost and constraint upon creative activity when it could so easily become an enabler of business flexibility, entrepreneurial activity and knowledge creation. Some companies have designed specific environments for particular purposes. Thus Cambridge Management Centres designed a purpose-built training suite with observation facilities, which was constructed in collaboration with the then Swallow Hotel group.

Many consulting companies now provide hot-desking staff between assignments with flexible environments that include meeting rooms, social areas and private workspaces. Consider companies that you are familiar with. Do the work environments offer personal space for reflection as well as opportunities for interaction with others? How easy is it for people to get the technology they may require for particular projects? What continuity is provided for those who like to develop a sense of identity and belonging?

# NEW SOURCES OF INSIGHT

Blood cannot be squeezed from a stone. So insights relating to the world of flexible network organizations may not always be obtainable from people and institutions whose experience, competence and literature have derived from a different environment. More relevant sources of insight may need to be tapped, in relation to conflict and co-operation as follows:

- Political scientists have long realized that nation states have interests in common, and that these give rise to opportunities for functional co-operation. Many managers concerned with improving co-operation along supply chains would benefit from examining how inter-state collaboration has grown and developed.
- Managers need to come to terms with the extent to which, in a market-place of network organizations, there is competition on the basis of attitudes and values. When these are in conflict, there are often problems of perception to address. The literature of international relations yields a rich heritage of material concerning competition between value systems, and how attitudes and values influence perception.
- Those seeking to understand the continuing global struggle between Coca-Cola and Pepsi might gain more insights from a history of the Punic Wars, or a study of the global struggle between capitalism and communism, than from a management textbook.

A manager seeking to broaden his or her perspective should not expect to seek inspiration in the 'usual places', or from people whose expertise relates to a world from which companies are planning to escape.

# DEATH BY CLONING

Tailored in-company programmes can result in the 'identikit' or 'clone' manager, 'introversion' and 'groupthink'. At the same time, as companies formulate distinct visions and develop attitudes and processes that distinguish them from the approaches of competitors, it may become more difficult to absorb 'general inputs' or 'standard solutions' from outside.

In Chapter 11 we saw that a common perspective can help to hold the international network organization together. However, a common culture should not be allowed to become a straitjacket. Exposure to different cultures and ways of doing things may enable people to see 'outside of the square'.

Management development that is too prescribed can encourage people to reproduce a standard response, or move forward in small incremental steps. What may also be needed is the corporate environment that enables people to link up and establish relationships between factors that were previously thought to be unrelated. The caterpillar moves incrementally, the kangaroo bounds ahead.

An international network organization should do more than tolerate diversity, it should actively encourage it. The author's view is as follows (Coulson-Thomas, 1992):

> Greater diversity and variety can and should be sought among those who share the vision as learning and change are more likely to occur where views are continually challenged and there is tension between alternative viewpoints. Debate can be more important than a consensus that is based upon uncritical acceptance…
>
> Different ways of doing things should be actively encouraged within an international network organization, so that different elements of the network may learn from each other.

Reference has already been made to the literature of politics. This may be very relevant to the executive seeking to create an open culture in which people are encouraged to question, and the right to dissent is preserved. It could also yield valuable insights into how the various interests of a network might be held together against external pressures and divisive forces.

# PUTTING IN AND TAKING OUT

A balance needs to be struck between individualism and collectivism, but also between taking out and putting in. Xerox Corporation has launched a thousand managerial careers. Its people applied what they learnt to advancing their own interests and achieved senior positions throughout the IT sector. Meanwhile, the company struggled and failed to exploit the core elements of contemporary technology invented by its own employees.

Many of the building blocks of an information technology revolution that transformed various areas of corporate operation in the last quarter of the 20th century derived from a succession of inventions from PARC, the Palo Alto Research Centre of Xerox Corporation. Local area networking, the mouse, icons, pop-up and pull-down menus are among the innovations of a creative team that used revenues generated by copier sales and rental income to create new technologies that would support the way they would naturally prefer to work and learn.

Yet despite the brilliance of PARC's researchers, many of the breakthroughs that occurred were first exploited by a variety of other companies rather than Xerox itself. The corporation failed after a five-year drive to derive a half or more of its income from integrated office systems and went on to outsource its own technology. Early in the 21st century, after a year of losses the ability of Xerox to meet its financial commitments could not be assumed. The very survival of a corporation that had launched a hundred growth businesses and a thousand successful management careers was in doubt.

The experience of Xerox Corporation is not unique. Relationships between individuals and organizations involve a precarious balance between putting in and taking out. Individuals who give a lot and receive little in return become disgruntled and disaffected. They switch off and move on. Considerable effort may be devoted to keeping valued people on board. However, there are also many cases of people taking out much more than they put in. Managers play games, pursue fads, and engage in activities to increase their own visibility while adding momentum to their own careers rather than building shareholder value.

The supply of fresh know-how is sometimes taken for granted. If too much is drawn from the knowledge well and insufficient effort is applied to replenishing the flow of new intellectual capital, the well may run dry (Coulson-Thomas, 1997 and 1998). A business can grow and develop only if its employees put in as well as take out. For companies that you are involved in or familiar with, examine what people put in and take out at various levels. Rank individuals and/or groups in terms of which put the most in and which take the most out. Identify people and groups who take a lot out in relation to what they put in and consider what might be done to increase their contribution. Steps may need to be taken to benefit those who take out relatively little in relation to what they put in. Are there particular individuals or areas in which people seem primarily concerned with their own interests?

## ACTIVE INVOLVEMENT

Involvement and participation are only of value if those who are to be involved and whose participation is sought are able to add value. To do this they must have the time and motivation to think.

Self-managed workgroups and new venture teams are pointless if people lack the capability to think for themselves. If they are not to draw upon a wide range of experiences, insights and perspectives, the benefits of giving responsibility to a group rather than to an individual will be lost.

A group might secure some understanding of the network as a whole, and particularly of its dynamics and tensions, by charging it with a task of producing a strategy and programme for taking over or killing the network. The outputs from such a development exercise may identify points of weakness and areas of vulnerability.

## THINKING AND LEARNING

Many losers experience intense competitive pressures upon prices and margins. Sharper and more determined rivals undercut them. In response, they pursue defensive or 'me-too' strategies. They fail to innovate, differentiate and build more value into their offerings. Hence they drift inexorably towards 'commoditization'.

Winners recognize that consumer expectations are rising. New ideas can quickly catch on. What is special today may become commonplace by tomorrow. Hence, they devote greater effort to questioning, challenging, innovation and creativity. Rather than merely match the moves of their better competitors, they create additional choices and alternative options.

Losers also tend to ossify. They become typecast and locked into certain roles within their marketplace. They become fenced in by self-imposed restrictions, constrained by prison bars created within their own imaginations. If knowledge management initiatives occur, training and development professionals are probably not involved in them.

Many are also confined by the limited expectations that others have of them. People do not suggest improvements or alternative courses of action to them on the assumption that they will not respond. When under pressure losers may simply redouble their efforts to sell their regular offerings, perhaps using traditional methods such as price reductions and special offers to clear stock.

Within companies that lose market share, people are invariably busy. Even when businesses go into liquidation, their employees are usually fully occupied right up until the moment of collapse. They attend meetings and process a steady stream of telephone calls and e-mails. However, much of this activity is reactive, uncontrolled and undisciplined. With the benefit of hindsight it will be judged to have concerned secondary tasks, while vital priorities were ignored.

Redoubling efforts and 'more of the same' may not be enough. Companies operating in sectors in which margins are being squeezed may need to introduce new lines of business while there is still time. Thinking as well as 'doing' is required. However, increased workloads and longer hours reduce the time that many people have available for deliberation and reflection. They lack the intellectual space to create escape routes and envisage viable ways ahead.

## WINNING CULTURES

The corporate culture of winners is more stimulating, positive and proactive. Their people are alert, open-minded and curious. They are resilient and mentally adventurous. They instinctively strive to push back the boundaries of what is possible. They will have a go and learn as they go.

Those who deal with people in winning companies expect them to try their hand at 'new things'. In addition to differentiating themselves from competitive suppliers of similar products and services, they also launch new ventures and develop additional offerings that give rise to incremental income streams. Some think outside of the box and transform how business is done.

Winning companies remain alert to novel ideas, monitor relevant debates and plug into emerging schools of thought. They recognize that as existing candles burn down, new ones need to be lit if the darkness of marginalization and irrelevance is to be avoided. They also exploit their know-how and recruit or develop and unleash information and knowledge entrepreneurs.

Winners are more likely to achieve a balance between securing further sales of current products and services, and the development of fresh and different offerings that will sustain future growth. Some have specific and demanding new product development objectives. People are allowed the time they may need to reflect and are encouraged to be innovative. The layout of premises may include social and quiet spaces for networking and thinking, respectively.

## LEARNING FROM EXPERIENCE

Learning from both triumph and disappointment is especially important. Some losers invariably deduce the wrong lessons from failure. For example, following an unsuccessful launch of a new product, they may conclude that in future such risks should be best avoided, when a more positive reaction might be to aim to do things differently and better the next time around.

Many losers rarely discuss outcomes – whether the acceptance of an offer or the rejection of a proposal. They do not build learning loops or feedback mechanisms into their processes. They may periodically re-engineer and redesign, but without learning whatever increased levels of performance are achieved may soon be overtaken by competitors for whom innovation is a way of life rather than an occasional challenge.

Winners go to work to learn as well as earn, particularly in the area of business development. They are more curious and resilient. Their culture and management style encourages knowledge sharing and responsible and thoughtful risk taking. Failure often makes their people more determined then ever to succeed.

People in winning companies learn from their experiences. They dissect and analyse what has happened and probe for root causes. Debrief questionnaires are circulated and reviews are held to uncover why a particular approach or proposal worked or flopped. They then discuss what needs to be changed or improved.

Winners do not expect to rest on their laurels. Like adventurous spirits, they look out for new challenges that will stretch them, open up different routes and widen horizons. They try out further options in order to assess whether alternative courses of action and another response might be more effective. An absence of disappointment could indicate a lack of ambition.

Winners keep a careful watch of trends and developments relating to their own performance. For example, they investigate how procurement and bid practices are evolving. They actively monitor the experiences of competitors without becoming fixated or mesmerized by them.

Successful business development teams are always open to suggestions for improving their approaches to winning business. They actively invite feedback and comments from staff, associates, business partners, customers and prospects. Having reflected, people in winning companies quickly implement whatever changes may be necessary to seize windows of opportunity and achieve their objectives.

## Losers

Losers:

- believe that senior people know best, and adopt a top-down approach to management;
- encourage people to follow standard procedures and processes;
- do not stray far from a well-trodden path;
- subject their people to training inputs that share existing knowledge;
- provide general training programmes in vague areas such as 'empowerment';
- treat people in a standard way;
- assume that training and development activities are beneficial;
- undertake activities that generally do not directly contribute to the achievement of corporate purpose, goals and objectives;
- do not have facilities to support learning and reflection;
- think they know best;
- avoid or rationalize bad news.

## Winners

Winners:

- believe that those closest to customers and problems should know best and encourage those in the 'front line' to produce innovative responses and bespoke solutions;
- allow people to work and learn in whatever ways enable them to be most effective;
- are always on the alert for new patterns, links and relationships;
- encourage their people to innovate, pioneer and discover, and produce whatever new knowledge and tools may be required to achieve novel outcomes;
- recognize that different people may learn in dissimilar ways;
- provide people with specific support as and when they require it;
- challenge training and development interventions and encourage learning and self-development;
- endeavour to link training, development and learning activities to the achievement of corporate purpose, goals and objectives;
- integrate learning and working, and have facilities and environments that are conducive of reflection and support a wide range of learning activities;
- form learning links and partnerships, and join learning networks;
- learn from mistakes and failures.

# LEARNING PARTNERSHIPS

During the SEMS survey (Coulson-Thomas, 1990) a requirement emerged for a range of services that effectively spans development and consultancy:

- Interviewees felt that much of traditional management education and development benefited individual students without offering corresponding gains for employing companies.
- A criticism of consultancy was that while corporate problems might be solved, little was usually done to increase the ability of internal staff to tackle related and similar problems at a later date.

Hence, there was a strong desire for project-based programmes which could be focused on significant workplace problems. Their solution in a development context might offer benefits to both student and employer.

There are opportunities for external partners to work with companies in the identification and definition of workplace-based projects that are both intrinsically important and offer development opportunities. The requirement can be met by the establishment of learning partnerships:

- The learning and development needs of the individuals or teams working upon the selected projects derive from their particular characteristics and requirements, and are facilitated by whatever means is thought most appropriate.
- The 'external' parties involved provide a varying mix of services depending upon the portfolio of projects being undertaken at any moment in time.

As a number of learning partnerships are created, the network organization metamorphoses into a learning network (Figure 13.1). When this becomes international, its members require sensitivity to cultural diversity.

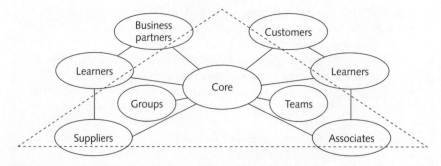

**Figure 13.1**   The learning network

Too often, students are encouraged to reach for their calculators and crunch the numbers, rather than observe and listen. The members of the international learning network, as one interviewee put it: 'Have to be able to look and listen in different languages.'

# BUILDING THE LEARNING NETWORK

Education and the technology that is used to support it should enable people to discover how they can best build their understanding. According to the IRL, the traditional 'black box' that produces an outcome without revealing why this has occurred 'deskills', while 'transparent technology' that allows the learner to observe processes at work can increase understanding with each application (Institute for Research on Learning, c1988).

The educational institution itself needs to evolve into a learning network (Figure 13.1) that can participate in learning partnerships. Resources should be switched from the campus and its buildings, to the technology and processes of the network. International learning networks can bring together learners and facilitators from around the globe.

Passing on experience and insights enables centres of excellence to consolidate and internalize what they have learnt. The experience of winners suggests that: approaches, processes, tools and techniques have been developed that can enable more companies to achieve a better return from training expenditure; there are cost-effective and flexible ways of managing and delivering training, and focusing training effort upon core activities, key objectives and critical success factors for competing and winning.

# THE KEY QUESTIONS

Persistent losers should subject their training and development activities to a critical review. From the point of view of the individual company there are two key questions that should be asked.

- If your company increased its expenditure on training by a factor of 10, would there be a significant improvement in performance?
- If the people within your company spent half their time on training activities, would there be a significant change in their attitudes or behaviour?

Evidence suggests that, for most 'loser' companies, the answers to both of these questions would be no. It is essential that companies identify what constitutes value to their customers, and understand how to deliver this value.

Many corporate programmes will continue to fail to achieve significant results until crucial missing pieces of the transformation jigsaw puzzle are put in place and critical obstacles to change are identified and overcome.

As we will see in Chapter 17, all the elements that are needed to turn the international network into the international learning network exist. The same, or compatible, processes and technology can support both learning and working across barriers of distance, function and time. They are available to those with the vision and will to use them.

---

# CHECKLIST

▶ Is the culture of your organization conducive of learning?

▶ Is there tolerance and the active encouragement of diversity?

▶ Do the members of the board and senior management team act as role models in terms of their commitment to learning?

▶ Are formal education and development programmes focused upon those processes and activities that add value for customers?

▶ Do these programmes embrace other members of the supply chain, such as customers, suppliers and business partners?

▶ What, if anything, does your company learn from customers and other supply chain partners?

▶ How willing is your company to refine and modify its objectives and processes?

▶ What is done to help the people of your company identify their learning potential?

▶ Are individuals encouraged to work and learn in ways that match their own preferences and potential?

▶ Are working and learning integrated?

▶ What does your company do to encourage informal learning?

▶ Is the reward system and are promotion and performance management decisions conducive of learning?

▶ Is learning focused on critical factors for competing and winning?

# REFERENCES

Coulson-Thomas, C (1990) *Human Resource Development for International Operation*, a Survey sponsored by Surrey European Management School, Adaptation Ltd, London

Coulson-Thomas, C (1992) *Creating the Global Company, Successful Internationalisation*, McGraw-Hill, London

Coulson-Thomas, C (ed) (1994), *Business Process Re-engineering: Myth and Reality*, Kogan Page, London

Coulson-Thomas, C (1997 and 1998), *The Future of the Organization: Achieving excellence through business transformation*, Kogan Page, London

Coulson-Thomas, C (1999), *Developing a Corporate Learning Strategy: The key knowledge management challenge for the HR function*, Policy Publications, Bedford

Institute for Research on Learning (c1988) *The Advancement of Learning*, Institute for Research on Learning, Palo Alto, Calif., undated

# FURTHER INFORMATION

Brochures describing *Developing a Corporate Learning Strategy* and *The Responsive Organisation* report, methodology and toolkit for introducing new ways of working are available from Policy Publications, 4 The Crescent, Bedford MK40 2RU (tel: +44 (0) 1234 328448; fax: +44 (0) 1234 357231, e-mail: policypubs@kbnet.co.uk; Web site: www.ntwkfirm.com/bookshop).

# 14

# Partnering with Consultants and Business Schools

*'People should not travel on the river after dusk'*

## AN UNPRECEDENTED OPPORTUNITY

One senses urgency and desperation. Given the importance attached to corporate transformation, and the range of problems being experienced, consultants should be having a field day. Notwithstanding an economic recession or slowdown in key world economies, people running corporations need help.

Across a wide range of companies there is a requirement to equip people to cope with the demands of a turbulent business environment and new threats such as global terrorism. There is also the continuing desire to become more flexible and responsive. For over a decade managers have sought to effect a transition from machine bureaucracy to organic network. However, in 'loser' companies the fundamental changes of attitude and perspective required to bring it about have yet to be achieved.

As part of the transformation process, companies have sought to hive off and subcontract. This has created further opportunities for external providers of services.

In tackling the lucrative openings in the marketplace, consultancies have access to 'the brightest and the best'. When it comes to promotion, presentations and the production of glossy brochures, the services of the slickest and the smoothest are at their disposal. After reading just a few consultants' 'mailshots' from the 1990s, it seems remarkable that many companies should have management problems at all.

## THE BLIND LEADING THE BLIND

And yet, in general, those who have been interviewed in the course of the surveys upon which this book is based are far from satisfied with the quality of external services they receive. On occasion, their purveyors are perceived as parasites rather than facilitators. As one managing director put it: 'If you get it right, don't tell anyone. If you do, every consultant will be trying to get hold of your ideas. They seem desperate for anything that works.'

Although many business schools and consultancies have a public commitment to learning from, and sharing, best practice, this has not stopped some of them, and those who use their services, from jumping at techniques such as 're-engineering' as if they represent a revelation. One director confided: 'We are into begging, stealing and borrowing like there is no tomorrow.'

Mindless copying can result in the spread of panaceas, hype and misunderstanding, and gives added momentum to the latest craze. While it may be good news for those who ride bandwagons, it is not so hot for those whose toes get in the way.

When external suppliers, such as consultants, do get hold of a best practice 'gem', their motivation is often to spread it around their client base as soon as possible. Thus the corporation's competitive edge can quickly become industry commonplace. One CEO of an innovative company mused: 'Sometimes I just feel as though we have been idea-stripped. We pay to be intellectually cleaned out.'

Some consultants receive as good as they give. Companies invite various experts to pitch for business and then 'do it themselves', using the best of the various ideas they have picked up. The 'learning organization' is a voracious and insatiable plunderer and consumer of intellectual capital. The wary choose their network partners with care.

## PEOPLE AND CORPORATE TRANSFORMATION

In essence, corporate transformation is a service activity. Its achievement is dependent upon 'reaching', motivating, coaching and counselling people; involving, empowering and supporting them; equipping them with the skills they need; sharing values with them; helping them to build new forms of relationships; and changing their attitudes and perspectives.

Involving people in workplace activities that lead to desired outcomes encourages 'positive' attitude and behaviour changes. Success leads to further success.

Coping with disappointment and failure can bring other qualities to the surface. It can lead to 'negative' behaviour such as concealment or the denial of reality, deception, deflection of the blame on to others, and the search for excuses and scapegoats. Hence the desire to close gaps between aspiration and achievement, and the need for help.

Collectively, consultants and business schools offer a wide range of programmes, including short courses and 'in-company' training. The faculties and staff of many individual suppliers represent significant concentrations of expertise. But how is this 'resource' perceived? Are organizations approaching consultants and business schools for advice on fundamental issues concerning corporate transformation, or to meet particular skill needs?

# DOUBTS AND CONCERNS

There are clearly potential openings for the services of consultants, business schools, and of education and training generally. But several surveys undertaken for the first edition of this book (Coulson-Thomas, 1992) suggested that if this opportunity was to be seized, a fundamental rethink, and new attitudes and approaches might be necessary:

- In a number of key areas the advice of consultants, business schools and their staff was not perceived as either relevant or desirable.
- Traditional skills and services were no longer perceived as being sufficient to bring about the corporate transformations that were required. Changes of approach, attitude and perspective were sought, not knowledge *per se* or technical skills. Holistic programmes were needed, not discrete 'products'.
- Many companies had become wary, if not distrustful, of external sources of advice and services, and were instead relying upon their own internal resources.

Two interview comments appeared to sum up common views and concerns:

*If it's standard and structured, I know I can go out and get any number of different techniques... [They will be] documented, and the manuals will be available. But how do you get the people all around you to think in new ways... to feel differently about things? That's tough for anyone else.*

*We used to buy things that were done to people... they were equipped with this and that skill. It's you and your colleagues who are [now] involved... Our relationships with people influence their attitudes... the way they see problems. We have to work it out with them ourselves.*

'Loser' companies attach excessive credence to the counsel of external and uninvolved experts while paying little attention to the views of their customers. The Shell.com Web site provides discussion group facilities that allow the international oil company to seek opinions from interested supporters whether they be allies or critics. Their response can be taken into account when policies are reviewed and decisions have to be taken.

New approaches, attitudes, perspectives and values are required. We saw in Chapter 13 that a growing number of companies have sought to integrate learning and working. Consultants need access to these learning environments in order to become learning partners.

## THE ADVISER AS LEARNER

Within many consultancies and business schools people still learn and practise as individuals within a framework of separate departments or practices. There is segregation by subject and specialism or section, rather than the cross-functional and multi-purpose team. Buildings contain lecture and seminar rooms and work spaces rather than learning areas and atmospheres. At many business schools classroom learning persists, along with various devices from case studies, through simulation to the introduction of virtual reality to emulate and imitate learning situations that abound in far richer forms in most companies.

The desire of some consultants and academics to learn about new and alternative approaches has given rise to the accusation that they are 'learning from' rather than 'learning with'. The 'learning from' approach can cause much resentment, while the 'learning with' approach can command respect. According to one CEO:

> I would respect a guy who came in and said 'Look, neither of us knows that much about this, but let's take a bite at it together'. ... I can't stand those who try to con you when they haven't a clue. I would prefer to trust someone with their eyes open and a willingness to learn.

We have observed the consequences and limitations of a narrow and mechanical approach to activities as varied as planning, communicating and problem solving, at a number of points in this book. Companies want practical solutions to real and evolving problems, rather than theoretical options and possibilities, or optimum outcomes.

We saw in the last chapter that because of a lack of faith in external providers, many companies have established their own colleges and corporate universities. Activity is related directly to the achievement of business objectives.

However, those with a strong preference for internal sources of expertise acknowledge the benefits of an independent perspective, given the dangers of a narrow corporate view emerging.

According to one quality manager: 'It's difficult to find an overview out there. Different people are good at different things. We have drawn bits and pieces from all over the place... You just can't go to a single source... we encourage people... to get different views.'

## MANAGEMENT OF CHANGE

In the main, management teams appear to consider the management of change to be an internal responsibility. The degree of commitment required, and the involvement of all employees, makes it difficult for many managers to identify other than specific tasks which could be undertaken by an external party. Consider the following comments:

*Role-model conduct is your responsibility... You can't go out and get a 'stand in'... [and] you need feedback from the people around you.*

*How can you smell what's going on around here, if you are not breathing the air?*

*Giving authority... taking out inhibitors, setting the scene and values... these all involve lots of different people. No outsider would have the clout.*

*The [change programme] is evolving... [Because] it's changing you need to be here to steer it. There is no value in handing over a blueprint and walking away.*

*Outsiders always have to explain who they are, and under what terms they are working... It takes time for people to assess where they are coming from.*

The management of change is regarded as a holistic or 'total' process involving people throughout an organization and its network of relationships. Winners retain ownership of change programmes, rather than abdicate this responsibility to external consultants.

## THE LIMITATIONS OF EXTERNAL ADVICE

Why are people sceptical of external advice? In many cases it is because they feel it is important to understand the distinct corporate culture of a company:

- It is thought to be difficult for a third party fully to appreciate the particular features of an internal corporate culture. Companies appear reluctant to hand over what are perceived as culture-specific problems to third parties.
- People also doubt that 'standard solutions and packages' are of much value. According to a managing director: 'Perhaps we do sometimes exaggerate what's different about us. But what was good down the road

may not work around here.'
- A frequent complaint of interviewees relates to the apparent reluctance of consultants to 'get to grips' with the unique situation and circumstances of individual companies. Instead there is a tendency to go automatic. As one director put it: 'Whenever I see earnest young people working their way through manuals or diagnostic kits that are inches thick, I worry. Someone somewhere is not thinking or asking basic questions.'
- Companies are finding it difficult to recruit experienced and competent practitioners who are able to move effectively between corporate cultures. Too often 'experts' turn out to be technical specialists, when the main problems to be overcome are managerial and attitudinal.
- There is a perception that much of what is provided is over-elaborate. One managing director expressed the view: 'If it's esoteric and you don't understand it, it probably misses the point. Working back from the customer reveals that complexity is often the result of a desire to justify an activity that is not generating value for customers.'

External suppliers are also thought to be too complacent. They uncritically apply packaged approaches without tailoring, testing and observation. A few moments spent examining actual outcomes might reveal that they are not working.

Many external consultants persuade insecure managers that they ought at least to pretend to know about fashionable concepts. They continually peddle new ideas to companies that would benefit from traditional remedies. Tesco has prospered at the expense of rivals by focusing unashamedly on the basics of successful retailing, particularly the creation of greater value for the customer, while at the same time moving into on-line shopping and expansion overseas.

Independence and objectivity can be extremely desirable qualities. However, in some cases, the maintenance of 'professional distance' can conceal a reluctance to become involved. One cynical interviewee suggested: 'If you provide a bit of what's required, and then stand back, you can avoid blame when things go wrong.' The fault can be ascribed to the whole, and how the individual change elements were combined or used.

Many people selling external services have an inadequate understanding of the internal context within which these could be used and applied. They 'push' their own services, rather than work with 'users or clients' to develop new approaches that confront marketplace realities and opportunities.

Many suppliers also still focus upon 'the short-term sale' rather than the building of longer-term relationships, even though there is widespread use of such pat phrases as 'in-company', 'tailoring' and 'finding solutions to customer problems'. Overall, the approach is that of external supplier rather than network member. As one director put it: 'There is a premature packaging of the product. The proposal is in while we are still trying to get to grips with what the problem really is. They want to supply to us... [but] they are not working with us.'

# THE MIGRATION FROM EXTERNAL SUPPORT TO SELF-HELP

Companies attaching most weight to external advice and support appear to be those that are relatively new to a corporate change or transformation initiative. The role of the external consultant as an initial catalyst is acknowledged. During the process of corporate transformation, many companies appear to rely increasingly upon their own resources. Consider the following selection of comments:

*We used external help to get off the starting block. But now we're implementing ourselves. Externals are an expensive way of getting the legwork done.*

*The key points came across in the various pitches and presentations. We ended up deciding to use our own people. You need to do it yourself, as this is the best way of learning and getting the attitude changes that you need.*

*I'm beginning to get an overview of how it all fits together. Our consultants are still focused on their individual offerings. They don't see the big picture.*

*I would prefer a longer term partnership, but we tend to quickly absorb what [consultants] have to offer, and move on. How come those who advise and counsel are so incapable of learning?*

In order to play a useful role in facilitating change, a process consultant needs persistence and a high degree of staying power. Organizational transformation is not a business for those with a penchant for working mechanically through a standard set of techniques and tools, and greeting the unexpected with the cry: 'What now?'

## THE NAÏVE AND THE INNOCENT

The management teams of companies that are starting out on 'change journeys' are drawn like moths to a light to those who promise results. Having committed the organization, they crave reassurance. They are anxious, and want to feel that they have done the right thing.

The focus of most consultants is almost entirely upon the lessons of success, and yet Bennis and Nanus have rightly drawn attention to the importance of learning from failure (Bennis and Nanus, 1985). The leaders they studied, 'simply don't think about failure, don't even use the word, relying on such synonyms as "mistake", "glitch", "bungle", or countless others'; and they concluded that 'early success' is 'the worst problem in leadership'.

Suave and beguiling consultants flatter and serve up great dollops of what they know or imagine their clients want to hear. Some may not even realize they are doing it. They 'keep in' by offering the reassurance that is so desperately sought, 'maintaining accounts' by avoiding reality and selling deception. Their life at court is only disturbed when the CEO is fired. They then have a successor to 'size up and work on'.

Companies that have made some progress appear more sophisticated:

- They are more aware of the unique nature and requirements of their own companies. By now they know that simplistic approaches do not work. As one manager put it: 'Those were the teenage years – now we've grown up.'
- Suspicion of generalized solutions and experience gained elsewhere grows as an approach to change comes to be seen as an integral element of a unique corporate culture.
- Their internal capability may have grown to match or exceed that of the external supplier. These are the companies that focus upon 'adding value' and raise the question: 'What's in it for us?'

As organizations seek to differentiate themselves from competitors, and develop strong and unique corporate cultures, they find it increasingly difficult to absorb 'external inputs'. Consultants invariably take time to adjust to the unique aspects of corporate culture.

In general, those with a few years' experience of implementing change within their organizations do not feel that the contribution of many external organizations would 'add much value'. More mature and holistic approaches are sought, which are substantially tailored to the needs of a particular corporate culture, and confront the need to change attitudes and perspective.

There is considerable suspicion of standard 'off the shelf' solutions. Many organizations are relying primarily upon their own internal resources because of growing awareness of the time it takes to achieve a significant change of attitudes. Some seasoned campaigners avoid those with solutions, and seek out those with the problems. They want to know how others cope with obstacles and overcome similar difficulties to those they encounter.

## SUSPICION OF THE EXPERTS

Those intimately involved in corporate transformation may encounter, almost daily, a variety of situations for the first time. They journey through a changing landscape, and are deeply suspicious of experts with maps.

Too many of the 'specialists', both internally and externally, are thought to be but one step ahead of those they advise.

Organizational change is very threatening to specialist groups that are reluctant to shift their focus and to put the emphasis upon 'working with' as a team member, rather than 'working for' as an expert adviser:

- Groups of experts in head office specialisms from personnel to IT have been slimmed down, with many central groups being wound up. As one CEO put it: 'Around here, if you don't take a holistic view, we're likely to take a holistic view of your job.'
- Specialist services have been contracted out, or delegated to business units where they are closer to customers, and it is easier to align professional priorities with commercial objectives.
- Those at the centre are expected to take a broader view, focusing upon strategies and policies, rather than operational matters. Many individuals have been reluctant to 'step up' to this challenge, their perspective remaining functional rather than extending to embrace the totality of the company and transformation challenge.
- Services may now need to be sold, rather than costs allocated. This means building relationships with possible users and understanding their priorities.
- Some professionals have found that their area of expertise is suddenly in demand and that the CEO has 'at last noticed'. Rather than respond by rushing out to claim their place in the sun, many professionals fail to rise to the occasion and lurk in the shadows instead.
- The reluctance of many professionals to venture beyond the confines of the narrowest definition of their skills means they watch from the sidelines while a succession of new groups claim centre stage.

Experts and specialists are a distinguishing feature of the machine bureaucracy. In the 'locust years' of cartels and 'barriers to entry' they could be afforded. The size of central staffs was a mark of status, rather like the number of cattle in the chief's kraal.

Years of service in bureaucratic organizations gave many professionals a reluctance to examine alternative approaches, or stray beyond the confines of role descriptions and process manuals. They remain inhibited and constrained, prisoners of the familiar, and victims of the routines and standards they administer and police.

Professional values put great stress upon reliability and predictability. Surprises are unwelcome and uncertainties are avoided. Too many managers, and those who advise them, are afraid to take risks. Confident companies encourage innovation and entrepreneurship.

# MANAGING WHAT ISN'T

Too much management attention is paid to modifying what is, rather than searching for what is missing. What is can be 'seen and suffered'. What is not there may appear to be something of an act of faith. Managers are often reluctant to devote time to pursuing what may turn out to be a mirage. Squeezing small, incremental improvements out of the familiar may appear to be a 'safer' option.

Similarly, much consultancy effort is devoted to the application of tried and tested tools and techniques to existing approaches and activities, rather than to identifying missing elements, and devising and adopting new approaches that may have greater relevance. Expertise, training and technology are devoted to what is, rather than bringing about what ought to be.

If the key processes that deliver the value sought by customers are cross-functional and inter-organizational, delays are hidden, and 'hinders' have not been explored, a company should expect relatively limited returns from departmental consultancy projects. A more holistic approach may be needed if more fundamental change is to be achieved.

A checklist along the lines of Figure 14.1 could be used to identify areas of external expertise that might be needed to support the introduction of a corporate transformation programme. Any external resource that is contracted should understand the contribution of its particular area of authority in relation to the programme as a whole.

When certain elements are implemented exceptionally well, and in the process demand and receive an excessive amount of attention, a programme as a whole can become unbalanced. Enthusiasts must know when to stop. Some areas may need to be reined back in the interests of balance, and so that complementary aspects can catch up.

# DANGERS OF SELF-RELIANCE

In certain 'loser' companies a suspicion of 'external' services in general has been taken to an extreme. A dislike of what are termed 'general' or 'standard' solutions, appears to be leading to an excessive and unhealthy reliance upon internal expertise. For example:

- Some companies, while readily admitting their own lack of speed and progress in tackling barriers to change, are drawing almost exclusively upon their own experience.
- Many companies acknowledge a reluctance to learn from others by, for instance, benchmarking themselves against non-competing companies or engaging in shared learning.

Self-help is most dangerous where there is complacency, and of greatest value where there is openness, trust and a willingness to learn. Winners

| Requirement | Own Capability | Develop Capability | Consultant on Network |
|---|---|---|---|
| Formulating vision | | | |
| Communicating/sharing vision | | | |
| Performance management | | | |
| Differentiation | | | |
| Allocating objectives/ Roles and responsibilities | | | |
| Entrepreneurship | | | |
| Self-managed work groups | | | |
| Individual learning | | | |
| Corporate learning | | | |
| Knowledge creation and management | | | |
| Team working | | | |
| Project management | | | |
| etc | | | |

**Figure 14.1** Consultants' checklist

display a sustained commitment to learning from both outside and within. External partnering and internal self-help are practised as integral elements of a comprehensive corporate change programme.

# PARTNERING

Mention has already been made in Chapters 5 and 6 of the fact that losers avoid intimacy in their relationships with customers. Instead they keep them at arm's length. Their people may take steps to protect corporate interests by means of 'no-go' areas, detailed legal agreements and a culture of secrecy that encourages hoarding rather than sharing.

Losers are risk averse and inhibited, if not timorous and constipated. They do not stray too far from what they consider to be their core areas of expertise. They have a fear of being rejected, burned or dumped. They are often constrained by limited vision and a lack of drive rather than a shortage of funding or a dearth of talent.

Losers will undertake specific and discrete tasks for which they are likely to be paid. However, they tend to avoid more general arrangements that lead to uncertain and performance-related outcomes. They may consider the broader picture to be of little interest or consequence.

Given such characteristics, it is not surprising that so many 'loser' companies become suppliers of commodity products and undifferentiated services. Winners are more adventurous and open-minded. They welcome opportunities to form close relationships and strategic partnerships, as do people associated with them. They believe that shared vision and values and common objectives will safeguard their longer-term interests better than either avoiding intimacy or relying on 'small print'.

People in winning companies do not mind venturing into the unknown and participating in both the risks and the returns that might result. They are happy to consider and conclude arrangements that allocate a proportion of any profits or cost savings that are generated to each party. They focus on how partners in the enterprise can best achieve the outcomes they individually and collectively desire.

## CORPORATE CREDENTIALS

The promotional materials and corporate presentations of losers tend to be dominated by whatever products and services are currently on offer. Little evidence may be presented of their underpinning know-how, potential or ability to do other things.

Potential partners find it difficult to determine what distinctive qualities and capability losers might be able to bring to the party. Directors and senior managers of 'loser' companies may themselves be unsure of what they might be able to contribute to a partnering relationship. The desirability of alternative courses of action may seem uncertain and they may struggle to choose between available partners.

Many organizations commit almost all of their public relations and marketing expenditure to product-specific promotions. Little emphasis is devoted to packaging and communicating strategic corporate strengths and core competencies. An analysis or explanation of central elements of corporate capability may be more important for people considering a strategic partnership than information on individual offerings.

Winners know what they are about and what they have to offer. They produce credentials likely to be of interest to potential partners. Executive presentations stress special qualities, distinctive resources and particular strengths.

# BUILDING PARTNERSHIPS

Partnering and mutually beneficial partnership relationships can enable companies to break out of commodity product traps into a cycle of ascent to higher profitability (Coulson-Thomas, 1997 and 1998). However, potential partners should be identified and chosen with care. For example, some academics are masters at stripping companies of good ideas, selling them to competitors and then writing about them in journals in order to enhance their personal reputations. Such 'prima donnas' should be avoided.

Collaboration can be rather like travelling down a river that twists and turns. People who travel in daylight and keep their eyes open are best able to stay clear of reed banks, shallows and overhanging branches. Winners keep their wits about them when building partnerships.

Ideal partners have available time and are free of conflicting interests and commitments. Flexibility, responsiveness, future potential and the importance of a relationship for each party should be taken into account.

Each of the various parties to an arrangement should play to their particular strengths. Thus within a learning partnership corporate contributions could include company-specific modules, while one or more of the traditional universities handles the common and more generic elements of a collaborative programme (Coulson-Thomas, 1999). Costs should be fairly allocated in relation to benefits obtained by the different participants.

Compatible objectives and complementary capabilities enhance bargaining power. An initiative with several partners, diversified sources of funding and a degree of self-governance may be more resilient in the face of short-term pressures than a more limited arrangement. An example is the Centre for Competitiveness based at the University of Luton.

Collaborative ventures can tap a wider pool of experience, avoid introversion and spread set-up and running costs. They can also bring together a critical mass. Thus each party alone might not be able to field sufficient candidates to justify a dedicated development programme. However, relationships need to be managed and the benefits obtained must exceed the costs of doing this.

Winners avoid arrogant and opinionated 'experts' operating from expensive offices in central business districts. Eager to claim credit and derive fees from the success of others, they run for cover whenever problems or potential embarrassments arise. Leading professionals sought Robert Maxwell as a customer and banked his fees. However, when companies he controlled folded they rapidly distanced themselves and claimed not to have been insiders.

# LEARNING RELATIONSHIPS

Many companies would benefit from the establishment of a wider range of learning relationships, in order to share experiences of tackling similar problems. Learning partners might be found in a wide range of sectors and locations, and could become members of the network organization. Networks of colleague and peer relationships can enable people with similar problems to learn from each other.

The global network form of organization allows certain territorial barriers to be overcome. Companies adopting it can enter into closer relationships with international customers and suppliers, in order to jointly explore change requirements, and establish collaborative activities. The right external party can contribute a broader perspective and an awareness of alternative approaches.

Those more 'secure' in their commitment to change appear more open to the value of benchmarking, partnering and a diversity of approaches. While many 'loser' companies seem to have adopted one approach and 'stuck to it', certain larger 'winner' corporations appear consciously to seek different and competing overviews, in order to 'challenge' their management teams.

The acid test of many learning partnerships is whether the shared learning that results leads to creation of new know-how (Coulson-Thomas, 1999). Expectations regarding the ownership and use of intellectual capital should be clarified. People and organizations with too much on, or preoccupied with solving *their own* short-term problems, should be avoided.

# MANAGING INTELLECTUAL CAPITAL

Many companies do not effectively manage the know-how they create (Perrin, 2000). At board meetings, financial, marketing and other directors could suggest formal reviews of corporate approaches to the management of intellectual capital, and advocate proactive strategies for harvesting more value from it. Incentives should be put in place to encourage this.

The focus should be on the areas of greatest opportunity. Many companies spread their IT and other investments too thinly and do not concentrate on where they can have most impact upon the critical success factors for achieving key corporate objectives. The 'Managing Intellectual Capital' research report (Perrin, 2000) and 'The Information Entrepreneur' guide (Coulson-Thomas, 2000) suggest some key questions to ask:

- How significant is know-how as a source of customer and shareholder value within your company's sector?
- Is its contribution assessed and tracked?
- Is the sharing of information, knowledge and understanding measured?

- Are sufficient resources devoted to thinking, learning and the acquisition, creation, management and exploitation of information, knowledge and understanding?
- Is intellectual capital identified, packaged, badged and protected?
- Is intellectual property valued and revalued, and appropriately treated in the annual report and accounts?
- Is an appropriate knowledge management framework like K-frame (www.K-frame.com) in place?
- Does this allow the company to capture, access, present and exploit intellectual capital quickly?

'Leaders' are far more determined than 'laggards' to exploit corporate know-how, and are much more effective at monitoring intellectual capital performance and revenue contribution. They are also more likely to identify know-how as a primary driver of shareholder value, to focus on the roles different management functions should play in creating and exploiting intellectual property, and to address the relevant people, culture, process and IT factors (Perrin, 2000).

---

## Losers

Losers:

- rely upon consultants to tell them what to do and how to do it;
- take a short-term and project view of relationships with consultants;
- are fixed in their views, resistant to new ideas and alternative courses of action, and reluctant to learn from outsiders;
- tend to fall back on existing approaches and tried and tested techniques;
- adopt standard solutions, methodologies and packages;
- seek general improvements in performance;
- employ consultants who work systematically through their firm's methodology manuals;
- become lost in the intricacies of complex mega-projects;
- do not understand how the products and services of different supplies interrelate with each other;
- focus upon what is immediately apparent;
- are reluctant partners and fail to exploit the full potential of their know-how.

## Winners

Winners:

- give consultants and external advisers a clear direction and seek specific help from those with relevant credentials;
- seek longer-term and partnering relationships with consultants who share their objectives;
- are prepared to learn from and with external parties they respect;
- will try new approaches and are prepared to develop their own methodologies and techniques;
- prefer to secure bespoke approaches to particular problems;
- endeavour to achieve specific and stated objectives;
- use consultants who understand and address what is unique and special about an individual company's situation and circumstances;
- try to keep management efforts simple and focused;
- understand how individual products and services complement and work with each other;
- attempt to understand and influence the drivers behind what is apparent;
- form mutually beneficial learning partnerships and manage and exploit the know-how that results.

## ROOTS OF INCOMPATIBILITY

Some consultancies and professional firms face particular problems when seeking to establish longer-term partnerships relationships with corporate clients. To take some examples:

- Their relatively flat organization, and the existence of many directors and partners, linked with consensus management and the reluctance to delegate power to managing roles, makes it difficult to agree a common vision and specific objectives.
- A high degree of specialism, and a practice unit culture, makes it difficult for multidisciplinary teams to be brought together. The brochures might refer to the various areas of expertise, but in practice there is often a reluctance to bring them together, due to billing problems, internal political and territorial issues.
- While corporate clients seek increasingly to link remuneration to the achievement of tangible outputs, many professional practices still cling obstinately to a preference for charging on an input or time spent basis.
- In the case of partnership structures, there may be a resistance to significant investment in IT and other requirements of creating a network and

global capability, as the monies required 'come out of the pockets' of the 'equity partners'.

- Many professionals are reluctant to stray from what they regard as their areas of expertise. Their focus is upon the accumulation of expert knowledge, when the client may be more concerned with its application in a particular and fleeting context, and the problems which arise may be difficult to 'pigeon-hole' in terms of professional specialisms.
- Professional practices also tend to maintain a 'hard shell', and are often reluctant to forge network links, especially with other firms in similar fields. In many professional firms there is enormous scope for cost savings, for example, through shared specialist services, as a result of network links. Because of professional values, codes of practice and familiarity with 'Chinese walls', professional firms ought to find it easier than many commercial enterprises to co-operate in some areas, while competing in others.

An early example of an international professional network was the Pacific Rim Advisory Council. The various law firms constituting the network, and located in a number of countries around the Pacific Rim, accessed each other's specialist skills as required.

Business schools have also had their problems. Their response to the changing requirements of network organizations for partnership relationships have strained their own links with host universities. Some have an 'uneasy' connection with the wider organizational setting in which they find themselves.

## PREPARATION FOR A CHANGING WORLD

Business schools have had to revamp their programmes to give greater priority to coping with diversity, turbulence and surprise; encouraging sensitivity to feelings, attitudes and values; building a holistic perspective, and multicultural and international awareness; and bringing about revolutionary change and corporate transformation.

The corporation is today more vulnerable to competition and challenges beyond its control. Opportunities are fleeting. Understanding these changes requires political and cultural sensitivity, and an acute awareness of underlying concerns and values.

In the past many business schools placed an excessive emphasis upon the internal functions of the corporate machine, with separate courses in production, marketing, personnel, finance, accountancy etc, and over-stressed rational approaches to decision making and optimization. In the 'real world' of 'global commercial warfare', terrorist attacks and partnership arrangements, a subject such as international relations, with its emphasis upon decision making in situations of stress and incomplete information, international negotiation, cross-cultural communication, crisis management and the establishment and break up of alliances may be more relevant.

The international network organization requires processes for identifying and anticipating change in the global environment. Managers require an awareness of contemporary international political, economic, financial, trade, environmental and moral issues and risks. It is important to appreciate the limitations upon corporate power and influence, and potential vulnerability to changing values.

## DIVERSITY AND THE NETWORK

To prepare people for movement around the network organization, they need awareness of different perspectives, and experience of various forms of partnership relationship. The packaged programme can encourage one way of looking at the world, and may deny an organization the opportunities to capitalize upon the rich diversity of backgrounds and approaches that might exist across an international network.

Some companies 'spend millions' wiping out diversity in the interests of instilling a common approach. The result can be the robo-corporation, peopled with clones with identikit attitudes, approaches, tools and techniques.

Diversity need not be incompatible with developing a shared perspective of corporate goals and priorities, and a common position on certain international issues. For many years companies such as Asea Brown Boveri and General Electric have brought groups of managers together to participate with senior management in issue-based seminars. People are exposed to each other's viewpoints and perspectives. Tolerance and respect for diversity should be a shared value.

## IMPLICATIONS

Many of those concerned with consultancy, training and development may challenge the validity of the perceptions of the 'external' supplier of advice and services which have been presented in this chapter. Yet the perceptions exist, and in the minds of a significant group of corporate decision makers. Suppliers of external and development services need to recognize the following in many companies:

- The emphasis has shifted from solving particular problems to achieving a more fundamental change of approach, attitude and perspective.
- There is considerable suspicion of external experts and consultants. They are perceived as offering short-term, simplistic and standard solutions, when the achievement of fundamental change is thought to require a sustained commitment that may be beyond the perspective of

the management team, let alone the 'assignment mentality' of the external supplier.

- Considerable effort has been devoted to creating distinct corporate cultures. This can make external inputs, and experience that has been gained elsewhere, more difficult to absorb.
- Internal sources of advice have become more confident. It is no longer thought that there are external experts who 'have the answers'. Strains of battle-hardened warriors have emerged that are more resistant to hype.
- The achievement of corporate transformation and remaining relevant and competitive are perceived as more complex and intractable than was thought a decade ago. Quick-fix merchants are being turned away.

If the advice and services of consultants and business schools are to be perceived as more relevant to the achievement of attitude and perspective change and to differentiation and winning, they will need to put more emphasis upon establishing and sustaining longer-term partnership arrangements with specific companies. They need to put away the presentations and prospectuses, roll up their sleeves and join the team.

They must also remember to focus upon what isn't – the key items that are missing from the change programme. Perhaps the parable of the 'lost sheep' is a prophetic and elegant appeal to search for the change element or relationship that will complete the corporate transformation jigsaw puzzle.

# CHECKLIST

▶ Does your company learn from its consultants or vice versa?

▶ Does your company regard consultants as external suppliers, or as elements of the network organization?

▶ Do the consultants that your company uses understand its vision, goals and values?

▶ How flexible and willing to learn are the people who advise your company?

▶ Do they listen?

▶ Are they willing to share risks and enter into partnering relationships?

▶ Do they have a holistic view of business problems, or are they 'functional' in approach?

▶ Do they apply standard tools and techniques, or are they selective in tailoring approaches to your particular problems?

- ▶ Do they describe and confront reality?

- ▶ Are their 'feet on the ground'?

- ▶ Are they 'telling it as it is', or saying what they believe you might wish to hear?

- ▶ How many of the things they talk about have been successfully implemented in their organizations?

- ▶ Are they as willing to come forward with 'lessons of failure' as they are with 'success case studies'?

- ▶ What value results from your company's relationship with business schools?

- ▶ What would be lost if business schools ceased to exist?

# REFERENCES

Bennis, W and Nanus, B (1985) *Leaders: The strategies for taking change*, Harper & Row, New York

Coulson-Thomas, C (1992) *Transforming the Company: Bridging the gap between management myth and corporate reality*, Kogan Page, London

Coulson-Thomas, C (1997 and 1998), *The Future of the Organization: Achieving excellence through business transformation*, Kogan Page, London

Coulson-Thomas, C (1999) *Developing a Corporate Learning Strategy: The key knowledge management challenge for the HR function*, Policy Publications, Bedford

Coulson-Thomas, C (2000) *The Information Entrepreneur*, 3Com Active Business Unit, Winnersh

Perrin, S (2000) *Managing Intellectual Capital to Grow Shareholder Value*, Policy Publications, Bedford.

# FURTHER INFORMATION

A brochure describing *Managing Intellectual Capital to Grow Shareholder Value* is available from Policy Publications, 4 The Crescent, Bedford MK40 2RU (tel: +44 (0) 1234 328448; fax: + 44 (0) 1234 357231, e-mail: policypubs@kbnet.co.uk; Web site: www.ntwkfirm.com/bookshop).

# 15

# IT, e-Business and Corporate Transformation

*'Even swans can get airborne'*

## THE NETWORK ORGANIZATION

Corporate organizations are transitioning to ever more flexible and responsive forms. We have seen that networks have been established that embrace customers, suppliers and business partners (Coulson-Thomas, 1992). These use information and communications technologies to facilitate new ways of working and learning, and new forms of relationships (Bartram, 1996).

At least this is the theory. In practice, the functioning global network that can support a diversity of virtual teams and entrepreneurial ventures can sometimes appear a long way away. The complexity is intimidating and difficult to understand, while the cost seems daunting and people worry whether it is affordable.

A vivid illustration of the gap between vision and reality in the IT arena is provided by the bag of plugs which many users of laptop computers have to take with them when they travel abroad. The 'collection' is needed to accommodate the range of voltages, and different sizes and configurations of socket that may be encountered.

# THE BOTTOMLESS PIT

For many companies the networked enterprise vision became the reality of what appeared to be a bottomless pit into which money was poured with little prospect of achieving the 'benefits' that were originally sought. The OECD concluded that the returns from early investment in IT were problematic (OECD, 1988). The potion turned those with aspirations to become princesses and fairies into frogs and goblins.

Much of past 'investment' in IT has been used to shore up existing ways of working. One chairman commented ruefully: 'We have used IT to set our organization in concrete. We have worked hard and spent millions consolidating a bureaucratic form of organization which we are now trying to break down.'

IT suppliers, with a mixture of cheek and bravado, have long been in the business of offering solutions to the many problems which their own products have created. They suggest that this or that upgrade may yet turn the lead boots they have supplied into winged slippers.

Paul Strassmann suggested that while, overall, the introduction of early generations of IT may have had little beneficial impact, it does appear to have widened the gap between the more and less efficient companies (Strassmann, 1985). There are 'winners', but for many IT from its origins to the dotcom era has been an 'honest mirror' that has confronted them with their own warts and wrinkles.

# IT AND CORPORATE TRANSFORMATION

Corporate transformation usually takes longer to achieve than is first thought. In many organizations a wide gulf emerges between expectation and achievement.

Past practices and entrenched attitudes are not easily laid to rest. The persistence of bureaucracy derived from its perceived advantages compared with other forms of organization. Applying IT to what is, as opposed to what ought to be, can further entrench a current model of operation and make it more difficult to change.

The struggle to change raises certain questions that will be examined in this and subsequent chapters. Why is IT so often part of the problem, a barrier to change, entrepreneurship, differentiation, knowledge creation and building more intimate relationships with customers? What is the role of IT in the achievement of corporate transformation? We will look at how winners use IT to facilitate and support the transition to the organic network form of organization.

# THE MISAPPLICATION OF IT

A decade ago, while IT may have transformed factory productivity, it was hardly touching the office in terms of improving the quality of management. In the office environment, IT was pervasive and visible without necessarily being beneficial. Some of those interviewed for the first edition of this book (Coulson-Thomas, 1992) suspected that the reasons for this lay not in the technology itself, but in its use and application. Consider the following comments:

*The processes that are important from a customer point of view tend to be cross-functional. Virtually all our IT is departmental.*

*People spend hours reading irrelevant e-mail. We struggle with information overload.*

*IT around here pushes information upwards... it is used for command and control purposes.*

*There is fragmentation... people and departments do their own thing and hoard their information. [Information] is not shared, either in groups or across departments.*

*If we have applied IT to the wrong things, why should anyone expect a positive return?*

By using IT to support re-engineered business processes, a significant improvement in managerial productivity can be achieved. But this requires looking at work and processes from a holistic rather than IT function point of view. Narrowness, introversion and departmentalism are not conducive of a vision-led approach.

Table 15.1 sets out the main elements that distinguished process simplification from process re-engineering (Coulson-Thomas, 1992). IT of itself,

**Table 15.1** Process simplification or re-engineering

| Process simplification | Process re-engineering |
| --- | --- |
| Step change | Radical transformation |
| Process-led | Vision-led |
| Within existing framework | Review framework |
| Improve application of technology | Introduce new technology |
| Assume attitudes and behaviour | Change attitudes and behaviour |
| Management led | Director led |
| Various simultaneous projects | Limited number of corporate initiatives |

and by itself, does not deliver the solution. Most of the benefits of simplification usually derive from changing the workflow and empowering people, so the challenge for IT may be relatively modest.

In the case of process re-engineering, the contribution of IT is often more significant. But the interrelationships between people, process and technology, within a particular goal and value framework, need to be understood. The IT person is likely to be but one member of the re-engineering team.

IT and re-engineering can facilitate or frustrate the task of corporate transformation, depending on what they are applied to, for what purpose and how they are managed (Coulson-Thomas, 1994, 1997 and 1998). An error of strategy can imprison a whole organization, tying people down with the chains of inappropriate technology. The flexibility of the network organization gives it the potential to spread, grow and evolve. This process of organic evolution needs to be assisted and not constrained by IT.

## ASPIRATION AND THE OPPORTUNITY FOR IT

There has been a genuine desire for change. For approaching two decades and in response to multiple challenges and opportunities (Table 1.2), CEOs have sought to create more adaptable and capable organizations. Externally, priority has been given to building closer relationships with customers, while internally the focus has been on harnessing human talent. There has been a strong desire to integrate working and learning.

The opportunity for IT derived from the fact that the technology that best supports new ways of working within network organizations is also often that which can facilitate new approaches to learning. If properly applied, IT can enable working and learning relationships to be built and sustained across barriers of function, distance, time and culture.

There is little interest in IT for its own sake. One CEO questioned: 'Why does everyone feel they need an IT strategy? IT strategies can develop a life of their own. I can understand a strategy focused on the customer that identifies where IT can make a contribution.' IT is only perceived as relevant where it can advance organizational goals. To do this it needs to support the critical success factors for becoming competitive and winning.

IT has been applied to support the development of international network organizations. The growth of international corporate networks has changed working patterns:

- Computer and video-conferencing, the Internet, groupware and mobile technologies support location-independent working and virtual teams.
- Tasks can be allocated on a global basis. Software development is undertaken 'offshore' in India.
- International units can be brought together that operate as international networks. VEBA found a decade ago that its research activities were

internationalizing to such an extent that a 'unit of research' was a network rather than a building.

- Information and relevant expertise can be assembled and accessed, transactions processed and relationships built on a global basis.
- Customer service support and relationships can be handled on a global and 24-hour-a-day basis.

The network can be much more than a basic 'one-to-one' electronic mail service. Information cannot be easily shared by people who need to work together but are based at different locations. Yet in 'loser' companies, single and isolated applications are not building new co-operative and group-working cultures.

## THE CONTRIBUTION OF IT

Potentially, IT can have a very significant impact upon patterns of work, relationship building, knowledge creation, entrepreneurship and the distribution of power within organizations. This excites certain people to the same extent that it makes others wary. While some seek to gain a competitive edge, their colleagues may be concerned about the loss of personal advantage.

The contribution IT is allowed to make will depend upon the context, and especially will, motivation and values. Scarce information can be a potent source of personal power in the machine bureaucracy. Ubiquitous information is the birthright of all the citizen members of the organic network organization. Decisions about how to use a corporate intranet or extranet can be very revealing of the extent to which senior management really believes in the concept of the open organization.

In the above, and other, areas the key questions should be the following:

- Can IT facilitate and support new 'network' relationships with customers, suppliers and business partners? Does it facilitate learning, adaptation and change, entrepreneurship and the integration of learning and working?
- Are investments in IT 'setting existing ways of operating in concrete', or are they enabling new alternatives and creating additional value and choice for customers?
- Does IT support new patterns of working and new approaches to learning and knowledge and value creation? Does it allow information, know-how and expertise to be easily shared within workgroups?
- Could IT enable new markets to be created and more intimate and inter-active relationships with individual customers to be established? Are the attitudes and patterns of behaviour that it encourages supportive or destructive of corporate transformation?

The leverage obtained from IT will depend upon how effectively its use is co-ordinated with that of other change elements.

The contribution of IT is often exaggerated. Revolutions in the means of communication have occurred at previous times in history. For example, the impact of Gutenberg's printing press was so profound that Ottoman rulers banned its use for more than two centuries.

The IT sector itself faces more severe challenges than many of its customers. Motorola and Ericsson have found themselves with excess capacity. Cisco Systems has failed to sustain its rapid rate of growth. From one year to the next there have been dramatic losses of shareholder value – well over £100 billion in the case of Vodafone.

While individual IT companies such as Dell have embraced e-commerce and e-business opportunities, others have been poor role models. BT has lacked imagination and entrepreneurial spirit. The company has also struggled under a burden of debt resulting from its relatively high payment for a third-generation mobile phone licence. Even if the rights acquired at such a high cost turn out to be the purchase of the century, it is doubtful whether the corporation's culture will allow it profitably to exploit them. If swans can get airborne, more of our applications of IT should fly. The trick is to apply technology to the critical success factors for business success. Too many investments are in areas that do not make the difference between winning and losing. Standard packages may be fine for non-critical activities, but bespoke development in crucial areas for competitive advantage can differentiate and result in the creation of new intellectual capital.

## THE NETWORK ORGANIZATION

As fewer companies are able by themselves to deliver 'total value' to customers, increasingly CEOs and their management teams have created networks of relationships, with electronic links forward into customers, backwards to suppliers and sideways to business partners (Figure 1.1). As networks and supply chains become global, bringing together all those who share a common vision or a particular mission, the formulation and implementation of IT strategy increasingly involves co-operation and collaboration across organizational and national boundaries.

Interest in rules and procedures has waned, but a desire for the identification of tasks, the establishment of teams, and new processes for generating value for customers, additional intellectual capital and new ventures, and achieving adaptation and change has grown. Richard Joyce, of 3Com believes the 'global network' of 'the vision':

*offers a 'complete infrastructure' that allows data and information to flow transparently, from computer to computer, regardless of type and location. Such 'arterial information highways' permit flexibility, faster decision making, and greater responsiveness to customers and suppliers. They allow*

*new ways of working and can change the role of managers... Whole func-*
*tions could be geographically dispersed across the globe to take advantage of*
*lower costs and proximity to customers.*

Many of the task and new venture teams that come together in the network organization have a requirement for access to appropriate technology 'on demand'. A particular technology is used according to the task, just as one's selection of clothes may depend upon the weather. In 'loser' companies the reality is different. One IT director described what appears to be a typical problem:

> *We have an absolute mess... every sort and kind of equipment, from every*
> *supplier you could think of. As part of the culture change, everyone has been*
> *encouraged to do their own thing... Any thought of gateways and interfaces*
> *has gone out of the window... Technology-wise we are now a collection of*
> *self-contained cells... It's horrible.*

A combination of devolution and contracting out has swept like a wave through many companies, leaving self-contained islands of technology in its wake. In the words of an IT director: 'I watched it break up... now I'm being asked to stitch it together again.' Another IT director touched upon an issue that could be added to the arenas of confrontation of Chapter 12:

> *A network needs some common infrastructure if flexibility is to be achieved.*
> *You can't cross functions and organizations if the equipment does not link*
> *up. But even raising the issue smacks of 'centralism'... people want their*
> *freedom. They have tasted freedom and are not interested in group things*
> *anymore... They just don't want to know or pay.*

Individual business units and ventures may only be interested in funding applications of IT that enable them to achieve their own particular objectives. The relatively high proportion of total IT spend that may be required to establish and operate the core network can be perceived as 'central overhead'. Too much local discretion could result in a network infrastructure that is not able to support cross-venture processes adequately, or enable expertise to be accessed independently of location.

Information technology provides the nerves and arteries of the network organization. Yet the very activity of identifying the processes that create and deliver value can result in battles for the allocation of the IT budget and the control of its people.

# EMBRACING E-BUSINESS

Conflicts can be resolved by focusing on shared interests and mutual advantage, and there have been successes. Many of these have featured in the e-Business Innovations Awards (www.ecommerce-awards.com). E-business technologies and principles are being used to create new markets and change how business is done (Coulson-Thomas, 2001). For example: procurement is undertaken electronically; intelligent agents search for suitable suppliers; opportunities are put out to electronic auction.

A company's Web presence can be used in many ways to build closer and interactive relationships with customers. Many IT companies allow their software products to be purchased and downloaded via the Internet. Guinness produced a screen saver version of its Guinness.com Web site that could be downloaded.

Electronic links can encourage intimacy and enable 24-hour trading and access to information, knowledge and opportunities. Responses can be made within seconds. Online visitors can be helped to diagnose problems, assess requirements and assemble or develop solutions. E-Business and mobile technologies are profoundly changing relationships between businesses and their customers, suppliers and business partners (Stone *et al*, 1999, 2000a, b, c).

There are so many opportunities to challenge and improve on current practices that all members of staff should be encouraged to consider the possibilities. Ford in the United States and Powergen in the United Kingdom have provided all their employees with a home computer. Senior managers believe the skills and experience they acquire will benefit their contributions during office hours.

Success can depend on the extent to which a Web presence is accessible, distinctive and memorable. Follow-up fulfilment processes and offerings need to be in place to ensure that, after an initial contact, interested visitors are converted into buyers and continuing relationships are forged.

Federal Express has redesigned its core business processes to allow the great bulk of its parcel shipments to be ordered, arranged and managed via the Internet. At any time during the day or night customers can log on and see exactly where each item is. The company's most valuable assets used to be its trucks and aeroplanes. Its value now primarily derives from its processes and supporting software.

## WINNING AND LOSING APPROACHES

Losers tend to adopt cautious, tentative and half-hearted approaches. They dabble and test rather than fully commit. For example, they may create a static Web site featuring background information about themselves and then use the lack of visitors that is likely to result as a vindication of the modest nature of their investment. The consequences of inaction are used to justify further lethargy and inertia.

When losers do act they are often naïve and give little thought to the likely reactions of others. They decide they too would like a Web presence and its establishment becomes an end in itself irrespective of whether it has a purpose or would help achieve certain objectives. Not surprisingly, the sites that result attract few visitors.

Winners are more positive, considered and open-minded. They use e-business to expand their customer base and provide additional support services to existing consumers. Some replace physical marketplaces with new electronic market spaces (Bartram, 1996).

People in winning companies get to know their Web site visitors and their interests, and endeavour to provide a complete, personalized and regularly updated service or experience. They start with a problem or opportunity from a user perspective.

Winners think about how new e-business channels might make it easier for customers to access the information and opportunities that they need. They examine ways in which selection and purchasing might be made simpler for suppliers, for example by providing online search, configuration, pricing and cost-justification tools.

Every effort is made to build an iterative relationship with each individual and to provide additional value to that which might be obtained from any alternative sources. Wherever possible visitors are enabled to help themselves. Electronic templates allow visitors to present their requirements, or any problems they might have, in a way that makes it easier to provide a relevant response. Online facilities could range from simple ordering and tracking systems to complex self-design facilities.

Winners invite feedback and comment from users and their people are encouraged to actively consider how they could make more extensive use of e-business applications. Reactions, comments and suggestions are sought, obtained and acted upon. The financial costs involved represent a minor element of the total investment of time and commitment in creating services and facilities that meet user needs and lock them in.

Winners create and actively participate in virtual communities. They encourage mutual sharing and support. By enabling interaction and introducing dynamic elements they encourage repeat visits. Regular reviews occur and findings are acted upon to help ensure that whatever is offered continues to be of interest, relevant and vital. Their involvement enables them to monitor trends, identify evolving concerns and spot emerging aspirations and requirements before they crystallize.

## Losers

Losers:

- are technology driven and regard enhanced technology as a laudable goal in its own right;
- are attracted by the prospect of upgrading their information technology and using the latest of whatever is available;
- find themselves easy targets for those selling information technology;
- initiate fashionable and technology-led approaches to corporate transformation;
- apply information technology to improve existing activities;
- focus on internal opportunities;
- endow information technologies with an element of mystery and entrust them to specialists;
- leave decisions about which technologies to adopt almost exclusively to technical experts;
- maintain separate and central information technology departments;
- develop static Web sites that replicate other channels of communication.

## Winners

Winners:

- are objective driven and view information technologies as a means to an end;
- endeavour to acquire only the information technology and level of functionality that is relevant to what they are setting out to achieve;
- are demanding consumers and users of information technology;
- implement relevant and objective-led approaches to corporate transformation;
- use information technology to undertake new and different activities and work and learn in new ways;
- concentrate on opportunities to improve key relationships;
- embed relevant information technologies into the fabric of the organization;
- encourage people to adopt whatever technology is most relevant to the achievement of their objectives;
- locate responsibility for information technologies where it is most appropriate;
- create interactive Web sites that provide new opportunities and additional possibilities.

# IT AND THE 'NEW ÉLITE'

While the rhetoric has been of empowerment and involvement, the IT investment decisions of some 'loser' companies are concentrating and excluding. New 'core' élites are emerging that have access to a wide range of network information and services that are denied to others. In the view of one director: 'If you are not "on the network" you might as well be dead.'

The members of the new élite gather together in their high-tech and air-conditioned offices, cars and homes rather like travellers on a hostile planet congregating at the 'moon base'. They peer into their screens, and check their e-mail 'in case they might miss something', rather than breathe fresh air and meet customers. Other people of the network organization, such as associates, isolated customers and small suppliers, can feel 'disenfranchised' or 'second-class citizens'. The 'money runs out' before the 'benefits of civilization' can be brought to the far-flung reaches.

# IT: AN ENABLER OR A BARRIER?

In the main, the concerns of CEOs relate to attitudes towards IT which inhibit its application to those activities and processes that are critical to competitive success. In particular, the IT community is not thought to have a holistic view of the role of IT in relation to other change elements in either the vision of the 'network organization' or how it might be brought about.

Cynicism, resulting from early experiences with technology that did not deliver the hoped-for benefits, has given way to a realization that what is important is the use and application of technology, not the technology *per se*. In the main, the major 'barriers' concern people, their skills and attitudes, and the management of technology, rather than the technology itself. Technology needs to be used, where appropriate, to support the way people prefer to work and think, and enable more of them to move closer to their full potential.

IT has been democratized. 'Universal' technology that is simple, reliable and cheap needs to be available to all members of the network wherever they may be. For one interviewee: 'Usable... unobtrusive technology must be the right of everyone [and not] the privilege of the office-bound few.'

Technology is neutral. Its application reflects the richness or poverty of our vision, the clarity or confusion of our objectives, and the utility or stupidity of our choices. For example, virtual reality could be used to open up an unprecedented range of learning opportunities and expose people to various experiences. Aspiration can, for a time, take on the appearance of reality. The dream can become the product. However, the same technology could be used to pander to a variety of unsocial instincts by enabling people to act out their wildest fantasies.

Appropriate IT has its place among the change elements that make up a corporate transformation programme. How relevant and significant it is will depend upon the situation and circumstances.

## CHECKLIST

► Do the IT specialists in your company understand its vision?

► Are their activities supportive of the changes that are sought?

► Have the key cross-functional and inter-organizational processes that enable new ventures, create know-how and add value for customers been identified?

► Are partnering relationships and tailored responses to individual customers being supported?

► Have particular individuals been made responsible for these processes?

► Is IT applied to support them, or to departmental activities that may or may not be generating value for customers?

► How fragmented is the IT of your company?

► Are there actual or latent conflicts within your company between the 'core' IT team, and those in new ventures, business units and divisions?

► Does the IT perspective and e-business strategy of your company embrace other members of the supply chain?

► Does your organization's IT network allow groups and teams to come together and work across barriers of function, distance, nationality and time?

► Does it support the way people naturally work and think, or do people have to distort their preferred behaviour in order to 'fit in' with the technology?

► Is it a learning network, able to integrate learning and working?

► Is it sufficiently flexible to allow various people to work and learn in different ways, and at a variety of locations, according to personal preferences and changing task requirements?

# REFERENCES

Bartram, P (1996) *The Competitive Network*, Policy Publications, Bedford

Coulson-Thomas, C (1992) *Transforming the Company: Bridging the gap between management myth and corporate reality*, Kogan Page, London

Coulson-Thomas, C (1994) *Business Process Re-engineering: Myth and reality*, Kogan Page, London

Coulson-Thomas, C (1997 and 1998) *The Future of the Organization: Achieving excellence through business transformation*, Kogan Page, London

Coulson-Thomas, C (2001) *Shaping Things to Come: Strategies for creating alternative enterprises*, Blackhall Publishing, Dublin

Organisation for Economic Co-operation and Development (OECD) (1988) *New Technology in the 1990s: A socio-economic strategy*, Paris

Stone, M *et al* (1999) *Managing Customers with e-Business*, Policy Publications, Bedford

Stone, M *et al* (2000a) *The Intelligent Supply Chain*, Policy Publications, Bedford

Stone, M *et al* (2000b) *The Intelligent e-Business*, Policy Publications, Bedford

Stone, M et al (2000c) *Customer Management on the Move*, Policy Publications, Bedford

Strassmann, P A (1985) *Information Payoff*, Macmillan, New York and London

# FURTHER INFORMATION

Brochures describing *The Competitive Network* report with its methodology for re-engineering supply chains with e-business technologies and the 'Close to the Customer' briefings on the use of mobile and e-business technologies to build customer relationships are available from Policy Publications, 4 The Crescent, Bedford MK40 2RU (tel: +44 (0) 1234 328448; fax: + 44 (0) 1234 357231; e-mail: policypubs@kbnet.co.uk; Web site: www.ntwkfirm.com/bookshop).

# 16

# Supporting the Network Organization

*'There are stones as well as mud beside the banks of rivers'*

## EMBRACING THE GLOBE

Where will it all end? The growth of the organic network is limited only by the bounds of where people can live. Quite small companies have the potential to operate as international networks. The limiting factor is generally awareness, vision and perspective. Most companies stitch their own blinkers and forge their own chains.

Increasingly network organizations, especially when composed largely of knowledge workers, are distinguished by their supporting technology and the extent to which they are able to harness human talent and forge intimate and mutually beneficial relationships. These are the areas we will explore in this, and the next, chapter.

## THE FEAR OF SCALE

Brave souls sometimes become timid at the thought of international operation. And yet, as a CEO pointed out: 'You may have much more in common with someone on the other side of the world than with the next-door neighbour.'

It is easy to become awed by the scale and complexity of many international networks. But they are not new. Back in 1990 the global network of Digital Equipment, for example, linked 57,000 computer terminals at 498 locations in 31 countries. Club Méditerranée operated a 2000-terminal global network which allows 24-hour-a-day bookings to be made for accommodation at any of its holiday centres. The total resources of the international organization are accessible from any single point.

Even the possession of a telephone opens up possibilities for direct contact with customers and suppliers throughout the world. It was possible in 1990 to direct dial 197 countries from the UK, and to thereby secure access to 99 per cent of the world's 700 million telephones. Today people can be reached on the move (Stone *et al*, 2000).

For over a decade it has been possible to monitor the extent of internationalization and interdependence, the pattern of economic activity, the location of interacting knowledge workers, or the degree of intimacy with customers or integration of particular countries into the global economy by examining the pattern of cross-border telephone calls. Today such analyses are undertaken of e-mail flows and Web traffic.

Bloomberg is the quintessential international network organization. The financial information and trading service provider operates via data terminals in 100 countries, radio reports, a 24-hour television service in seven languages and the Internet. A thousand reporters in offices around the world feed stories into the network.

The focus of this chapter is not on the technology itself, but on how it has been, can be and ought to be used, and crucially on how winners and losers vary in their attitude towards building relationships. The creative use of information technology focuses upon the search for competitive advantage and differentiation, changing internal and external relationships, overcoming barriers and transforming the nature of the marketplace. We need smart heads not smart suits.

Simple technologies may succeed where more complex ones fail. People use SMS text messaging to keep in touch with each other, while manufacturers have struggled to find cost-effective applications for more-expensive WAP technology.

# THE VALUE OF THE INTERNATIONAL NETWORK

Does your IT pass the 'So what?' test? The use of any technology should be justified in terms of its impact upon creating value and new choices for external customers. In order to be responsive to the changing requirements of customers, companies need to enter into a dialogue with them. To do this, and to facilitate a relationship based upon two-way communication, customers, suppliers and business partners need to be incorporated into the network.

Early adopters were active in the 1980s. Xerox equipped many of its office products with a self-diagnostic capability to monitor their own performance. A built-in Remote Interactive Communications (RIC) system enabled the machine in the customer's office to 'call' a Xerox or Rank Xerox technician when it sensed that it needed attention. The supplier knew before the customer that the customer had a problem.

For many years the cost of establishing a complete global network appeared prohibitive. However, where a network is operated on a co-operative basis, the development and operating costs can be shared. The Bank of Scotland pioneered direct customer access by terminal to account information. It also developed an Edipay system that allowed international companies to electronically exchange payments through the international automatic bank payment system, and remittance information through the global information system of General Electric.

The 'IT solution' may also be available to the 'one location' business that joins a network consortium. The centralized reservation system run by Consort Hotels Consortium was an early example. Most of the members of this consortium were single hotels. For them, access to, rather than ownership of, the network was a key to marketplace success. The e-Business Innovations Awards Web site (www.ecommerce-awards.com) lists many awards that have been given for collaborative ventures.

Intriguingly IT suppliers themselves have sometimes avoided the networks of collaboration they help their customers to support in favour of relatively self-contained operation. Hewlett-Packard prized its product and technology independence until a market downturn in its sector forced it to enter into merger and acquisition negotiations with Compaq.

# SPEED OF RESPONSE

In competitive markets, the technology that allows a faster and tailored response to customer requirements can be decisive. In the late 1980s, National, a Japanese bicycle manufacturer, combined flexibility and speed of response to produce made-to-order machines in about two weeks.

During the 1990s competition was increasingly between networks or clusters of co-operating companies, rather than between individual enterprises. Within such networks companies can be both customers and suppliers.

Many networks are composed of companies with complementary resources that can be harnessed by compatible computing and telecommunications networks. Network partners may operate in different industry sectors. For example, members of a cluster composed of a financial institution, IT supplier and management consultancy could access each other's complementary resources.

Care needs to be taken to ensure that network members satisfy certain core membership criteria. Employees of Huntingdon Life Sciences have been subject to physical attacks by animal rights activists opposed to the company's use of animals for research purposes and have had their cars firebombed. Suppliers and business partners of targeted companies can also find themselves exposed. Bringing a company that is under threat into a network might put other members at risk.

Historically incompatible networks have put barriers between companies that would otherwise work together. In the UK, it was not possible in 1985 to complete a merger between the Woolwich and Nationwide building societies because the two companies had built networks with the products of different suppliers, and it would have been both difficult and expensive to link them up.

## INFORMATION AND UNDERSTANDING

The quantity of information available to people in many organizations has increased dramatically. In some business sectors it has become a commodity, accessible on demand. However, too much information is neither relevant nor timely. It does not always flow easily between organizations and the systems of different suppliers. Nor does its content and presentation improve the quality of decision making. It may be impossible to work with it, or share it, in order to improve understanding. Consider the following comments:

> We are just swamped with information. No one has time to read it... You get to the meeting and more of it is handed out. You see people's eyes just glaze over. It's ridiculous... people are killing themselves to produce this stuff [and] it's killing us.

> I could spend all day reading and responding to e-mails that have nothing to do with my priority tasks.

> People used to come to meetings with piles of slides. Now we have a standard format. All we ask for is trends, root causes, comparisons and some options... We've got a grip on it and are managing the business again.

Information and knowledge of themselves may be of little or no value. In a business context, they are usually required for a purpose. Their value ought to exceed their cost. IT is also a means to an end and is rarely acquired as an end in itself. As a CEO put it: 'I'm beginning to think it's like castor oil... we take it, thinking it's doing us some good.'

Those who circulate and receive information and knowledge have a shared responsibility for ensuring that what is transmitted is relevant and understood. Information and knowledge are of strategic value only when they increase understanding at the point at which important decisions are made. Information and knowledge that is understood by experts and specialists, but not by management colleagues, or in the boardroom, is not of strategic value.

A director summed up an interview theme: 'We still churn out more when we don't understand what we have already got.' Information technology can improve the generation and availability of information and knowledge to such an extent as to cause an excess or 'overload'. It can do this without improving understanding. This creates enormous opportunities for information and knowledge entrepreneurs (Coulson-Thomas, 2000).

## SOWING THE SEEDS

Why has such an imbalance between information and understanding arisen? Why are there so many glum faces, tired eyes and empty bank accounts? The answer lies in the history of the use of technology in the office explored in the first edition of this book (Coulson-Thomas, 1992), and in particular its application to routine and structured tasks rather than unstructured, bespoke and entrepreneurial activities and relationship building.

The effectiveness of such 'unstructured' activities as researching, analysing, thinking, challenging, conceptualizing, learning, refining, collaborating, changing and adapting can depend critically upon the ease with which relevant information and knowledge can be accessed, manipulated, assimilated, shared and exploited. These activities are the essence of the network organization, of critical importance in the achievement of competitive advantage, and can be facilitated and supported by appropriate technology.

## CHANGING ATTITUDES

In the early 1990s, research in such centres as Xerox PARK focused on human learning, effective team working and 'interaction', or the interface between person and machine. Office systems technology has become increasingly pervasive, user friendly and less obtrusive. The technology is being adapted to the needs of teams and groups, and the requirements of individual users and learners.

Business decision makers need no longer be victims of whatever emerges from the corporate information system. They can become proactive, viewing the technology as a crucial enabler, rather than as a threat. The technology can support new ways of working, shopping and learning. It is changing the business environment, creating new competitive threats and fresh business opportunities (Coulson-Thomas, 2001).

The realization is beginning to dawn. One interviewee exclaimed: 'I've been beaten around the head long enough with this stuff... I can now see a way of doing something useful with it.' The light can be seen, but many companies still have to climb out of a deep pit and change attitudes in order to get to it.

Justification is shifting from decision support to the extent to which system capability and intelligence can complement and enhance human contribution in improving decision making and management processes, in order to cope with challenges such as internationalization and corporate transformation. Justification is now concerned with the value delivered to customers, and the quality of relationships and of the learning that can be facilitated.

Intimate and mutually beneficial relationships are the key to bespoke responses and sustained knowledge and value creation. The effective use of IT has become very dependent upon attitudes towards such relationships, and towards 'external' parties and customers in particular. The key question is the extent to which they are perceived and treated as full members or citizens of the network.

## HOW LOSERS APPROACH CUSTOMER RELATIONSHIPS

Reference was made in Chapter 5 to the different approaches that winners and losers take to customer relationships. A survey undertaken for the Developing Strategic Customers and Key Accounts report (Hurcomb, 1998) reveals a wide gulf between their attitudes, approaches and results. For example, winners consider three times as many of the key processes identified to be 'very important'. Significantly for this chapter, winners are five times as likely to be intending to make use of emerging technologies.

People in 'loser' companies tend to live for the moment. Tomorrow is another day. They are driven by the prospect of immediate business and its impact on achieving their short-term sales targets. When dealing with customers, they focus on their own requirements. Essentially they use their clients to attain their personal ends. Within such companies key account relationships are also largely left to sales and marketing staff. Business development is regarded as their responsibility.

People employed by losers, and those who associate with them, use the rhetoric of customer relationship management. They mouth generalizations about the importance of 'building closer and longer-term relationships with customers' but in practice do little to make them happen. They avoid making personal commitments and shun the integration of processes and systems. The risk of exposure to viruses, temptation and hacking is used to justify their reluctance to provide direct electronic links.

Losers play their cards close to their chest. They like being 'insiders' who are in the know. They instinctively collect and hoard information, rather than disseminate and share it. Hence they avoid open-book accounting and granting access to corporate databases.

People in loser companies are also intolerant of 'exceptions' and reluctant to depart from standard procedures. Variations to help particular clients are seen as a cause of additional work and extra costs. Little effort is made to categorize customers, who tend to be treated in the same way irrespective of their requirements or significance.

If and when losers do designate certain customers as key accounts, this tends to be on the basis of their current significance rather than their future potential. People simply rank existing customers in order of the revenue or profit obtained from them and select those at the top. Even then major customers may be 'key accounts' in name only, as they receive few advantages or favours over customers in general.

Losers continue to use sales and negotiation techniques that fail to recognize either 'buyer power' or 'key account' status. Terms of business, including price, are still employed as a selling tool. Entrepreneurial customers on learning of their new standing realize their importance and endeavour to exploit it. They demand price reductions or special discounts, seek favours and request additional services.

Relationships with 'key accounts' may be put exclusively in the hands of a dedicated manager, who may have little influence over colleagues. Customers who enlist his or her help may find that he or she is unable to reach decision makers and powerless to short-cut procedures. The dedicated manager in turn may find it difficult to cope with more-demanding clients.

Personal connections can be tentative, conditional and ephemeral. Lazy key account managers cultivate few points of contact with customer organizations. When people move to a new role or different employer, particular relationships may be lost. Replacements may be difficult to find. Links may be broken at a time when they are most needed.

The contrast between 'winners' and 'losers' is particularly stark in relation to locking out the competition. Winners rank 11 out of 17 'lock out' factors identified in the 'Developing Strategic Customers and Key Accounts' report (Hurcomb, 1998). The losers do not rank any. The bottom quarter of companies in the survey sample do not appear to protect their key accounts from competitors. Not surprisingly, they lose important customers and generally fail to realize the benefits of strategic relationships.

## HOW WINNERS DEVELOP STRATEGIC CUSTOMER RELATIONSHIPS

People in winning companies take a longer, lifetime view of customer relationships. They consider aspirations and future prospects when categorizing accounts. They value their clients and are prepared to make special arrangements for them. Procedures are seen as a means to an end and not as an end in themselves. If they get in the way, they are changed.

Winners are not saving themselves for tomorrow. When they see an opening they may well go for it. They take advantage of e-business and mobile technologies to offer new services and better support to customers, and learn more about them (Stone *et al*, 1999, 2000). But they think before acting. The allure of opportunities does not blind them to the risks involved. The boater in search of an overnight mooring knows from experience that rocks are sometimes to be found along the edges of the most attractive riverbanks.

People in winning companies are open and eager to build personal relationships. Their focus is on customer requirements and buyer expectations. They understand their customers' businesses, industries and buying processes and look out for opportunities that might benefit them.

Winners encourage a broader range of contacts at multiple levels between their own staff and those of their key account customers. Managers encourage their teams to work with their peers. Everyone feels responsible in some way for business development.

Effort is made to ensure that arrangements entered into are mutually beneficial and are underpinned by supporting processes and systems. Joint working parties, supply-chain review groups and supplier–client teams may be established. As a consequence, valued relationships are normally not prejudiced or lost when particular individuals change jobs or employers. Customers are locked in.

Senior managers demonstrate the significance of certain relationships by participating in important negotiations. Their involvement supports rather than undermines client managers. People generally are prepared to differentiate and depart from the norm in order to deliver greater value and benefit their customers' businesses.

Whereas losers mouth generalizations, winners concentrate upon specifics. They are prepared to commit resources and do things differently. Partnership embraces the terms of business. They integrate processes and systems to achieve a degree of intimacy that may be difficult to unscramble without disruption and pain.

Traditional sales techniques are largely ignored. Winners influence buying rather than overtly sell. They endeavour to help customers and prospects achieve their procurement objectives and underlying aspirations. Ultimately they realize the many benefits of strategic customer relationships that elude 'loser' companies (Hurcomb, 1998).

# TECHNOLOGY TO MANAGE INTELLECTUAL CAPITAL

Successful strategic partnerships lead to the creation of additional know-how. Because there are many different forms of intellectual capital, staff responsible for keeping records and protecting knowledge assets increasingly need knowledge management frameworks and repositories that can handle a diversity of formats. The various categories of know-how range from electronic databases, printed documents and slides, through designs and other visual images, to audio and video material and animation. One example is K-Frame (www.k-frame.com), winner of the 2000 eBusiness Innovations Award for Knowledge Management.

K-Frame allows intellectual capital from text and spreadsheets to multimedia and information off the Internet to be captured and stored within a single portable framework. Fuzzy searches can be undertaken, including on audio and video material. The search function can cope with spelling mistakes and even look for words in audio files and voice-overs. Knowledge creation tools and report and presentation generators can be included.

Such a knowledge management framework can support other activities that various members of the board are involved with, such as the production of corporate credentials or annual reports. Thus multimedia content could be issued to interested parties by means of a CD ROM. Laptop-computer-based sales support applications for companies like call centre technology supplier Eyretel incorporate a pricing engine and proposal generator.

Expertise can be assembled, captured and presented in a form that is accessible via the Internet or CD ROM technology. For example, a consortium of eight leading professional firms led by Hill and Knowlton developed a risk-assessment tool called PROMPT-RPS. Its contents include report templates, diagnostic questionnaires and contact arrangements. These enable people to form a basic understanding of the situation they are in and to identify when and where more specialist assistance is required.

Users of tools such as PROMPT-RPS can prepare more structured and better thought-through requests for guidance and support. The knowledge workers they approach save time because they do not have to collect basic information. This enables them to devote a higher proportion of their chargeable hours to more 'added-value' activities and higher-margin work. They may also receive a wider range of enquiries, especially when they are among the first to offer packaged knowledge in a particular area.

## Losers

Losers:

- become intimidated by large-scale requirements and difficult challenges;
- pass up opportunities they cannot afford to address;
- suffer from information overload and drown in an excess of e-mails and other forms of communication;
- adapt how they operate to match the requirements of changing technology;
- experience a conflict between the demands of technology and the preferences of their people;
- replace people with technology;
- regard networks as an internal capability;
- apply technology to structured situations;
- address the technical problems of introducing new technologies;
- are reluctant to extend network membership and services to customers, suppliers and business partners.

## Winners

Winners:

- are willing to tackle complex issues and confront demanding situations;
- seek collaborators and partners to exploit opportunities that would otherwise stretch their resources;
- draw a distinction between information and understanding, and manage the former to enhance the latter;
- adopt technologies that support how they naturally prefer to work, communicate and learn;
- view people, processes and technology as complementary and endeavour to achieve a harmonious relationship between them;
- support people with technology;
- use networks to facilitate relationships with customers, suppliers and business partners;
- adopt technologies that enable them to deal with both structured and unstructured situations;
- address the attitudinal, behavioural and technical problems of introducing new technologies;
- use network membership to build intimate relationships with customers, suppliers and business partners, and lock them in.

# THE OPPORTUNITY FOR THE IT BUYER

The information technology buyer is relatively well placed. The problems of suppliers have created opportunities for customers. Falling levels of demand mean competitive prices. As the pace of technological advance continues, more can be obtained for less.

A range of financing and facilities management options are also available to users who wish to contract out and focus upon their core activities. Although the buyer is in a relatively strong position, there is still a need to be cautious. The availability of accessible technology does not mean it will be sensibly used. Companies will still make mistakes in their search for competitive advantage and new market opportunities.

# SUPPORTING RATHER THAN REPLACING PEOPLE

The use of technology is very revealing of how people are perceived by senior management. It communicates attitudes and expectations. Management teams who regard people as components in a machine, and treat them as extensions of the technology, should not be surprised if some of them behave as alienated robots.

The emphasis has shifted to the use of technology to attract, develop and update people and facilitate their value-added contribution. People and their supporting technology are increasingly viewed as an investment rather than a cost.

The flexible and adaptable network organization is quickly able to bring relevant information and knowledge to bear in a hectic environment of interruption, changing views and assumptions, and constant pressures of time. Knowledge workers face unpredictable demands upon their time and expertise. In this environment work is inevitably 'unstructured'. IT must be able to cope with chaos and uncertainty, and improve the effectiveness of people engaged in creative and entrepreneurial activities.

In the network organization there is less emphasis upon processing standard transactions, and more emphasis upon manipulating and refining information and knowledge to build and share understanding, allow a more flexible response to individual requirements, and support new ways of working and learning.

The process of working effectively in a team involves more than just sharing captured knowledge on a corporate intranet. It must also be possible to share thoughts, ideas, insights and concepts. The technology that is used should allow them to be refined and amended. It should facilitate learning and development, and should itself be capable of learning and development.

Full citizens of the network organization should have access to all relevant information and knowledge. To enhance understanding or add value, this information and knowledge must be assimilated, shared and correct conclusions drawn. Subsequently, what has been achieved, learnt or refined must be presented to decision makers or customers in a form to which they can relate.

The network should also embrace customers, business partners and suppliers. It should be capable of organic international expansion. Seamless access is required to relevant internal and external repositories.

## MAKING THE VISION HAPPEN

Winners put basic building blocks in place. Documents and templates are the currency of the network organization. They sit on Web sites and flow along business processes, making things happen for customers.

Knowledge work is largely based upon documents. The effective network needs to be able to capture physical documents in electronic form, access, share and manipulate electronic documents, and enable them to be created and managed. The technology needs to embrace scanning, creation, refinement, storage and document management.

The commissioning, assembly, structuring and external presentation of information and knowledge are all stages of the publishing process. Traditional publishing can be slow, relatively expensive, remote from users and not easily controlled by them or responsive to their individual needs. The publishing process can now be interactive at the point at which needs and creative ideas originate.

Understanding can be further enhanced through the use of a network not only to collect and organize information and knowledge in a variety of formats, but also to browse through what has been collected and discovered. Expert systems can enable relationships to be established and 'logic checks' made for coherence. Persuasive arguments to support a point of view may be constructed by using logical relationships discovered in a variety of formats.

The enhancement of understanding is an interactive process. The output of one knowledge worker is another's input. An effective office system allows information and understanding to be shared, circulated, refined and applied. It empowers, develops and enables contributions to be received from many minds. The prospect of growing, sharing and exploitation on a continuing basis encourages people to seek membership of the network.

The technology of the network should be capable of capturing the sum total of available information, knowledge and understanding and bringing it to bear at the point of decision or need. By allowing direct access, intermediaries, 'gatekeepers', and sources of confusion and distortion can be cut out.

# ASSESSMENT CRITERIA

How should information technology investment proposals be assessed? Much will depend upon the situation and circumstances of the company. Key considerations that have applied to communities of knowledge workers include the following:

- the extent to which a proposed system can cope with mobility, threats such as viruses and hacking, 'unstructured' activity; and allow refinement and integration;
- whether it is flexible, simple and reliable; compatible with the equipment of multiple vendors; and allows adaptation and migration to the employment of intelligent agents and expert systems.

Sophistication for the sake of it should be avoided. A premium should be placed upon ease of access and interaction. The more open an office system, the more flexible and adaptable it will be in accommodating technological advances.

The aim should be to introduce cost-effective elements of technology employing a suitable architecture that may be compatible with past investments, and which may allow for adaptation to achieve and maintain a fully integrated global network.

If this advice sounds like 'techno-speak', consider supplementing it with some 'hard-nosed' first principle questions. The following approaches were used by interviewees to concentrate their minds:

*I always say to myself, what would I do if this were my business? Would I put my hand in my pocket?*

*We ask the people putting up the proposals how much they are going to contribute from their divisional or departmental budget... You see them melt away. The ones left in the room are those who think it will do them some good.*

*What does it all mean for customers? Is it about them, or about us and what we would like to have? That's the approach to take.*

*Stand back from it and reflect. If we do none of this, what would happen to customer satisfaction? What business objectives would suffer?*

To build flexible and international networks that meet a distinct set of requirements requires partnerships between suppliers and users of IT. Rather than 'packaging' and marketing IT goods and services, IT suppliers enter into strategic relationships, making their underlying technology available and working in joint supplier–customer teams to customize both hardware and software to the requirements of particular networks.

Any process that is used to determine global network requirements should satisfy the criteria set out in Table 16.1. Independence and objectivity

**Table 16.1** Suggested evaluation process

| A process to formulate and implement a global network should: |
| --- |
| Understand the corporate vision and mission |
| Take account of business goals and objectives |
| Concentrate upon the activities and processes that generate and deliver know-how and value |
| Be independent, objective and authoritative |
| Identify and confront barriers and obstacles |
| Focus on the application, use and management of technology |
| Involve customers, suppliers and business partners as required |
| Be representative of the various interests involved |
| Be sensitive to the diversity of requirements and perspectives |
| Access relevant research on learning |
| Tap best practice experience |
| Have the necessary commitment and support |
| Be empowered and equipped to deliver |
| Draw upon implementation experience |
| Allow for agreement in stages |
| Incorporate a 'learning loop' and quality review |

are particularly important when suppliers are involved. Often, it is the project management expertise which is the most critical, the ability to deliver what is required to budget and on time.

# COMPLETING THE TRANSFORMATION JIGSAW PUZZLE

It is worth repeating a key conclusion of Chapter 15, namely that barriers to the successful introduction of technology tend to be attitudinal and behavioural, rather than technical. How IT is introduced and used can influence both attitudes and behaviour. It could be applied for this purpose.

The correct application of IT also demonstrates commitment to people and to business objectives. Equipping people with the right technology can help turn the rhetoric of empowerment into a reality. People are involved and not excluded. They can access information and knowledge, and make their contribution. Objectives may not appear to be just 'words on paper' when the means to turn aspiration into achievement are visibly being put in place.

The most effective technology is often that which is relatively unobtrusive. The technology of the network organization increasingly will merge into the background to become an accepted feature of the living environment. It should be as reassuring, and no more disturbing, than the crackling of a log on an inglenook fire.

# CHECKLIST

▶ Does your company have an international information technology strategy and how compatible is this with its international vision?

▶ How important are speed and intimate and iterative relationships with individual customers?

▶ How might your company's relationships with its customers, suppliers and business partners be transformed through the use and application of IT?

▶ Does your company's IT network facilitate multifunctional, multi-location, and multinational team working?

▶ Does it allow flexible access to all relevant external sources of knowledge and skill?

▶ Does your company's IT network facilitate the building of understanding, as well as the acquisition of information and knowledge?

▶ Is it supportive of 'all-channel' communication, and the integration of working and learning?

▶ Is the technology of your company appropriate to its strategy, organization, people and management processes?

▶ Can it handle intellectual property in a variety of formats?

▶ Is it supportive of continuing adaptation and change?

▶ How 'user friendly' is the technology of your company, ie is it compatible with, and supportive of, the way people naturally work and think, and conductive of 'interfaces' with, or links to, other networks?

▶ What are the main barriers to the more effective use of IT in your company and how might these be overcome?

# REFERENCES

Coulson-Thomas, C (1992) *Transforming the Company: Bridging the gap between management myth and corporate reality*, Kogan Page, London

Coulson-Thomas, C (2000) *The Information Entrepreneur*, 3Com Active Business Unit, Winnersh

Coulson-Thomas, C (2001) *Shaping Things to Come: Strategies for creating alternative enterprises*, Blackhall Publishing, Dublin

Hurcomb, J (1998) *Developing Strategic Customers & Key Accounts: The critical success factors*, Policy Publications, Bedford

Stone, M *et al* (1999) *Managing Customers with e-Business*, Policy Publications, Bedford

Stone, M *et al* (2000) *Customer Management on the Move*, Policy Publications, Bedford

# FURTHER INFORMATION

A brochure describing the *Developing Strategic Customers & Key Accounts: The critical success factors* report and the 'Close to the Customer' briefings on the use of mobile and e-business technologies to build customer relationships are available from Policy Publications, 4 The Crescent, Bedford MK40 2RU (tel: +44 (0) 1234 328448; fax: + 44 (0) 1234 357231; e-mail: policypubs@kbnet.co.uk; Web site: www.ntwkfirm.com/bookshop).

# 17

# Creating the International Learning Network

*'If too much water is taken out and not enough put in, a canal pound will drain'*

## THE CREDO AND THE BACK ALLEY

A commitment to tapping more of the potential of people is an integral element of the credo of the new organization. The rhetoric proclaims the central importance of empowered people who are counselled, mentored, supported and facilitated in creating know-how, launching new ventures, building relationships with *their* customers, and delivering value to them.

The potential and the talents to encourage, nourish and build are not just the ones that are known about. They should include the latent capability that has been smothered and concealed, and the hidden strengths that people do not even know that they have. Beneath the job titles, and other labels and trappings, are attributes and qualities that should be brought to the surface.

We saw in Chapter 13 that the well-meaning efforts of many educationalists, trainers and developers destroy the innate drive of millions of people to explore and learn. Rather than being 'released', their ambitions and prospects are crushed in a vice of misunderstanding, mass deception and unintended consequences. Some accept their categorization, 'settle down' and grumble about a humdrum existence, tinged with the occasional thought that they might have done better or glimpse of what might have been. Others rebel and seek an alternative route to peer recognition in the alley or the street.

## BRINGING LEARNING INTO THE NETWORK

How can the reality of active and universal learning be brought into the network organization? This chapter will examine the different approaches of winners and losers to learning, and the creation of international corporate networks to support both working and learning.

Learning is not a panacea. It all depends on what is learnt, for what purpose and how it is used. Rover sought to become a learning organization and considerable effort was devoted to the establishment of learning processes throughout the company. Yet Rover failed to become competitive within the car industry and ended up being acquired by BMW.

Under British Aerospace the commitment to learning shown by the setting up of Rover Learning Business was not matched by complementary investments in physical resources. Little was spent on ensuring that Rover's plant and machinery remained at the cutting edge. BMW endeavoured to address these deficiencies but failed to understand the learning culture it had acquired. The renamed group training function replaced learning with traditional instruction.

British Aerospace did understand the nature and potential value of the learning culture within Rover that had been established under the leadership of Sir Graham Day. Individual learning champions and much of the know-how created were retained to help with the subsequent transformation of the remaining aerospace businesses.

## LEARNING ISN'T WORKING

Internationally, people have been concerned about learning for a generation (Coulson-Thomas, 1992). Governments recognized (Coulson-Thomas, 1992) that the relative performance of national economies can reflect the relevance and adaptability of skills.

The roots of many learning limitations and inhibitions lie in early experiences at school. Traditional approaches to education have been challenged. In a demanding and changing international marketplace, individual initiative and creativity need greater encouragement.

The deficiencies of traditional education have led to many ambitious initiatives to introduce new learning environments that will use various technologies, and a variety of approaches, to better meet the needs of learners. Internationalization has encouraged cross-border comparisons. What was once uncritically accepted is now questioned.

In the case of many educational applications of IT there has been too much emphasis upon the technology. In others, it has been used to 'automate' traditional approaches to learning that are of questionable value. The focus should be upon the nature of the learning process and how this can best be facilitated for individuals and groups, with or without IT.

# THE LEARNING PROCESS

How do people learn? In the past this was assumed rather than understood. For many years at centres such as the Institute for Research on Learning (IRL) in California, relatively small and multidisciplinary groups have examined how people learn – not just those who are academic, but all people.

The findings are consistent with many of the learning preferences of companies we considered in Chapter 13, in particular the integration of learning and working.

The most effective learning occurs in life generally, as a result of doing things and observing the outcomes. When left to themselves, people do not 'reserve' learning for certain hours and locations. The classroom is, for many people, one of the least effective learning environments. They feel cut off, estranged or distanced from normal life, and do not relate to many of the abstract symbols and concepts that are used. They talk of a 'fear of courses', an 'alien environment'.

One manager summed up the misgivings: 'I like to be on my own ground, somewhere where I feel at home.' Learning at institutions, with teachers 'pouring knowledge into people', is unsatisfactory for the majority of people. The context is wrong, and relevance and purpose are not perceived. There is a need for learning situations that enable the practical relevance of concepts and ideas to be more easily grasped.

# DIVERSE CORPORATE REQUIREMENTS

The nature of the work and life for which people need to be prepared will vary across countries, according to such factors as culture and stage of development. Learning materials and approaches may need to be adapted to be relevant to local needs. The ability to communicate internationally should not obscure the need for local tailoring.

Team activity and group learning can be particularly effective, yet educational institutions generally require people to learn and be assessed upon an individual basis. Little attention is given to understanding group processes, supporting group learning or improving outputs from teams, each of which may have distinct learning needs and preferences.

Research over a decade ago at IRL revealed that not all of us learn in the same way. Each of us has a distinct potential as a learner. We need to be able to respond flexibly to groups of people who may learn in a variety of ways. These findings suggest questions which people with development responsibilities should have addressed:

- How can development be responsive to the learning and development needs of the individual, and of particular groups?
- How should the role of facilitator of learning differ from that of subject teacher?
- What are the implications of how different people learn for the roles of mentor and coach?
- How should technology be used to facilitate team activity and group learning?
- How could a learning network be used as a catalyst for the transformation of the corporate system and culture as a whole?
- How could collaborative venture and learning partners be incorporated into the network?

The empowered person should be enabled to do more than harness the information, knowledge and resources of the company on behalf of customers. People should be able to reach into their own minds and those of colleagues. The stimulation, release and application of learning potential is true empowerment.

## LEARNING AND TECHNOLOGY

The results of early research into how people learn still have important implications for the use of IT to facilitate learning (Wenger, 1987a). The traditional 'black box' that produces an outcome without revealing why this has occurred can 'deskill'. A more 'transparent technology' that allows the learner to observe processes at work can increase understanding with each application. This has been called 'glass-box' technology, and can assist the 'merging of learning and doing' (Wenger, 1987b).

Virtual reality technology can create a wealth of learning environments that may adapt to the needs, interests and capabilities of the individual learner. IT that can facilitate interaction, team activity and group learning, is particularly valuable. However, there are practical and attitudinal barriers to address. Consider the following comments:

*We had presentations in the boardroom, and saw the learning potential of the technology. By the time you go down two or three layers in the company, the vision gets lost... Our people went out and bought the cheapest boxes.*

*I have to focus on... problems to be fixed. There are short term targets to be met... I just don't have time to think about the wider implications.*

*If people would pay for it and use it, I would go for the learning solution... But the benefits are not immediate... Other things are more immediate and get the priority.*

*Suppliers are the problem. We all agree on the concept... [but] they go away and come back with whatever it is they want to sell. It's never what we want... we cannot progress things.*

When a cost-saving approach to purchase decisions is taken, the 'commodity' technology that is acquired can sometimes fall short of what would most effectively facilitate team working and create a rich and distinctive learning environment.

A 'user-friendly' technology is required that does not distort too much the way people naturally learn. The technology that suits one group may be inappropriate for another that learns in a different way. There are alternative approaches that could be adopted according to learning aptitudes, styles and preferences. For example, we saw the following in Chapter 13:

- Traditional approaches to learning assumed that we all learn in a similar way. It was best suited to the 'academics', those who operate in a world of logic and structure, and who proceed by means of small incremental steps from an understood current position.
- Breakthroughs and revolutions in thought challenge the frameworks, the tidy boxes within which academics and others work. They occur when 'connections are made'. These 'other' approaches to learning are based upon the establishment of links, patterns and relationships, and may release qualities in people hardly touched by the academic knowledge-based approach.

Creativity should not be 'something different', confined to those upon whom 'the gods have smiled'. It is too often treated as an exception or a surprise, rather than as part of everyday work. As one CEO put it: 'My customers demand creativity. ... I don't want to pay extra for creativity – I want to assume it.'

## MISSING ELEMENTS

Creativity does not 'just happen'. Throughout this book, considerable stress has been put upon the importance of the attitudinal aspects of corporate culture. The technological environment can also be an important element of the 'learning culture'. Consider the following questions raised by interviewees:

*Can't we use technology to make everyone more creative?... Isn't there software we can load on to our boxes?*

*There must be a way of magnifying people. Should we be using technology and 'know-how' to blow up their strengths?*

The artificial intelligence (AI) environment offered the prospect of a universal and affordable complement to human intelligence that can support both learning and working. However, just when the potential was within grasp, attention 'moved on'. Word got around on the 'groupthink grapevine' that AI was 'overrated' and 'hasn't delivered'. What it isn't should not blind us to what it is.

The AI environment suits those who are sensitive to potential links and relationships. The 'academic' who imposes assumptions and frameworks may cut himself or herself off from possibilities that the environment is suggesting. Those without formal academic qualifications, but who are receptive to patterns and possibilities, may, with an appropriate induction, become innovation superstars.

An accessible learning environment should have sufficient flexibility to support different ways of learning. It should allow each individual to become aware of how he or she most effectively learns and, subsequently should facilitate such learning. The aim should be to enable individuals to discover what their relative strengths as learners are, and how they might best build their understanding.

## SELECTING THE TECHNOLOGY TO APPLY

Just as it is 'horses for courses', when it comes to facilitating the learning of individuals, so it is with making use of IT. Different technologies and their underlying architectures have distinct strengths and weaknesses. Use can be made of each, as appropriate, so long as interfaces exist.

The dilemma for companies is that they may need both the incremental or procedural, and the relational or process approach to learning, along with some others. For one director, the concept of the learning organization presents a dilemma:

*The notion is attractive... It sounds good. When you think it through, all sorts of possibilities open up [but] the implications and potential costs can be intimidating. To get there means dramatic changes... another revolution, when we have yet to accomplish the first. It's a question of how true you want to be to the vision.*

Given the diversity of people that may be found across the network organization, winners focus learning support on the key factors for becoming and remaining relevant, creative, distinctive and competitive.

When considering the application of information technology to support new approaches to learning, a set of objectives should be established. An example of one such set is given in Table 17.1.

**Table 17.1** Objectives of a learning network

Improve win rates and increase sales force productivity
Support shared learning partnerships
Enhance knowledge creation and exploitation
Allow individuals, venture teams and work groups to manage their own learning
Match learning need to appropriate learning activities and resources
Enable flexible access to relevant learning opportunities and environments
Overcome shortages of teachers and experts
Use specialists as facilitators and managers of learning
Integrate learning and working
Allow international access and expansion
Be integrated into the corporate and value chain network
Be 'open' to multivendor technology
Offer advantages to network partners and learners over known alternatives
Create and maintain a migration path regarding future technologies and alternative
    approaches
Be capable of organic growth and development

A technology that is sufficiently flexible and adaptable to support individual and participative approaches to learning is preferable to one that is structured and rigid, and offers a standard approach. It needs to support a diversity of individual and shared learning requirements across a network of electronic links, forward to customers, backwards to suppliers and sideways to business partners.

Developments in technology have been supportive of the creation of integrated working and learning networks. The whole of western Europe can be within the footprint of a single satellite, while interactive Web-based services can be accessible to people all over the world. A variety of public and corporate electronic learning networks have been in existence for over a decade (Coulson-Thomas, 1992).

A gradual switch of expenditure has occurred from the 'campus' and its classrooms to the terminals of the 'enabling' electronic network, as 'learning' has been taken to the 'learners'. In certain 'knowledge industries' the quality of the 'network' embracing and linking learners and facilitators of the learning process can become the key competitive differentiator. A possible development framework, or set of guidelines, is presented in Table 17.2.

Schools networks such as Campus 2000 and electronic universities with students who communicate with each other and contact their tutors via computer terminals have over a decade of experience. Students in various locations log on at convenient times and interact with each other. They can access relevant material, bounce ideas and drafts off others by electronic mail, and produce and deliver reports, essays and presentations using a terminal located at home or on an office desk. Such a learning environment can itself 'learn', as previous learning material, knowledge and assignments can be accessed, updated and refined.

**Table 17.2** Integrated learning environment development framework

Articulation and agreement of common vision
Establish framework and guidelines
Set attainable objectives
Ensure compatibility with likely future developments
Reflect mixed technology environment of the real world
Access relevant knowledge, competence and experience
Establish basis for seeking internal and external participation and support
Open to multivendor and partner involvement
Preserve international operation, growth and development options

# MANAGING THE LEARNING NETWORK

The form in which learning opportunities and materials are presented can reflect the capabilities and interest of each student. Learner and facilitator become partners in the learning process. Each point of contact, or terminal, is able in theory to draw upon the resources of the whole network.

The technology can also record contributions, track progress, co-ordinate diaries, and monitor assignments, project groups and teams. It can determine who is 'living off the system', and who is putting most into the network. Geographic dispersion need not result in less awareness of what is going on.

How many companies assess and reward learning? The assessment of both work and learning could be based on demonstrated competencies and delivered output. Rewards could be linked to the effective facilitation of the learning of others. Learning environments can also be used to identify facilitator development needs.

A learning network can advertise its mission, or particular focus, and call for partners to work on individual projects, perhaps for named clients, rather than specific 'job' vacancies or opportunities. Similarly, those with particular skills and interests may advertise them, and the sort of projects upon which they would like to work, and on what terms. Specialism could be by learning process or barrier, rather than by subject or discipline.

Both quality management consultancy, and world-class management education have become increasingly expensive. As a consequence, companies desire to get the best of each, namely personal and team development, and a value-added contribution to a corporate problem. In effect, what is sought is neither management consultancy nor management education, but a combination of the two. The requirement is for access to a flexible resource that can help to:

- define corporate tasks in the form of projects which could be undertaken by individuals and groups in the working environment;
- identify related development needs of the individuals and teams concerned; and

● provide help and support, as required, to facilitate the acquisition of the required skills and knowledge, and the successful completion of the project tasks.

Many corporate networks established for effective international communication can be used to support international distance learning. Table 17.3 sets out a suggested programme for the establishment of a collaborative and interactive learning network. A first step for many companies is to link up their own internal training facilities and centres of expertise to form a corporate network, which can then link up with a variety of external networks at local, regional and international levels.

Information technology can make an important contribution to the development of network organizations. But without relevant skills, attitudes and learning partners, its role may represent an aspiration rather than a reality. Technical competence has to be matched with awareness, empathy and sensitivity.

## CORPORATE EXPERIENCE

How aware of the above possibilities and sensitive to the diversity of learning requirements are those who formulate corporate learning strategies? A decade after the formulation of the vision (Coulson-Thomas,

**Table 17.3** Suggested international learning network programme

Discuss possibilities and options with customers, suppliers and business partners
Establish purpose and focus
Identify possible collaborative partners
Explore shared learning needs and requirements
Share hopes and expectations
Agree common vision, values and goals
Set measurable objectives
Allocate roles and responsibilities
Contact relevant projects, research institutes, experts and authorities
Agree learning principles and approaches
Specify systems framework architectures and standards
Agree guidelines covering the curriculum development and creation, protection and sharing of intellectual property
Determine means of project management and coordination and management of the network
Secure commitment of the core parties
Refine implementation plan
Articulate benefits of proposed learning environment to potential members and partners
Implement, trial, test, review and refine

1992) are integrated learning networks creating new knowledge and additional choices for customers?

We saw in Chapter 8 that too many approaches to knowledge management focus excessively on the sharing of an existing stock of knowledge and pay inadequate attention to the determination and development of the new knowledge required for achieving priority objectives (Coulson-Thomas, 1997 and 1998). Knowledge creation is becoming increasingly important. Let us consider examples at different ends of the standard-bespoke knowledge set continuum.

As e-business erodes barriers of distance and time, physical markets are being replaced by electronic market spaces. Increasingly, purchases of commodity products will consist of impersonal transactions via intelligent agents accessing integrated supply chains through Web sites. Their evolving requirements will become a more important determinant of the information that will need to be presented, updated and refined.

Moving up the value chain will require new forms of differentiation and additional ways of adding value (Coulson-Thomas, 2001). More bespoke responses to the requirements of individual customers will require new attitudes, skills and tools, as well as redesigned processes and supporting technology. Efficiency and cost-cutting drives need to be complemented by efforts to generate higher margins and incremental revenues.

In particular, as the proportion of final value delivered to customers that is represented by know-how continues to increase, people will need to become more effective at creating, packaging, sharing, applying and generally managing and exploiting information, knowledge and understanding. In short, companies need knowledge entrepreneurs, and fast (Coulson-Thomas, 2000).

## CORPORATE LEARNING STRATEGY

Smart investors are becoming more sensitive to corporate will and capability to learn. In many businesses large and small there is an urgent need for mentors, counsellors, 'trainers' and 'developers' who can quickly rise to the challenge and encourage and support knowledge creation. Today's training activities, development preoccupations and learning priorities are likely to be a significant determinant of tomorrow's attitudes, skills and knowledge.

Companies should urgently assess whether training and development inputs are resulting in knowledge and intellectual capital outputs. Do they contribute to innovation and intrapreneurship, new business wins and better key account management, or the imaginative use of e-business? Maybe software is being bought to help capture existing knowledge, but are people learning and creating new knowledge?

In many companies training and development is at a watershed. Many existing courses and facilities have reached the end of their useful life. As we have seen, there are new approaches to learning and emerging technologies to evaluate.

Enthusiasts of e-learning can quickly locate online material to access. So much is available they need to select carefully. Even British Telecom's Openworld provides newscasts on a growing range of business topics. Some sources are more authoritative than others. The prestigious Massachusetts Institute of Technology is investing $100 million in making the learning materials that support its 2,000 courses freely available over the World Wide Web. How should companies take advantage of such opportunities?

There are also other important questions to address. Could business development and the processes of value and knowledge creation be better supported? Should a corporate university be set up? Could particular training activities, or the whole function, be made a revenue centre, a separate business, or simply outsourced? Then there are the 'acid test' questions: If all existing courses ceased, would users, clients or customers notice or care? What would be lost if 'central training' were closed down?

# REVIEWING APPROACHES TO CORPORATE LEARNING

A two-year examination of corporate learning plans and priorities has addressed such questions. The investigation included corporate visits and 69 structured interviews with individuals responsible for the training and development of some 460,000 people. The results with case studies, checklists and key action points are summarized in the report 'Developing a Corporate Learning Strategy' (Coulson-Thomas, 1999a).

The findings are sobering and they demand urgent attention. Many courses have passed their 'sell by' date, while essential requirements and critical corporate priorities are largely ignored. Millions are being spent on fashionable concepts such as empowerment, grandiose 'leadership' initiatives, and general 'teamwork' training, yet only one of the organizations surveyed is equipping its people to be more successful at bringing in new business.

Key areas such as the attitudes, knowledge and skills required for succeeding in competitive bid situations are being overlooked. This omission is unnecessary given that the specific skill requirements of bid team leaders and other business development professionals have been identified (Kennedy, 1999) and a suite of tools for bid teams has also been produced (Bartram, 1999).

As we saw in Chapters 5 and 16, relationship and account management skills are becoming particularly important because of the greater emphasis being given to developing partnerships and the search for opportunities to widen the range of services offered to individual customers. The need has been recognized, and relevant critical success factors have been identified

(Hurcomb, 1998), but specific steps, such as defining the competencies and role-model behaviours of account managers, have yet to be undertaken in many companies.

Trainers are 'following fads' and buying 'off-the-shelf' learning resources packs, rather than addressing specific situations and circumstances. People receive standard courses regardless of individual interests and needs. Enormous sums of money are spent exposing diverse people, working on very different activities, to common experiences that have little relevance to their particular requirements and priorities. Yet, the analysis of the atypical, rather than replication of the normal, is often the key to differentiation.

With value increasingly delivered by supply chains rather than individual companies, more shared learning also needs to occur. However, the organizations examined focus overwhelmingly upon the internal training of employed staff. The external development needs of customers, contractors, suppliers, supply chain partners and business associates are being ignored. The focus is on the intranet rather than the extranet.

Overall, little effort is devoted to business development and relationship building, e-business or knowledge creation. Entrepreneurship seems a no-go area even though companies need new ventures and guidance on what companies can do to stimulate enterprise and create entrepreneurs (Coulson-Thomas, 1999b). Overwhelmingly the emphasis is on squeezing and cutting costs, rather than income generation. Corporate learning should embrace the creation, sharing, application and exploitation of knowledge, and new multidisciplinary approaches are needed.

Companies such as IBM and Microsoft regard customer education as a major global business opportunity. However, in general, education, training and development are not perceived as a source of incremental revenue. Nor are they used as a means of building relationships with key decision-makers in strategic customers, suppliers and business partners.

Education, training and development expenditures are still widely viewed and treated as costs rather than vital investments in the creation of knowledge, intellectual capital and value for customers. With trainers focusing upon corporate preoccupations, the aspirations of individuals are being largely overlooked. Switching the emphasis from cost cutting to innovation, business building and value creation would result in enhanced corporate performance and greater personal fulfilment (Coulson-Thomas, 1999b).

## HOW LOSERS APPROACH TRAINING AND DEVELOPMENT

Senior managers in losing companies have little interest in integrated learning networks. They have a resigned attitude towards traditional training and development. Expenditure on them is viewed as worthy and an inevitable cost of being in business. However, when cash flow is squeezed they are among the first areas to be cut back.

Losers tend to lack rigour when analysing training requirements. They provide general and standard courses in areas such as 'quality'; 'empowerment' or 'diversity' rather than develop more specific ones aimed at named individuals in order to support the achievement of particular objectives. Such offerings are in the 'nice to have' rather than essential category.

They may also be made available on a number of dates. There is no particular urgency about them and people attend as and when they can. Programmes remain listed in prospectuses and handbooks until everyone has been through them. Long before this happens in larger companies they may already be past their 'sell by' date.

Losers imitate and follow fashion. The training furnished tends to reflect what other companies are doing and the areas and topics considered trendy at the time of its inception. What is supplied rarely addresses the different interests, aspirations and priorities of the various people and personalities involved. Nor does it accommodate their individual learning styles and preferences.

The training provided can also be divisive. Employees are welcome but contract staff and 'associates' may be excluded from training and thus made to feel second-class citizens. Home-based and itinerant staff may simply be forgotten. Joint activities are suspended and customer and business partner representatives read the papers, drink tea or delete unwanted e-mails while the 'home team' goes into the conference room.

Losers are essentially selfish. They give reluctantly and only in order to receive. They focus almost exclusively upon their own objectives. Those responsible for training and development are also departmental in their thinking and approach. They wrestle in isolation with problems that feature on many corporate learning agendas. They fail to collaborate and join training consortia and other collective arrangements. Hence they do not benefit from collective purchasing, resource sharing and specialization.

## HOW WINNERS SET OUT TO LEARN

Winners are more discriminating and selective. They reflect the learning network vision in their attitudes. They adopt bespoke approaches and provide specific support that addresses particular learning needs and is intended to be helpful to those involved.

The learning costs incurred by winners are more likely to be perceived as investments in building strategic capabilities and the creation of knowledge and customer and shareholder value. Plans and policies are designed to enable the organization to accomplish key elements of whatever it is seeking to achieve. Results are carefully monitored and corrective action taken as appropriate.

Winners address individual as well as corporate requirements. Personnel, learning and IT specialists, business unit teams and infrastructure managers work together. They also cooperate with other organizations. They open up learning opportunities to customers, suppliers, associates and business partners. Learning occurs within and across value and supply chains. It is a differentiator and as a source of incremental income becomes an area of business opportunity in its own right.

# CREATING AND EXPLOITING INTELLECTUAL CAPITAL

We saw in Chapter 8 that there is considerable scope for information and knowledge entrepreneurship (Coulson-Thomas, 2000) and in Chapter 16 that professional firms are packaging basic know-how on CD ROMs and Web sites. Users can access them and work through diagnostics in order to better understand their problems and home in on the areas in which they need advice before they contact the relevant experts suggested.

The sale of specialized knowledge, or the licensing of intellectual capital such as particular approaches or techniques can contribute additional income streams. The report 'Managing Intellectual Capital to Grow Shareholder Value' suggests that most organizations fail to properly manage and fully exploit the 20 categories of intellectual capital examined (Perrin, 2000).

Many businesses could do far more to generate additional income streams by packaging and exploiting their knowledge and understanding. Maybe they could help other people to assemble the information, knowledge and understanding that they might need to create and deliver value for *their* customers. Perhaps they could use the Internet to reach a wider geographical spread of customers or license particular approaches or techniques or offer personalized online counselling and support.

The education, learning, training and updating markets are among the most exciting of contemporary business opportunities. The 'Developing a Corporate Learning Strategy' report (Coulson-Thomas, 1999a) identifies no fewer than 25 different categories of learning support services that could be offered. Intellectual capital from simple tools to advanced techniques can also be licensed or sold. There is enormous potential for income generation, higher margins and knowledge entrepreneurship.

Despite the opportunities, most trainers are not directly supporting the creation, sharing and application of knowledge and understanding. Explicit knowledge management initiatives tend to be conceived and to operate quite independently of the training and development team (Coulson-Thomas, 1999a). Many human resources professionals are leaving the running to IT specialists and vendors of software for capturing, structuring and managing existing knowledge, when the emphasis should be upon creating and exploiting new know-how.

Managing current stocks of information, knowledge or understanding might or might not be relevant to individual aspirations, customer requirements or corporate objectives. But new insights, discoveries and breakthroughs, the dynamics of the creation and application of pertinent knowledge, are often the keys to leadership in competitive markets. IBM devotes significant resources to creating new intellectual capital and actively exploits its patent portfolio in its contracts with customers and partners.

## LOSERS AND KNOW-HOW CREATION AND EXPLOITATION

Innovation and the creation of new alternatives are a key source of competitive differentiation (Coulson-Thomas, 2001). We saw in Chapter 8 that losers tend to be consumers rather than producers of knowledge, understanding and intellectual capital (Coulson-Thomas, 1997 and 1998). They are fashion followers, not thought leaders. They tend to work almost exclusively on current projects and opportunities, and rarely, if ever, consider how what they do might be packaged to generate additional income flows that are independent of day-to-day operations.

While losers may attempt to manage existing stocks of information and knowledge, little effort is devoted to ensuring that they are relevant and current. People tend to be passive and unquestioning recipients. What is learnt tends to be applied to improving current operations. Learning takes place at defined times in dedicated places. Learning inputs lead to quantified outputs, such as the number of managers put through particular courses.

When they do find themselves owning intellectual capital, losers are among the corporate laggards at managing and exploiting it (Perrin, 2000). While some forms of know-how may be packaged, badged and protected, most of their senior managers are unaware of the variety of different forms of intellectual capital that can occur. Most are also ignorant of frameworks such as the award-winning K-frame (www.k-frame.com) that can handle and search for a variety of formats from text, presentation slides and electronic data stores to animations and audio and video material.

## WHAT WINNERS DO DIFFERENTLY

Winners are much more likely to develop, document and use their own ideas and approaches. Their people consider how bespoke responses to particular customer requirements might be packaged to form a generic product or service, or a distinctive capability that could be offered to other clients. As a consequence, they create their own intellectual capital that can represent balance sheet value in its own right and be licensed or sold (Coulson-

Thomas, 2000; Perrin, 2000). Capturing, sharing and applying knowledge enables them to move up value chains and achieve higher margins.

People in winning companies are concerned with flows of information and knowledge – innovations, discoveries and breakthroughs that add to and extend what is already known. They learn with and for customers and review, critique and refresh whatever know-how, resources and facilities are provided in the search for new marketplace offerings and alternative ways of operating. Learning and working are integrated and learning inputs are expected to lead to demonstrable business outputs.

Many winners pay particular attention to the valuation and management of intellectual capital. They are always alert to opportunities to exploit what they know and apply how they go about doing things in other contexts.

Key members of staff recognize that there are many different types of know-how. They may take the trouble to acquire a knowledge management framework such as K-frame that can handle them and allow easy and rapid storage, access and utilization without the need for expensive investments in new technologies or specialist support. They are also catholic in their search for possible applications.

Various central services can be offered to the members of a learning network. Support could be provided for individual learners and particular shared-learning communities. Cover could be provided during holidays, illnesses or periods of peak workload. Advice could be offered on assessment, validation, the selection of learning technologies, or assembling a combination of complementary elements to address particular learning needs.

Learning activities in different locations and time zones could be coordinated and monitored and appropriate reports generated. Shared resources from virtual classrooms, specialist learning environments and stores to online bulletin boards, presentations and discussion groups could be provided. Periodic audits and reviews could be undertaken of the adequacy of a knowledge bank. Like the supply of water to a pound on a canal, it may not be adequate if there are too many users. Steps may need to be taken to plug gaps and access new sources of supply.

## TAKING REMEDIAL ACTION

The existing state of affairs in 'loser' companies cannot continue. Those interviewed derive little satisfaction from the current situation. One head of training explained in exasperation that: 'It's like going along to the stadium to play any one of a number of new games whose rules you do not understand and not knowing whether your kit, equipment or technique will be relevant or acceptable.'

The 'Developing a Corporate Learning Strategy' report (Coulson-Thomas, 1999a) suggests a way ahead. Let's start with learning. Winners venture beyond the passive importation and sharing of existing information, knowledge and understanding. Rather than merely observe or imitate, they investigate and innovate.

Boards and managers should actively champion enterprise and learning. Knowledge development should be explicitly rewarded. As we saw in Chapter 9, pioneers do not play 'me-too' or 'catch-up' according to yesterday's rules. They are energetic creators, imaginative innovators and restless explorers. They devise and set up new games with different rules.

The creation, capture, valuation, sharing, use and application of knowledge and intellectual capital are vital. When tailoring responses and differentiating, the ability to learn quickly and effectively is a source of both value and competitive advantage. The most successful enterprises will evolve into communities of knowledge entrepreneurs (Coulson-Thomas, 1999b, 2001).

Learning processes can be created, improved or re-engineered, and learning support tools acquired. For example, a framework for managing intellectual capital in its various formats may also be required. Learning should also be built into work processes, and standard training offerings should be abandoned in favour of specific and tailored interventions to support learning and knowledge entrepreneurship. 'The Information Entrepreneur' (Coulson-Thomas, 2000) provides practical checklists which entrepreneurs, investors, managers and individual members of the board can use to create customer and shareholder value by packaging and exploiting knowledge.

Knowledge creation should start with what an organization is setting out to do. Next, roles and responsibilities, processes, and ways of working and learning to achieve the desired objectives have to be designed and agreed. Role-model behaviours and, importantly, the knowledge, experience and understanding likely to be required can then be determined, along with any additional tools, techniques and methodologies that may be needed.

Centres of excellence, or panels of experts, could review certain areas of a company's 'body of knowledge' to keep them up to date. Individuals could be given responsibility for recording what they have learnt, and ensuring that their CVs and learning logs are current.

The tangible consequences of knowledge creation and exploitation include improved employee and customer satisfaction, an enhanced image and an increased share valuation. HRD activities should contribute to enterprise, and business and knowledge development. If a causal link to fresh know-how, greater customer value, or additional business cannot be demonstrated, they should be discontinued.

## KEY QUESTIONS TO ASK

Many corporate training teams are missing a historic opportunity to make a strategic contribution to knowledge and value creation and the achievement of corporate objectives. Hence the critical importance of developing new strategies for corporate learning.

Those responsible for training and development should consider whether their current portfolio of courses and their coaches and mentors are contributing to uniformity and resulting in a standard attitudes, knowledge and skills set or stimulating diversity and knowledge creation (Coulson-Thomas, 1999a):

- Do training and development objectives make explicit the need for knowledge creation and the creation of new and distinct alternatives?
- What proportion of the training budget is devoted to the support of individual development and diversity as opposed to standard courses?
- Is each person enabled to play to their particular strengths and to achieve their personal aspirations?
- How much emphasis is placed upon consensus, 'middle way' and 'lowest common denominator' approaches?
- Do training activities help to build the personal qualities and skills needed to develop new knowledge and craft novel offerings?
- Do they address barriers to creativity, innovation and discovery?
- What is being done to support enterprise and entrepreneurship?
- How much emphasis do courses and counselling place upon role model behaviour and conformity to corporate norms?
- How much importance is attached to imitation, benchmarking, competitor analysis and teamworking, as opposed to innovation and individual discovery?
- Does the corporate culture encourage discussion, stimulate thought and foster inspired individuality?
- Are employees, associates and business partners encouraged to question and dissent from prevailing opinions?
- What proportion of training and development resources are devoted to helping them become more effective at playing existing activities and games?
- What proportion is designed to help them create new and alternative activities and games?
- What steps are being taken within the training and development community to make a more significant contribution to knowledge and opportunity creation?

There is no need for training and development to be regarded as a cost of being in business. Training teams could be tasked with becoming separate and profitable ventures. Individuals could become 'customers' with personal learning accounts.

Knowledge and experience-sharing can present an attitudinal and cultural challenge. Where people are reluctant to 'give away *their* knowledge' new mentoring and counselling roles with associated status and financial rewards may need to be created.

Targets and measures should reflect these changes. Input indicators such as 'bums on seats' should be replaced by demonstrable or verifiable outcomes. For example, by how much has the 'win rate' in competitive bidding situations increased? What proportion of turnover is accounted for by new products and services? What value is ascribed to newly packaged intellectual capital? How many accredited qualifications have been obtained?

# SUPPORTING ENTREPRENEURSHIP

More emphasis needs to be put upon creativity, imagination and innovation, and exploration, discovery and problem solving. Avoidance, rationalization and passive learning must be replaced by the active creation of opportunities, solutions and value.

Standard competencies and 'training' to provide people with a common experience should cease. The emphasis should switch to self-directed learning and creating learning environments, such as a corporate university, that can respond to the particular interests and aspirations of individual members of staff and encourage innovation and knowledge creation.

Corporate universities can access specialist expertise, develop new competencies, create imaginative approaches, or develop additional capabilities. Staff can be seconded for specified periods to work on strategic learning projects. Think tank environments can be conducive of 'blue skies' thinking, and the open-minded, systematic and imaginative consideration of alternatives.

If companies are to become incubators of entrepreneurial activity (Coulson-Thomas, 1999b), 'human resource' professionals must work more closely with information technology specialists, business units, new venture teams, facilities managers, and learning partners in the stimulation and support of knowledge, value and enterprise creation. Work environments should inspire. They should enable learning, innovation and creativity.

---

## Losers

Losers:

- consider learning and thinking as exceptional and specialist activities;
- regard innovation and learning as distinct and separate activities;
- assume most people learn the same way;
- instruct and teach;
- move forward incrementally from what is known;
- adopt technologies that automate existing approaches to learning;
- attempt to manage the learning of their people;

- provide internal training programmes;
- operate dedicated corporate training centres;
- respond to requests for sponsorship from local traditional universities;
- fail to create and exploit new know-how;
- rarely subject their learning strategies and practices to a periodic and independent review.

## Winners

Winners:

- build learning and thinking into people's roles;
- integrate learning and working;
- recognize that people do not all learn the same way;
- facilitate, enable and support learning;
- encourage people to identify links, patterns and relationships and establish the connections that may result in revolutions and break-throughs in understanding;
- adopt technologies that enable new and better approaches to learning;
- allow individuals to manage their own learning;
- encourage their people to join international, collaborative and shared-learning networks;
- operate international learning networks;
- establish corporate universities and learning partnerships with relevant universities;
- are active information and knowledge entrepreneurs;
- keep their learning strategies and approaches current, relevant and vital.

# RECOGNIZING CONTRIBUTIONS

The use of learning and knowledge creation networks awards an enhanced 'premium' to those who are professional and academic 'superstars' in comparison with their more 'average' colleagues. Information technology has had a major impact upon the 'knowledge bases' of both the professions and academic disciplines, as well as upon patterns of work and approaches to learning. Companies stress the unique features of their cultures as they strive to differentiate. As a more 'situational' or 'contextual' view of the nature and relevance of knowledge and of expertise emerges, networks must become more tolerant of diversity.

Multiple part-time contracts can allow a number of institutions and learning networks to access a 'scarce resource'. Companies will have to compete to attract the 'stars'. Those who are mobile will be the people networks strive to attract and retain, while the 'inflexible' and 'low performers' cling like limpets to a diminishing set of tenured havens and secure job titles. Traditional subject teachers will become fewer in number, as demand grows for facilitators of the learning process whose skills cross discipline boundaries.

As their customers become more discerning, individual institutions and learning networks will need to demonstrate 'relevance' on a continuing basis, and establish a distinct focus and vision in order to differentiate themselves. Individuals who do not commit to the continual refinement and updating of knowledge will experience a steady erosion of their relevance and value.

One CEO commented: 'We fight a continual battle to match the forces that erode our capabilities and skills.' This is why vision, values, attitudes and perspective are so important. They can survive storm and drought.

Networks of collaborating institutions will need to persuade those in their target marketplaces that their own grouping is able to enhance skill, competence and experience to a greater extent than the alternatives available.

# DIRECTORS OF LEARNING AND THINKING

In order to turn the rhetoric of the learning organization into a working reality, companies are entering into new forms of relationships with learning partners. The international networks, structures and processes that are emerging need to be directed and managed. Companies, and their professional and educational partners, are becoming learning networks. Their *raison d'etre* is tapping human talent through the facilitation of learning, knowledge creation and entrepreneurship.

Preparation for a role in directing a network could involve a journey between and around customer, supplier, academic and professional organizations in order to gain experience of each of its elements. Moving between significant roles within very different organizations, and bridging barriers of prejudice, misperception and misunderstanding, these managers and directors of learning or thinking will be both project leaders and diplomats.

Our leaders and champions of learning will not be easy to find. As when mining gold, it may be necessary to work through a ton of dross to obtain an ounce of what you want. However, if they succeed in their new roles we will have to reassess our views of what is dross, base metal and gold. A combination of learning culture, environment and network could yield an outcome more magical than that sought of the philosopher's stone.

# CHECKLIST

▶ How committed is your company to harnessing human talent on an international basis?

▶ How critical is the concept of the learning network to the achievement of its vision?

▶ Does your company understand the learning process and how people learn?

▶ Who, within the company, is responsible for learning?

▶ What is being done to ensure that all members of the network discover their learning potential and how they as individuals might best build their understanding?

▶ If it has not already done so, should your company appoint a director of learning, understanding or thinking?

▶ How relevant is more appropriate technology to the facilitation of learning in your company?

▶ Should your company be more extensively linked up to national, regional and international learning networks?

▶ What needs to be done to ensure that the company itself takes on more of the attributes of a learning network?

▶ Does your company understand how the changing nature of educational and professional institutions, and the emerging requirements of the knowledge worker, will impact upon its own relationships with them?

▶ Have your company's managers and professionals been equipped to act as facilitators of learning?

▶ Are you prepared to act as a catalyst in encouraging the adoption of new forms of working and learning, and the integration of working and learning?

# REFERENCES

Bartram, P (Editor), (1999) *The Contract Bid Manager's Toolkit*, Policy Publications, Bedford

Coulson-Thomas, C (1992) *Transforming the Company: Bridging the gap between management myth and corporate reality*, Kogan Page, London

Couslon-Thomas, C (1997 and 1998) *The Future of the Organisation: Achieving excellence through business transformation*, Kogan Page, London

Coulson-Thomas, C (1999a) *Developing a Corporate Learning Strategy: The key knowledge management challenge for the HR function*, Policy Publications, Bedford

Coulson-Thomas, C (1999b) *Individuals and Enterprise: Creating entrepreneurs for the new millennium through personal transformation*, Blackhall Publishing, Dublin

Coulson-Thomas, C (2000) *The Information Entrepreneur*, 3Com Active Business Unit, Winnersh

Coulson-Thomas, C (2001) *Shaping Things to Come: Strategies for Creating Alternative Enterprises*, Blackhall Publishing, Dublin

Hurcomb, J (1998) *Developing Strategic Customers & Key Accounts: The critical success factors*, Policy Publications, Bedford

Kennedy, C (1999) *Bidding for Business: The skills agenda*, Policy Publications, Bedford

Perrin, S (2000) *Managing Intellectual Capital to Grow Shareholder Value*, Policy Publications, Bedford

Wenger, E (1987a) *Artificial Intelligence Tutoring Systems*, Morgan Kaufman, San Pateo, Calif

Wenger, E (1987b) *Glass-box Technology: Merging learning and doing*, IRL Research Abstract 1, Institute for Research on Learning, Palo Alto, Calif

## FURTHER INFORMATION

Brochures describing the *Developing a Corporate Learning Strategy* and *Managing Intellectual Capital to Grow Shareholder Value* reports are available from Policy Publications, 4 The Crescent, Bedford MK40 2RU (tel: +44 (0) 1234 328448; fax: +44 (0) 1234 357231, e-mail: policypubs@kbnet.co.uk; Web site: www.ntwkfirm.com/bookshop).

# 18

# Springing the Trap

*'Too much sun burns, a little at the right time and place can be magic'*

## BREAKING OUT

Throughout this book we have shared the frank views of those who are struggling to 'make it happen'. There are others who, with varying degrees of confidence, believe that they are on the right track. There are enough 'real world' examples to suggest that dramatic and sustained breakthroughs in performance can be achieved. These are occurring not just in 'quoted cases', such as General Electric, but in other companies that jealously guard their new-found sources of competitive advantage from external eyes, while 'going all out' within.

The champions of corporate transformation are creating organizations that are fluid, where change and learning occur naturally. What people learn, how they work, and the approaches, tools and technology that are used by groups and teams depend upon customer and new venture requirements. Opportunity determines the evolution of the network. The people and members of the network are held together by shared vision, values and goals, and work and learn harmoniously and co-operatively to the extent that human nature allows.

# ALLURING PROSPECTS AND PERSISTENT UNCERTAINTIES

A rush of questions often precedes and heralds the dawn of a new age. People are thinking and forming conclusions. Consider the following selection of comments:

*We cannot lower expectations, so we must increase our capacity to deliver.*

*Why should achievement match aspiration, when people rarely think through the implementation barriers and requirements?*

*There is no point in activity for its own sake. Do not start any major programme until all the elements needed for success are identified and lined up.*

*Try the 'So what?' or 'what is the point' test. There is no point having the best of this or that if it does not add value for customers.*

The flexible network organization can be achieved, but it requires total commitment. A company that picks and chooses which survey lessons to apply, or which success factors to adopt, will probably fail. The picture is not complete until every piece of the transformation jigsaw is in place (Coulson-Thomas, 1992, 1997 and 1998). When many pieces are missing, and a likeness or guide is unavailable, the eventual image may be uncertain. Enthusiasm or desperation is preventing many companies from taking a holistic and considered approach.

Corporate transformation is not a role for hermits in caves. The complexity of combination in large organizations and degree of effort needed to assemble certain change elements demand the efforts of a group, and may involve many teams.

A visitor from Mars who surveyed our commercial world might be pardoned for believing that our winners and losers in the battle for competitive survival constitute two quite distinct corporate species. Companies in both categories are easily recognizable. A ratchet effect appears to operate. Losers with deeply ingrained habits and entrenched practices sometimes find it very difficult to become winners, while very successful companies can quickly founder.

Just as effective transformation cannot be assumed, so continuing success should not be taken for granted. Before the terrorist attacks in New York and Washington on 11 September 2001, BA was losing business customers, the very people it was endeavouring to attract. The company appeared to have lost its touch and way since its British Airways days when it claimed to be the 'world's favourite airline'.

Sometimes a form of Greek wheel of fortune appears to operate as companies at the top descend the ranks of competitive performance.

Perhaps, like boxers, they absorb so much punishment from rivals that their managers become punch drunk and no longer see and react to obvious threats. Marks & Spencer represents a sad example of how entrepreneurial instinct can appear to vanish as rapidly and comprehensively as attractive looks or good health.

## MANAGING CHANGE

The management of change and corporate transformation is a critical differentiator. Organizational change is assumed to be desirable and beneficial. Its necessity is taken for granted and losers uncritically assume that change is invariably advantageous. 'The management of change' has become a lucrative area of consultancy. Managers are assessed and rewarded in relation to the amount and nature of change they bring about.

However, expectations of the benefits of change can rise faster than its achievement. Also, many organizational changes are not met with universal approval. They can be stressful and destructive if mismanaged. There may be both winners and losers. The satisfied may favour the status quo, while the frustrated, ambitious and blocked may desire a new regime. Debates may occur in the boardroom between those who are for and those who are against particular changes.

The impacts of change are not always immediately apparent. Some people who advocate particular action may be ignorant of its consequences. In contrast, the disadvantaged may be very aware of adverse effects. When benefits are widely spread their recipients may not even be conscious of them. Or they may lack the motivation to prevent the blocking action of sectional interests. The indifferent or ambivalent may simply 'go with the flow'.

Change can be disorienting and disruptive, even when beneficial. It may be that people can take only so much of it. Without some variety they may go to sleep, but subject them to too much that is new or unfamiliar and they may suffer stress and become unable to cope. The last change 'initiative' might break the manager's back.

## THE RATIONALE FOR CHANGE

The visions and rationales for change that are offered by many losers are excessively general. People should be expected to make demanding changes only for good reason. Will they enhance competitiveness? Effort should be concentrated where it is most likely to make a difference (Coulson-Thomas, 2001).

Justifiable changes could relate to critical success factors for achieving key corporate objectives and delivering greater customer and shareholder value (Perrin, 2000). For example, the key factors for winning competitive bids and building successful key and strategic account relationships in various commercial sectors and professions have been identified in a series of practical reports produced by the Winning Business Research Programme team (Kennedy *et al*, 1997–2001).

Winners think deeply about the purposes of change and the capacity of the people involved to adapt. Directors of winning companies question the rationale and justification for proposed changes, and ask whether an impact analysis has been undertaken of the likely implications (Coulson-Thomas, 2001). Are the potential consequences of proposed changes for employees, customers, suppliers, business partners and investors adequately assessed? Are harmful results and implications usually foreseen?

Winners ensure that people are equipped to achieve the changes they are expected to bring about. While general 'change' programmes have become more common, specific and bespoke initiatives and tools to help individuals bring about particular changes are few and far between (Coulson-Thomas, 1999a). In general, our perceptions, and individual and collective actions, will determine whether certain changes are beneficial or harmful.

## MATCHING STRATEGY AND CAPABILITY

The key to closing the gap between rhetoric and reality and aspiration and achievement is to match transformation capability with change strategy. Figure 18.1 illustrates some possible outcomes:

● When strategy is right in relation to the situation and circumstances of the company, but the various change elements cannot be assembled in such a way as to 'make it happen', people experience frustration.

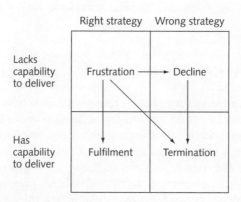

**Figure 18.1** Strategy and capability

- When the capability to deliver is created, perhaps by assembling some missing pieces of the transformation jigsaw puzzle, frustration can turn to fulfilment.
- Nothing may save the company with the wrong strategy. The capability to deliver could actually bring about a quick termination rather than a slow decline. The efficiency with which erroneous objectives are pursued and mistaken policies are implemented brings management into contact with the destructive consequences of its decisions more quickly than might otherwise be the case.

## CONSIDERING THE IMPLICATIONS OF CHANGE

The 'tide of events' can be hard on minorities and tough on the atypical. Over time, once those adopting an innovation reach a critical mass the provision of alternatives may be stopped. Supplies and spare parts may no longer be made available. Since most people have acquired CD players, many albums are no longer made available in the vinyl or magnetic tape formats. Winners gain credit and allies by identifying and protecting the interests of significant, important and disadvantaged minorities.

Introducing changes without thought as to their costs or consequences can do great harm. Many losers lack foresight and an 'end-to-end' perspective. Altering a task at one point in a process, or introducing a new activity, may cause problems for those operating elsewhere, either within the same process or in a related or dependent one.

One way of spreading responsibility for determining how much of particular forms of change should occur is to create new markets for the areas in question. Entrepreneurs will set up and launch a multiplicity of them (Coulson-Thomas, 1999b, 2001). Early adopters will be able go ahead without having to first wait for an organizational or board consensus to form in favour of a proposal or development.

Implications of change can be consciously made explicit or surreptitiously concealed. The cynical influence opinions by emphasizing the advantages of proposals while playing down their drawbacks. Opposition may be bought-off and neutralized, or even eliminated, by those who are determined to bring about particular changes.

Assessing the impact and contribution of subordinates and colleagues by the amount of change they introduce can sometimes encourage change for change's sake. In reality, the preservation of an existing reputation and core values may be what is required. However, preventing unnecessary activity in order to protect what is important and prevent compromise of beliefs is less glamourous and may be more difficult to evaluate.

# CONTINUITY AND CHANGE

Both individuals and organizations will have to distinguish between goals, values, objectives, policies and activities that need to be changed and those that should be continued and perhaps cherished (Coulson-Thomas, 2001). Some people will 'follow the herd' without thinking for fear of being left behind. Whenever a clear majority appears to favour a particular course of action, there is a tendency for the uncommitted to climb aboard the bandwagon.

Members of the majority may be naïve or mistaken in relation to what is in their best long-term interests. The respective merits of different options can also become confused amidst competing advertising and marketing claims. In the case of the battle between video formats, technologies that many considered superior to VHS (which became the de facto standard) were abandoned, simply because they came to command a minority market share.

Views, preferences and priorities can alter as situations evolve, circumstances change and fashions come and go. Nothing is more frustrating than to find that certain options have been forgone because a selected course of action cannot be reversed. After it has been cut down, the rainforest may not regenerate itself. Because their habitat is destroyed particular species may also cease to exist.

Winners strike a balance between change and continuity (Coulson-Thomas, 2001). A degree of continuity is desirable for those who need something to hang onto in an uncertain world. Companies sometimes attempt to change too much. Is there sufficient continuity for people to have a sense of identity, belonging, direction and purpose? Are conscious efforts made to provide enough continuity for people not to feel threatened and insecure?

Network organizations need wise and respected individuals in 'guardian' roles (Coulson-Thomas, 2001). By 'holding true' to core values and safeguarding what is collectively agreed to be important they may be able to protect us from ourselves. Independent directors can perform this duty and question whether changes are resulting in the loss of strategically important knowledge and understanding, and whether sufficient effort is devoted to building longer-term relationships with customers, suppliers, investors and business partners.

Change may have its opponents and saboteurs. Whereas losers may be naïve, winners tend to be politically astute. They are aware of who is slowing down, undermining, blocking or campaigning against what they are seeking to achieve. They make arrangements to deal with vociferous and vested interests – and determined but unrepresentative minorities.

# MANAGING THE TRANSFORMATION PROCESS

There are a variety of individual change elements and requirements that a formal transformation programme could embrace. People need to be equipped, enabled and motivated to manage change. Changes of attitude, awareness, approach and perspective are generally required.

Once all the pieces of the jigsaw puzzle – the various change elements – have been assembled, the change programme itself needs to be project managed. Among losers, there is insufficient recognition of the distinctive nature of project management competences, and their importance in the achievement of corporate transformation.

In the view of one chairman:

*We could do all of that... specific objectives, roles and responsibilities, teams... the lot. [But] we wouldn't have the project managers to run the projects. There's not much chance that we would deliver, given all the people from different areas that need to work together.*

Transformation project management can involve the sequencing and juggling of disparate change elements. Some pieces of the transformation jigsaw puzzle need to be put in place before later pieces can be added. To use another analogy, all the elements needed to build a house may be lying about in a builder's yard, but they still have to be brought together. When they are, people feel confident. According to one manager: 'You feel that collectively we are going to make it happen, because it is all there... We have thought of all the angles, and it's been pulled together.'

Until the various elements of a comprehensive change programme are put in place, those who trumpet visions are riding for a fall. They are raising expectations with little hope of delivery.

The impacts of corporate transformation activities are sometimes difficult to distinguish from those of other programmes such as a diversification strategy, or from the consequences of changes in the market and competitive environment. As the initial transformation experience of BP demonstrated, commitment to corporate transformation will not result in commercial success if other policies and initiatives do not match the situation and circumstances of the company.

# MANAGEMENT REQUIREMENTS

Table 18.1 presents some of the attributes of bureaucratic and network organizations identified by interviewees for the first edition of this book (Coulson-Thomas, 1992). Only a selection of the many points of difference and various contrasts which emerged are given. Nevertheless, they illustrate the profound impact that corporate transformation has had upon the role of the manager and the need to strike new balances between contending forces (Coulson-Thomas, 2001).

**Table 18.1** Perceived attributes of the bureaucratic and network organizations

| Bureaucratic organization | Network organization |
|---|---|
| Managers | Leaders, facilitators and entrepreneurs |
| Decision-makers | Counsellors and mentors |
| Departmental specialism and values | Shared vision and mission |
| Rivalry | Interdependence |
| Rules and procedures | Processes |
| Jobs and organization charts | Roles and responsibilities |
| Hierarchy | Project teams |
| Status | Contribution |
| Homogeneous | Diverse |
| Privilege | Democracy |
| Committees | Taskforces and teams |
| Vertical communication | Horizontal and all-channel communication |
| Central direction | Individual initiative |
| Control | Empowerment and support |
| Narrow specialism | General awareness |
| Strong head office | Effective customer interface |
| Competition, office politics | Co-operation, mutual trust |
| Factions | Common interests |
| Continuity | Change |
| Loyalty | Participation |
| Generalization and standardization | Responsive to individual customers and employees |
| Automate | Support |
| Centralization | Decentralization and delegation |
| Closed and secretive | Open and transparent |
| Suspicion and monitoring | Trust and encouragement |
| Hoarding expertise | Sharing experience |
| Sophistication | Simplification |
| Inflexible and fixed | Responsive and dynamic |
| Teaching and talking | Learning and listening |

People must believe that there is the prospect of a better life for themselves and for others. If not, why bother? The importance of encouraging and motivating people to act was recognized by one chairman at the eleventh hour:

> *It was all there and people said – 'Yeah, great'... It was interesting and probably right, but they were not that happy. There wasn't any incentive... We motivated them to do other things, but not to change how we operate.*

Too much faith should not be put in reward and remuneration, or indeed in any single change element. But a supportive approach can help. A decade ago General Electric rewarded people for learning. However, many companies actually encourage people, through the 'incentives' they provide, to act in ways that undermine the purposes and values of their transformation programmes.

Key priorities and activities should be continuously reviewed, and may need to be adjusted during the course of a corporate change programme.

## COMMITMENT TO CHANGE

People who 'really believe' can be so committed that it melts the rubber soles on their shoes. However, many of those who are committed appear unable to communicate it, or to demonstrate it, in a convincing way. The perceived 'commitment gap' is a serious problem in loser companies.

We have seen that too many boards lack vision, and are short-term oriented. They craft strategies that have little chance of implementation. The board itself is the source of much misunderstanding and distrust, and the cause of arenas of conflict in many companies. Corporate change programmes are generally incomplete and inadequately thought through. Some boards of loser companies appear to be 'clutching at straws'.

## CHANGE AND CONTROL

Many change programmes are over-managed and under-led. Having abandoned a 'command and control model', control may still need to be exercised, but in new ways. The challenge is not whether or not to 'give up' control, but to determine more appropriate ways in which it could be exercised. The successful management of change may depend upon the extent to which chosen methods of control match what is required at each stage of the transition.

## COMMUNICATIONS SKILLS

The transformation vision must be shared, the purpose of change communicated, and employee involvement and commitment secured. Personal attitudes and actions, the symbols people protect, the prejudices they perpetuate, and the conduct they display, often 'speaks volumes'. The combined effect of these, amplified by the leaks, rumour and gossip of the informal grapevine, 'drowns out' the anaemic, bland and sanitized prose of the hired scriptwriter and hacks.

In communicating the vision of flexible network operation, shared learning, creative partnerships and entrepreneurship, winners make considerable use of images. The clear image can be a powerful aid to understanding. At the same time, the power and persistence of an image, and how it might colour and distort perceptions, should not be overlooked. People should understand the thinking behind the portrayal of the concept, and the reasons why a particular form of organization and operation is being sought.

## CONSEQUENCES AS OPPORTUNITIES

The consequences of change may represent a business opportunity. Thus those offering specialist services could work on a flexible basis to provide support and outsourced help to start-up and transforming companies and e-business ventures. The nature of the assistance required can alter significantly as an enterprise changes, grows and develops. Hence companies that supply people with distinct skills and interim executives face a growing demand for their services.

In the age of mass markets, and long production runs of identical goods, those who were on the 'receiving end' of 'adverse trends' had every reason to feel abandoned and unloved (Coulson-Thomas, 2001). With suppliers clambering to get out of declining markets, minority consumers found themselves under pressure to switch. In many cases, manufacturers simply discontinued the provision of 'old models' or stopped holding spare parts.

An exodus of mainstream suppliers from a marketplace creates opportunities for niche suppliers to fill gaps and exploit 'tail ends' (Coulson-Thomas, 1999b, 2001). Some of these will be enthusiasts for the products and services in question. Perhaps there will be enough of them to form owners' clubs, open swap shops, establish steam railways or restage historic battles. Some companies discover when it is too late that their customers may have more regard for their offerings than most of their senior managers.

Changes are occurring all around us and may or may not represent challenges or opportunities (Coulson-Thomas, 1999b, 2001). Winners identify significant trends and developments, consider who are likely to be 'gainers' and 'losers', and assess whether there are alternative offerings that would mitigate undesirable impacts and enable people to take fuller advantage of whatever is likely to occur. Those affected might be sufficiently numerous and motivated to represent a potential target market for products and services tailored to their particular interests.

Consistently rapid development sometimes can be easier to handle than sudden discontinuities in growth rates. Those who ride the crest of a technological wave may feel confident that they are 'in the right place at the right time'. They may come to assume that they will have plenty of time in which to accumulate stock options and to cash them in before the tide turns. Small setbacks may be masked by a generally favourable trend of events. However, even corporate stars like Cisco Systems, which expanded at a frantic pace, have faced adverse market conditions and the need to retrench.

Those employed in smokestack industries may become reconciled to change for the worse and accustomed to a succession of bad news. Yet there will be some individuals who stubbornly refuse to give up. So long as actual or potential customers exist there is hope.

# REGRESSION AND NOSTALGIA AS AN ARENA OF OPPORTUNITY

Certain trends continue for longer than others. Some lose momentum, stop and eventually go into reverse. A small minority of like-minded people may be sufficient to safeguard what remains or to cause a renaissance. Communities of enthusiasts can be assembled via Web sites that issue 'calls to arms'. They also enable supporters to coordinate responses and allow other interested parties to monitor developments.

On occasion, advance may result from regression to desirable aspects of past periods. Addicts and the ardent may decide that 'enough is enough'. The vision of a replica of a steam engine or fully rigged tall ship in sail may stir emotions that could never be reached by anaemic 'corporate communications', a fancy new job title or the latest restructuring.

Astute entrepreneurs look for preoccupations and interests of previous ages that met deep-seated needs and which could be reborn (Coulson-Thomas, 2001). It has become progressively cheaper and easier to make direct contact with those who share our enthusiasms. With the dramatic growth in the Internet, like-minded people will be able to contact each other and initiate collective action.

Conditions have never been more favourable for minority interests to flourish. Traditional barriers to entry are falling. Systems and processes are becoming more flexible. Many people in developed countries are more prosperous. Because they are healthier and are living longer, they will have more time for further careers, additional causes, new enthusiasms and fresh obsessions (Coulson-Thomas, 1999b). And they will be able to enjoy the results of lifestyle changes.

The future is likely to be characterized by greater diversity, as those who are against certain combinations of changes take positive steps to safeguard what is threatened and to recreate what has been lost (Coulson-Thomas, 2001). Rather than meekly resign themselves to marginalization, they will actively set out to find locations and establish arenas in which they will be able to live life on their terms. Recognizing opportunities to cater for minorities will be a more important skill than the ability to replicate me-too provision.

Corporate leaders will be unable to become directly involved in the many and varied activities that more bespoke and imaginative responses to a greater variety of requirements will need. As we saw in Chapter 9, corporations need to transform themselves into incubators of enterprise and communities of entrepreneurs (Coulson-Thomas, 1999b). Different venture teams will be empowered and enabled to determine and bring about whatever changes are required to enable them to achieve their objectives and deliver value to *their* customers.

# CHANGING ATTITUDES AND BEHAVIOUR

The 'acid test' of the extent to which corporate transformation is taking place is the degree to which attitudes and behaviour have changed and are continuing to change to reflect evolving and diverse requirements. For 'loser' companies, ingrained attitudes have proved to be stubborn. Not only do they persist, but they resist reason and have a habit of bouncing back. In some companies, they must seep out of the walls, or enter the consciousness like bad spirits when people are asleep.

Winners achieve changes in attitudes and behaviour that elude other companies. The approaches, tools and techniques that have been used are usually simple and straightforward. They could be considered common sense, but the 'litmus test' is performance. In the harsh reality of the global marketplace there is little requirement for 'cosmetic' programmes. Wishful thinking and 'make-believe' may fool some faithful retainers, but they do not keep the teeth of competitive wolves from flabby corporate flesh.

To close the gap between aspiration and achievement, and influence attitudes and behaviour, winners build upon firm foundations. A host of worthy initiatives should not be left to topple over because the essentials have not been attended to.

It is logical to start with the clarification of vision, goals and values, measurable objectives and a performance management framework. Subsequently, attention should be given to the various elements that need to be in place if objectives are to be achieved, the pace and direction of change maintained, and accomplishments consolidated.

A well thought-out programme appears to be 'cumulative', as incremental elements both reinforce, and take advantage of, attitude shifts that are beginning to be achieved. A change element that jars, or does not seem to fit, may feel rough in the mouth. As a result of its introduction, it may be spat out and other elements may be 'thrown up'.

Losers have a tendency to exaggerate benefits, while failure is played down or concealed. After all, in the words of an interviewee: 'You don't sell ways of doing things less badly... You sell success.' A willingness to openly discuss disappointments is a harbinger of winning attitudes.

Success can bring as many problems as failure. Complacency, slackness, arrogance, becoming sidetracked with trinkets and irrelevancies, forgetting the customer, or just falling asleep are all towards the top of the list. Losers tend to be their own worst enemies, and to come to the gallows with their own rope.

# CHANGE AND TRANSFORMATION LOSERS

The distinction between winners and losers is clear and stark. We know when a board has lost the plot and its members are no longer in control. They become obsessed with trivia, distracted with fads, and bamboozled by surface appearances. They sustain the illusion of achievement while preparing the ground for substantial compensation payments when reality catches up with them and either non-executive directors act or shareholders decide they have had enough.

They become reactive and defensive, get lost in complexity of labyrinthine proportions and the more activities they engage in to break free, the more they become entangled. They introduce changes for changes' sake. They become neutralized by their lack of imagination and entangled in barbed wire created by their own words and actions. The trick they try to play is to retire or to move on at a high point.

Losers in the battle to become and remain competitive:

- are 'in their own space' and relatively oblivious to the needs of others; they do not anticipate and remain unaware of significant external developments and pressing requirements to change;
- lack self-confidence and self-worth and hold back; they are diffident, can be indecisive and find it difficult to commit themselves;
- do not have a compelling rationale and purpose; they are not unique, special or even distinctive;
- are not noticed by people; they are grey and dull, and hence fail to stand out or have an impact;
- copy and follow others; they do not innovate or differentiate themselves from their competitors;
- respond to events; they react to incoming approaches and invitations to tender;
- do not prioritize and focus; they fail to address what is important as a result of being distracted by trivia;
- hoard information and hold on to the reigns of power; they are reluctant to delegate and to trust and involve others;
- remunerate people according to their seniority and status in the management hierarchy;
- are driven by internal personal goals and corporate targets rather than by customer requirements;
- play other people's games rather than live on their own terms; they become pawns on other people's chessboards;
- adopt standard approaches and are rigid and inflexible;
- follow fashions and have a penchant for fads;
- search for panaceas and single solutions;
- define their capabilities in terms of the tangible assets they own and the people they employ;
- are consumers rather than producers of knowledge, understanding and intellectual capital;
- respond unimaginatively and mechanically to business opportunities;
- rely on traditional 'hard-sell' techniques and undertake win-lose negotiations;
- make little effort to learn from either their experience or that of others;

- hold back and stay aloof; they avoid personal commitments, partnering arrangements and inter-organizational links;
- are selfish in relationships and put the minimum of effort into maintaining them;
- use their customers to achieve their own short-term objectives;
- are cautious and half-hearted in their approach to e-business;
- mouth generalizations and platitudes; they indulge in self-deception and spin;
- live for the moment; they have short time horizons;
- do little to keep competitors out of their key accounts;
- leave the building of customer relationships to specialist sales staff;
- ignore organizations that are supplied by competitors;
- prize their freedom and independence; they prefer to operate alone;
- attempt to protect their interests with small print and avoid the assumption and sharing of risks;
- are secretive and defensive; they build internal and external barriers to create a hard shell;
- offer their employees general training and development that is viewed as a cost;
- fail to equip their people to win new business, create new offerings or build customer relationships;
- are complacent and set in their ways; they are reluctant to think, question and learn;
- confuse the roles of owner-shareholder, manager and director;
- fail to distinguish between operational matters and strategic issues;
- become typecast and locked into certain roles; they tend to end up as commodity suppliers.

Losers adopt a combination of attitudes, approaches and priorities, from a limited vision and a short-term and internal orientation, through cutting corners, to attempts to protect corporate interests, and this locks them into a 'spiral of descent' (Coulson-Thomas, 1997 and 1998). The almost inevitable outcome of their actions and inaction is a struggle to remain viable as a supplier of low-margin commodity work.

## CHANGE AND TRANSFORMATION WINNERS

Winners are very different. Their longer-term view, customer focus and external orientation launches them into a 'virtuous spiral of ascent' (Coulson-Thomas, 1997 and 1998) towards increased margins and profitability. They build their capability, 'work smarter', deepen relationships, develop their people and add more value to become trusted business partners of their clients and consumers (Coulson-Thomas, 1997 and 1998).

Winners assemble the elements needed to ride out the storms of commercial life. Most importantly, they succeed. They carry on exploiting the host of business opportunities that surround us. They identify them by challenging assumptions and asking fundamental questions. Their responses are sometimes basic and direct. Wal-Mart became the largest retailer in the United States as a result of a simple strategy of minimizing costs in order to reduce prices.

Winners are persistent. James Dyson spent 10 years trying to interest backers in his innovative alternative to conventional vacuum cleaners. Forty companies turned down Chester Carlson's invention of the plain-paper copying process. Jim Clark's sustained commitment to entrepreneurship saw him founding both Silicon Graphics to exploit his designs for a new form of computer chip and Netscape to help people navigate around the Internet.

Winners in the battle to become and remain competitive:

- relate to others and empathize with them; they live in their customers' worlds, monitor trends and react quickly to challenges and opportunities;
- are confident; they can be resolute and determined when the going gets tough;
- differentiate themselves; they have a distinctive rationale and purpose that is rooted in the requirements of customers and prospects;
- stand out; they are distinctive – people notice them and are attracted to them;
- explore, create and discover; they are innovative, develop new offerings and pioneer alternative approaches;
- are proactive, driven and inwardly directed; they sustain themselves and others through adversity;
- prioritize; they focus on the areas of greatest opportunity;
- share information, knowledge, resources and opportunities with others whenever it is likely to prove mutually beneficial;
- trust other people when it is reasonable to do so; they delegate responsibly;
- create enterprise colonies that tap, build and release latent talents and the entrepreneurial potential of their people;
- inspire and motivate; they recognize the primary importance of non-monetary rewards but are also prepared to link remuneration to the development of intellectual capital and the creation of customer and shareholder value;
- understand, value and address their customers' requirements;
- tailor; they develop bespoke offerings for individual customers;
- are proactive; they are willing to go out in front – they initiate relationships with those they would most like to have as customers, suppliers or business partners;
- take control of their destinies; they define issues, set agendas and initiate debates;
- are very selective; they choose associates, partners and opportunities with care;

- value variety, extend choice and encourage diversity;
- are versatile, adaptable and resilient; they can be tolerant and can handle uncertainty;
- adopt pragmatic combinations of whatever elements and factors enable them to achieve their objectives;
- define their capabilities in terms of mutually beneficial and productive relationships and flexible access to the resources, skills and business partners they require;
- develop, share, manage, apply and exploit knowledge and intellectual capital;
- create and respond to business opportunities with commitment and clear objectives;
- influence purchasing by understanding how buying decisions are made and supporting them; they initiate and undertake win-win negotiations;
- invite and welcome feedback; they actively learn from both successes and failures;
- subject their key processes and their approaches to winning business to independent review;
- work hard to establish empathy and build trust; they try to match their culture to that of customers, prospects and business partners;
- invest in relationships and endeavour to ensure that they are mutually beneficial for all of the parties involved;
- value their customers and want them to do well; they pass on ideas, insights and leads – they are always on the look out for ways of delivering greater value to them or of helping them to achieve their business objectives;
- enthusiastically embrace e-business; they focus on improving access to people, information and offerings and making business transactions easier and more enjoyable for their customers;
- focus on specifics; they take concrete steps to benefit, protect and lock in their key accounts;
- look ahead; they have a longer-term perspective;
- create multiple points of contact with strategically significant customers; everyone feels responsible for business development and value creation;
- develop account capture plans to break into customers that are supplied by competitors – there are no no-go areas;
- actively collaborate with dissimilar and complementary partners according to the aims and requirements of the various parties and comparative advantage;
- agree common values and objectives with their people and collaborating organizations;
- take and share calculated risks; they are willing to enter into partnering relationships and are able to manage them;
- are open and transparent; they cooperate, undertake shared learning and carry out peer reviews;

- offer bespoke approaches to development that meet individual needs and view the costs involved as strategic investments in building capabilities and the creation of knowledge, intellectual capital, and customer and shareholder value;
- specifically equip their people to win business and build customer relationships;
- actively question and challenge; they encourage thinking, support reflection and learn from both successes and failures;
- understand the distinction between direction and management and the differing roles and responsibilities of owners, directors and managers;
- build effective boards and develop competent directors;
- push back the boundaries of what is possible and become sought-after business partners.

Winners proactively address realities and the substance of what is at stake. They cut through distractions and trappings and get down to the fundamentals of issues and opportunities. They think things through before they act, and they prefer simple solutions and direct courses of action. They remain focused, flexible and free.

Loyalty and continuity of commitment, core relationships and essential values are also highly prized. Winning companies encourage their people to make considered moves and avoid cosmetics and unnecessary activity. Changes are made only when they are justified and beneficial.

## Losers

Losers:

- implement specific corporate change and transformation programmes;
- often lack the capability to implement their chosen strategies;
- initiate incomplete transformation programmes;
- still operate as bureaucratic organizations;
- find their change programmes undermined by reward and remuneration policy;
- do not necessarily believe that transformation objectives can be achieved;
- avoid confrontation and modify objectives to match their accomplishments;
- stifle changes with inappropriate controls;
- are hard upon those who struggle to adapt;
- change slogans and jargon;
- redouble their efforts or give up when they confront obstacles and barriers;

- tend to 'go off the boil' or become sidetracked unless continually challenged and periodically motivated;
- conceal disappointments and rationalize failures;
- leave out crucial elements of the transformation jigsaw puzzle.

## Winners

Winners:

- regard change and transformation as normal activity;
- endeavour to balance strategy and capability;
- ensure that all the pieces of the jigsaw puzzle required for successful transformation are in place;
- endeavour to operate as flexible networks;
- use reward and remuneration policy to facilitate desired changes;
- work to achieve transformation objectives;
- confront barriers and hold true to their visions;
- modify controls to ensure that they are appropriate for, and supportive of, each stage of the change process;
- equip their people to achieve successful transformations;
- successfully change attitudes and behaviour;
- pursue their visions purposely over time;
- remain sharp and stay focused on reality, flexible and motivated;
- learn from failures and celebrate and reinforce success;
- ensure that all the elements required for transformation and sustained competitiveness are in place.

# PRESERVE DIVERSITY, STAY FLUID AND KEEP LEARNING

Winners aim to keep on winning. Clones and crawlers should be discouraged from joining the network organization. The organic network thrives on argument and debate, and is made more vibrant by variety and diversity. Common and standard approaches should not be allowed to solidify the criss-cross pattern of communications into the bars of a prescribed cage.

In Chapters 13 and 17 the emphasis was upon the integration of working and learning. People should be encouraged to find themselves, and not forced to hide themselves, in the work environment. The author has long believed that the most fulfilled individuals are those who are self-aware and true to themselves (Coulson-Thomas, 1989):

*Those who focus upon what they enjoy doing and do best, and are able to work at a location and time of their choice, find it easier to close the gap between actual personal performance and their maximum potential. Career development should be managed to build a personal combination of competencies, experiences and qualities with a market value. This is more easily achieved by those who understand how they as individuals learn most effectively, and consciously seek to draw lessons from their experience... individuals likely to be in the greatest demand will be those who are open minded, flexible and adaptable, willing to learn, and who have something distinct to contribute.*

We saw in Chapter 13 that approaches to learning and development should be adapted to reflect the unique capability and potential, and the preferred learning style, of each individual and build upon their natural strengths. The bringing together of people from a variety of cultural backgrounds into international groups and teams offers the opportunity to create a diversity of learning environments. Individuals can be encouraged to build up a personal network of learning relationships that match their own unique attributes, interests and preferences.

Too often, the single-minded pursuit of 'the concept' against opposition and caution results in passionate advocates of change losing touch with reality. For example, the 'learning network' and the 'learning partnership' may appeal as concepts, but they have to be thought through in order to realize their value in a particular context.

Setting up links and relationships does not automatically result in their use for learning purposes. Not all the members of the network organization will be equally committed to learning from their network partners. A health warning about the intellectual voraciousness of the 'learning organization' was issued in Chapter 14. What to some is openness and receptiveness, can appear to others as mental banditry and the piracy of ideas. The naïve and unguarded can quickly become the victims of plagiarizing parasites.

Where behaviour is changed and is seen to be effective, attitudes may follow, even though they may have been initially hostile. How does one judge the extent of such changes? More basically, are people for it, or going along with it? Duplicity and an eagerness to please combine to confuse our senses.

We need new ways of putting a finger on what is going on. The signs that may reveal what is happening in the organic network organization are likely to be different. For example: progress will be marked by creating know-how, launching new ventures or joining teams that are working on more complex and critical problems, rather than by job titles and the dimensions of an air-conditioned office.

# REINFORCE SUCCESS

Success can encourage further success, if the overall culture is supportive of innovation and change (Figure 18.2). The favourable climate is an inducement to innovation and entrepreneurship. The success of these can reinforce a positive commitment among core members of the network, while shared learning can help other ventures and business units to follow in the path of pioneers.

Entrepreneurial cultures encourage venture teams to learn from each other and identify missing elements of the transformation jigsaw puzzle. They should focus on the critical factors for differentiation and becoming and remaining competitive, and be sufficiently flexible to reflect the situation and circumstances of the particular opportunity.

# GO FOR IT

If you are fighting a war against entrenched 'loser' attitudes, interests and prejudices, blather, deception and hype, you cannot afford to use one weapon at a time. The various barriers and obstacles need to be simultaneously overwhelmed with carefully selected combinations of 'change element' weapons in your armoury.

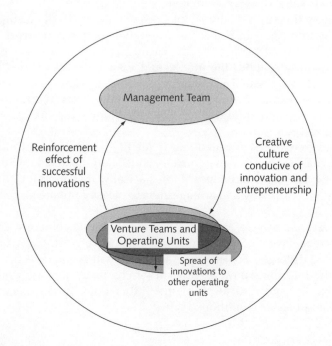

**Figure 18.2** The innovative culture

Some potential winners are very hard on themselves. They should take heart if some pieces of the jigsaw puzzle have been put in place as a result of their efforts, even though enough elements have not been assembled to achieve a 'breakout'. By standing on the next brick made up of critical factors for competitive success they might, for the first time, be able to see over the top.

Many good people have lost their jobs as a result of a perceived failure to deliver. Many of these 'victims of transformation' could not have produced the results that were sought for a variety of reasons. Generally, this was because some other piece of the jigsaw puzzle, for which they were not responsible, needed to be in place if their own efforts were to bear fruit.

People need to understand the key factors that distinguish winners from losers. They must line up the change elements that are required to 'make it happen'. They must come to the conclusion: 'This is going to work.' This is when they become believers and committed converts.

Having got this far you should now be more realistic and better informed when assessing whether your company is, or is likely to become, a winner or a loser in relation to the particular challenges and opportunities it faces. How would it fare when encountering a serious setback, confronting a formidable obstacle or working with an exciting but demanding prospect? Where does it stand in relation to each of the identified success factors? Asking such questions should enable you to locate areas of relative deficiency that must be addressed.

The key issue for you and your colleagues may be whether you have the determination to put in place the attitudes, approaches, capabilities and practices needed to compete and win. No one can be sure of what may lie around the next corner. Nirvana, nemesis or more of the same may lurk and beckon. What you do now and how you undertake the process of review and transformation will determine which it is to be.

The various elements that need to be brought together lie all around us in corporate organizations. We have identified the critical success factors. In some cases, the programmes are already in place that could be managed to overcome what technical or financial barriers remain. For many people, all that lies between them and their dreams is their own reluctance to venture forth, and to think and feel, share and trust, and listen and learn.

The coming together of a compelling and distinctive vision, shared values and the capability to deliver is a potent combination. There is no limit to the sacrifice and commitment people will make for their deeply-held beliefs. No end of disappointment and disruption, or privation and pain, will be suffered if the imagination is captured, the purpose is right and the cause is just.

Innovations across a range of products and services have the potential to transform our daily lives, hopes and aspirations. By enthusing and harnessing the capability of network organizations and the potential of their members, those who are alive and awake today have the means to achieve impact, at a speed and on a scale that would dwarf the wildest imaginings of the most fertile imaginations of past ages.

The payoff from running the extra mile can be enormous, exciting, rewarding and fulfilling. Today's caterpillar can become tomorrow's butterfly. Go for it!

---

# CHECKLIST

▶ Have you thought through what you are trying to achieve?

▶ Has it been expressed in terms of opportunities, requirements and clear objectives?

▶ Are these agreed by the key players and partners?

▶ Are they committed to their achievement?

▶ Is the commitment visible and palpable?

▶ Can the objectives be measured and performance managed?

▶ Have the 'vital few' tasks which need to be done been identified?

▶ Are roles and responsibilities relating to key tasks understood?

▶ Have the opportunities, requirements and objectives been shared with all those who need to contribute to individual and collective achievement?

▶ Do people understand their individual contributions?

▶ Have they been empowered, enabled and motivated to act?

▶ Do they understand the critical factors for becoming and remaining competitive?

▶ Can and will relevant, productive and shared learning occur?

▶ Are the rewards and the performance management framework consistent with what you are all seeking to achieve?

▶ Do they have the knowledge and skills to make it happen?

▶ Are they winners or losers?

▶ What are the likely obstacles and barriers to success and fulfilment?

▶ What needs to be done about them, by whom and when?

# REFERENCES

Coulson-Thomas, C (1989) *Too Old at 40?*, BIM, Corby

Coulson-Thomas, C (1992) *Transforming the Company: Bridging the gap between management myth and corporate reality*, Kogan Page, London

Coulson-Thomas, C (1997 and 1998) *The Future of the Organization: Achieving excellence through business transformation*, Kogan Page, London

Coulson-Thomas, C (1999a) *Developing a Corporate Learning Strategy*, Policy Publications, Bedford

Coulson-Thomas, C (1999b) *Individuals and Enterprise: Creating entrepreneurs for the new millennium through personal transformation*, Blackhall Publishing, Dublin

Coulson-Thomas, C (2001) *Shaping Things to Come: Strategies for creating alternative enterprises*, Blackhall Publishing, Dublin

Kennedy, C, O'Connor, James M *et al* (1997–2001) *Winning Business*, the critical success factors' series of reports, Policy Publications, Bedford

Perrin, S (2000) *Managing Intellectual Capital to Grow Shareholder Value*, Policy Publications, Bedford

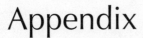

# Appendix

# 'Winning Business'
# Best Practice Programme

## Project Leader: Prof. Colin Coulson-Thomas

To shape the future, businesses need to establish and build relationships with customers. The 'Winning Business' best practice programme is identifying the critical success factors for winning and retaining customers in competitive markets. Over 2,000 companies and professional practices have participated. The business practices of 'winners' are compared with those of 'losers' to reveal why some companies are so much more successful than others. The investigating teams are led by Prof. Colin Coulson-Thomas, an experienced chairman of entrepreneurial and award-winning companies, Director of The Business Development Forum and chairman of the judges for the e-Business Innovations Awards (www.ecommerce-awards.com).

Recent outputs include 'critical success factors' reports, 'best practice' case studies, practical bidding tools and techniques, key business development skills, in-house training, winning business audits and reviews, and a benchmarking service that provides professional firms and practices with bespoke reports highlighting where they most lag behind successful competitors.

Published best practice reports that are currently available include:

- *Winning Major Bids: The critical success factors*, which examines the processes and practices for winning business in the competitive situations of 293 companies.

- *Bidding for Business in Construction, IT & Telecoms, Engineering and Manufacturing, etc*, best practice resource packs which include reports on critical success factors for winning business in particular sectors.
- *Bidding for Business: the Skills Agenda*, which covers the top 20 skills required.
- *The Contract Bid Manager's Toolkit*, which contains 30 practical tools for winning contracts.
- *Winning New Business in Management Consultancy, Advertising, Accountancy, PR & Marketing Consultancy, Engineering Consultancy, IT Consultancy, Law, etc*: the Critical Success Factors, which covers particular professions.
- *Developing Strategic Customers & Key Accounts: the Critical Success Factors*, which examines the experiences and key customer relationship practices of 194 companies.
- The '*Close to the Customer*' series of 28 management briefings on particular customer relationship management issues and best practice in different business sectors.
- *Developing a Corporate Learning Strategy*, which examines training and development practices and priorities, and information and knowledge entrepreneurship.
- *Effective Purchasing: the Critical Success Factors*, a European study of issues and trends.
- *Managing Intellectual Capital to Grow Shareholder Value*, an examination of how the better management of intellectual capital might generate incremental income.

All of these reports and the '*Close to the Customer*' series of briefings on customer relationship management are published by Policy Publications Ltd. Full details, including free brochures about each report and related benchmarking services, can be obtained from Policy Publications, 4 The Crescent, Bedford MK40 2RU (tel: +44 [0]1234 328 448; fax: +44 [0]1234 357 231; Web site: www.ntwkfirm.com/bookshop; e-mail: policypubs@kbnet.co.uk). Further information about the 'Winning Business' Best Practice Programme can be obtained from Prof. Colin Coulson-Thomas (tel: +44 [0]1733 361 149; fax: +44[0]1733 361 459; e-mail: adaptationltd@cs.com).

# Index